RIVERS *of* GOLD, LIVES *of* BONDAGE

Rivers *of* Gold, Lives *of* Bondage

GOVERNING THROUGH SLAVERY IN COLONIAL QUITO

Sherwin K. Bryant

The University of North Carolina Press *Chapel Hill*

Publication of this book was supported by a grant
from the Northwestern University Research Grants Committee.

All rights reserved. Manufactured in the United States of America.
Set in Calluna types by codeMantra. The paper in this book
meets the guidelines for permanence and durability of the Committee on
Production Guidelines for Book Longevity of the Council on Library Resources.
The University of North Carolina Press has been a member of the
Green Press Initiative since 2003.

Cover illustration: "Histoire naturelle des Indes," manuscript, ca. 1586, fol. 100 recto.
The Pierpont Morgan Library, New York. MA 3900; bequest of Clara S. Peck, 1983.

Library of Congress Cataloging-in-Publication Data
Bryant, Sherwin K.
Rivers of gold, lives of bondage : governing through slavery in colonial Quito /
Sherwin K. Bryant.
pages cm
Includes bibliographical references and index.
ISBN 978-1-4696-0772-6 (cloth : alk. paper) — ISBN 978-1-4696-4566-7 (pbk. : alk. paper)
ISBN 978-1-4696-0773-3 (ebook)
1. Slavery—Quito (Audiencia)—History. 2. Slaves—Colonization—Quito (Audiencia)—History.
3. Africans—Quito (Audiencia)—History. 4. Quito (Audiencia)—Politics and government.
5. Quito (Audiencia)—History. I. Title.
HT1136.Q58B79 2014
306.3'6209866—dc23
2014019787

THIS BOOK WAS ENABLED BY THE GENEROSITY OF

Jewish Federation *of* Greater Hartford

For Aliyah *and* Naiyah

CONTENTS

ILLUSTRATIONS AND TABLES

ACKNOWLEDGMENTS

The seeds for this book were sown many years ago. As an undergraduate at North Carolina Central University, I had the distinct pleasure of taking my first Latin American history course with Professor Lolita Gutiérrez Brockington. Not only was she one of the most captivating professors I had ever encountered, but she inspired my interest in Latin American history. It was in my first course, a survey of colonial Latin American history, that she assigned Colin A. Palmer's *Slaves of the White God: Blacks in Mexico, 1570–1650.* Reading that book started me on a journey into the study of slavery, race, and colonial Latin American history. Lolita also invited Professor Palmer to guest lecture on the themes of *casta* and race in colonial Latin America. Those talks catalyzed my interests in the history of the region. I thank her for noticing whatever it was she saw in me and for insisting that I attend The Ohio State University to study with Kenneth J. Andrien. Over the years, she has supported me every step of the way, serving as an encouraging voice and a constructive critic. Her scholarship and pedagogical example continue to guide me.

I feel extremely fortunate to have been able to work with Kenneth J. Andrien and Stephanie J. Shaw during my graduate training at The Ohio State University. From the start, Ken served as a responsive, supportive, and engaging mentor. Over the years, he helped shape my thinking in the areas of Latin American historiography, historical methodologies, slavery, economic history, and the Andes in countless ways. Ken's ability to provide incisive yet constructive criticism is something I did not even know I could hope for in an advisor, mentor, and friend. His encouragement and advice gave me the confidence to develop areas of inquiry and follow them. His scholarship continues to guide my thinking on the Andes, Quito, the economic and social history of the region, and the stakes of colonial governance. I learned from him as a teacher, an editor, and a colleague. He is one of the most widely read historians I know, one to whom I happily owe a debt of gratitude for his dedication to this project and his continued support.

Stephanie Shaw guided my study of African American history and slavery. Her admonishments to read widely and pay attention to the details remain with me. It was Professor Shaw who taught me about slavery, slave life, gender, and African American history writ large.

Tom Klubock informed my critical engagements with labor and modern Latin American historiography. Randy Roth taught me much about historical methods and historical writing. Margaret Newell nurtured my interests in ethnohistory. Donna Guy and Stephanie Smith pushed me to read widely and remember my audience.

Friends and colleagues in Colombia and Ecuador made the many months spent in the archives enjoyable and productive. Susana Cabeza de Vaca, Susie Chiriboga, and others at the Fulbright commission in Quito and Guayaquil offered research support and helpful advice about caring for a family in Quito. Juan Miguel and Lorie Espinoza of the Andean Studies Programs offered hospitality and counsel about life in Quito. Alejandra Andrade, my Quiteña host mom, spoiled me with wonderful meals and a beautiful tour of coastal Manabí, Puerto Viejo, and Monte Christí. Marcos and María Cruz, along with their children Juan Carolos, Jacqui, and Kathy, proved enduring friends and generous hosts. Jacqueline Pavón, María Alexandra Ocles, Davíd Reyes, Raquel Quevedo, Andres Reyes, and the entire Reyes family provided a home away from home. In Colombia, I thank Juan de Dios Mosquera and Daniel Garcés Aragon de Arara, who taught me much about Afro-Colombian history and politics. I thank the Cantóras for sharing their time, poetry, and songs and for teaching me about the history and culture of the Palenque Patía.

Colleagues and students at Kenyon College offered an enriching environment for teaching and writing. Bruce Kinzer proved a generous chair and encouraging senior colleague. Wendy Singer, Jeffrey Bowman, and Glenn McNair all helped orient me at Kenyon. And who could be a more enthusiastic and engaging mentor than Roy T. Wortman? His intellect, good cheer, and seemingly instant support of my work remain deeply appreciated. Conversations with Kris Kennelly, Marla Kohlman, and Ted Mason were also highlights of my time teaching at Kenyon. At the University of Notre Dame, Erskine A. Peters fellows Brandie Brimmer, Paul Minafee, Dorian Warren, Jessica Wormely, and Reana Ursin offered community, camaraderie, and helpful suggestions. Richard Pierce and Hugh R. Page Jr. remain heroic examples of engaged university citizens and generous academic hosts. Over the years, I have admired their grace and dedication in building Africana studies at Notre Dame as a department and an intellectual community. Their commitment to that project and their celebration of the legacy of Erskine A. Peters have been nothing short of exemplary and meaningful to so many of us now working in the academy.

Graduate school comrades Lawrence D. Bell, Jason Chambers, Alcira Due-ñas, Stephen Hall, Cecily McDaniel, Leonard Moore, Ana María Presta, Ti-wanna Simpson, and Anna Travis taught me the ropes, shared thoughts on literature, and read drafts of grant proposals and papers. David Alford, Brian Millen, Jalani Favors, Derek White, and Sowande Mustkum added good humor and lively debates along the way.

Colleagues and students at Northwestern University offered expertise and support. Darlene Clark Hine provided mentorship and nurtured this project along with others from our first encounter as colleagues. Martha Biondi read and commented on early drafts. Mary Patillo and Celeste Watkins Hayes offered encouragement and laughter. E. Patrick Johnson offered support and insisted that I seek out Elaine Maisner at the University of North Carolina Press. Nitasha Sharma and John Márquez read early drafts of the manuscript, offering helpful suggestions about organization and style. I am indebted to Suzette Denose and Marjorie McDonald for their generous assistance with various stages of preparing the manuscript and for securing image permissions.

Over the years, Barnor Hesse, Richard Iton, Dylan Penningroth, and Rudolph Ware each asked questions that sharpened my thinking on race, slavery, law, governance, and African history. Team teaching and discussions with Butch Ware about Atlantic Africa, religion, and embodied knowledge influenced my thinking for the better. Barnor Hesse and Richard Iton continued to ask me questions about resistance, sovereignty, slavery, and the politics of the enslaved. Conversations with each of them about political theory and the African diaspora always proved enlightening and generative. Richard Iton, a colleague of tremendous integrity, grace, and generosity, provided encouragement and incisive criticism, all the while remembering those human elements such as birthdays and good music. Barnor Hesse, an impassioned and critical interlocutor, also read drafts of chapters and engaged me in a series of conversations about political theory. Mark Hauser offered good humor and insightful conversations about Atlantic slavery, contraband circuits, and even the subtitle of this book. Thanks also to Mark for producing and granting me permission to use the slave-trading map in the book. Badia Ahad, Ana Aparicio, Hollis Clayson, Huey Copeland, Jorge Coronado, Brodie Fisher, Marla Frederick, Lucille Kerr, Michelle Molina, Frank Safford, David Schoenbrun, Krista Thompson, Tracy Vaughn-Manley, Mary Weismantel, and the members of the Midwest Colonial Latin American History Group will always have my gratitude for their community, warmth, and encouragement. Students in my classes, especially AFAM 390 (Spring 2011) and AFAM 342 (Spring 2012), read portions of chapter 2 and proved to be great interlocutors. Caitlin Bruce and Camille Edwards were very capable and productive research assistants.

Release time from teaching and service obligations, thanks to Northwestern's Weinberg College junior faculty fellowship, allowed me to develop early ideas about slavery in colonial Quito and New Granada. The Newberry Library, the John Carter Brown Library, and Northwestern University's Alice Berline Kaplan Center for the Humanities each provided funding, important intellectual space, resources, and release time for research and writing at critical junctures in the process. The communities of scholars I encountered in each of these rich settings offered cherished dialogues and ongoing intellectual engagement. Michael Hamerly shared his expertise and insight on the history of Guayaquil and the Andes along with hospitality and good cheer during my stay at the John Carter Brown Library.

Herbert S. Klein and Jane Landers read an early draft of the manuscript, providing pages of constructive criticism. Herb, especially, reminded me of the importance of thinking comparatively within Latin America. Although I did not take Herb's advice to write a separate chapter on the "free colored" populations, I did accept his admonitions as an invitation to extend my thinking about the deep entanglements of colonialism, racial slavery, and black freedom.

Kathryn Burns and James Sweet revealed themselves to me as the readers for UNC Press who read the manuscript twice and made important suggestions for revisions. Both offered invaluable, generative insights. Kathryn Burns provided close and careful readings, which made this an infinitely better book. James Sweet's detailed suggestions also improved the book in countless ways. Herman L. Bennett's detailed comments on earlier drafts of the entire manuscript sharpened my thinking. He has served as a formidable interlocutor and generous critic, pushing me to consider what it meant to exist as a slave within an early modern Catholic order. I met Kris E. Lane in the archives of Popayán many years ago, and I have been struck by his generosity of spirit as well as his passion for historical inquiry and his deep knowledge of the colonial archive. He also read the full manuscript, offering a level of detailed suggestions that only Kris can offer. Rachel O'Toole and Marcela Echeverrí both read drafts of the entire manuscript and helped refine my thinking in important ways. Kym Morrison, Michelle Reid-Vázquez, Charles Beatty-Medina, Kristine Huffine, and Ben Vinson, comrades on another project, became generous interlocutors and companions on journeys within the academy. Guadalupe García read portions of the manuscript multiple times. She engaged me in many conversations about the project and encouraged its completion to the bitter end. Kristin

Huffine, Laura Matthew, Jovita Barber, and colleagues in the Midwest Colonial Latin American History Working Group read early drafts of chapter 2 and provided valuable feedback. I thank friends in Bogotá, Columbus, Durham, Evanston, Quito, and Leland for their love and support over the years—Melissa Davis, Cheria V. Dial, Scott Hunter, Mark Innis, and Anthony Trotman. Ericka M. Hicks offered friendship and assistance with map drafts and administrative help in the final stages of the manuscript preparation. Ruth Homrighaus, Alisia Shelton, and Micaela A. Smith edited portions of the manuscript in preparation for publication.

I thank scholars from the 2012 Tepoztlán Institute for Transnational History of the Americas meeting for comments on chapter 2. Many important questions and points of connections were raised during a session that featured my work alongside that of Denise Ferreira da Silva and Adam Warren. Thanks to Maria "Sasha" Woolson and E. Gabrielle Kuenzli for their generosity to my girls and me and for their supportive engagements while I was at Tepoztlán. Micaela A. Smith and I met late in the process, but she has become a patient and generous reader, an incisive critic, and a dear friend. Special thanks also to Joe and Sandy Smith for the many delicious home-cooked meals, laughs, and a quiet space to read, write, and relax in their home in Ramona, California. Going far beyond the call of duty, they read chapters 2–4, offering careful comments, questions, and suggestions. E. Gabrielle Kuenzli engaged me in countless conversations about the book and the colonial Andes. She read multiple drafts of various parts of the manuscript, offering useful criticism, suggestions, and encouragement. I can only hope the final product justifies the generous efforts of so many. Any errors of fact and interpretation that remain are, of course, my own.

Elaine Maisner, my editor at the University of North Carolina Press, guided the manuscript through its various stages. Her patience, enthusiasm, and good cheer helped to make the publishing process lively and enjoyable. I thank Elaine for believing in this project. Her fame as an editor of choice, especially for first-time authors, is well known and much deserved.

In the process of writing this book, I published an earlier version of chapter 4 as "Enslaved Rebels, Fugitives, and Litigants: The Resistance Continuum in Colonial Quito," *Colonial Latin American Review* 13, no. 1 (2004): 7–46. I thank the editors for permission to reprint this material.

A special thanks goes to my family. First, to the ones who have gone before. I thank Sondra Kay Wilson for her support and her example of scholarly engagement. While she departed this life long before I could complete this project, she remains a tremendous source of inspiration. I will forever cherish her generosity, grace, and guidance throughout my time in graduate school and early musings on this book. My maternal grandmother, Essie Mae Clemmons, passed away during the writing of this project, and though she was ill during much of the writing, she showed me a great deal of love, care, and inspiration in my own parenting. The knowledge and stories of family history of my maternal grandmother, Bessie May Bryant, captivated me as a child. The story of her washing the whip-scarred back of her formerly enslaved grandmother, Katherine Hazzard, continues to haunt me as I research and write histories of enslaved Africans sent along another passage. I miss them both dearly. At the very end of this project, a dear colleague, mentor, and friend, Richard Iton, passed away. It is still difficult to believe. Richard also read drafts of this manuscript, offering generous criticism and prodding as only he could. I hope the appearance of this work will serve as something of a testimony to his collegiality and the reach of his thinking on diaspora and coloniality.

I thank my sister LaShonda C. Lewis for believing in me, for her dedication to family, and for many encouraging words and supportive gestures during the research and writing of this book. Thanks for the many birthday visits, for the advice on shopping for growing young girls, and for your listening ear. To my brother-in-law Steven Lewis and my nephew Tyrese, thanks for many holidays and family times filled with laughter and cheer. A special welcome to our new bundle, Christopher Bryant Lewis, who arrived just before the completion of this book. To Arthur T. Hicks III, Ingraham Cephus, and Joseph Kevin Carpenter III, thanks for lifelong friendship and gentle inquiries about the book. To Michael-Bryant Hicks, a thinker, critic, and gifted writer in his own right and more of a brother than a friend, thanks for your thoughtfulness, generosity, and encouragement over the years. And to the rest of the village that raised me—my aunts, Barbara and Laura Mae, and uncles, Anthony, Curtwright, Gregory, Landon, Nathaniel, and Wayne—thank you for the fun times, affection, and wise counsel.

I thank my parents, Joe and Connie Bryant, for their love, sacrifice, guidance, and hard work in raising me, for supporting my parenting, and for their enthusiastic support of this book. Memories from my childhood of weekly family dialogues on education, hard work, and sacrifice remain with me. I thank them for the chores and great expectations and for loving and supporting me throughout life's triumphs and tragedies. Both have come to Evanston at various times during this book's writing and production to assist with childcare as I worked to write and publish as an ambitious, part-time single dad. You continue to anchor our family in ways that words can hardly express. I remain in awe of your partnership, comforted by your love, and guided by your wisdom. Finally, to my girls, Aliyah and Naiyah, who have grown up with this book, in addition to the love, companionship, and inspiration that you have provided me over the years, I thank you for your forbearance and confidence. Yes, Naiyah, Daddy has finally finished the book. And although hardly recompense, I dedicate this book to the two of you as a token of my love, devotion, and gratitude.

RIVERS *of* GOLD, LIVES *of* BONDAGE

Slavery and Governance

The Governor wrote to me that you had sent him seventeen black slaves and
that you ought to send more. It seems to me that you ought to send one hundred
black slaves and a person in your confidence ought to go with them.
—King Ferdinand, 1507

Slavery is the punishment even of the greatest crimes. . . .
But those who bear their punishment patiently, and are so much wrought
on by that pressure that lies so hard on them that it appears they are really more
troubled for the crimes they have committed than for the miseries they suffer,
are not out of hope but that at last either the Prince will by his prerogative,
or the people by their intercession, restore them again to their liberty.
—Thomas More, *Utopia*, Book 2, 168–69

In 1592, Francisco Auncibay, one of the three royal justices (*oidores*) serving on
Quito's high court (*audiencia*), penned a treatise to King Philip II. The treatise
concerned the indigenous population and territories of Popayán and proposed
that the king invest 1 million pesos of gold to subsidize the importation of
2,000 enslaved captives from the "land of Guinea" to colonize the area and
mine area riverbeds laden with gold.[1] Describing the region's humid climate;
horrible roadways; multilingual, ungoverned, and rapidly declining "*indios*"
(indigenous populations); and rivers with gravel beds laden with gold, Auncibay's petition reads more like a treatise on government than a mere economic
rationale regarding economic capital and labor.[2]

Auncibay's petition points to a scarcely considered aspect of slavery—the
ways that enslaved Africans were fundamental to claiming New World territories and the development of colonial sovereignty. The justice's petition reveals racial slavery as a settlement of foreign, deracinated (removed from their
homelands), and non-European subjects. It reveals conquest, enslavement, and
slave trading as early modern modes of constituting colonial societies and systems of rule. Auncibay's proposal suggested more than a labor arrangement

aimed at replacing fleeing or otherwise unavailable indigenous subjects. Instead, the justice proposed to further colonize Popayán and govern the region through slavery. For the judge, colonial slavery promised to help claim this new territory, harness its natural resources, and thereby prove elemental to the establishment of its estates, towns, markets, and good governance. Making the region productive and improving its miserable *indios* were requirements of colonial sovereignty and legitimacy. The message was clear: to claim proper dominion over Popayán's rivers of gold, the crown would need lives of bondage.[3] For Auncibay, slavery was an early modern practice of *buen gobierno* (good governance).[4]

Drawing upon sixteenth-century European political theory, the high court justice referenced Thomas More's *Utopia* directly in his proposal by suggesting that masters and slaves organize themselves into small royal "colonies."[5] As chief stakeholder and initial owner, the crown indicated the terms of their organization, management, manumission, and movement within the realm. Promising to enrich the royal coffers, Auncibay projected that the slaves might produce a return of 520,000 pesos of gold within six to eight years of the initial investment, repaying his majesty with interest. To these 1,200 men and 800 women of an average age of seventeen, priests would administer the sacrament of marriage, and owners would purchase them in gangs of twenty.[6] Concerned with social discipline and internal governance, Auncibay suggested that a portion of the slaves be adults forty years and older. They would serve as authority figures for these slave towns. Owners would not be allowed to remove the children whom, Auncibay anticipated, enslaved women would reproduce.[7] This, he feared, would lead to the births of black *ladinos* (hispanicized), who might leave the mines, never to return.

In all, Auncibay proscribed twenty-seven norms and regulations for governing both the enslaved *and* those who would rule them. If "slave masters ruled," they were expected to do so within the conventions of early modern dominion.[8] They were not to allow their slaves to learn to read and write; there would be no swordplay, riding of horses, or bearing of arms. These were all Christian-European entitlements. Black men would marry black women exclusively. Tools would be collected at night, and harsh punishments would befall any who challenged the peace and sanctity of the kingdom through flight, rebellion, or both. These slaves were not to contract services, exchange goods with Spaniards, or trade and live with Amerindians. The most compliant slaves would be able to purchase their liberty but could do so only after the king recovered his initial investment. Even then, they were never to leave the region of Popayán, nor were they to cease work except in the case of old age or infirmity. Those freed would remain black and captive, receiving a small payment for their labor yet forced to remain in the territory.[9] Over time, Auncibay's freed blacks would come to occupy a coerced *jornalero* (day laborer) status, paid workers with tributary obligations to remain in these territories at the behest of his majesty, revealing what scholars commonly call freedom as an early modern juridical privilege, *fuero*, or exemption from the most abject form of colonial subjection. Auncibay's utopia envisioned edicts and colonial officials harnessing territories and governing colonial development in part through the colonial imposition and governance of slavery.

Auncibay's request, along with many others like it coming from Quito and the greater Andes, situates slavery as a governing practice within an emerging colonial order. It points to slavery as a fundamental aspect of colonial practice, sovereignty, and governance. The petition also reveals the juridical logics of slavery as a mode of dominion as they permeated daily life, social norms, and Quito's power matrix.[10] Slavery was not merely a labor system, nor was it a separate institution.[11] Rather, it was one of the chief governing practices and juridical claims that constituted Castile's colonial relation to New World territories, subject peoples, and natural resources. In short, it was one of the chief European technologies used to exercise dominion over the Indies. By governing the importation, distribution, sale, management, and use of enslaved Africans, the crown and its officials conducted the development of colonial authority and over time colonial state formation.

Auncibay's request highlights a range of issues and perspectives concerning the study of slavery and slave life during the early modern era. First, it calls attention to the centrality of slavery to law, settler colonialism, and the development of government. Second, it points to the ways that slaves and slavery were elemental to territorial claims, the harnessing of natural resources, the subduing of indigenous subjects, and thereby the establishment of dominion over the Indies. Third, it showcases an obvious and important tension within the law. The fantasies of slaveholders and the emergent colonial state depended upon and sought to produce silent, dependent, compliant, unlettered, non-European subjects whom they would *improve* through good government and proper Christian discipline. Nevertheless, enslaved Africans and their descendants challenged and shaped the boundaries of colonial servitude, thereby limiting the effects of their subjection as people within the order. In short, slaves marked off the fragmented sovereignty that Castile sought to install within the Americas by contesting authority and making requests of their masters and colonial officials that were never enshrined in law. In choosing spouses, making kin, and participating in colonial religious communities, enslaved people

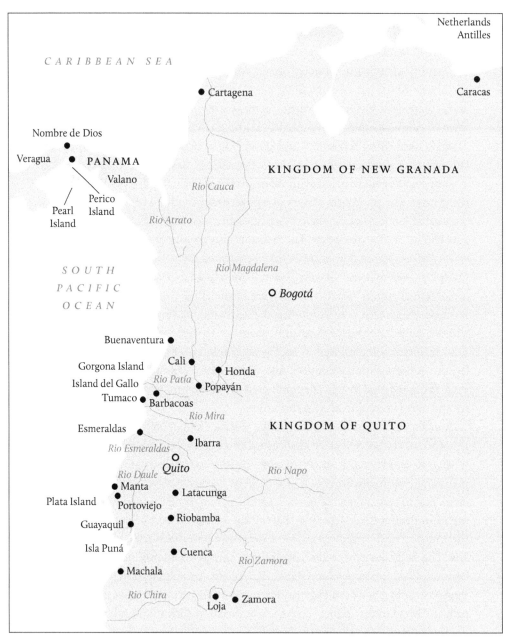

Kingdoms of Quito and New Granada.
Based on a map drawn by Carol Cooperrider; map is not to scale.

confronted the vulnerability of their kinless and abject status. Along the way, they gave shape to colonial law and disorder. As they lived and moved within the interstices of Quito's colonial power matrix, some were able to carve out a modicum of possibilities for themselves and their loved ones.[12]

Examining the role of slavery and the lives of the enslaved in Spain's Kingdom of Quito (Ecuador and southern Colombia), *Rivers of Gold, Lives of Bondage* argues that scholars must break with the labor metaphor of slavery in order to apprehend its centrality to colonialism, colonial authority, social practice, and the constitution of race. It explores the ways that enslaved colonials conditioned their servitude through a series of strategies and daily practice that included waging contests before colonial courts and engaging in violent rebellion, the politics of escape, and private negotiations. Along the way, this book reveals slavery as a fundamental feature of colonial practice, political economy, and social life within early modernity rather than a replacement of a labor system used primarily in response to declining indigenous populations. Tracing slavery as a feature of law and governance establishes it as embedded in shifting and contingent colonial settings.[13] Conceptually, this brings into relief the features of slavery and slave trading as practices constituting race through modes of governance and colonial subjection of Africans as black, deracinated, kinless, and vulnerable colonial subjects, who as such innovated identities and associations within the racial order of Spanish colonialism.

While the study of slavery and black life in diaspora in Latin America has grown dramatically over the last two decades, the study of slavery in the North Andes (Ecuador and southern Colombia) remains marginal to the broad and expansive field of comparative slavery and the African diaspora. This is due in part to the fact that the population of enslaved Africans was small in colonial Quito. Slavery *as labor* did not drive the economic engine of the colony. This has led some scholars to insist that Quito was merely a society with slaves rather than a slave society.[14] This study departs from such dichotomies since they are based upon a limited, materialist-driven conceptualization of slavery via labor and economic outputs. Scarcely considered in such formulations are the ways in which "human captivity in various forms were central pillars— perhaps *the* pillars of life in early Quito, city and colony."[15]

By and large, debates and studies on slavery have examined its predicament and value through the lens of economic capital, labor, and the transition to freedom. Property and labor continue to stand as the chief metaphors or points of entry into the study of slavery and slave societies. Consequently, within comparative slavery scholarship the imperatives of work and the scale of the slave population have served as the chief metrics through which scholars examine the importance of slavery within a given society. Likewise, a focus on capital, the North Atlantic world, and plantation societies continues to predominate, leaving transoceanic sites within the Pacific and Andean territories undertheorized as spaces for studying slavery and African-descended life in diaspora. Although correctives are under way, the study of slavery in Spanish America remains marginalized in national histories and scholarship on the African diaspora.[16] The case of slavery in Quito reveals, however, the centrality of slavery to colonial development and the emergence of race as a modality of early modern colonial governance. Understanding slavery as more than labor has required situating it alongside other colonial practices aimed at claiming new territories and subject peoples.

Consequently, this book narrates conquest, slaving, commerce, and governance as mutually constitutive processes that helped to forge colonial sovereignty through violence and juridical enclosure. More than laborers, enslaved subjects were, by will of the king, conscripted colonial subjects, assembled as non-Europeans and subject to differentiated governance and social life under Castilian monarchs. As such, they were constituted over time as differentiated colonial assemblages forged within and mutually constitutive of European-derived colonial rule. Enslaved Africans were abased and subjected to a slavery wherein their only hope of liberation was conditional, muted, and forever tied to the colonial race relations of governance that Castile constituted through practices such as slavery and slave trading. Through slavery, the king and his regents installed sovereignty within territories, thereby constituting colonial authority and Europeanness. This returns the analysis of slavery and society to its basis within Mediterranean household dominions and Roman law.

According to Roman law, slavery was first and foremost a legally structured personal relation that marked the enslaved with the legal status of "enslaved captive subject of servitude" ruled through the dominion of a Pater, or head of household, a feature of slavery that Castile extended to the Americas from the beginning of colonial development.[17] This legal designation of household subject endowed slaves with more than a value indexed to the market and its corresponding labor needs. It marked the sovereign claims that the monarch held against the bodies of all enslaved subjects and the right to govern the multiple uses and values that the enslaved carried within their bodies. In Quito, slaves worked in gold mining, sugar cultivation, shipbuilding, domestic and skilled trades, and transit, among other industries. But they did far more than that. Here, slavery served as a form of display of the Spanish sovereign's power. Not only did colonial governance and economic exploitation often go hand in hand; they were constituted mutually through slavery as governance.[18]

Understanding how slavery helped to shape European colonization and its unique form of *race governance* (the colonial constitution of non-Europeans through differentiated rule) requires an examination of slave status within the political economy of early modern monarchies. Since the thirteenth century, legally, a slave was the one the sovereign had preserved (*servare*); enslavement was by definition a sovereign act, one that saved rather than beheaded foreign captives who were said to deserve death. Slaves thus owed allegiance not only to their master but also to the king, as they were obliged to inform the king of impending danger.[19] Consequently, the crown held a stake in all slaves, thereby allowing the crown to encroach upon the dominion of masters, who imagined their power over enslaved subjects as household property to be absolute.[20]

Slavery marked dominion, conferring prestige value and a kind of majesty upon slaveholders while inscribing colonial rule within new territories.[21] More than labor, economy, and capital, slavery conferred this authority to Christian heads of households (patresfamilias). It involved placing deracinated foreign dependents and subjects under European Christian household dominion. Enslaved subjects, much like land, marked sovereign territories for differentiated Christian rule. By the fifteenth century, slaving, slave trading, and slavery were modes of conquest used to install sovereignty. Ultimately, slaving and the slave status of foreign others were culminating events in Castile's ritualized *toma de posesión* (taking possession).[22] Slavery, therefore, established a regime of governing practices that constituted "ceremonies of possession."[23] Claiming the New World and installing Castilian sovereignty were two related yet distinct processes. The first depended upon ritualized claims—knowledge of the place, its location, geographies, peoples—while the second process depended upon the literal marks on the bodies of new territories.[24]

In economic terms, the value of enslaved men, women, and children proved far more complex than numbers and production would suggest. The broader economy accounted for slavery in myriad ways, indexing slavery and its multiple values and uses within the circulation of currency and goods, lending, property values, the moral economy of piety, and the cash and goods that circulated within parish coffers, convents, and monasteries. Enslaved Africans often served as the endowment for *bequests*, funds that paid for prayers to be made for deceased souls, who apparently could afford slaves in life and death.[25] Aside from providing labor and specie, enslaved subjects were living, heavily regulated people whose good governance further legitimated the crown and the broader web of power that structured the social order. Slavery was, in this sense, an apparatus of colonial governance that installed colonial sovereignty, allowing the crown access to the household dominion and personal affairs of a range of colonial actors through its regulation.

This work joins a growing literature addressing slavery and the law in transoceanic perspectives.[26] Throughout Spanish America enslaved subjects were endowed with a series of legal opportunities and possibilities and a modicum of rights, most notably the right to a royal audience wherein they might denounce illegal practices of their owners such as the failure to instruct them in the faith, gross mistreatment (*sevicia*), or infringements upon their rights to marry and live a conjugal lifestyle. Over the last three decades, scholarship addressing slavery and the law has expanded from a focus on questions regarding the law as a tempering force within slavery to an analysis of the complexities of colonial practice and the ways in which legal practice changed over time in response to enslaved litigants and the shifting concerns of the colonial state in regulating slaveholders.[27] The law has been seen as a site of both resistance and subjection for the enslaved. Over time, throughout Spanish America, enslaved legal action produced formal changes within legal practice, enshrining in law and legal practice the customary norms and practices that slaves negotiated with their masters within diverse colonial settings. The field is now characterized by microhistories of slavery, law, and jurisprudence that pay careful attention to the ways that changing legal and bureaucratic processes created spaces of opportunity for enslaved litigants to have an audience and denounce the bad governance of their masters, even as slaves appear to have been only moderately successful at influencing legal change over time.[28] In the eighteenth century, Bourbon officials created the position of sindicat (*sindico*), a legal agent representing enslaved litigants in their pleas before colonial courts. This work argues that while this development constituted a more formalized intrusion into the masters' authority, it was enslaved litigants who made the law work to the degree that it did.[29] Even then, in many instances the enslaved benefited from clashes within legal regimes, struggles between masters and royal officials, conflicts around jurisdiction, and the daily and material circumstances that made legal redress contingent and delimited.[30] Slavery as racial rule was inherently unstable as subalterns behaved in ways that challenged the limits of law and colonial order. As legal historian Michelle McKinley notes, "Enslaved litigants did not possess conventional sources of political or social power that would have swayed courts."[31] And even when they did "prevail against their owners," they did so as slaves. Indeed, their possibilities before courts were few. But the politics of the powerless took on many forms.[32] The enslaved sent many messages to those responsible for governing and meting out justice. As McKinley notes, "Locating the cause and effect, the grounds for [slave] agency, co-optation and resistance is difficult given the hegemonic force of colonial modes of paternalistic social control, patron-client networks, and the intricacies of the power matrix."[33] Nevertheless, moving within the interstices of the colonial web of power, enslaved captive subjects of servitude had an impact upon the establishment of law, colonial legal cultures, and the judicial debates of their day. This work suggests, therefore, that we see slaves, slaveholders, magistrates, and other colonial actors as conditioning the development of an absolutist state and personal patronage. Along the way, this study sheds new light on the ways in which these colonial participants engaged in broad dialogues about good governance. It suggests that we see the enslaved as the principal colonial subject worthy of spectral violence, subjection, and bondage within the law, but one who also spoke back and otherwise practiced a politics aimed at subverting colonial modes of dispossession and power. Apprehending these practices and their colonial contexts requires understanding the juridical category of slave within the broader practices of race governance that characterized early modern colonial rule.

Defining Race as Governance

Historians have long looked to early modernity for signs of an emergent racial ideology regarding bodies, blood, and fixity. Discourses on the body as indexed through the nomenclature of *casta* and *raza* have conditioned our entry into the archive of race and its groundings in early modern thought regarding the body, nature, and the human condition. This book argues, however, that race was inscribed and conditioned through early modern practices of differentiated rule, insisting that it is possible to recuperate an early modern history of race as constituted over time through a series of colonial governing practices. Early modern juridical monikers, racial designations, and color-coded referents to geohumoral origins (*casta*), nations (*naciones*), and religious or moral attributions such as blood purity (*limpieza de sangre*) and social/reputational rank (*calidad*) were multivalent and reflexive modes of marking and governing populations of diverse territorial origins. Each of these monikers aimed to identify Indians and Africans and bind them to specified territorial lineages for differentiated governance through the elaboration of Christendom's imperial power. *Indios*, for example, mapped onto specific territories within the Americas, as well as specific kinds of juridical standing (wards and slaves—both indicative of subhumanity and disorder) within Castile's emergent global order. *Reducciones*, Spanish use of *mit'a*, and *ecomienda* were all modes of race governance applied exclusively to Amerindians.[34] These served to bind them to a geopolitical heritage of non-Europeanness, structuring colonial authority and Spanish American vassalage. Africans, on the other hand, were deemed foreign and mapped onto specific territories of enslavability within Africa and the colony. For this reason, Atlantic slave-trading designations of *naturaleza*, *casta*, and *nación* reveal more about the ways in which slave traders and the Spanish colonial authorities constituted subjection of Africans by marking and governing them as enslavable in relation to their corporeal, political, and territorial origins.[35] Through forced migration, colonials installed enslaved Africans in the Americas as colonial subjects against whom the Spanish monarchs held an ownership stake. Claiming Africans and the rights to govern the slave trade, Castilian monarchs laid claim to the ocean sea, colonial ports, markets, and the actual territories wherein royal agents licensed and governed Africans' forced migration and importation.

Although bodies over time became the privileged metonym of blackness, slavery, and race, race governance was constituted as a set of colonial practices meant to brand, bind (geopolitically), mark, and distinguish peoples *and* territories for colonial governance.[36] Drawing upon work on the colonial state, studies of governance, and political theorist Barnor Hesse's formulation of race as the constitution of Europe and non-Europe through systems of governance, this book insists that early modernity was racialized not due to ideology, biological notions of blood or fixity, or a definable logic of race thinking. Rather, the colonial horizon of early modernity was racial because European colonial practices deemed the territorial origins and political and cultural practices of those they considered non-Europeans as a basis for dispossession. Over time, these practices established and legitimated European sovereignty, European normativity, and whiteness in all their guises and implications.[37] This sovereignty was based upon the conceit that white, old Christian lineage (as indexed in part by the metaphor of blood purity) entitled Castilians to a higher degree of humanity within a cosmology or economy that included the Christian god's trinity of father, son, and holy spirit, who were venerated by lords of all angels, saints, sinners, infidels, pagans, savage barbarians, and demons of an evil underworld.

Bodies, unlike territories, *moved*, carrying both royal majesty and the potential to undermine colonial sovereignty. In this way, enslaved subjects represented the contingencies of colonial sovereignty. Indexing bodies to territories was, therefore, a way of harnessing labor, raw materials, and capital. But more importantly, it was also a way of marking territorial claims and sovereign power. Consequently, the aim of race governance was not isolated to early modern scientific differentiation or the coloring of European rule. After all, early modern black subjects could and did achieve positions of power and prestige within the emergent white hegemonic monarchical orders of European colonialism. Thus, far more important than biology and color (although these would matter greatly over time) was the proclamation, achievement, maintenance, and defense of European sovereignty through the extension of an early modern Spanish Catholic order. Race governance, therefore, was foundational to and constitutive of Spanish sovereign claims over the Americas and, over time, became a quintessential characteristic of the emergent colonial state. This book insists, then, that colonial practices aimed at regulating the slave trade and governing the spiritual lives of the enslaved demonstrate the ways that colonial officials constituted assemblages of non-Europeanness. Slave-trading *casta* categories, sometimes referred to as ethnic monikers, which became the basis for the formation of *cofradias*, marriage, baptismal parties, and black social life, were fundamentally ways of assembling differentiated collectivities for colonial surveillance and rule. These practices, born of the imposition of the white gaze, were modes of subjection that constituted racial difference and legitimated governance on this basis.[38]

Slavery, Early Modernity, and the Development of Race Governance

The story of racial slavery has it beginnings in Atlantic/Mediterranean settings. In 1441, Portuguese knights kidnapped the first black captive subjects of "Guinea" (northern Senegambia) and took them to Iberia.[39] Bartering for and buying additional subjects, they intentionally marked them in relation to Castile's Muslim enemies. Guinea's subjects were, thereby, deemed infidels, bound within territories Iberians read increasingly as *black* and sovereignless and worthy of subjugation through *buena guerra* (just war) and its corollary, enslavement.[40] Historian Nancy E. van Deusen notes that enslaving non-Christian enemies dwelling in non-Christian lands had been a modus operandi for the expansion of Christendom and, one might add, Islam for centuries.[41] By the end of the fifteenth century, a vibrant trade in enslaved peoples of varying origins characterized the Mediterranean world.[42] Sovereignty was asserted, installed, and maintained in the Mediterranean world through wars initiated increasingly for the purpose of slaving within pagan, infidel, or otherwise non-Christian, non-European territories.

It was during this moment of conjuncture that medieval modes of personhood collided with new Atlantic slaving practices to produce new forms of subject making.[43] For Christians, the image of the "Moro" popularized as *the* slave in late medieval and early modern Mediterranean literature tied slave status to non-Christian, infidel, foreign, pagan, and barbarian status. Deemed as deserving of death, the enslaved avoided temporal death in exchange for a life of alienation under the dominion of the Christian paterfamilias. Captured, purchased, and cut off from their natal communities and familial ties, Tartars, Circassians, Russians, and Greek Orthodox Christian women and children were incorporated, yet differentiated, within Iberia's kingdoms. Along with enslaved Africans and Canary Islanders, they were labeled and governed through the idiom of color and slavery. Free Muslims (Mudejars) living within Christian kingdoms were sentenced to perpetual servitude for crimes. Slavery, therefore, offered errant Muslims chastisement, reproof, and correction, placing them under the dominion of Christian patriarchy.[44] Iberian rulers asserted that the enslaved's proximity to Christian discipline would improve them and their progeny along with the good of the order and its sovereign claims upon the Americas. As a category of governance and subjection, slavery also marked captives (whether Muslims, blacks, or others) as a distinct subcategory of persons unfit for life within the commonwealth or city. Early modern slavery emerged less as a pure economic system than a mode of discipline and a corollary to warfare.[45] Slavery was a means of conferring personalistic power upon Christian vassals and a method of enclosure and differentiation that Castile imposed upon captives within its sovereign order.[46] Enslavement, the juridical constitution of slavery, enclosed these newly deracinated colonial subjects under the dominion of legitimate Christian vassalage. In short, slavery was a feature of law, an early modern governing practice that Europeans imposed upon the Americas as a mode of marking people and territories and extending the boundaries of early modern monarchical orders.

By the end of the fifteenth century, Iberians were beginning to establish practices that governed sub-Saharan Africans distinctly relative to other Iberian subjects. This practice was a political provocation by Portuguese knights and monarchs in their efforts to claim the territories that the Papal States had granted them.[47] Drawing upon Aristotelian notions of the Tropics, Castilians employed theological-political practices based in science to mark and govern Africans due to their territorial proximity to Islamic kingdoms within sub-Saharan Africa. Castilians labeled these as *black lands*—torrid zones, where location and proximity to the sun was said to affect people's skin pigment, tendencies, and physical disposition. Iberians based their determination of sub-Saharan Africans as sovereignless, black, and enslavable on three factors: first, their *naturaleza* or place and condition of birth; second, their spiritual heritage as non-Christians (and suspect Muslims or possibly pagans); and third, their sovereignless corporate status as individuals lacking a king or sovereign territory that Castile was compelled to recognize. Iberians used these pretenses to rule sub-Saharan Africans as *black* and enslavable. Over time blackness came to signify a people so debased that they deserved the unnatural and legally reprehensible status of slave.[48]

Consequently, throughout the Mediterranean, terms such as *blanco* (white), *negro* (black), *loro* (brown), and *mulatto* (black lineage) all pointed to territorial origins deemed worthy of dispossession. During the late fifteenth century Islamic and Christian slaving circuits tied blackness to slavery as territorial lineage, thereby launching practices that over time constituted race.[49] In short, before the coming of Columbus and the decimation of indigenous populations and before a perceived need for labor, slaving, slave trading, and slavery were modes of governance that marked individuals in relation to territories, corporeality, and Castilian sovereignty. In order to see slavery as a method of installing sovereignty and governing foreign territories and subject peoples, we must break with the labor metaphor of slavery and contemplate what slavery signified and occasioned before the so-called discovery of the Indies as well as during its conquest. In the absence of a proper foundation, the violence of seeing, marking, writing, and slaving imposed Castilian sovereignty and governance on the Americas.[50]

Blackness and Colonial Possession

In October 1492, on the beach of Guanahani, Columbus went ashore and unfurled the royal banner and two captain's flags, marking the location with the royal insignia. In the presence of the royal notary and at least two witnesses, Columbus performed possession, marking the islands and declaring them possessions of his lords, the king and queen of Castile and Aragon. These acts—seeing land, descending from the boat with notary in tow, installing boundary markers, renaming, cutting branches from trees, pulling up twigs, digging into the land, and wading into the sea to unfurl the royal banner—were all juridical acts meant to claim and bind territories to Castile for governance.[51] In 1492, conquest, expansion, religious warfare, dominance, and trade were all fundamentally and inextricably linked to slavery and, increasingly, blackness and color.

By enslaving the inhabitants of the Americas, Columbus marked New World peoples and their corresponding territories in a manner peculiar to Castilian sovereignty. Initially taking ten Amerindians captive, Columbus returned to Iberia with them in hopes of training them as translators for subsequent voyages. But it was through his dispatch of 550 *indios* to Cadiz as slaves for sale in Andalusia that Columbus provoked the principal question of governance for the sovereigns of Castile: "Can we with good conscience sell them?"[52] Slavery, or slave status, was the juridical marker through which indigenous subjection was first filtered, interrogated, and established. Thus, slavery as a juridical category of Castilian law held profound implications for early modern claims of good governance and the construction of the colonial horizon. Slavery was a critical axis for the creation of new forms of rule and power as European monarchies stretched across oceans and continents.[53]

Responding to Columbus's first sovereign acts, Ferdinand and Isabella of Castile and Aragon initially offered sanction for the enslavement and sale of those he called "*indios*," suggesting that he might fetch handsome returns for their sale in Andalusia. But by the time caravels carrying approximately 350 enslaved Tainos landed at Cadiz, the sovereigns decided to inquire of their *letrados* (theologians and canon lawyers) if these captives could be sold. The question was, were these natural slaves? Answering this question required that the jurists interpolate the enslaved into Castilian presumptions regarding their territorial, political, and cultural origins. In other words, they were read through Castile's Christian and scientific understandings of the globe or through the terminology of *naturaleza*, *nación*, and *casta* that was coming to inform Castile's relationship to the people who resided and originated outside of the Iberian Peninsula.[54]

As captives arrived on the peninsula from diverse locations around the globe, Iberians read them against Muslims and Jews who had by then been the subjects of war, forced baptism, and suspicion. Increasingly, Christian absolutism aimed at creating a pure, Catholic order in the face of a broader Islamic imperial vision and introduced slaving as an inextricably entangled component of expanding the Christian colonizing missions and contests over sovereignty.[55] Properly adjudicating slave status amid an expanding and prosperous trade in captives was, therefore, an inherent concern of Spanish governance. Hundreds of thousands of captives were "deracinated" (taken from their home territories and stripped of their natal social and political standing) to serve as slaves and servants between 1503 and 1543.[56] Shipped as commodities, curiosities, domestic servants, and military auxiliaries throughout the Iberian colonial world, slaves were mobile forces of Castile's emergent empire. Masters, seamen, and merchants brought slaves from a wide array of geographic locations into Iberia and Castile between 1492 and 1592. Others were buffeted within an illegal slave trade that dispersed them throughout Castile's kingdoms on the Iberian Peninsula. Nancy van Deusen states, "These slaves globalized Iberia in both literal and conceptual ways."[57] Slavery and questions of slave status marked the contours of the emergent global European order, establishing a colonial horizon constituted through racial governance.

By 1501 Queen Isabella I declared *indios* free vassals.[58] While the queen had instructed Governor Ovando in Hispaniola that *indios* were free and subjects of the crown, edicts that were codified through the laws of Burgos in 1512, she had allowed for the enslavement of "rebel cannibals" and those taken in a just war. Castilian monarchs established sovereignty over New World territories in part through claiming the "right to decide" between granting their subjects a life of colonial servitude or free-subject status.[59] In declaring a just war and installing new sovereign authority, Castilians read the *requerimiento*, a declaration of war read to subjects of new territories granting them the choice between accepting Christian authority and the pretense of "protection" under the dominion of Castile or facing imminent war and enslavement. A first prerogative of the sovereigns, indeed the first juridical imposition of Castilian rule in claiming the Indies, was their assumption of the right to decide who would be enslaved, under what conditions, and how that servitude would be governed.

Deeming the region's indigenous peoples *"indios miserables,"* the justice folded them and the territories they indexed into an expanding discussion of colonial sovereignty based upon theological-political discourses of government inscribed over the Indies through ongoing practices of conquest, pillage, and slaving. These were weighty matters of law and good governance. According to the judge, the many peoples he deemed *indios* lacked a king and possessed no unifying cosmology ("no tenían rey ni le ni superstición alguna").[60] Far from valiant, the justice insisted that Popayán's *indios* were sovereignless people who preferred flight to fight. Consequently, they and their territories represented subjects and spaces that Castile not only rightfully claimed but also were in need of proper dominion.

In spite of these observations, slavery is often narrated as an appendage of colonialism, resulting in the curious formulation of colonialism and slavery as distinct phenomena, one a mode of governing and the other an economic and social institution. This formulation showcases the ways in which the notion of slavery is already embedded in concepts of "the market" and as such constitutes a conceptual appendage to society and colonial governance. Nevertheless, indigenous forms of subjugation such as *encomienda*, *mit'a*, and reducing are all understood as foundational to the very making of the colonial governing apparatus and the formation of the indigenous commonwealth.[61] The corporate standing of the indigenous, the range of protections they were accorded within the law, and the relative lack of the same for Africans and their children seem to have seduced some scholars into formulations that disentangle slavery and colonialism, when in fact slavery was a constitutive practice of colonial governance and thereby deeply embedded within colonialism. Indeed, statements such as "*encomienda* and colonialism" or "*mit'a* and colonialism" ring as redundant formulations, at best. Yet all of these forms made use of indigenous subjects' labor and governed them in part by requiring them to labor in order to produce tribute. Whereas enslaved Africans and slavery are often studied in relation to the market, social control, and cultural productions, Amerindians are viewed as both laborers and vassals constituting the colonial state, colonialism, and coloniality. This book seeks to correct this view, examining slavery at the level of political economy and through the lived experiences of those subjugated through the subject status that bondage conferred.

By 1513, anticipating the growing commerce in enslaved Africans to the Indies, the crown imposed a head tax of 2 ducats on any black slave arriving in the Indies. In 1517 the crown authorized the first direct shipment of enslaved African captives to the Americas. Distinct from *ladinos* (Spanish-speaking, acculturated slaves) in their territorial, national, and religious heritage, 4,000 enslaved captives known as *bozales* (recently arrived Africans), would arrive over an eight-year period, as mandated by the crown. These were among the first sovereign acts that Castile's monarchs undertook, and they did far more than underscore the profit motive of conquest.[62]

Enslaved blacks vividly displayed the powerful advance of Christian sovereignty emerging out of the Kingdoms of Castile and Aragon at the end of the fifteenth century.[63] Although the intrinsic nature of slavery in Iberia was not yet reduced to bodies read as "black," slave status was indexed increasingly through the geopolitical frame of color, especially "blackness," which Castile used to deem them enslavable. The bodies that Europeans marked and constituted as black were already becoming emblematic of prestige, wealth, royal power, and majesty.

Slave trading and slave labor marked the ascendancy of Western nations and economic conglomerates within the early modern global economy. Dutch images, in particular, showcase the ways that slavery became a central trope in performing and producing European cosmopolitanism and majesty. By 1648, for example, Dutch visual culture was beginning to reveal how black slavery was already a part of Dutch domestic life. Enslaved blacks were, thus, a part of the imperial sociocultural horizon that produced both European metropoles and their early modern colonies.[64] Similarly, by the seventeenth century, enslaved blacks were also "fashionable" in England, accompanying aristocratic

Christóvão de Morais, *Portrait de Jeanne d'Austriche, 1535–1573, fille de Charles Quint*.
Musées Royaux des Beaux-Arts de Belgique.

displays in art along with fruit, pets, and other articles of luxury, signaling that the enslaved represented far more than labor.[65] They were foundational to early modern European claims of legitimate authority and normativity. Early modern legal cultures and notions of lordship and bondage were tied directly to the very thing that formed the basis of household authority and power—slaves. Extending Castilian Christian households and the rights of patresfamilias to import their enslaved subjects to the Americas also marked the extension of slavery to the New World before the legal sanction of the transatlantic slave trade. In short, extending slavery was a royal grant and a legal characteristic of the coming monarchical order.

Slavery and Social Practice in Colonial Quito

The Kingdom of Quito held a small enslaved population compared to broader and perhaps more familiar Atlantic patterns. At the beginning of the seventeenth century, there were only a few thousand enslaved Africans and blacks in the kingdom—no more than 1,000 in Guayaquil, 300–400 in Quito city, less than 2,500 in greater Popayán, and probably no more than 500–1,000 dispersed throughout the central highlands. Thus, a principal aim of this study is to explain how and why a relatively small number of slaves mattered to the society, culture, and economy of colonial Quito. Doing so requires rethinking what slavery is, what it provides societies, and what societies like Quito can tell us about early modern race governance. In other words, it requires an attention the political history of slavery as a practice that constituted colonial law and governance. Indeed, this work argues that you cannot understand Spain's colonial project without apprehending how the practice of slavery shaped the development of colonial authority and juridical practice.

As a result of the Kingdom of Quito's large and resilient Andean population, which rebounded over the course of the seventeenth century through migration and developed biological immunity to Old World diseases, Quiteños never acquired large numbers of enslaved Africans. Consequently, slavery never achieved the economic or labor dominance in Quito that it held in nineteenth-century plantation societies or urban centers of Spanish America, such as Lima and Mexico City. Indeed, at no time did enslaved Africans constitute a majority. At the end of the eighteenth century Quito's overall enslaved population was approximately 28,000, less than 5 percent of the total population of approximately 573,000. Most slaves were held in Popayán (in southern Colombia).[66] Yet enslaved Africans are found throughout Quito's colonial archive as members of society and crucial players within the region's various economies and

Vicente Albán, *Distinguished Woman with Her Negro Slave* (Quito, 1783).
Museo de America, Madrid. Photograph by Erich Lessing/Art Resource, NY.

social settings. This study takes the reader into the gold-mining frontier, the agropastoral estates in isolated Andean valleys, an urban administrative center, and a coastal port city and enclave. From the very beginning, the proliferation of slavery proved an intrinsic feature of the colony's economic and social life.

As juridical subjects, currency, mobile capital, and people caught up in a complex web of material and spiritual capital, slaves became intrinsic to Spanish colonial establishment. Indeed, African slavery offered a method of producing *and* performing wealth and status in society. A slaveholder could mortgage a slave to fund a dowry for his daughter while gifting his daughter another slave as a personal servant as part of the deal.[67] This same slaveholder might also will two slaves to the church to offer prayers for his soul. Therefore, slavery served, in life and death, to facilitate the production and performance of wealth in this life. For slaveholders, it helped to ease racial life within the realm while serving their souls in route to a more celestial kingdom.

Slavery's majestic quality was evident throughout multiple aspects of colonial life. From Popayán in the north to Loja in the south of the kingdom, performance of wealth and standing involved matters of display, strolling entourages that featured enslaved subjects.[68] Imagine an elite family and its entourage on a stroll about town, a procession featuring a slave or two. Since slaves were among the most observed members of a society, even the clothing and adornment of a slave as he or she moved about town on behalf of an owner signaled the family's wealth and status.[69] The colonial archive is filled with comments on the slaves' presence, social importance, prestige value, and circulation. The arrival of slaves at a dock; their sale in the market; the ledgers; the sales tax revenues; the branding; the sound of their punishment at the lash; references to them in sales, wills, and testaments; their participation in the legal system; and their presence within the religious culture of the kingdom suggest that slavery was so interwoven into colonial life that it was inextricable from social practice throughout colonial Quito. The slave symbolized a disciplined and ordered body, as well as the majesty that held the order together. If the power held by the state was represented not by might but by display, the slave must have been elemental to that display, as slaves signified the most violent, "spectacular and discontinuous interventions of power."[70] Enslaved Africans were branded, watched, whipped, castrated, and otherwise made to announce their presence in the form of a belled iron collar. In short, slaves embodied "exemplary, because exceptional, punishment."[71]

As a feature of conquest, governance, social formation, and commerce, slavery was an early and deeply ingrained feature of colonial life in Quito. Not only were enslaved blacks part of early conquest campaigns, but magistrates and town councils quickly issued legislation concerning how slaves and slavery would be governed. Indeed, slavery was not an afterthought or a mere response to declining indigenous populations, as it is often considered. While few slaves came to Quito in those early years, by the late 1530s the preference for slave ownership was becoming increasingly apparent in the city of Quito. By 1538, for example, several *encomenderos* (holders of land grants) based in the city of Quito were mining the region's ore deposits with gangs of Andeans and small numbers of enslaved Africans. For many of those early arrivals, life would take them away from the highland capital to the gold mines of Santa Barbara, a small town near the city of Cuenca located in the south-central highlands.[72]

To the far north in the Gobernación de Popayán, Amerindians and blacks were already producing some 30,000 gold pesos annually by the 1540s.[73] Slaves were mining gold in the towns of Arma, Cartago, Caramanta, and Anserma. In the early 1550s, there were some 2,000 blacks and Amerindians mining in the town of Almaguer. Some estimates suggest that the African population of Almaguer had risen to almost 1,400 by this time.[74] As Payanese elites came to depend increasingly upon enslaved Africans, they crafted elaborate proposals aimed at generating royally subsidized shipments of African slave laborers.

While elites in the city of Quito were not as quick to develop a large slave population, by the late 1570s the enslaved black population had reached upward of 100 individuals amid an overall population of 400 property owners and 2,000 *mestizos* (indigenous people of Spanish lineage).[75] In subsequent years, the enslaved population would grow exponentially, both through natural births and through the importation of ethnic Africans. Between 1580 and 1600, some 250 enslaved Africans and Afro-Creoles were exchanged, marking the beginning of slavery's rise in the north-central highland area more generally.[76]

Similar to Popayán, by the 1570s, the coastal port city of Guayaquil boasted a slave population of 333 individuals (216 men and 117 women); by 1600 the number had grown to 1,000 individuals.[77] But whereas Popayán's slave population found itself panning for gold in the region's river- and streambeds, laborers in Guayaquil filled the high demand for domestics, lumberjacks, polemen, carpenters, and shipbuilders. They, along with indigenous subjects, built the four *templos* (temples), three small convents, and sixty-one houses that stood out in the geographic landscape of the city in the year 1605.[78] In addition to providing labor for seemingly never-ending public works projects, Africans worked as pearl divers off the coast of Guayaquil in those early years.[79] By the late sixteenth century, the usefulness of African slave labor had been well established throughout the kingdom. In Quito's lowland coastal district, the town of Puerto Viejo possessed thirty-three enslaved men and fourteen enslaved women, outnumbering the ten "married Spaniards," fifteen "married Creoles," and three Spanish bachelors of the port. Jipijapa, situated in the central coast of modern Ecuador, was said to be home to "some slaves." Even Jaén de Bracamoros, situated at the southern tip of the kingdom, registered at least ten slaves. The presence of these enslaved laborers showcases elites' efforts to bring African slavery from their old Iberian world to this region of the Americas while drawing simultaneously upon Amerindian labor charges in the region.[80]

Chapter 1 explores slavery as a facet of early colonial development. Beginning with slavery as a feature of conquest and law, it traces the legal, social, and economic development of the region, delineating how slavery helped to structure laws and colonial order and to claim territories and otherwise came to constitute a mode of race governance. Woven throughout are the three countervailing contexts of slavery in the kingdom: the sordid cities of Quito and Guayaquil, the sugar-producing valleys of the Chota-Mira Rivers north of

Quito city, and the rivers of gold that flowed through greater Popayán. A guiding concept for this chapter's treatment of slave life is the way that slaves' lives, labor, and location were mutually constitutive.

The remaining chapters treat slavery thematically as both a set of conditions and a set of predicaments.[81] Chapter 2 explores the juridical subjection of enslaved blacks, revealing branding, baptism, and practices of bondage as modes of legal practice in the constitution of racialized enslaved subjects. These legal markings along with the reading of enslaved bodies through slave-trading practices served to inscribe blackness upon African captives as they entered the order. Over time, a growing association between blackness and slave status served to inscribe such relations in law. Grounded in the story of slave trading to and within the Kingdom of Quito, this chapter details the incremental expansion of slave trading and racial governance throughout the kingdom. By the late 1680s, a confluence of social, political, and economic factors prompted local elites to employ African slave laborers at unprecedented levels, causing the exponential expansion of the colony's African population. As slavery expanded, existing populations of enslaved people, mostly Afro-Creoles (New World–born), were integrated with new arrivals of ethnic Africans from a range of ethnoregional backgrounds throughout West and West-Central Africa. This chapter pays particular attention to how and why certain demographic transformations occurred, contextualizing the social worlds of enslaved Africans and their Creole descendants among African-descended peoples as slavery expanded in the region.

The final two chapters explore the contours of slave life, outlining how enslaved men and women made their lives both within and in opposition to slavery. Chapter 3 details slave marriage, family, and formation of sacred communities. Even as the church and canon law sought to discipline the behavior and beliefs of slave laborers, enslaved Africans and their descendants chose marriage partners and kin, creating communities that defied the impositions of labor and landscape. In the midst of colonial servitude, Africans and Afro-Creoles formalized social relations in part by participating in spiritual community. Where some forged alliances, others were enemies. A signal aim of this chapter is to explore the tension between the contexts of work and geography and the human actors who affected colonial spaces and constituted "rival geographies."[82] Implicit here, again, is the dialectical relationship between the slaves' lived experiences and the predicament of colonial racial servitude.

Chapter 4 approaches slavery through the lens of the law, examining the legal actions of the enslaved and those who would be free. This chapter draws extensively upon the testimony given in slaves' lawsuits against their masters for *sevicia* (gross mistreatment) and *libertad* (freedom). It charts the expanding dialogue between abused slaves, those who would be free, and slaveholders, while analyzing the ways that this dialogue changed as the institution expanded and as masters responded to new sociopolitical and economic pressures at the end of the eighteenth century. As the political and economic environment changed just before the wars of independence, slavery remained critical to gold mining and the burgeoning agro-export economy emanating from the coastal port city of Guayaquil. New economic pressures translated into more brutal experiences for slave laborers and increased activity for colonial courts.

The litigation struggles between masters and slaves reached their highest expression during this era, as slaves brought an unprecedented number of cases against their masters. In the end, however, the colonial state that was once thought to mediate royal justice and serve as a check against the gross mistreatment of slaves became simultaneously the single largest owner of slaves and the most negligent and abusive master in the colony. This occurred even as slaves and masters continued to debate and redefine the meaning of slavery and the legal limits of mastery. This chapter also features spectacularly brutal and subtle aspects of master dominance, showcasing the ways that shifting sociopolitical winds could impact slave life in oppressive ways.[83] Chapter 4 explores slavery and the law, the legal regimes that governed slavery, the ways that restive slaves gave legal action context, and the actions of enslaved litigants. Here, too, are the processes of manumission, tales of the free colored, and the elusiveness of freedom in colonial Quito. In considering these subjects, the chapter further elucidates how legal struggles between slaves and slaveholders determined conditions of life in the North Andes.

Ultimately, this work offers the first comprehensive analysis of slavery and slave life in the North Andes. It advances an interrogation of African diasporic life and struggle under colonial racial slavery in a region heretofore thought, by most historians, to have lacked enslaved Africans in a number substantial enough for slavery to have mattered significantly to the colonial enterprise.

CHAPTER ONE

Slavery and Colonial Development

On December 6, 1534, representatives of the crown of Castile established a *cabildo* (town council) in the Inka city of Quito. Renaming the site the "very loyal city" of Saint Francis, Spanish conquerors blessed and baptized the city with a Christian name. This ceremonial pause within an era of colonial warfare signaled Spain's attempt to install colonial sovereignty. It revealed the matrix of race governance characteristic of Spanish colonial practice vis-à-vis those deemed "*indios*," "*negros*," and "*castas*" for differentiated status and social life within the order. It was an act of Spanish possession and conquest that inscribed the violence of law over a region that Spaniards were claiming through bloodshed and slaving. Weeks prior, while crossing the Andean mountains, Spaniards had depended heavily upon enslaved conscripts as they invaded the northern Inka outpost of Quito. In the process, Spaniards enslaved many indigenous war captives, making some of the new servile subjects wives and concubines.[1] Entering the Quito Valley in December 1534, an army of enslaved blacks and Indians along with Spaniards gave chase to the Inka general Rumiñahui. They encountered and subdued a people already compromised by disease, death, and shifting social and political alliances within the context of warfare between competing successors for the Inka empire, Huscar and Atalluapa (1527–32).[2] On that day in December, Spaniards stood triumphant with their army comprised mainly of enslaved subjects and subjugated indigenous vassals.[3] There, they installed Castilian colonial claims over new territories and peoples for an expanding, slaving Christian monarchical order, sealing in law what they had enacted through invasion, conquest, and slaving and reducing human beings to servitude.[4] Castile's advancing order was a slaving project, one based on the propagation of war and making slaves of captives.

The Castilian slave-based army's advance represented one of two methods of claiming new subjects and territories: installing foreign enslaved Africans and reducing indigenous war captives to slavery.[5] The other means was the *encomienda*, a royal grant of indigenous towns to a slaveholding Spanish lord (*encomendero*). *Encomienda* was a mode of constituting Native Americans as Indians—subjugated vassals under Euro-Christian authority. *Encomienda* and slavery were thus dual modes of establishing colonial authority, extracting tribute, and extending Christian discipline within the colony. Labor, in this sense, was as much a method of subjection and establishing colonial sovereignty as it was a system of extracting produce and labor for the colonial order.[6] African slavery, enslaving Amerindians, and *encomienda* were colonial practices of race governance that constituted blacks and Indians as servile colonial subjects and established European, Christian colonial authority.

Any peace Spaniards had envisaged for Quito's founding on December 6, 1534, was short-lived. Immediately, Spaniards set about dividing indigenous communities and settlements into *encomienda* grants given to the lords of conquest. In the process, runaway slaves and periodic indigenous rebellions undermined the consolidation of Spanish rule. Early frictions developed between the conquistadors over the spoils of war, erupting into open hostilities and a civil war between the Pizarro and Almagro clans between 1538 and 1554. These tensions between royal control and *encomendero*/slaveholder authority were brought into sharp relief with the arrival of Peru's first viceroy, Blasco Núñez Vela (1544–46), in Quito.

Blasco Núñez Vela arrived in May 1544 carrying royal instructions, including the infamous New Laws, which challenged conquistadors' unrestrained exploitation of reputedly free indigenous vassals. The most controversial aspects of the New Laws of 1542 addressed the *encomienda* system. Among other things, the New Laws declared an end to Amerindian slavery (except for Amerindians taken in just war); that no Amerindian be sent to labor in the mines without proper cause; the establishment of a fair and honest system of taxation for all Amerindians; that all *encomienda* grants held by public officials and the clergy revert to the crown; and, most critically, that all *encomienda* grants revert back to the crown upon the death of the holder. *Encomenderos* resented such encroachment upon their domain within territories they had claimed.[7] The viceroy's quarrelsome disposition offended the powerful clans of Peru, especially his position on the New Laws. Lima's powerful rallied increasingly around Gonzalo Pizarro, who, late in the year 1544, raised an army including 1,000 enslaved blacks in Cuzco to march on the viceroy in Lima. Viceroy Núñez Vela fled northward into the province of Quito on January 18, 1546, just two leagues north of Quito city, with a small, slave-based force of 400 soldiers.[8] There, he faced a battalion of 700 soldiers, which by some accounts featured as many as 600 enslaved soldiers and 100 Spaniards. The viceroy fought valiantly but was mortally wounded on the battlefield. As the viceroy lay dying, one of Pizarro's lieutenants ordered a slave to behead him. Severing the head of the viceroy and mangling the beard of the king's embodied presence, the slave-based army carried the head back to the city of Quito triumphantly and, in the presence of many, hoisted it on a pike. Reports of the event differ concerning who ordered the beheading and who carried the head and largely focus on whether or not the viceroy received a proper burial.[9] In at least one report it was a slave who carried the head as he marched behind his master while entering Quito's central plaza. Here, the slave is front and center in this juridically significant ceremony of repossession. Upon beheading the viceroy, the slave-based army reportedly placed a string through his mouth, carrying the head triumphantly on their march southward to Lima as they announced the death of bad government in the kingdoms.

The silence around this case is deafening. Although the viceroy was clearly battling a cadre of enslaved soldiers, few have taken up this early expression of slavery in the constitution of personalistic power among masters or meditated upon the slave's centrality to our understanding of early colonial political economy and political theory, or, simply put, colonialism.[10] Yet the image of a slave beheading the viceroy and carrying the head triumphantly into the city of Quito after disgracing this representative of Castilian power, signaled the stakes of governance and showcased one of the many reasons why the very basis of colonists' power in the kingdoms had to be checked and limited. The beheading also laid bare slavery's constitutive value and role within the colonial power matrix, including the threat slaves posed to colonial development. Indeed, any of the 600 battle-hardened slaves might have chosen to behead the vice king without an order from Pizarro's lieutenants. According to Andrés de Ariza, a citizen of Panama, the centrality of the slave's role in executing the viceroy predominated. Ariza's testimony from the Isthmus of Panama just months after the incident highlights the circulation of news about the event as well as ongoing concerns about warrior slaves. This incident shows that slaves conveyed power and prestige to their owners even as they represented a claim of the king and a threat to colonial order and that a slave served as the central actor in this moment of political transition.[11] Just as the viceroy's severed head captured the audience's attention, so does the centrality of the slave and his potential as both servant and assassin. At this major moment of upheaval, crisis, and transition, the presence and pivotal role of the enslaved was on full display, revealing slaves as emblems of power and might, pivotal players in political transitions, and people in need of governance.

Although the colonialists struck a decisive blow against the royalist forces at the battle of Añaquito, in which the viceroy's head was severed, divisions emerged once again among the colonists as slaves continued to fight, resist, and take flight. The crown dispatched Governor Pedro de la Gasca, who raised a slave-based army and ultimately defeated Gonzalo Pizarro at the battle of Ja-quijahuana in 1548.[12] After the battle, Gasca ordered Pizarro's execution along with some of his slaves and compatriots. Other enslaved subjects belonging to Pizarro and some of his comrades were confiscated, auctioned for the royal cof-fers, and passed along as prizes to the crown's most prominent supporters. In 1550, for example, seven of the most prominent royalists received 1,700 duty-free slave licenses as compensation for their expenses in supporting the Spanish crown during the time of war. [13] The case also reveals slavery's currency as a royal favor granted to trusted vassals such as Gasca.[14] Such grants aimed to honor those who helped to consolidate power among the *encomendero*/slaveholding elites. They reveal slavery as one of a set of privileges or *fueros*, inducements, and royal grants.[15] Slaves continued to form the base of colonial power, under-scoring the tensions that slavery contained for local masters, monarchs, and colonial officials.[16] Governing through the very subjects over whom royal vassals claimed dominion was tantamount to the insertion and maintenance of colo-nial sovereignty within this slave-based order. In their final efforts at resistance, colonists only confirmed this reality. It was not, however, until after putting down another slave-based colonist uprising (1553–54), this one led by Francisco Hernández Girón, that the crown established a tentative peace over the region.

Francisco Hernández Girón, the last among a series of beleaguered yet defi-ant Pizarrists, knew all too well the personalistic power that slave subjects con-tained. Girón relied extensively on slave conscripts in his last battle against the crown, even as he faced royalist forces comprised of enslaved squadrons.[17] In the past, Girón could have counted on other *encomenderos* to bring their slaves to war against the royal government, but by the mid-1550s, most *encomendero* families in Peru had sided with the royal effort rather than the Pizarrists.

Offering slave conscripts "vague promises of freedom and the immediate inducement of military trappings," Girón doubled the size of his enslaved forces, taking slaves from Arequipa, Guamanga (Ayacucho), and Nazca.[18] The contingent was trained and commanded by General Juan, a black carpenter credited with "disciplining and dividing the group into companies, with ban-ners and drums, armed with pikes and harquebuses."[19] The crown also made use of enslaved blacks, and as it consolidated power among the colonists, they also brought their slaves to aid in the battle, decisively defeating Girón and his slave-based battalion. Colonial authorities hung Girón, sentencing some of his enslaved comrades to death while gifting others to loyal Spanish vassals. Simultaneously, municipal governments released a series of admonishments and reminders against the arming of enslaved subjects.[20]

In the midst of crackdowns on arming slaves, runaways, and death sentences against those involved in the colonist uprising, Francisco, one of Girón's slave lieutenants, made his way to Quito and into the dominion of a Spanish patron. Francisco had fought with Girón at the battle of Purcará north of Lake Titicaca in 1554. On September 8, 1557, amid the festivals honoring the accession of Philip II, the governor of Quito, Gil Ramírez Dávalos, commuted the death sentence of Francisco, an enslaved black who had fought with Girón in the last rebellion during Peru's civil wars. Father and guardian Fray Francisco de Morales had secured the slave's pardon on behalf the Convent of San Francisco, insisting that the slave be forgiven the crimes committed by those in the company of Francisco Hernández Girón. With the prior approval of Viceroy Hurtado de Mendoza, Marqués de Cañete, the slave Francisco was to be sold at public auction. The proceeds of his sale were designated for the Colegio of San Andés for *mestizos* and poor children institutionalized within the convent. The pardon was finalized on July 15, 1558, allowing Francisco to avoid the gallows in exchange for a life of colonial captivity and black subjection. Meanwhile, the Franciscan monastery's charitable aims would be served by saving the life of this slave warrior.[21]

The case of Francisco recalls slavery's fundamental association with warfare, captivity, and redemption; regional economic development; and law and order. Here stood Franscisco, an enslaved war captive who, like the slave who beheaded the viceroy, had waged war against loyal Christian vassals and threatened the public peace. For him, the most heinous aspects of colonial discipline had been reserved. Perhaps more importantly, the case points to the two overlapping legal regimes that governed slavery and those who practiced this form of racial rule. Governing officials, including magistrates, governors, judges, and priests, all participated in slavery and slave trading and all demonstrated their colonial authority in part through overseeing the entrance, circulation, and governance of slaves and slavery throughout the realm. The governor, with the backing of the viceroy, represented the king and the dispensation of royal justice, in this case mercy. Likewise, Fray Francisco de Morales recalls the importance of the clergy in the establishment of colonial sovereignty and ecclesiastical governance and the ways that enslaved people circulated as servile subjects in convents and monasteries in cities and towns from Popayán to Quito, Guayaquil, Lima, and Cuzco. In this sense, slaves like Francisco were elemental to the "moral economies" of cities such as Quito and Cuzco, circulating as capital while laboring in the region's gold mines, on agropastoral estates, and in *obrajes* (textile mills) owned by monasteries, convents, and religious orders such as the Franciscans and the Jesuits.[22] Finally, it reveals priests as figures of authority who were elemental to colonial law.

Law in this sense was the order itself, enclosing prince, pontiff, citizen, subject, and territory within a system of royal and local decrees, doctrine, and doctrinal codes emerging from medieval Roman codes, customs, practices, and social values. Law was inherently theological, grounded in a dual economy of government that referenced divine and human duties without distinction.[23] Counter to formulations of church and state, public and private, religious and secular, or canon and civil law, colonial law encompassed church, territory, city, prince, and the people, thus comprising an order from which an economy was derived and constituted. Law was practically created in specific moments of conflict that prompted justices to discover the law on the one hand and implement it on the other.[24] All decisions replicated the divine order of things. As historian Tamar Herzog states, "This order was dictated by god, held by the king (God's lieutenant on earth), and implemented by the king's judges."[25] Earthly, priestly intercession was "thy will be done on earth as it is in heaven." Fray Francisco de Morales served as an earthly advocate and intercessor for the most unworthy of slaves in need of royal mercy. In short, the pardoned slave points again to the central role that even a few slaves could play in colonial practice and daily life.

Structuring Laws and Colonial (Dis)Order

In the midst of warfare and attempts at settlement, local town councils turned their attention to regulating slavery. Much of the legislation concerned both controlling the enslaved and regulating slaveholders' uses of their chattel. In the year 1538, for example, Quito's town council turned its attention to governing cimaroons or runaway slaves and their owners. Amid developing war between the conquistadors, the town council taxed slaveholders two pesos of gold for failing to report absent slaves. The town council noted especially that runaways must be kept out of indigenous villages, decreeing that slaves discovered living in indigenous villages be punished with 100 lashes for the first offense. The second offense carried the penalty of losing all toes on the right foot, and the third called for the slave's death without compensation to the master.[26] If masters stood to lose their dominion and financial entitlements, slaves risked life and physical punishment. Blacks found in the indigenous marketplace (*tianguez*) would receive 100 lashes at the post.[27] Early slave codes aimed to keep the enslaved under the watchful eye of their masters. Keeping them out of the indigenous marketplace was about both curbing slave mobility and limiting colonist access to indigenous territories. It also aimed to undermine the development of dangerous alliances between the enslaved and Amerindians living in villages. The code, however, governed slaves and slaveholders alike. Slaves who ran away would be subject to the most gruesome aspects of the law, while slaveholders who could not exercise dominion would be sanctioned and fined. Such laws were designed in the main to protect Spaniards and establish colonial authority. Slavery in this sense was elemental to colonial economic aspirations and labor/status designs, but it emerged also as a crucial feature of colonial order and governance aimed at limiting aristocratic authority and maintaining the crown's rights to adjudicate and have a say in a range of matters in daily life. Enforcing such laws through investigations and fines conditioned colonial authority, added to the local treasury, and generated information about slaveholders' dealings with their slaves for the emergent colonial state. Laws governing slavery aided, therefore, in the extension of royal sovereignty. But as personal subjects of their masters' estates, slaves owed their personal power, time, and resources to their captors and immediate lords.

In January 1551, the *cabildo* declared that any female runaway found after being absent for more than eight days would receive 100 lashes. Male runaways found after this period would have their "genital members and testicles cut off."[28] This was in spite of a 1540 Reál Cedúla, in which the crown declared, "We demand that in no case shall you punish black maroons by cutting their parts, which honestly one cannot name, and ensure that they are punished consistent with the law [*derecho*], and laws [*leyes*] of this text."[29] Local officials, however, reserved in law the most heinous and grotesque punishments for bodies marked as black. These were applied especially when blacks were charged with the most offensive infractions, such as chronic flight, sleeping with indigenous women, or violent confrontations and robberies. Further evidence that these penalties were generally accepted is found in Licenciado Francisco de Auncibay's 1596 declaration regarding the care and control of a proposed crown-subsidized shipment of enslaved ethnic Africans. Auncibay stated, "The punishments administered to blacks will be lashes and the loss of ears, and for three-time runaways, they shall be stripped [*desgarronarles*], placed in shackles, leg irons, pillories, and the *campanilla* [iron collar with a hanging bell], but not exile nor the galleys, and if the crime is heinous, death." This accompanied Auncibay's 1596 petition to the crown for subsidy in the development of Popayán's goldfields. Among other things, Auncibay requested that the crown purchase 1,000 Africans, including an equal number of males and females.[30]

Spanish representatives also strove to curtail slaves' actions in daily life in the colonies. By midcentury, the crown spoke incessantly about the disruptive force and formidable threat that black rebels and fugitives posed against the public peace of its American colonies. On numerous occasions, the crown addressed the threat of blacks "walking the city streets at night" beyond the watchful eye of their masters.[31] Edicts emanating from Spain echoed decrees made by municipal governments throughout the empire that outlined the penalties for maroons and delinquent slaves or those who ran off and hid for periods of time.[32] One notable code began by stating, "In the province of Tierra Firme [Panama] there have been many deaths, robberies, [and] injuries, committed by runaway blacks in mobs, and hidden in frontier regions and fortified or secure locations [arcabacas]."[33] While chiding slave masters for failing to provide adequate supervision of runaways and slave armies during war, the crown also condemned the practice—widespread among masters, especially in the age of exploration and conquest and during the Spanish civil wars—of arming enslaved blacks, saying, "Blacks, loros [people of African and Amerindian heritage], and free blacks [must] not carry weapons." Those who failed to comply would face hefty fines and stiff penalties.[34]

From the beginning of the sixteenth century slavery offered the crown a distinct set of governing possibilities as well as a series of governing challenges and concerns. Already the crown had conceded the free vassalage of indigenous subjects of the Americas. In spite of this, Spanish slaving of indigenous subjects and brutal attempts to dominate and reduce them to colonial service persisted, leading to indigenous population decline and ensuring that proper indigenous subjection would remain a royal concern of good governance. Claiming and holding legitimate sovereignty over the Indies rested upon according indigenous subjects proper status and ensuring their proper governance and fair treatment. But the need to check the rise of a conquistador aristocracy capable of challenging the crown's authority in the Indies prompted the crown to govern through the regulation of colonial subjection, subject making, and access to servile labor.

The New Laws of 1542–43 that had exacerbated earlier colonist tensions, like many other edicts and forms of legislation emanating from the crown and its surrogates in the Americas, reflected the moral and political goals of the crown and were designed to limit the power of an emergent class of Spanish Christian vassals. Although a spate of civil wars between the Pizarrists and the Almagros abrogated this legislation in Peru, the policies it espoused emerged alongside a series of laws around slavery and its governance to reveal the ways in which the crown sought to regulate colonialism. In the case of the New Laws, Indian slavery was again prohibited by royal edict, except for those who proved bellicose and resistant to Christian authority.

Simultaneously, through policy and practice, the colonial government naturalized slavery's association with blackness. In so doing, it mapped blackness and slavery onto foreign African territorial subjection in relation to subjugated indigenous vassalage. Both were duly placed in the care and under the dominion of Christian vassals, who were obligated to wield proper dominion to the benefit and betterment of the order. Slavery, *ecomienda*, *mit'a*, and the resulting status of Andeans (*yananaconas*) who sought to avoid their tribute payments by fleeing to Spanish estates and cities throughout Quito were foundational to colonial modes of governing diverse and mobile populations and determining the limits and responsibilities of Spanish and Creole authority throughout the Americas. These policies were designed to channel indigenous subjection and place the indigenous in the service of colonial development. They were also aimed at the proper enclosure of Christian vassals for the proper structuring of the Spanish commonwealth through limitations placed upon developing New World estates and elite "houses" or patresfamilias. Consequently, in the New Laws and during the Toledo Reforms of 1569, *encomenderos* were forbidden to demand tribute in the form of unpaid labor, with the crown fixing the other amounts of tribute they could collect. In 1569, King Philip II dispatched Francisco de Toledo with a series of reforms for the viceroyalty of Peru in response to an emerging crisis in the Andes over governance. The reforms contained three principal elements: first, congregating or "reducing" indigenous peoples into large, strategically located towns—the Reducción General de Indios; second, imposing a more regularized taxation system; and third, establishing a regime of forced labor to support the silver mines of Peru and Upper Peru (Bolivia).[35] The crown limited the holding of *encomienda* grants in perpetuity and installed *corregidores de indios*, royal officials who exercised judicial and political authority over the indigenous. These *corregidores* aimed to govern Indian areas not unlike governors in the Spanish areas, thus reducing *encomenderos'* power over the indigenous such that by the 1570s, the message was clear: the crown, not conquistadors and their descendants, was to hold ultimate sway over the servile populations of Indian vassals and African slaves.

Regulations around slavery emerged, therefore, within this context of race governance. Like the crown's attempts to rule Indians, its interests in structuring authority, promoting commercial relations, and maintaining public peace influenced the development and rationales of these regulations. From the moment the first enslaved subjects arrived in the Americas, resistance was expected and began to shape colonial governing designs and practices. Restive captives took flight and formed a contingent of "counterconquistadors," even as many of their would-be comrades helped to advance the march of the Spanish order. Confronted by multiple challenges—internal conflicts among Spaniards, rebellious Amerindians, and the need for a tighter grip on the empire in the face of piracy—the crown stood to lose the empire if it failed to check rogue elements within its territories. Something had to be done to shore up the authority of the crown and its agents in the Indies. As a result, municipal governments, in concert with the crown, issued numerous pieces of legislation, many of which responded directly to resistance and rebellion by the enslaved. Royal decrees and municipal ordinances provide evidence of elite fears, underscoring the fact that rebels and fugitives helped to form the evolving judicial context wherein laws were made and judgments were rendered.

Royal edicts and admonishments also emphasized the crown's pragmatic approach to the regulation of slaveholding. In concert with harsher social controls, royal admonishments to American courts included, for example, the command that judiciaries ensure that free blacks who adhered to the rule of law were not molested or provoked to unruly behavior. The royal edict of 1540, for example, ordered American courts to "hear and provide justice to those [blacks] that proclaim free status . . . and do justice, and rule, that in this they are not mistreated by their masters."

In addition to these prohibitions, the crown and the clergy extended to slaves the rights to marriage and good treatment, the right to own and inherit property, and the right to self-purchase—all concessions designed to curb male slave discontent. Such concessions, while based on medieval-era law, as well as canon and civil law, were voiced during the early colonial era as essential means of promoting the peaceful coexistence of slave and master by tempering slave resentment.[36]

From the 1550s to the 1640s, rebels and fugitives, along with "unruly" and "disruptive" subjects more generally, found themselves within a shifting imperial context. Royal attempts at absolutism coincided with a renewed emphasis on an "imperial" de jure order to circumscribe the lives of all subjects while promoting an increasingly racialized discourse that cast all persons of color into the category of things wild and potentially subversive.[37] The need for various forms of regulation had spawned strict controls aimed at all potentially disruptive subjects.[38] In the case of the enslaved, conciliatory slave codes—granting the right to marriage, property ownership, inheritance, and merciful treatment—rewarded complicity in hopes of quelling all potential for violence. On the other hand, restrictive legislation, with its corresponding punishments—whipping, castration, and lynching—served to encode the hopes and fears of the crown and its American surrogates.

Early colonial slave regulations, therefore, signaled the pervasiveness of actual imperial threats, providing a twofold approach to social control. Complicity would be rewarded by inclusion in the form of access to the law; flouting royal authority, however, rendered one worthy of the most brutal aspects of the *reconquista*. In several codes addressing runaways, we find the crown using phrases such as "war on maroons" and "campaign to search out maroons." In many ways this was a true war and/or campaign from the earliest moments. The crown went to great lengths to administer this "war" or "campaign" on maroons, prescribing in 1624 that those who worked in this service in Cartagena receive six reales for each maroon they apprehended. While setting forth legislation aimed at governing this war, the crown also provided incentives for slaves who returned voluntarily and even "better" incentives for those willing to bring in other runaways. On the island of Cuba, for example, officials sent out armed militias accompanied by search dogs (*perros de busca*) to seek out and apprehend runaways. Apparently this measure caused just as much confusion as it sought to quell. These bands often forced free blacks into slavery and/or extorted cash, goods, and services from them. This became such a problem that in 1623 the crown demanded that these bands not "molest" free blacks ("que los rancheadores no molesten a los morenos libres, que estuvieren pacificos").[39]

In Cartagena, slaves aided in religious instruction and the imposition of Christian discipline; hunted down runaways; and worked as overseers in mining communities, *obrajes*, farms, and estates. These examples suggest enslaved subjects participated in the ordering of colonial society. Slave governance, slave subjection, and the personalist power they embodied suggest that slaves were formidable subjects whose governance and use as subjects were far too important to leave solely to those who claimed direct dominion over them. They point to the peculiarities of slavery's institutionalized and bureaucratic formation. Slavery in this sense was neither an appendage of the market nor a strange institution that arranged labor and economy. Rather, it was a royal concession that produced subjects, authority, and land claims as well as critical aspects of the colonial bureaucracy.

If applied, such codes proposed to condition both mastery and slavery, governing owners and the enslaved alike through slavery. Ownership, the right to properly possess and subjugate enslaved captive subjects, required, nevertheless, the proper exercise of dominion. Ultimately, good governance legitimated rule, just as it did for sitting sovereigns. This was at least the principle enshrined in the law, one that allowed pontiffs and monarchs alike to dispossess wayward masters and reallocate enslaved subjects through public auction.

By the early seventeenth century, the juridical context of colonialism had been established. Imperial and municipal slave codes had emerged over the course of the early colonial period as responses to the cumulative effects of slave flight and rebellion. Though functioning within *derecho* (the legal tradition and system) and while extending the boundaries of the royal court, royal edicts and municipal ordinances constituted judicial reactions to radical resistance by the enslaved—reactions that were predicated upon elite fears and assumptions about blacks, both enslaved and free. The crown and its representatives in the New World had articulated a legal discourse that sought to be both conciliatory and restrictive in an effort to achieve and sustain social order. The dividing lines were clear, as all were cast as either "insiders" or "outsiders" in relation to an expanding imperial order. Those who conformed and performed the duties of the loyal would be accorded certain conciliatory measures; those who failed to comply would suffer the harsher side of the law. In this way, sixteenth- and early seventeenth-century antecedents laid the groundwork for managing colonial Spanish America and controlling errant slaves. They also signaled the crown's claims to govern the Indies—slaveholders, indigenous vassals, free blacks, and the enslaved alike—through the very systems of authority and production. If slaveholders ruled, it was within the same limits that constrained the dominion of the crown and clergy. In short, the concern for good governance enclosed all within the realm.

On March 8, 1650, in the city of Guayaquil, the town council expressed the need to continue the ongoing practice of using arriving African captives to clear the mangroves that surrounded the city while they awaited purchase. Mangroves presented a potential health hazard to residents already plagued by diseases. They reduced ventilation, posed a risk of fires, and provided possible cover for pirates, marauding Indians, and African runaways threatening the city. The council called upon local slaveholders as ruling elites wielding dominion to assist in remedying the problem of growing mangroves and carrying out the overall improvement of the city's built environment. Over the course of the next two days, the city commissioned the conscription of fifty slaves, including their time, labor, and rents, in order to clear the mangroves. Council records reveal that a range of slaveholders from city authorities to poor colonials donated their slaves or rents for periods ranging from a few days to a week or more.

A willingness to donate enslaved subjects' time and physical labor in the service of the colonies varied from owner to owner.[40] Some, such as Captain don Antonio Calderón, sent two blacks for the period of one week. Others sent as many as four enslaved blacks for one week. The governor, don Juan María de Guevara y Cantos, donated the service of only one "*moreno*" for one week, while the Convent of San Augustín sent two *morenos* for eight days, along with an ax. Some citizens sent no more than three pesos or barely more than the rent of one slave for three days. One sent "one black for one day," while a few sent slaves for an unspecified amount of time.[41] These examples showcase the ways in which even the "labor" of slaves mapped onto a broader field of colonial governing concerns, not the least of which was how to keep the city safe from fires and marauding pirates and otherwise ensure its development and productivity. They also illustrate the ways local authority and standing were demonstrated by dispatching subjects and providing necessary laborers for civic needs—in this case slaves to assist in urban improvement and town safety rather than individual profit—and reveal the ways legislative and governing bodies used slavery to structure colonial life and urban planning.

On October 1, 1652, General don Francisco Vasquez de Silva, *corregidor* and *justicia mayor* of the cities Guayaquil and Puerto Viejo, conferred the title of lieutenant general upon don Antonio de Castro y Guzman. Runaway slaves and Indians were allegedly causing insufferable harm to the city's Spaniards and Indians, "robbing women, cattle, setting fires, and engaging in petty theft with great excesses."[42] Guzman was already a member of the Santa Hermandad of Guayaquil and heir to a shipbuilding operation based in the royal shipyards of Guayaquil. Just two years prior, on August 9, 1650, Guzman and other *cabildo* members issued an edict against the practice of masters using slaves to steal wood. Those who continued to do so would face a penalty of having the wood confiscated and having their slaves receive 100 lashes.[43] In this context, slavery proved quite generative for Guzman, helping him to raise his social standing. Owning slaves promised Guzman material resources even as hunting down slaves, vagabonds, and rebellious Indians furthered his social standing as an act showcasing his valor at arms. Now elevated to the rank of lieutenant general, Guzman increased his colonial standing both by forcing enslaved carpenters to build ships and by policing the region's roads, brush, and coastline for pirates, runaway slaves, vagabonds, and rebellious Amerindians.

On September 22, 1650, Guayaquil's town council enlisted the leadership of Antonio Hidalgo, a former municipal councillor or member of the town council. Both municipal leaders (*alcaldes*) were outside of the city tending to important matters of business and justice. One was away in the valley of Baba and the other in the valley of Yaguache. The council members noted that the city was found with only the bailiff's lieutenant. They wished to deputize Antonio Hidalgo in order that he might corral and punish "*negros y mulatos*" who "disturb this republic." This, they claimed, was not possible with only one lieutenant. As a result, the council proposed to empower the former city council member. The challenges of slave resistance and rebellious Indians provoked several governing concerns, prompted the council to undertake specific forms of policy and authority, and affected the society in ways that a focus on slave population size and economic outputs obscures. They defy, thereby, prevailing notions of slavery and slave societies. Ultimately, the actions of the enslaved conditioned the social order and the development of colonial authority.[44] Policies such as those enacted in Guayaquil reveal slavery's imprint upon the ordering of society in ways that suggest that even a small number of slaves could help to constitute a slave society.

Slavery was not the sole concern of seventeenth-century municipalities but was often involved in other royal imperatives and local interests. On July 23, 1654, for example, the Guayaquil town council convened local property holders and prelates due to their failure to pay sales taxes and import tariffs associated with incoming slaves. Among those in attendance were a local major and judge, prominent landowners, priests, members of the town council, and those in the service of the crown at the royal shipyards. Prior to this convention, Viceroy Conde de Salvatierra had dispatched two official notices, one to the town council concerning remittances to the royal treasury and the other to the Real Audiencia in Quito, which had failed to remit sales taxes for four months.[45] Among other concerns and possible areas needing oversight that were discussed was the observation that city clerics and *religiosos* were failing to submit sales taxes when importing enslaved captives into the port of Guayaquil.

Just a decade earlier, in the year 1644, Guayaquil's town council heard a dispute concerning financial interests bound to the enslaved Juan Angola. His owner, Captain Hernando Alonso Holguín, owed the city 1,000 pesos in principal. Interest was accruing. The town council had confiscated Juan Angola, denying Alonso access to his subject and thereby restricting his ability to extract rents, labor, or economic value from Juan, whom the town council described as an axman or a hewer or wood "*hachero*." When Alonso suggested that the city hire out the slave and make use of his rents, the council insisted that it had already done so, noting that his rents barely covered the cost of his food and care during his time in the city's custody. Consequently, the city council confiscated other possessions of Alonso, ceding Juan's rents to the slave himself in order that he might support himself until such a time as the council might sell him at public auction. The full weight of early colonial historiography shows that viceregal, provincial, and municipal governments dispossessed unworthy slaveholders of their dominion, even as they legitimated slavery and maintained slaves in their condition of colonial servitude. In so doing, they claimed the right to govern colonial vassals through the subjects over whom they claimed dominion. Slavery was, therefore, fundamental to a particular kind of governance that over time drew the king into the most intimate affairs of individual subjects throughout the kingdom. Slaves circulated as royal symbols, sacred yet disposable bodies, and commodities long before they were put to work. These concerns made the enslaved and the territories they mapped essential to colonial rule as abiding concerns of colonial governance.

Through conquest, pillage, slaving, and the onslaught of Old World diseases, Iberians, Africans, and Indians constituted the colonial horizon of the Atlantic

World, producing a new and vast regional system of governance that connected the three continents. Iberians forged these connections through the practices of subjugation aimed at indigenous populations while developing new modes of slaving, slave trading, and enslavement aimed in an increasingly exclusive fashion toward those of African descent. These practices and processes of governing new territories, subject peoples, and markets conditioned the extension of early modern legal regimes and the emergence of new governing norms that developed in tandem with new intellectual discourses about bodies and territories as well as new modes of commercial exchange. While elements of this narration of early modernity are familiar in Atlantic colonial history, the role of slavery as a mode of governing colonial development remains less recognized. Even in areas of the Americas where it never came to dominate the local labor regime, African slavery was a part of the juridical ordering of society, a coveted possession, a marker of prestige and personalistic power, and consequently a conveyer of multiple values and interests. This cultural, social, political, and aspirational value of slavery came with conquistadors, noblemen, and women arriving from Iberia over the course of the sixteenth century. The right to rule captive subjects was by this time already part of the general pattern of Iberian ambition and a growing elite conceit throughout Europe.[46] As conquistadors, noblemen, clerics, and merchants fanned out across the Americas in the wake of conquest, they brought with them entourages comprised of enslaved blacks while harboring aspirations to own and rule over more. Merchants and speculators also carried enslaved Africans, ensuring their growing presence while developing cash for other pursuits. Elemental to early modes of commerce, capital, and commercial valuation, enslaved subjects (blacks and some Indians) provided Castilian sovereigns with another set of royal concessions for their Christian vassals with their penchant for slaving and wielding dominion. Limiting the growing dominion of conquistadors, noblemen, clerics, and merchants was a part of the general pattern of this expanding absolutist order. Governing slaving, slave trading, and slave-based colonial authority was, therefore, an early aim of Politica Indiana and proved interstitial to the emergent colonial apparatus.

In the Pacific and Andean territories, slavery catalyzed and conditioned early modern Atlantic governmental development and commercial exchange and served to legitimate imperial claims. After the legendary 1545 silver strike at Potosí, Spanish fleets carried enormous sums of precious metals from profits extracted from the great mountain of Potosí to the royal treasury in Spain.[47] The removal and transferal of such vast sums of silver, first from the red mountain to Arica and then on through Callao and across the Isthmus of Panama, drew Andean territories and subject peoples into contact with increasing numbers of ethnic Africans emerging from Atlantic commercial and legal cultures. These processes spurred commercial action, provoked judicial oversight and legislation, and informed mercantilist policies that over time grounded the racial subjection and subject status of indigenous and African-descended subjects. The sheer magnitude and scale of indigenous demographic decline, silver extraction, gold mining, and judicial action point to the multiple meanings of labor for colonialism and subject making. In short, making laboring subjects of Amerindians, Africans, and their *casta* descendants proved elemental to defining colonial subject status while honoring Spanish Christian vassalage and structuring colonial authority. Consequently, over the course of the sixteenth century, Castile sought to legitimate its claims to the Americas through governing every aspect of colonial development, including the proper use and treatment of even the most subordinated of colonial subjects.

In Quito, the quest for metallurgical deposits shaped territorial advancement and settlement patterns and spurred the material aspirations of conquistadors. In the 1540s this search for El Dorado lead them first to the southernmost regions of the kingdom at the sites of Zaruma and Zamora and shortly thereafter on to Quito's northern hinterland of Popayán. As Europeans enslaved Afro-Iberians, Africans, Central Americans, and some local indigenous populations, they made use of them in their quest to claim new territories, harness natural resources, and subjugate laboring vassals.

Obrajes and indigenous labor have dominated explorations of Quito's socioeconomic history and the development of the colonial state, while African slavery is understood to have been marginal to the kingdom's economy and state formation. Beginning in the 1560s and 1570s the kingdom developed a vibrant regional economy based on the production of woolen textiles. Silver mining at Potosí drew Spanish Andean colonial development into the international economy.[48] Smaller regional markets like Quito produced foodstuffs, wine, liquor, cloth, and labor for the mining zones. Over the course of the seventeenth century, textile production in the north-central highlands allowed Quito to play a crucial role in a series of evolving secondary regional markets. Fertile lands found within Quito's narrow Andean valleys and wide expanses of *páramo* pasturelands allowed for the establishment of agropastoral estates and numerous textile mills stretching from Otavalo in the north to Riobamba in the central highlands. Reliant upon indigenous labor charges, not enslaved Africans, these mills supplied woolen textiles for the mining markets of Peru and New Granada in return for silver, allowing a small but powerful elite to enjoy European cosmopolitan pleasures and conceits.[49] The use of pasturelands combined with royal labor grants and oppressive tribute measures gave mill owners cheap access to the labor of a growing indigenous population.[50] Textiles along with cheap and available indigenous labor, we are told, drove the economy, making Quito a "society with slaves," one in which slaves were present yet economically inconsequential, rather than a "slave society," in which slave labor overwhelmingly determined the economic trajectory of the colony.[51]

Yet, upon further inquiry into the overlapping circuits of commerce, laws, and legal cultures that crisscrossed and governed the region, we see the ways that slavery shaped colonial practice in the North Andes as it proved elemental to economic development and the integration of secondary regional markets. Over the course of the sixteenth and seventeenth centuries, the colonial state licensed and governed the incremental expansion of slavery into new territories such as Popayán and Barbacoas, allowing for the introduction of enslaved blacks. Colonial officials licensed the enslavement of some of the region's *indios*, such as the Pijaos and the Paez of the Cauca Valley, while subduing others such as the Sindaguas of the Pacific lowlands as *encomienda* charges. The region would not have been claimed or made productive, however, were it not for the presence and physical force of slaves. Enslaved captive subjects of servitude were, therefore, more than a labor remedy; they were part of a larger colonial advance and marked off new territories of governance for colonial authorities in Santa Fé and Quito. Enslaved African subjects stirred the aspirations of miners, *audiencia* justices, tax collectors, priests, nuns, and a host of colonial subjects within the advancing order. The expansion of slavery, therefore, did more than provide the colony labor for gold or agricultural exports. Slaves also served to develop markets, claim new territories, and established a range of social and political networks crucial to establishing territorial sovereignty. For example, the *asiento*, paying sales taxes and tithes, and rendering the royal fifth were all forms of tribute collection, royal grants, and modes of subject making, not unlike *encomienda* and *mit'a*. Slaves also conditioned colonial rule. They took flight, established maroon settlements, rebelled violently, and negotiated the terms of their servitude with masters. In the process they helped to shape the development of laws and practices of governance designed to control slaves and regulate their masters' power in the colonies.

Enslaved subjects played multiple roles: they circulated within society as cash, capital, and accoutrements of the wealthy.[52] Slaves were passed along in the most prized and respectable dowries, dressed in finery for proper placement within the retinues of the wealthy taking pious strolls, or mortgaged and exchanged for some other coveted piece of property.[53] Bequests of slaves to the church and deathbed manumissions funded a moral economy that enriched the *religiosos* of the kingdom while facilitating baroque expressions of piety.[54]

The circulation and regulation of enslaved bodies drew both the pontiff's and the crown's concerns into daily life in specific and intimate ways. Possession and dominion of slaves communicated status, but it also necessitated good Christian mastery. This included the proper feeding and clothing, religious instruction, and comportment of the slave for the sake of God and the order.[55] Enslaved blacks became marked Christian subjects, who literally moved throughout the kingdom with the king's brand on their bodies. If majesty and power were communicated through display, ceremonies of governance, and royal symbolism, the symbolism of the royally marked and sanctioned slave body must have offered a powerful icon of royal authority in daily life. This reminds us again that before the late eighteenth century and the development of an economic rationale of governance, economy as a governing concept was bound up in governance and claims of European sovereignty. The structuring of commerce was a mode of governing exchanges made between patriarchal authorities and communities within the realm, even as it was a mode of producing wealth. Thus, slavery was fundamental to a particular kind of governance that over time drew the king into the most intimate affairs of individual subjects throughout the kingdom. In Baroque Quito and well into the late eighteenth century, enslaved blacks circulated as royal symbols, sacred yet disposable bodies, and commodities long before they were put to work, preceding or during the decline or disruption of indigenous populations. These concerns made the enslaved and the territories they mapped crucial in the structuring of colonial rule, law, and jurisprudence.

Claiming Territories in the Pacific Lowlands: The Next Frontier

In the year 1650, an unidentified observer wrote to the crown:

> Your Majesty has in this Gobierno de Popayán certain provinces that fall at the margins of the South Sea, named the Barbacoas. They are situated in the western *cordillera*, in the part that faces Gorgona, island of the said sea. In these provinces one finds when one enters the *gobierno*, that a town has been founded under the title of Santa María del Puerto, something of a detour from the sea, yet in canoes over a navigable river, named Telembí and others in the same coast of the said sea, just beginning to be populated, that they named, the port of Santa Bárbara of the Island of Gallo. This one founded here for the grand ease that one can have with the said port since it is very large and accommodating, and since it is not farther than a five-day trip to Panamá over the said sea, to

which they can board large ships in large quantities and there they will
be well guarded and secure in all instance. . . . Close to this port there
is a province named el Sindagua, whose Indians after giving peace and
obedience to Your Majesty, they live beyond 60 years; and all of them
are in such [condition] that they do not fall into decline, neither can one
pacify them because they are bellicose people and very cannibalistic,
inclined to eat human flesh and make a thousand assaults.[56]

This *relación* or royal report grew out of attempts to see, know, and properly
claim the territories known as the Barbacoas (Taíno for "Land of Stilt-Houses")
situated in Colombia's southwest Pacific littoral. The area was one of the first
districts of the Pacific that Spaniards explored. Francisco Pizarro had put in at
the islands of Gorgona and Gallo in 1526 but was discouraged by the rainforest climate of rain, mangroves, and humidity and moved southward. Likewise,
Popayán's second governor, Pedrarías Davila, explored the perimeter of Barbacoas from various points in the 1520s and 1530s.[57] But while it was legend that the
region was home to rivers of gold, Barbacoas, along with its northern neighbor
Chocó, remained independent until well into the mid-1630s and 1650s, respectively.[58] The various indigenous groups of the region—Boyas, Chupas, Nulpes,
Guapies, and Sindaguas—succeeded at keeping the Spaniards at bay in spite of
expeditionary campaigns comprised of enslaved Africans and highland indigenous conscripts who fell victim to kidnapping and executions at the hands of
reputed head-hunters and cannibals. Similar to Esmeraldas, Mercedarian and
Jesuit missionary campaigns were also pushed back violently, as labyrinths of
mangrove swamps and rapid and often unnavigable rivers bordering junglelike
forests served as natural barriers to Spanish incursion. The dense rainforest and
mangroves of the wet Pacific littoral were also home to poisons, vipers, mosqui-
toes, and an abundance of human parasites.[59] An important Spanish settlement
was established at Santa María del Puerto around 1631 in the form of a small village along the Telembí River, some 80 kilometers from the Pacific Ocean. Other
permanent settlements emerged slowly along the Patía, Iscuandé, and Timbiquí
Rivers. These settlements followed renewed expeditions authorized by Governor don Lorenzo de Villaquirán of Popayán, who was determined to press the
region's indigenous inhabitants into service and punish rebel Sindaguas.[60]

Villaquirán authorized an expedition lead by Francisco de Prado y Zúñiga.
And by 1632, a Panama-based mine owner had arrived with twenty enslaved
Africans to work the Telpí River near Santa Barbará de la Isla del Gallo. Although they found gold, the group soon fell ill and died. Soon thereafter, Cris-
tóbal de Aguilar, another Panama-based associate, sent "a black confidant" to

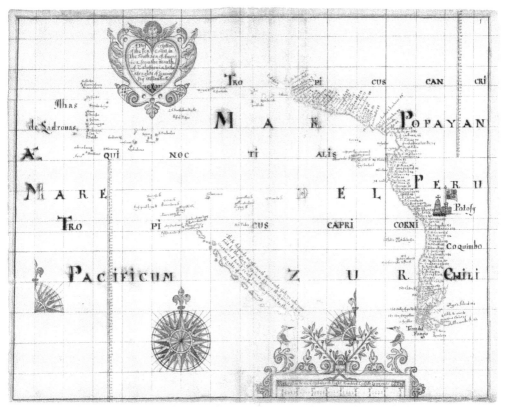

Mare Pacificum. From William Hack, *An Accurate Description of the South Sea* (1698). John Carter Brown Library at Brown University.

prospect for gold along the Timbiquí River. This resulted in Aguilar sending 150 enslaved Africans in three of his own vessels.[61] Aspiring mine owners who did not own enslaved blacks or could not yet afford to purchase them sought *encomiendas*, which gave them access to people who could mine the region's rivers of gold and negotiate life in the region's dense rainforest ecosystem. In this case, *encomienda* offered status to third-generation elites from Pasto and served as a bridge to the incremental expansion of slavery into the region.[62] For over a century, gold-mining operations in the Cauca Valley had driven wealth accumulation and status claims in greater Popayán. There, slave-based gold-mining operations shifted and expanded as owners installed enslaved Africans in mining centers in the north (Caloto), west (Chisquío), and south (Almaguer). Increasingly, as cattle-ranching and agropastoral enterprises expanded to supply the region's mining settlements with foodstuffs and agricultural goods, they also gradually used enslaved Africans as servile laborers.

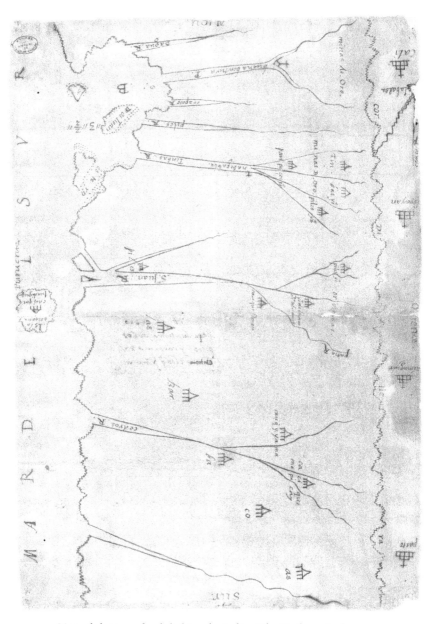

Mapa de la tierra donde habitan los indios, Piles Timbas y Barbacoas.
AGI, MP-Panamá, 30. Archivo General de Indias.

By the 1650s, mine owners were settling the region of Barbacoas in increasing numbers. Some had very few enslaved subjects yet held considerable collections of specialized mining tools.[63] In addition, as of 1658, one Barbacoan mine owner purchased enslaved blacks, including three men and one woman: Manuel Santa Fé (*nación Angola*), his wife Lucía (also *nación Angola*), Juan Philupo de los Ríos, and Juan Razón, an Afro-Criollo, aged 40, 35, 35, and 16, respectively.[64] These enslaved subjects aided in the claiming of vast stretches of territory, ensuring that Popayán and Barbacoas would not be colonial backwaters.[65] By the close of the century broad swathes of new territories were in the process of being incorporated and large sums of gold were being smelted. By the 1680s Barbacoas was registering 20,000–30,000 gold pesos (*castellanos*), an amount valued at approximately 40,000–60,000 silver pesos (*patacones*).[66] Conquest of the region, however, was not a fait accompli. Restive Amerindians continued to flee Spanish service, avoid work, rebel, and take legal action. Likewise, enslaved Africans marked off the fragmentary colonial sovereignty, forming *palenques* (runaway settlements) up the Patía River, southward into the district of Esmeraldas, and in the foothills of the western Cordillera between Barbacoas and the upper Patía River valley. The largest and best-known *palenque* in the Pacific lowlands was El Castigo (The Punishment), which was formed during this period of incremental settlement and expansion between 1635 and 1726.[67]

The colonization and settlement of Quito's northern hinterlands reveal slavery as instrumental in the making of black colonial subjects and the constitution of colonial governance over new landscapes, peoples, markets, and economies. Along the way, these processes evidence racial slavery as constitutive of the colonial order and emergent notions of sovereignty, order, economy, and government. They reveal a crucial link between slavery and the making of the colonial state. This suggests the need to better conceptualize slavery as a foundational facet of colonialism. Whether in Mexico City or the Yucatan, Lima or the highland valleys of Quito, these were slave-based societies. Consequently, their legal regimes and practices developed in tandem with slavery and the circuits of commerce and authority were mutually constitutive of colonial rule. In short, this is why slaves were so important to so many aspects of colonial law and legal practice, why the law indeed mattered in significant and yet dispersed and uneven ways for slaves across the kingdoms, thereby obscuring the urban/rural divide. Whatever justice there was for a slave, slave subjection was understood through and marked severely upon the body of the enslaved. Brands, baptism, and bonds (fetters, lashings, castrations, amputations, etc.) were all modes of subjection meant to govern slaves' comportment within Christian discipline. This was colonial race governance.

CHAPTER TWO

Marking Bodies

Brands, Baptism, and the Body as Text

Indians were conquered. Negroes were enslaved—constructed categories
of colonial subjection occurring over the sixteenth century relationally.
—Eric Wolf, *Europe and the People without History*

Race was the colonial sedimentation of the political.
—Barnor Hesse, "Creolizing the Political"

On May 6, 1699, in the town of Popayán, Captain Don Sebastían Torijano registered the arrival of 65 enslaved African Spaniards dubbed *bozales*. The newly arrived group of Africans, known variously throughout the diaspora as "saltwater
slaves," "Guinea birds," or *bozales*, were a diasporic people; they had emerged
from the deadly and turbulent currents of Atlantic commerce and governance.[1]
Like those before and after them, these 37 women (*negras*) and 28 men (*negros*)
landed at the Magdalena River port of Honda on February 16, 1699.[2] Forcefully
dispersed throughout the Gobernación de Popayán into the administrative
heartland of Quito, these enslaved Africans joined growing numbers entering
the kingdom.[3] Africans' diverse origins, ports of embarkation, varying rates of
arrival, and points of entry were constitutive of their roles in conquering the
region, claiming territories, and establishing its governing norms. Slave trading,
much like other forms of commerce, established Castile's colonial sovereignty
within the new region. Yet, as Castile consolidated its control over the land,
spaces of contention opened up within the very process. The mechanisms of
slave trading to and within Quito helped form Castilian governance based on
race relations, marking the bodies of enslaved Africans as foreign subjects from
distant, non-Castilian territories. These enslaved subjects merited a specific kind
of governance and structured specific forms of authority within the colonial matrix of power. The formation of interior lives or attempts to forge kinships occurred in the midst of colonial race governance as enslaved subjects lived and
labored within the various modalities of racial slavery.

While enslaved blacks created kin and forged meaningful social lives, their movements within empire were governed through colonial assemblages of territoriality, corporeality, culture, politics, and religion.[4] In this sense, race, less than an ideology or a scientific notion predicated upon blood lineage, proved to be a colonial governing practice that circumscribed black social life and interiority.[5] As a colonial practice of governance, race inscribed the juridico-political status of the enslaved and governed their movement, treatment, and life within the order.[6] Suffering social death and gross alienation upon arrival, deracinated and enslaved Africans, otherwise marked as "black," formed social lives as diminished, subjugated, and excluded subjects. Their colonially inscribed lineage, dispositions, and subject status mapped onto territories Castilians and other Mediterranean peoples had traditionally considered uninhabitable, malevolent, non-Christian, degenerative, and therefore as legitimate sources for enslaved captives. Marked as utterly alien, these Africans entered the Americas not as property, capital, or labor per se, but as people identified by the sovereigns of Castile as having "black" territorial origins, dubious "national" affiliations, as well as physical and moral qualities that legitimized their enslavability. In short, Castilians used what they deemed to be African origins (geohumoral and territorial) as a pretense for enslaving and governing Africans differently in relation to Castilians.[7] Colonial practices of racial governance were, thus, bound within and productive of racialized modes of mapping, claiming, and governing non-European territories and their adjacent transoceanic regions in the wake of exploration, conquest, and colonization.

In declaring certain captives "black," *bozal*, and of a particular African *casta/nación*, Castilians did more than identify people and bodies in relation to Castilians and Christian blood lineage. These practices delineated landscapes and territories, mapping geographies in relation to Castilian sovereignty for the extension of imperial rule. At the beginning of the sixteenth century, Castile was but a conglomeration of kingdoms with fractured sovereignty. Having barely wrest control of the Iberian Peninsula from Muslims by 1492, Christian kingdoms defined themselves increasingly in relation to lands, territories, and peoples. Based in part upon Aristotelian notions of space and place, Europeans deemed themselves inherently superior in their *naturaleza* and their political theological concepts of Christian blood heritage. Although these concepts were not in and of themselves tantamount to "race thinking" or postenlightenment biological understanding of "modern bodies" and fixity over time, Castilian colonial declarations and acts of race governance mapped entire regions of the Americas and Africa as *black and enslavable*. Race was, therefore, less a mental condition and more a political provocation that over time deemed Guinea and its inhabitants as non-Christian, barbarian, and unworthy of self-governance and territorial dominion.[8] Over time, these practices in dialogue, including those aimed at governing indigenous subjects, served to naturalize black as slave and slave as fundamentally, if not increasingly exclusively, black. By the time Torijano's captives had arrived, Castilians had elaborated a system of racial slavery that installed captive deracinated non-European populations in their early modern colonies, obliging them "under law and practice to comport themselves within the social contours of their designated assemblage of race."[9]

In this sense, Castilians' use of slavery to govern both deracinated populations from sub-Saharan Africa and those indigenous to the Americas was the quintessential colonial practice to establish populations *and* territories as non-European/nonwhite. This form of racial governance, in tandem with that occasioned by the *encomienda*, the Inquisition, and the *sistema de castas*, defined geographies, territorial origins, and the bodies of non-Europeans. Consequently, slavery and Castilian mechanisms of determining and legitimating slave status did far more than facilitate the arrival of people commodified as labor and capital. Over time, as an early modern European governing motif, slavery constituted the European colonial horizon. This was a process born during the age of exploration, conquest, and global expansion, based in part upon notions of religious heritage, but founded upon Mediterranean geopolitical and scientific discourses of geography, environment, and nature.

Over the course of the sixteenth century, Castilians deployed a broad lexicon of difference to justify the enslavement of colonial subjects and establish the European colonial horizon that characterized Castilian governance. Three interrelated Mediterranean notions guided the development of these practices defining belonging and status—*naturaleza, nación,* and *calidad.* These notions indexed early modern scientific readings of geographic zones, geopolitics, nature, and their impact upon human fitness for self-governance and life within the commonwealth. For centuries, Mediterranean understandings of the world distinguished geographic zones based on their proximity to the sun. Habitats, or *naturaleza,* acted upon human bodies, producing distinct characteristics used to identify individuals as *naturales* of a particular geographic zone or habitat. Chief among those characteristics was physiognomy. Cold, warm, dry, or humid environments and their proximity to the sun were understood as crucial to determining the geohumoral natures of people. This included the *calidad,* complexion, and overall health of *naturales.* In short, the complexions, health, and moral tendencies of a people correlated to place and a region's land, even its air. White, brown, and black were understood as geohumoral complexions that categorized environments somewhere between cold, moist, and thereby phlegmatic, stagnant and white, on the one hand, and dry, hot, and black, on the other. Ultimately, this early modern science of physiognomy insisted that it was possible to "read" and distinguish an individual's character and qualities through personal features of complexion, language, bodily marks, and other physical symbols understood as peculiar to specific environments. In this sense, Castilians used "color" to "read" habitat and *calidad*.[10]

Whereas *naturaleza* provided a method of reading people in relation to geographic origins, *nación* indexed geopolitical origins, or nation. Nation was a nonpejorative reference to sovereign claims over individuals that indexed practices, laws, and legal cultures within a given sovereign territory, which could be used to justify war, dispossession, and enslavement. Thus, to speak of one's nation was an attempt to read, mark, and govern subject peoples in relation to corporeal affiliations. It also referenced political and cultural practices that framed geographic and religious belonging, not completely unlike *naturaleza*.[11]

As historian Herman Bennett argues, Africans were not initially identified as savage or barbarian, but rather read through the juridico-political lexicon meant to establish corporeal groups and territories as either sovereign or sovereignless. *Nación*, or the practice of reading and defining national affinities, offered Castilians a method of deeming people of African descent as black, yet sovereign subjects, or black, sovereignless and enslavable. Before the middle of the fifteenth century, all people were entitled to live beyond a state of grace. But thereafter, Christian monarchs increasingly encroached upon the foreign domains of non-European/nonwhite populations, colonizing, capturing, enslaving, and interpolating them into their emergent imperial order through a lexicon of *naturaleza* and color, *nación* or sovereign status. Those judged to be lacking in both, whether through physical attributes that mapped upon degenerate locations on the earth or because of their pagan, infidel, or sovereignless nationality, were marked territorially and corporeally as *de color* and *slave*. For Castilians, *nación* offered a way to distinguish non-European foreigners living in their domains. To speak of *nación de negro* was to point to people from sub-Saharan African habitats. Both *moro* and *mora* indexed Moorish peoples. *Nación de loro* and *berberiscos* pointed to deracinated peoples from territories and corporate communities in North and West Africa.

Over the sixteenth century, as Castilians adjudicated the slave status of foreign captives living within their territories, *nación* came to be used interchangeably with the term *casta*, pointing to the ways that Castilians fused concerns about religious lineage, mixed ancestry, and geohumoral features in an effort to interpolate foreign subjects into their emergent Catholic colonial order. Historian Nancy van Deusen notes that "*nación* could also refer to a genus or group of distinguishable peoples, such as *moros*, *negros*, *loros*, and *indios*, with distinctive characteristics based on lineage." These neologisms, rooted in concerns around incorporating and distinguishing, or otherwise governing Jews and Basque peoples, combined with the bureaucratic concerns of parental lineage, were mapped onto religious, geographic, and cultural pedigrees. Imperial or corporate identity, blood lineage, and cultural inheritance were all indexed through the terms *naturaleza*, *nación*, *casta*, and *calidad*. During the sixteenth century, "a gradual emphasis on geohumoral attributes *and* lineage emerged, used especially to pinpoint enslaved status. But these descriptors had not yet developed into protoracial exclusionary categories that translated into a more rigid system of classification known as the caste system."[12] Castilians did not yet have "a homogeneous set of terms to denote individual physical differences or a template that established hard-and-fast distinctions among identifiable groups of people in bondage." Instead, these practices born primarily in efforts to define nonwhite/non-European, non-Christian, and slave status, produced a race relation of governance that structured slavery and constituted Castilian sovereignty in the Americas. A governance based on race relations marked in part by slave status formed the context within which Africans and their descendants developed diasporic kinship practices constituting what Trey Proctor calls diasporic ethnic affinities, or ethnicities.

In Quito, small yet diverse groups of Africans arrived in the kingdom through highly randomized trade processes. Theirs was an increasingly atomized and alienating existence characteristic and productive of the peculiar diasporic predicaments they lived as colonial subjects defined within a system of practices that constituted difference and the legality of slavery by inscribing *naturaleza*, *nación*, and *calidad*. These practices produced the predicaments within which Africans formed kin, reformulated political and cultural practices, and otherwise developed lives that produced and inaugurated Spain's early modern Catholic order and its sovereign claims over the Pacific North Andes. Africans and their descendants produced these subjectivities while buffeted within the region's slave trades and their corresponding governing motifs of inspection, declaring and determining subjects and territories for governance.

Ultimately, enslaved Africans were deemed incorporated, foreign captives of non-European, non-Catholic, and uninhabitable territories. All of this established black as a subcategory of human beings worthy of decapitation, yet forced to live within an early modern purgatory—a space constituted through social death, and incorporation through the discipline of a life lived within racial governance. As Europeans practiced slaving, slave trading, and enslavement in the Americas, they associated slavery and slave status with territorial assemblages of politics, culture, and religion, installing the captive subjects they marked legally as "black enslaved captive subjects of servitude." Racially constituted slavery was both a technology of colonial governance and a practice that declared and governed racialized subjects of empire. Racially constituted slavery pointed, therefore, not merely to labor, capital, and economy, but rather to a fragmented sovereignty constituted through, and upon, bodies ascribed as black, unworthy, and morally threatening to the body politic.

Early modern slavery as a colonial practice proclaimed, and dialectically produced, Europe and Euro-colonial sovereign claims by marking the subjects of Guinea through *casta/nación/naturaleza*. All of which could point to, and confer, slave status, non-Christian origins, and non-Europeanness. The colonial spectacle of power was predicated upon the simultaneous incorporation and exclusion of bodies defined as non-European and potentially conquerable and enslavable territories. Social death relied upon the living processes of racial governance. It relied upon the marking, constitution, and governance of non-European bodies for the elaboration of imperial power. Consequently, efforts to account for black life in diaspora must situate the enslaved within the predicament of life in an early modern Catholic order. This requires a proper reckoning with slavery and its constitutive practices—*blackening*, *branding*, and *baptizing*.

Blackening modes of incorporation and differentiation aimed at binding subjects to territorial origins and assemblages of power in the Americas. This is not to reenact the violence of colonial racial servitude, or to gaze upon its grotesque spectacle. Rather, it is to account for blackness, slavery, and processes of racialization at the level of governance and formation of an early modern state. More than a reproduction of colonial taxonomies at the expense of early modern bodies and lives, analysis requires a complex engagement with the dialectics of slaving, slavery, and everyday life. It requires attention to the very colonial practices that were ultimately productive of racial governance and ideologies of race. These practices began with a distinct reading and identification of African landscapes, territories, and bodies. As the crown sanctioned the chains, brands, and financial ledgers of specific European trading companies, Castile rendered African captives-turned-saltwater-slaves black upon arrival, tying them to Africa while installing them as distinct categories of human beings for the claiming and governance of colonized territories and subjects. Incorporating African captives within the order through specific practices, slave trading established Spanish colonial authority and Catholic order. It established commercial nodes and networks (clandestine and official), which gave way over time to a capitalist economy produced in dialogue with Castilian sovereign claims and efforts at governance, processes that expanded and contracted at the point of converting "saltwater slaves" to "black enslaved, captive subjects of servitude" within Castile's American-based kingdoms. The transition from "saltwater slavery" to Spanish America's *slaveries* was conditioned by a singular set of judicial frames.[13] Whether entering the kingdoms legally, as Torijano's slaves apparently had, or clandestinely, as many others did, three juridical acts of domination and rituals marked them and incorporated them differently— *blackening, branding,* and *baptism.*

Blackness was not a given; neither was it a simple descriptor of a perceived difference. It was an act of archival inscription that marked slave status in relation to *naturaleza,* nation/*casta,* and *calidades* that indexed Africans' non-European territorial origins.[14] The practice of subjecting the bodies of enslaved African captives to inspection, documenting their "marks," including scarification, wounds received in the transatlantic passage, smallpox marks, brands of the licensed trading companies, and their overall physical conditions were more than acts of power, these were ways of forming, expanding, and legitimating the race relation of governance that slavery installed. Documenting their geopolitical and cultural origins through the practice of reading their "*nación*" and "*casta*," notaries and royal officials marked Africans as non-European, nonwhite, people born within the alterity of climates, territories, lands, politics, and cultures of sub-Saharan Africa. Priests and royal officials in Cartagena used *nación* and *casta* to construct previously distinctive groups under a singular moniker of imperial alterity for incorporation and distinctive governance. These were the initial processes and practices that constituted blackness upon, and within, both the bodies of the enslaved and the territories from which they hailed. These legitimating practices made licit an otherwise illicit trade in people that the Spanish monarchs and local priests enslaved knowing they had not been acquired through a just war. These practices naturalized the European colonial horizon that constructed Africa as slave territory and Africans as slaves unless proved free. These acts constituted their foreign and legitimately enslaved juridical position in relation to Castilian sovereignty over the ocean sea and the American territories.

Having established their slave status, priests and royal officials subjected the enslaved to acts of royal incorporation *and* differentiation aimed at binding and redeeming the black body into a life of Christian service, compliance, and obeisance within Castile's early modern Catholic order. These acts or juridical classificatory *fonts* baptized the enslaved as newly incorporated, yet debased subjects of servitude bound thereby to Spanish kingdoms. These were the marks used to constitute and govern slave subjectivity. It was within this context, and that of the localities to which they were installed, that enslaved Africans and their descendants refashioned lives within racial slavery as social death. The following discussion charts the entanglement between these three acts—blackening, branding, and baptism as modes of installing and inscribing racial slavery upon Africans and within the Kingdoms of Quito and New Granada in an effort to contextualize the juridico-political and geographic contexts within which people of African descent took lovers, formed families, and sustained social lives as alienated captives who were now imperial subjects placed under the rule and dominion of Castile's colonial American vassals.[15]

Not all slaves entering Quito experienced fonts of incorporation equally. Some, for example, arrived without having been baptized, such as an enslaved *bozal* woman sold in Guayaquil by Don Roque García Salgado, or the *bozal* man of "casta no conocida" sold for 475 pesos.[16] These were, after all, juridical fonts. Slaves arriving illegally would have missed these or been subjected to attempts of counterfeit branding. Notably, slaves could be imported legally without having been baptized. Baptism was almost always mentioned, however, in the bill of sale and/or accompanying sales papers that accompanied slaves' arrival at ports like Guayaquil. Scribes and merchants usually took care to note when slaves had not been baptized. In some instances, these could have been contraband slaves they were trying to pass off as legal. It certainly begs the question of how regular baptism was for slaves passing legally through Panama or even Cartagena during the eighteenth century. We know Alonso de Sandoval and his agents, many of them enslaved multilingual Africans, were actively involved in conversion and baptismal rituals in Cartagena during the early seventeenth century.[17] It was clearly a royal mandate going back to the sixteenth century that *bozales* be baptized upon arrival. The Portuguese crown, for example, mandated that all slaves entering the slave trade be baptized.[18] Some were; some were not. Nevertheless, the act or lack thereof conditioned the legal incorporation of slaves. They could shore up their master's proprietary claims or invite inquiry from royal officials, revealing the contested nature of majesty in Spanish America and simultaneously the enslaved body as text.[19]

Enslavement through Three Routes

From the circum-Caribbean, there were three principal seaborne and overland routes that took enslaved Africans into Quito's many slaveries. First was the largely sanctioned trek that led from Cartagena upon the Magdalena River and overland into Popayán. This path continued into the south Pacific littoral of the Barbacoas and southward toward the Ibarra-Quito corridor. For those headed to Barbacoas, this was a voyage filled with serious shipping costs and far too many hazardous risks, including slaves absconding permanently along the way, as well as environmental challenges that included predatory animals, vipers, and pestilence—all of which awaited them on the jungle floor in Barbacoas.

But for those looking to import slaves into Barbacoas, the more sensible choice was one of two contraband trade routes that developed out of Panama. One carried slaves overland from Panama through the province of Darién southward via the Atrato River. The other hugged the Pacific coast of New Granada into Isla Gorgona near Barbacoas. This route serviced a long stretch of gold-mining operations that stretched south through the Chocó and Barbacoas just north of Esmeraldas. Spinning off the gold-mining enterprises of the tropical jungle, where rivers seemed to flow with gold, was a hidden economy—a complex commercial web that included complicit and participating local authorities. As shown in chapter 1, governing this region was frustrating for officials in the kingdom's capital city of Quito and Santa Fé, both of which sought to impose increased colonial oversight upon the collection of the royal fifth and other taxes in the region, forcing Popayán to change jurisdictions several times over the course of the century. Contraband slave trading was not a minor concern in these administrative shifts.

Ultimately, the Panama-Guayaquil trade routes took just as many slaves into Quito as the two routes that led through New Granada. In the late sixteenth and early seventeenth centuries, slaves were normally taken directly to Lima, then transshipped via the Pacific to Guayaquil or overland via Loja, Cuenca, and up the mountain chain to Quito. During the eighteenth century, however, though slaves did continue to arrive by way of Lima, many came directly from Panama along with other trade goods and passenger cargo vessels arriving at the port.

The Cartagena-Magdalena Passage

Over time, in connection with the Magdalena trade, Popayán became the northern slave market for Quito's north-central highland core. The incremental growth of slave sales within the market allowed for a regular, albeit inconsistent, slave trade to solidify in the town and region of Popayán. Popayán's slave sales were significant for a moderately successful gold economy. As capital, they added buoyancy to the local economy. As their numbers increased

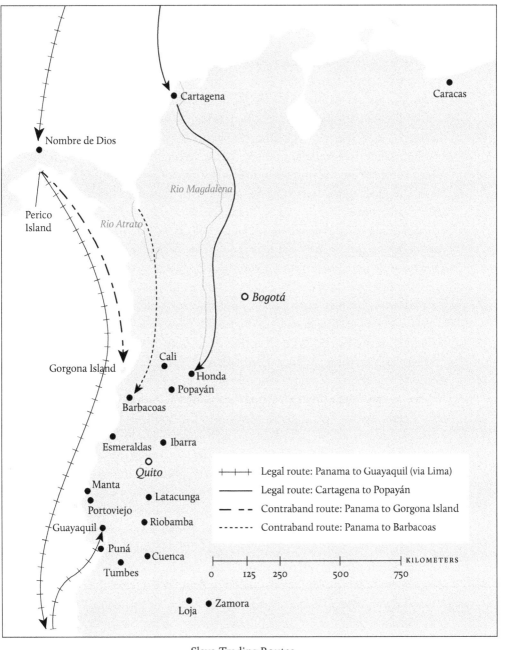

Caracas

Cartagena

Nombre de Dios

Perico
Island

Rio Magdalena

Rio Atrato

O Bogotá

Gorgona Island

Cali

Honda

Popayán

Barbacoas

Esmeraldas   ● Ibarra

O
Quito

Manta

Latacunga

Portoviejo

Guayaquil

Riobamba

Puná

Cuenca

Tumbes

Loja   ● Zamora

	Legal route: Panama to Guayaquil (via Lima)
	Legal route: Cartagena to Popayán
	Contraband route: Panama to Gorgona Island
	Contraband route: Panama to Barbacoas

KILOMETERS

0   125   250   500   750

Slave-Trading Routes

incrementally, they were formed into groups and installed in newly conquered regions, where they provided far more than needed hands in the search for new gold frontiers. They represented the advance of the colonial regime, constituting as they did the personalistic power of miners, merchants, and royal officials looking to pacify the area. Indeed, it was through the incremental expansion of slavery into the Barbacoan and Pacific lowland communities that Spain claimed these new territories, harnessed its natural resources, and established sovereign claims therein. Facilitating this process were local and regional *factors* (individual slave traders) connected to slave-trading networks within the Atlantic and circum-Caribbean. Individuals such as Captain Don Matheo del Masso supplied miners and would-be mine owners' seemingly insatiable desire for African captives.

Responding to local demands, on January 18, 1700, Masso appeared before Popayán's notary to certify the legality of some fifty-nine enslaved Africans whom he had purchased from Captain Don Gaspar de Adrade, treasurer and administrator general of the Portuguese Cacheu Company, stationed in Cartagena. Masso's group of men, women, and children (one small child, and one infant) was composed principally of individuals from West Africa's Slave Coast, including twenty-two adult female *castas* Ardas (one listed as *casta* Mina) and thirty-seven male *negros barones*, all between the ages of twenty-five and thirty.[20]

Masso wasted little time dispersing these slaves. Immediately following this registration, he sold two of these Africans to Captain Don Diego Ignacío de Aguinaga (*alcalde y vecino encomendero of Popayán*) for 1,010 patacones. Just nine days later, on January 27, 1700, Masso sold fourteen of the Africans to Joseph Veltran de Carzedo (*vesino de Popayán*), along with six more to Christobal de Mosquera Figueroa for 10,100 patacones, or 505 patacones per slave.[21] Later that year, a local factor, Don Juan Damian de la Torre, also purchased sixty-five enslaved Africans from Captain Don Gaspar de Adrade.[22] De la Torre stipulated that they were "bags of bones whose souls lay within their mouths," dispersing them quickly through a series of sales.[23] Although slaves had spent some time recuperating in Jamaica and Barbados, often there were several slaves who literally lay dying (*algunos casi murriendo*), making the baptismal font all the more spiritually necessary in Cartagena through the optic of church officials. Apparently, de la Torre's captives had not benefited sufficiently from the eighteenth-century practice of "seasoning," or allowing slaves a bit of rest and rehabilitation in the Caribbean before moving on to Cartagena or Porto Bello.[24] Had de la Torre fallen victim to the notorious camouflaging techniques employed to disguise the ill conditions of disease-ridden, emaciated, dying souls?[25] Slave mortality conditioned market realities, resulting in significant losses for traders. For his part, de la Torre would be forced to adjust the final price, calculating the sale for sixty-three captives rather than sixty-five.[26] Still, his financial losses paled in comparison to the loss of community, family, and even life that enslaved men, women, and children suffered during and after the harrowing transatlantic journey.

Itinerant merchants, miners, and small-scale traders also supplied Popayán's slave market. During the late seventeenth century, Popayán had become *the* slave-trading center of Quito's northern borderland. And slave trading punctuated life in the town well into the eighteenth century. Between 1694 and 1748, representatives of companies holding Spain's *asiento* sold sixty-one licenses to various merchants who passed through the town of Popayán, carrying 4,000 slaves into the region. A little more than half of the group was sold in the town of Popayán.[27] In total, these licenses represented 22 percent of all slaves entering Cartagena. These sales featured 288 lots, totaling 840 individual slaves. Miners purchased nearly 30 percent of these, while secular clerics purchased 11 percent. Convents and monasteries such as Santo Domingo, the Convent of the Sisters of Encarnación, the Jesuit Colegio of Popayán and Ibarra, and the Convent of Merced were among the main purchasers, with merchants, local property owners, landholders, and functionaries purchasing the remaining enslaved African captives.[28]

The number of captives sold within Popayán's market was small compared to large-scale plantation society standards, yet significant for a diversifying regional economy like Quito's, where enslaved subjects were in high demand. Efforts to settle, claim dominion, and harness the natural resources in areas of Barbacoas and the Chocó depended increasingly upon enslaved subjects. And Payanese merchants did their best to meet this need through official and unofficial means. A random sampling of Popayán notary records reveals that, between 1698 and 1757, Popayán received an average of 9.4 percent, or 2,847 out of 30,444, of all recorded sales occurring in Cartagena. (See table 2.1.) These numbers reflect the ongoing demand for slavery in Quito, and the incremental ways the markets responded to these demands.

Wars in the Atlantic theater and tensions between the British and Spanish disrupted *asiento* trade agreements that would supply the Spanish kingdoms according to royal mandates. In addition, supplying enslaved captives to the lowland Pacific littoral proved an expensive and increasingly dangerous proposition. Prices, therefore, remained high as a result of low supply and high demand, especially in desired locations within New Granada and Quito. Heavily leveraged miner owners were forced to grow their labor gangs slowly, using

Table 2.1. Percentage of Cartagena Slaves Sold in Popayán, 1698–1757

Years	Asiento	Sales in Cartagena	Years	Sales in Popayán	%
1698–1702	Cacheu (Port.)	2,538	1699–1703	383	15.0
1703–13	Guinea (French)	4,251	1704–15	320	7.5
1715–18	South Sea Co. I	1,430	1716–20	120	8.4
1722–27	South Sea Co. II	3,949	1722–28	248	6.3
1730–36	South Sea Co. III	4,919	1730–38	991	20.1
1746–57	Mayort-Noriega	12,957	1746–57	765	5.9
	TOTALS	30,044		2,827	9.4

Source: Colmenares, Historia económica y social, 34.

laborers of mixed statuses (e.g., enslaved, leased, commissioned) in their search for new gold frontiers. Wealth in gold developed slowly. The low supply, combined with the associated taxes, tariffs, and inconsistent shipments along the Magdalena, all converged to keep slave prices relatively high in Popayán. Cycles of boom and bust coincided with the usefulness of a hybridized system of labor organization, leading to the incremental growth of slavery in the region. All of this worked against huge surges in slave imports, which in any case were largely unavailable by way of Cartagena.

During the period between 1698 and 1727, Popayán sold an average of only 34.50 slaves per year. The period between 1730 and 1738, however, demonstrated an increase in slave sales: the figure jumped to 110.11 per year, then dropped to 69.54 sales per year between 1746 and 1757—still double the figure from the first three decades of the century. Available data on Popayán's market suggest that imports continued well beyond the 1760s, sometimes characterized by significant increases in sales. Still, these were punctuated by prolonged periods of decline in slave sales and moments of near inactivity in the trade. The randomizing, alienating, and atomizing experience of this trade defined the predicament of enslaved African diaspora peoples. These processes structured their entrance into the Spanish kingdoms, while generating economic opportunities and governing challenges all of their own.

Like any other commodity, the sudden inactivity within the slave market revealed a great deal of information, just as rumors or evidence of new African arrivals for sale must have catalyzed activity spinning off the market. This was a slave market with a pulse and temperature all its own, embedded in a live and active economy, and productive of slavery. Merchants supplying enslaved captives along the Magdalena made use of the labor of enslaved subjects who worked as polemen, manned canoes, and provided labor around the market in Honda. The arrival of large batches of enslaved people could sometimes draw more laborers into slave life along the river and within its market. Likewise, lower levels of activity or the absence of slave arrivals produced important silences that punctuated life along the routes leading to slavery in New Granada and Quito. Such fluctuations left an indelible imprint on the society, reinforcing the visibility and surveillance of slaves in the region. Indeed, one might ask, who failed to notice talk of the arrival of newly marked Africans from the Caribbean? What of those leaving the area bound for Barbacoas or Quito? Who would not know of any commotion or challenge that groups or individual slaves posed during transit? It was the enslaved Africans, however, who lived life along slavery's passages into the kingdom. Along the way, they learned the terrain firsthand and came face to face with colonial officials while forming affinities and kinships that constituted slave life in the Afro-Andes.

Southward to Quito: The Popayán-Ibarra-Quito Passage

Apart from demand within Popayán and that emanating from Barbacoas, the north-central highland core was a destination for bound Africans arriving from Cartagena. Large-scale *obrajeros* such as the Jesuits had tied their textile operations to slave-based sugar estates in the Chota-Mira Valley, just as they had within the Cauca Valley. The incremental increase in the availability of slaves served to bring growing numbers of African and Afro-Creole slaves into the north-central highlands and the urban center of Quito in the last decade of the seventeenth century.

On December 3, 1701, Don Joseph Blaco García reserved and purchased 54 of the 104 slave laborers that Don Juan Damian de la Torre had purchased and imported to Popayán.[29] Purchased under the *asiento* of Cacheu, all had been branded with the seal of the company and the crown. Although the corresponding documents do not feature the captives' assigned ethnoregional monikers, slave-trading data show that the group would have emerged from the Gold and Slave Coasts of West Africa.

That a little over half of the shipment had been earmarked for the Quito market was quite informative. Within one year, a total of ninety-one slave laborers had been imported into the region, and many more were en route. The slaves' varying origins and the circuitous routes they traveled offer some insight into the diversity of the kingdom's slave population and the contexts within which they formed their diasporic identities. If the Cartagena-Magdalena passage offered more diverse groupings of Africans in a highly randomizing fashion, a useful parallel process is found in the journeys of those in the legal trade between Panama and Guayaquil, one of the three routes for those headed to Quito city. By the turn of the eighteenth century, there were two well-developed parallel trade networks emerging out of Panama and running along the Pacific coast of the kingdoms of New Granada and Quito. One was legal, the other clandestine.

From Guayaquil to Quito and Back

In 1713 Don Andres Martines de Castro sold five slaves to Don Roque Garcia Salgado, who in turn contracted with Don Bartolome de Alba Yvarrientos in the city of Panama to transport five slaves from the Playa Amaral and sell them somewhere between the ports of Barbacoas and Guayaquil. Although Salgado had given Ybarrientos power of attorney to sell the captives as far away as Lima, both Barbacoas and Guayaquil were short distances from Panama, and a quick sale would bring both men a rapid return on their investments. Gold could be had in Barbacoas, but Guayaquil was a port that connected Ybarriento to trade networks running down Peru's northern Pacific coast into the Port of Callao that led into the city of Lima. Merchants routinely forced enslaved captives arriving in Guayaquil up the mountain chain into Quito city and the heartland of the kingdom. And this is where Ybarriento took these enslaved captives.[30]

Bypassing Barbacoas, Don Bartolome de Alba Ybarriento landed in Guayaquil. Given the prevalence of contraband slave trading in coastal Barbacoas, as well as officials' ongoing attempts to police the region, it is easy to understand why he bypassed Barbacoas. While the captives might have constituted legal merchandise, the contraband market was sure to cut into his profit margins. Guayaquil also offered the most accessible point of contact for the highland, where Bartolome's brother, Don Estaban de San Ybarrientos, was living in the town of Ibarra—the very epicenter of the burgeoning Jesuit estate complex. Salgado sold one of the slaves, leaving the other four in his brother's care. The Jesuits continued to staff their extensive agropastoral complexes, often making small purchases such as the four enslaved Africans the Ybarrientos brothers offered for sale. But the Jesuits also often opted to bypass middlemen like the Ybarrientos brothers.

On September 28, 1700, in the Caribbean port of Cartagena, Father Juan Ruíz Bonifacio, the ranking Jesuit priest for all of Quito, purchased thirty-six enslaved Africans—two infants, twelve women, and twenty-two men—for the Colegios of Popayán and Quito.[31] In 1722 the Jesuits purchased Maria de la Cruz (described as a twenty-two-year-old woman *de nación* Guinea) directly from her previous owner in Guayaquil.[32] Now Maria was headed to the north-central highland court, joining others whom Father Francisco Ruíz had purchased for the Jesuits directly from Cartagena. Seven years later, the Jesuits purchased Bonifacio, an eighteen-year-old who had been working during the previous ten months on the Colegio Maximo's Neblí hacienda. They paid a mere 250 pesos for him, tax free.[33]

As these sales suggest, Quito's emerging slave population hailed from all over the Atlantic World, most emanating first from the Gold and Slave Coasts of West Africa. Note the 1710 sale of Salbador (twenty-four-year-old *de nación* Arara), his wife, Theresa (twenty-four-year-old *de nación* Popo), and their son, Manuel (an Afro-Creole of two years and ten months) from a Popayán elite to Doña Mariana Guerro De Salar.[34] In addition to these Gold and Slave Coast African captives, others emerged from the region, including Juana de la Crus (a thirteen-year-old "Mina" girl); Catharina *de casta* Mandinga;[35] Domingo *de nación* Popo sold along with María *de nación* Lucumí;[36] and the sale of Francisco Arara (twenty-eight years of age), Antonio Basofia *de nación* Arara, Casimiro Arara, and María Colorada *de la mesma nación*. [37] Random sampling of Quito's notary *protocolos* for the period between 1692 and 1750 reveals that in 229 sales of slave laborers, 150 were ethnic Africans.[38]

Apart from the Panama-Guayaquil route (and that of Popayán), others arrived from as far away as La Plata.[39] Other slave laborers, such as Josepha (twenty-five, *de nación* Loango) and Maria ([same nation] *otra nombrada*), emerged from West Central African by way of the city of La Plata.[40] Many more emerged from the port city of Guayaquil. Still others arrived in the kingdom's heartland from Puerto Viejo (a port town north of Guayaquil), the village of Riobamba, the Asiento de Latacunga, Santa Fé de Bogotá, and the "Portuguese Empire."[41] In short, during the eighteenth century, Quiteños, with the help of itinerant merchants and large-scale slaveholders like the Jesuits, expanded the scope of slavery by drawing into the colony a multiorigin population of enslaved Africans and Afro-Creoles from diverse catchment sites in West and Central Africa as well as varied locations within the Americas, who arrived through circuitous routes in Africa and the Indies.

Merchants such as Joan Lanzagorta, one of Guayaquil's major slave traders, contributed to these processes. Between 1694 and 1695, Lanzagorta sold sixteen African captives who carried the ethnic moniker of "Loango" or "Congo" for an average of 340 pesos y ocho reales; his combined revenues for these sales alone reached 5,445 pesos.[42] Lanzagorta had provided various Quiteños with seven ten-year-old African males and three *negritos de casta* Congo.[43] Other merchants were selling captives like Lazaro (*criollo de esta ciudad*), Luisa *casta*

Congo, Joana Josepha de *casta* Congo, and Manuel Bozal. Despite the drastic increase in the supply, however, prices for slaves remained high, rising at times to 525 pesos for a healthy adult female (the price of the "Conga" women listed above). The average price of 340 pesos for a ten-year-old African male was quite expensive, as well.

In addition to the Central Africans in the city and colony of Quito, West Africans arrived throughout the kingdom in intermittent and relatively small shipments. Arriving at the river port of Honda over the next few years were several shipments of African captives carrying the ethnic identifiers Arara, Popó, Mandinga, Mina, Lucumí, Bambara, Chalá, and Caramantí.[44] Their presence, along with those of Afro-Creoles from various locations within the colonies, only added to the complex array of origins that marked Quito's slave communities.

The kingdom's diverse African population is reflective of the broader trans-atlantic slave trading patterns that supplied captives to the two principal ports for the region—Cartagena and Panama. In 1712 the ship the *Comte de Lamoignon* purchased African captives in the Bight of Benin at the port of Whydah before stopping first in Cartagena to deliver 398 of the 465 captives before continuing on to Panama. In 1704 the *Badine*, also destined for the "Spanish Mainland," purchased slaves first along the Slave Coast and then some at Whydah, but the trip was unsuccessful because of a slave uprising. The *Galant* purchased slaves in Senegal before making a delivery of 273 captives at Panama in the year 1711. Similarly, the English ship the *John*, traveling from Jamaica in 1719, tried to deliver 300 captives undoubtedly gathered largely from the Bight of Benin and the Gold Coast but was thwarted by Spanish capture. The *Leusden* (a Dutch ship) in 1723 purchased in the Bight of Benin the majority of the 535 African captives it delivered to the "Spanish Mainland." The *Fortune* had purchased 190 captives from the port of Bonny in the Bight of Biafra, stopping in Kingston before traveling on to Panama in 1754. Finally, even more emblematic of the overall trade, particularly to Cartagena and Panama, the *Jonge Issac* delivered some 514 African captives to the Spanish Main in 1758 after having made purchases in the Windward, Ivory, Gold, and Benin Coasts.[45]

The knowledge of the kingdom's roads, rivers, and passages, legal and clandestine, that this group of enslaved African captives possessed collectively remains an undertheorized aspect of slavery, legal history, and the study of identity formation within the realm. For example, what did it mean for knowledge production among slaves in Quito city that Central Africans, West Africans, and Creoles from sugar-producing towns like Buga and others from Bogotá, the "Portuguese empire," Riobamba, and Porto Viejo were now included in their ranks? What meaning did their pasts hold for them, their comrades, enemies, lovers, and friends in any of the kingdom's principal slaveholding regions? What contrasts did they draw between the spaces they had left and the Andean worlds they had entered? The realities of moving, mourning, and encountering other diasporic people conditioned their predicament, contextualizing their selection of kin and communities of association.[46]

Contextualizing Diverse and Atomized Africans

Enslaved Africans were simultaneously many things—foundational concerns of governance, signifiers of sovereignty, and possessions of royal majesty. In raw economic terms, they had always been property owned and enclosed within the pater's domain (an estate permeable to the intrusion of the pope and crown). They had been commodities, circulating as cash and capital capable of leveraging wealth and status while demonstrating honor and even piety. Without sufficient consideration or speculation, however, all of these possibilities, all of these fantasies of the enslaved, were somehow marked by the ceremonies of possession and by the very ironic grandeur with which slavery was treated. For elites, enslaved women eased the lives of would-be nursing mothers, whereas privileged males subjected others to their sexual predations.[47] Their labor had performed many grueling, dangerous, yet productive chores associated with gold mining, shipbuilding, and agricultural tasks. Scholars have scarcely considered slaves as more than commodities and laborers, or beyond economic reductionist terms. Alternatively, one might ask, what impact did the regulation of the slave trade have upon the advancement of royal authority into the region?

Findings from the Kingdom of Quito suggest that the examination and marking of African bodies represented emblems of power over royal subjects to be governed within the overlapping juridical spheres.[48] Indeed, these fonts presaged the multiple uses of slaves and the ways that mastery was encumbered from the moment a slave was either marked upon arrival or born within the realm. For Africans, having their bodies handled, examined, poked, prodded, and branded signaled the first stage of their captive life in the New World. Reading, marking, treating, and baptizing black bodies came to signify not only individual ownership but also political and commercial ownership. These were "ceremonies of possession" that all Europeans deployed as they endeavored to transform people into commodities.[49] Brands confirmed the king as sovereign of both slavery and regional market economies. In the process, they formalized the rendering of the captive body as a source to be examined, read, and interpreted. Historian Walter Johnson has remarked, "slaves' bodies were shaped to their slavery." "Slave children," he relates, "learned to view their bodies through two different lenses, one through their masters, the other belonging to themselves."[50] Hence the black body became a site to inscribe and endow meaning, making it both text and repository for master and slave. For Africans and Afro-Creoles, the marked bodies of Africans, and the relatively less marked bodies of Afro-Creoles, must have offered important clues and cues in the making of ethnicities in the diaspora.

How slaveowners defined ethnicity and discerned the most profitable method of identifying "Africans" on the continent and throughout the diaspora remains a critical concern among scholars.[51] The formulation and description of ethnic diversity presented here depends upon a rather specific reading of ethnic monikers. The point, however, is not to give a specious interpretation of the complex nature of such labels but rather to contextualize African ethnic identity by discerning the descriptive, yet highly suggestive, ethnic monikers that Europeans applied to native Africans.[52] Although these labels were derived largely from the names of port cities or points of embarkation, we can consider them as "signposts" that lead to disparate locations, as well as fluid and dynamic notions of ethnicity and "belonging." These labels, so-called African *castas* or nations (*naciónes*), affixed often as surnames of sorts, represented Europeans' best approximations regarding individual points of origin and Africans' perceived relationships to one another (i.e., their ability to communicate with one another or their possession of similar scarification patterns). While they fell short of precision in defining African ethnic identity, these monikers, when read with slave-trading data and observer commentary from the period, provide a window into the very complex and multivariate dynamic of West and West Central African ethnicity.[53] They chart a diasporic path that moves through the Atlantic World into the rivers, lands, communities, and states of West and West Central Africa, where ethnicity was produced and reproduced.

Moving from Atlantic coastal trading posts into the interior of Africa, the vision of ethnicity becomes even more obscure. According to historian Douglas Chambers, "Diasporic named groups did not signify specific political identities or known aspirations for separate nation-states, and generally did not have their own written languages. But they appeared to have been affinity groups, or intentional communities with a shared proper name, language, cultural identity, links to a homeland, collective memories and, as significantly, 'shared amnesias.'"[54]

Chambers prefers to view these groups as *ethnies*, "a named human population with myths of common ancestry, shared historical memories, one or more elements of common culture, a link with a homeland and a sense of solidarity among at least some of its members."[55] "Ethnicity," he contends, "refers to that cultural intangible which members of an ethnie have in common, recognizing of course that any group or individual has no *single* identity, but a variety which overlap to a lesser or greater degree, depending on the situation."[56] Consequently, he argues, "ethnies and ethnicity . . . exist only when people are in direct contact with others unlike themselves, and are used to distinguish 'us' from 'them.'"[57] Arguably, this was the case in colonial Quito. Quito possessed ethnic Africans drawn from "discrete" locations throughout West and West Central Africa. The small size of the population served to exacerbate ethnic diversity, making it difficult for individuals to form communities based on Old World cultural contexts.

The diversity that characterized Quito's slave population correlates closely to that among *bozales* arriving in Cartagena, who were far more diverse than those arriving in Veracruz during the same period. The African population concentrated at the port of Cartagena, the port from which Quito received almost all of its African slave laborers, was ethnically more diverse than many other ports throughout the circum-Caribbean, especially Veracruz, which extensively served Mexico and Meso-America. Historian Enriqueta Vila Vilar found, for example, that between 1595 and 1640, Angola was the port of debarkation for 84 percent of all ethnic Africans entering the port of Veracruz, with Cape Verde and São Tomé providing 6 percent and 7 percent, respectively. On the other hand, in Cartagena, Angola was registered as the port of debarkation for only 46 percent of all slaves, while Cape Verde registered 44 percent and São Tomé 3 percent.[58] Much like Panama, Cartagena represented a secondary market or shipping point for slave traders working within the circum-Caribbean and, therefore, imported slave laborers from a wider range of trading companies and itinerant merchants, working both legally and clandestinely at the nexus of the Atlantic, Pacific, and circum-Caribbean.[59] In short, data from all points that could have provided slaves to Quito reveal diverse ethnic mixes.

The opening of the Pacific lowlands, witnessed in the pacification of Barbacoas by the 1650s and the Chocó in the 1680s and 1690s, allowed slaveholders to end an era of forcing their slaves to migrate over long distances in search of mineral deposits. From the 1690s on, there would be an emphasis on growing large, relatively stable groups of laborers who would mine gold within a close radius of the camps along the riverways that crossed the district of Barbacoas. The transition to mining in the lowland Pacific littoral also created the necessity of large importations of ethnic Africans and thus changed slave community morphology in ways that must have held interesting implications for the process of ethnogenesis. Throughout the seventeenth century, Afro-Creoles had accounted for the majority of Popayán's slave population. Interspersed within this group were ethnic Africans, most of whom had emanated originally from regions within Central Africa and the Upper Guinea coast of West Africa. Many of these ethnic Africans became *ladinos*, who spoke Spanish, "professed" Catholicism, and understood the inner workings of Spanish colonial societies. Newly arrived ethnic Africans (most of them from the Bight of Benin, the Gold Coast, Central Africa, and, to a lesser extent, the Bight of Biafra) would have to find a space within this ethnically diverse population as they entered the Kingdom of Quito at the end of the century.

Considering the previous movements of slave laborers who came to Quito reveals at least four factors: the disruptive process of slave distribution, the increasing volume of slaves entering the region, the importance of Popayán as a marketplace for slaves going to greater Popayán and the Chocó, and the sporadic timing of large shipments of Africans entering the region. Although at different times, various ethnic groups might represent the majority group in the principal transatlantic shipments. Once the laborers arrived at the Magdalena River port of Honda, traders like Torijano and others dispersed them quickly without regard to ethnic or familial arrangements, thrusting them into environments where they seldom constituted the majority. Since the mid-eighteenth century, Afro-Criollos became the majority members within most mining gangs. And even in instances when Afro-Criollos were not the majority, ethnic Africans typically found themselves within an ethnically diverse mining community—a point well illustrated by the 1695 testament and appraisal of Don Pedro Fernandez de Novia's property.

At the time of his declaration, Novia's estate included fourteen slave laborers, of whom eleven were adults (seven ethnic Africans and four Afro-Criollos) and three children, two of whom were born to African–Afro-Criolla unions, and one born to a mixed African union; no child was born of an endogamous union between two ethnic Africans carrying the same ethnic moniker.[60] Moreover, amid the Africans cited, there were three Minas, two Golofos, one Congo, and one Popo, a picture that further underscores the inevitability of broad ethnogenesis in the formation of Afro-Quiteña communities. While Antonio Golofo and his wife, Elena, were apparently of the same ethnic persuasion—Golofo—Manuel Congo and his wife, María Popo, enjoyed no such distinction, a reality that more closely characterized the African experience in the city of Quito.

The specific origins of Popayán's slave community were changing, however. Ethnoregional diversity would continue to characterize these slave populations, but how did Africans and Afro-Creoles read and interpolate one another into ethnocultural mores already in process?

Bound Africans: Historicizing African Identity

On February 18, 1712, four large canoes carrying 166 enslaved Africans arrived at the Magdalena River port town of Honda, just northeast of Popayán.[61] Among the group were ninety-five men and thirty-seven women, twenty-nine boys under the age of fifteen, four girls under the age of twelve, and two infants who were listed with their mothers (*crias de la teta* or *del pecho*).[62] Among the group there were thirty-five Arara, forty-four Mina, four Luango, sixteen Lucumi, seven Caramantí, four Congo, thirteen Chala, seven Popo, fourteen Mandinga (upper Guinea Coast), one Hablar, one Prama, one Bandu(bi), one Poropue, one Boama, two Bambara, four Barbara, seven Ibo, three Mondongo, three Chara, and one Yupo.[63] All were noted to have "all marks with the royal insignia *coronilla* burned on their right breast and the mark of the *asiento* on the left side of their back."[64] The reading of bodies was such an integral part of making commodities of people that even the would-be marks of little babies and young children had to be accounted, even if only symbolically. Confirming this reality, the scribe remarked, "As expected the mark of the two babies and the small black boy, these are included in the number of children who are not marked."[65] In the early modern world, there was an obsession with marking bodies and the act of literally wearing one's state on one's sleeve. In the case of Africans, their skin was physically branded, while the white skin of *castas* marked them with privilege, wealth, and freedom of movement.

The body as a textual source for reading and marking belonging was not lost on Africans but was, in fact, a concept that held great currency among West African body artists and those initiated into the dynamic cultural mores of the diverse region. Country marks, or scarification, which usually took the form of varying types of incisions but could also appear as a tattoo, could signify conditions of birth or a particular rite of passage or serve simply the purpose of beautification. Other incisions that might have appeared to Europeans as "country marks" were used for the injection of various medicines into the body. Among the "Yoruba," some of the marks themselves were thought to have had curative and empowering objectives, apart from any medicinal properties that may or may not have been injected. While the process and meaning of country marks varied regionally, changing over time, the phenomenon draws attention to "the bodily basis of experience and knowledge," a "sense-based" approach to learning and making one's way in the world, or a "bodily, multi-sensorial basis of understanding."[66] Although much has been made of "country marks" or ethnic scarification and body art as indicators of ethnic distinctions and "Africanity," few have emphasized these aspects in the context of ethnic identity formation in Spanish America.[67] While African scarification has many cultural implications, country marks (*señals naturales*) are noted here as signals of the changing context of ethnic identity formation in early eighteenth-century Popayán and the *audiencia* more generally. They are noted to highlight the fundamental ways that Africans *sensed* their world and those around them, as body markings of all kinds helped form the context for New World ethnic identity formation.

Internal customs clearances, *visitas de despacho*, reflected two of the more formal customs reports completed at Cartagena and other Spanish American ports: the *visita de palmeo* and the *visita de sanidad*. Together, these reports revealed both the legality of the group and the general impression of health determined by officials in the Caribbean. Slave ships arriving in the Indies were subject to at least five standard searches: the *visita de sanidad* (health inspection), *visita de reconocimiento e inventoria* (inventory inspection), *visita de fondeo* (anchorage inspection), and *visita de entrada* (the entry inspection).[68]

In the late sixteenth century, officials had instituted these reviews and health inspections with the governor's ordering of the *protomedicato* (royal health officer) to inspect all crews and cargoes of African captives for signs of epidemics or "dangerous" diseases. Inspections varied in their degree of thoroughness. Nevertheless, some proved to be quite complete. In one example from 1742, the Mahotori *asiento* introduced 116 African captives who were found to be "completely healthy."[69] In this instance, the *protomedicato* based his diagnosis upon the captives' "appearance and their pulses." Others were more circumspect, reporting that slave laborers "seemed well" and appeared to be without disease with infectious potential.[70] But if the general reports issued by physicians to governors were at times vague, others contained information that suggests great attention was paid to the captive body. At a minimum, it seems that attention was paid to three bodily concerns: the marks of the crown and *asiento*, bodily signals of disease, and—most important here—ethnic scarification. The *visita de despacho* translated and reproduced from the import records of the 1712 trade in 166 captives, noted earlier, offers a rare glimpse at slaveholders' attempts to read African bodies (see table 2.2). It reminds us of the text that Africans (and Afro-Creoles) maneuvered, bodily distinctions signaling cultural similarities while marking differences.

The intent of these *visitas* was to help identify the overall physical well-being of the enslaved. Attention was paid in great detail, therefore, to myriad facets of the imported slave body as the slave entered the social hierarchy. This was the fundamental condition of the early modern black body: subject to display, viewing, marking, inspection, description, and use. Moreover, the black body was an object of desire and great interest. In short, these inspections allow us

Table 2.2. Translation of the *Visita de Despacho* for the 166 Slaves Who Arrived in Popayán on February 18, 1712

One [enslaved] black male of Casta Arara 18 years of age, more or less, with lines upon his temples and cheeks

Other Arara 22 years of age with incisions in the temples and one small hole in each cheek

Other Chala 18 years of age without any natural markings or country marks

Other Casta Luango 24 years of age with confusing lines in his temples

Other Arara 20 years of age with small lines in the temples

Other Arara 18 years of age with very subtle (nearly faded) lines in the temples

Other Lucumí 20 years of age with piercing lines in the cheeks

Other Popo 30 years of age with a full beard "very closed [*la barua*]"

Other Arara 24 years of age with the forehead and temples pierced and both cheeks pierced and one in between the eyebrows

Other Arara 16 years of age without country marks

Other Caramante 24 years of age without country marks

Arara 18 years of age with a row of lines in the temples

Other the same

Other Arara 18 years of age without country marks

Other Caramantí 26 years of age with a scar (likely a lash) [*ramalao*] on the left side of the face

Other Arara 25 years with the forehead and the cheeks [*picados*, normally followed by the term *viruelas*]

Other Arara 18 years of age with large spots [*piquetos gruesos*] in the forehead and temples

Other Congo 25 years of age with a few smallpox spots [*poco picado de viruelas* "*birbuelas*"]

Other Arara 18 years of age without any natural markings

Other Lecumí 15 years of age with four piercing lines in each cheek

Other Arara 15 years of age with the forehead and temples "spotted" [*piqueteadas*] [from smallpox]

Other Chala 18 years of age with three lines in each temple, one in the forehead and cheeks

Other Arara 18 years of age with a small line in the temples

Other Arara 16 with many lines in the temples

Other Arara 22 years of age with rows of piercing [*piqetillos*] in the temples and throughout the forehead

Other Arara 16 years of age with *muchos piquetes gruesos* in the temples, cheeks, and between them

Other Caramantí with a line in the middle of the forehead

Other Chala [no age listed] with a piercing in the forehead and cheeks

Other Mandinga 25 years of age without any country marks

Other Chala 26 years of age with a welt [*berdigon*] in the left temple and wrinkles between the eyes

Table 2.2. *continued*

Other Chala 25 years of age with the entire face and forehead filled with large lines

Other Chala 18 years of age with a welt [*berdigon*] in both sides of the nose through to the *quifadas*

Other Mina 20 years of age "I mean to say 26" [*digo veinte í seis*] very scarred from the pox [*mui picado de birbuelas*]

Other Arara 25 years of age with many marks in the forehead and face

Other 25 years of age with a small mark between the temple and the left eyebrow

Other Mandinga 22 years of age with several lines in the temples and forehead

Other Caramantí 30 years of age with confusing lines in the temples

Other Mandinga 26 years of age with a line between the eyebrows

Other Casta Luango 25 years of age with a scar [*señal de herida de vafo*] over the right eye

Other Mandinga with three very large lines in each temple and throughout the chest and a scarred belly

Other Popo 25 years old with a full beard [*serrado de barara*]

Other Lucumí 26 years with many very subtle lines throughout the face, forehead, and the mark of ˜v y ˜c over the left breast

Other Arara 18 years of age with two small piercings in the forehead and many lines in each temple

Other Lucumí 20 years of age with several scars resembling lash marks [*unas ramalasos*] on the left side of the face

Other Lucumí 26 years with fine lines on the left cheek

Other Lucumí 22 years without country marks

Other Arara 25 years of age with piercing in the temples

Other Arara 26 years with the forehead and checks marked [*picados*] [from smallpox]

Other Lucumí without any country marks

Other Lucumí 22 years of age with rows or long lashes [*ramalasos*] in the temples and three piercings in the each cheek

Other Mandinga 25 years with a row of marks all over the forehead and on the top lip [*endido*]

Other Mandinga 25 years with a large scar near the throat

Other Mina 25 years with lines in the temples

Other Mina with a blot or splotch [*borron*] between the eyebrows and four lines in each cheek

Other Chala 20 years with very thin lines in the temples and one wide line in the forehead

Other Mina 25 years with several fading lines in the forehead

Other Chala 20 years of age with many lines in the cheeks, temples, and forehead

Other Mina 20 years with lines in the temples

Other Mina 22 years of age with six lines in each temple, three in the left cheek, and one between the *sejas* and right cheek

Other Mina 26 years of age with six lines in each blot or splotch [*baron*] between the eyebrows, three [blots] in the right cheek, and a cross on the left cheek

Other Mina 22 years of age with five lines in each temple, other in the right cheek, and a cross on the left

Other Chala 25 years with very faint lines in the face, temple, and forehead

Other Caramantí 18 years of age with small marks like two lines on the left cheek

Other Popo 26 years of age without country marks

Other Barbara 18 years of age without country marks

Other Casta Bandubi, with three lines in each temple

Other Mina with very faint lines that one can barely recognize on the temples and cheeks

Other Mandinga 20 years of age without country marks

Other Chara 18 years of age with a welt [berdugon] above the right temple

Other Mina 28 years of age with six lines, three between the eyebrows, with two crosses in the right cheek and four lines on the left

Other Lucumí 25 years of age without country marks

Other Luango 18 years of age with a country mark or line [atrauesada dessajos] over the right eye

Other Casta Poropue 28 years of age scarred from smallpox along with a line in the middle of the forehead

Other Mina 26 years of age with four lines in each temple and a cross on the right cheek

Other [Mina] of 18 years of age without country marks

Other Casta Barbara 26 years of age with a line on the forehead

Other Casta Boama 22 years without country marks

Other Mina 25 years of age with confusing lines on the temples and forehead

Other Mandinga 22 years of age with lines in each of the temples

Another the same

Other Mandinga 20 years of age with three long lines in each temple

Other Mina 18 years of age with seven lines in each temple

Other 25 years with two scars from wounds [señales de herida] in the forehead

Other Mina 26 years with three lines in each cheek and several other small ones above the eyebrows

Other Arara 18 years with three lines upon each temple and very scarred from smallpox

The following are women:

One Lucumí 21 years with two rows of lines on each temple

Other Lucumí 18 years with faded lines on her temples

Other Lucumí 20 years with three lines on each temple

Other Conga 25 years with her baby

Another of 25 years with another baby with lines on the forehead and temples

Other Mina of 15 years with three lines on each temple

Other Mina of 25 years with lines on the forehead, temples, and cheeks

Other Popo of 21 years with five lines on each temple and four on the right cheek

Other Mina of 26 years with many lines on her temples and forehead

Other Popo of 24 years without any natural markings

Other Mina of 24 years with lines on her temples and forehead and one blotch [boron] in the middle of her forehead

Table 2.2. *continued*

Other Mina of 21 years with lines on her temples and a small blotch [*boron*] between her eyebrows

Other Chala of 20 years without any natural markings

Other Casta Babara of 24 years with lines on her temples and face pockmarked

Other Mina of 20 years with four lines on each temple and with three on her right cheek and a cross on the left

Other Mina of 24 years with five lines on each temple and three on the left cheek

Other Casta Babara of 22 years without any natural markings

Other Chara of 24 years without any natural markings

Other Casta Ibo of 26 years with lines on the temples

Other Caramanti of 24 years with a birthmark on the left cheek

Other Popo of 22 years of light skin [*color claro*]

Other Casta Ibo of 26 years with no natural markings

Other Casta Mondongo of 24 years with no natural markings

Other Mondongo of 24 years with no natural markings

Other Mina of 20 years with lines on her temples

Other Mondongo of 25 years with *medias lunas en la frente*

Other Chara of 22 years with six lines on each temple and one blotch [*un boron*] on each cheek

Other Lucumí of 30 years with lines on her temples

Other Mina of 20 years with three lines on each temple and one between her eyebrows

Other Arara of 26 years with her whole face and forehead *raiada*

Other Casta Prama of 25 years with five lines on her forehead

Other Lucumí of 20 years with no natural markings

The following are male children [segun muleques barones primeramente]:

One Casta Ara of 12 years more or less with the forehead and face pockmarked

Other Chala of 12 years with no natural markings

Other Arara of 14 years with some pockmarks on the face and temples

Other Ara of 10 years with no natural markings

Other Arara of 10 years of light skin [*color claro*]

Other Ara of 14 years with two small lines on his temples

Other Mina of 14 years with no natural markings

Other Ara of 11 years with a few small lines on his temples

Other Arara of 14 years with many lines on his temples

Other Mina of 14 years with many small lines on his temples and *carrillos y en medio de la frente*

Other Mandinga of 12 years of light skin [*color claro*] and with no natural markings

The following are female children [segun mulecas embras]:

Other Chala of 15 years with a small marking on the right side of her face

Other Casta Luango of 13 years with many lines on his temples and others on each cheek

Other Casta Ibo of 12 years of light skin [*color claro*] and with no natural markings

Other same

Other dark skin and same
Other Lucumí of 10 years with no natural markings
Other Mina of 10 years with no natural markings
Other Mina of 10 years with no natural markings
Other Mina of 8 years with no natural markings
Other Mina of 7 years with no natural markings
Other Mandinga of 6 years with no natural markings
Other Mina of 6 years with two lines on her temples and one on her face
Other Mina of 6 years with no natural markings
Other Mina of 7 years with three lines on each temple
Other Mina of 6 years with no natural markings
Other Mina of 5 years with no natural markings
Other Mina of 6 years with no natural markings
Other Arara of 12 years with many pockmarks on the forehead, temples, and cheeks
One Casta Ibo of 11 years more or less with a line on each temple
Other Ibo of 16 years with lines on her forehead
Other Conga of 11 years with no natural markings
Other Casta Yupo of 16 years with a small scar over her left eyebrow
Alusta dos a saver ohos negros ciento y sesenta í dos cabesass

---

Source: Archivo Central del Cauca, Primera Notaria, tomo 22, 1713, folios 63–68v.

to narrate the ways that the governing structure of Spanish slavery and commerce bound enslaved bodies to the webs of power within the colonial order.

Consequently, the *visita* provides a text within a text, highlighting the fact that enslaved bodies were a first indicator of how and where the person might be integrated into an evolving complex of community and identity formation. Intentional scarification suggested regional and ethnic origins just as the involuntary *picados de viruelas* (smallpox scars), served as reminders of the horrors of the passage. They encoded a person's history on the body. Bodies must serve as references for reconstructing cultural histories of early modern African-descended populations precisely because those bodies were sources to the people who made those histories. For Africans, body art and scarification must have spoken just as loudly as smallpox scars did for European medical examiners.[71]

The *visita* document highlights, quite forcefully, the diverse origins of the new Africans arriving in Popayán's slave communities and, to a greater degree, those origins in the kingdom. What did it mean that some "Araras" had incisions on the temples or that some carried one small hole in each cheek? Or that other Araras, usually those who fell below the age of eighteen, were found without their country marks? Or that still others of the same age were cited as having at least one small line on the temple, and another, age sixteen, many lines at the temples?

Table 2.3. Regional/Ethnic Breakdown of Slave Laborers Listed in 1712
Visita de Despacho

Gold Coast	Bight of Benin/ Bight of Biafra	Upper Guinea	Central Africa
Chaba (16)	Arará (35)	Mina (44)	Ibo (7)
Caramantí (7)	Lucumí (16)	Popo (7)	Congo (4)
	Mandinga (14)	Barbara (4)	Luango (4)
	Mondongo (3)		Boama (1)
	Poropue (1)		
	Bandu(bi) (1)		

Sources: ACC, Protocolos, PN, tomo 22, 1713, folios 63–71v; Hall, *Slavery and African Ethnicities*; Miller, *Way of Death*; Soares, *Devotos*; Law, *Slave Coast* and "Ethnicity and the Slave Trade"; Sweet, *Domingos*; and others have noted that "Mina" shifted in meaning over time and space. One could easily say "Bight of Benin," especially in the early eighteenth century. For a useful discussion of the Anlo-Ewe dispersal and gender, see Greene, *Gender, Ethnicity, and Social Change on the Upper Slave Coast*. For an introduction to cultural zones and points of departure for ethnic Africans during the slave trade, see Thornton, *Africa and Africans*.

To the uninitiated, the precise meaning that ethnic scarification held for the individual was likely to have remained illegible. Underscoring this perspective, Minas were found to have "lines in the temples"—some six, others three and four. Some appeared to be "of age" without any marks at all. Others were described frankly as having "confusing lines on the temples and forehead," a comment that highlights the scribe's or the medical inspector's uncertain gaze but also suggests that the recorder, at least to some extent, understood the pattern of other markings. Mandingas, too, had "several lines along the temples and forehead." Other Mandingas' lines were to be found "between the eye brows," "throughout the chest cavity," or "in a row over the forehead and on the lip *endido*" (see table 2.3).

Nevertheless, examining this group indicates that large numbers of Araras and Minas were present. This reflected a trend that began in the last decade of the seventeenth century, when the region of the Slave Coast made the transition from slave importer to slave exporter in response to shifting regional geopolitical realities and the sustained presence of the Dutch as a trading partner.[72] Although diversity remained the rule, slave laborers carrying the ethnic monikers Mina, Arara, Caravalí, Lucumí, Congo, and Cetre would maintain a significant presence in Popayán's slave market throughout the eighteenth century. Recall that Don Mateo del Masso's January 18, 1700, importation of fifty-nine captives included twenty-two Araras and thirty-seven Minas, all reputedly close to the age of twenty-five.[73] This should come as no surprise, since the Royal African

Company drew well over half of its African captives from the Gold Coast (31.2 percent) and the Bight of Benin (39.6 percent) during the period around 1713.[74]

But much like the transatlantic trade that fed Popayán's slave market, the origin of slave laborers fluctuated over time. During the early years (1705–13), most slave laborers emerged from the Bight of Benin, Senegambia, and Central Africa. Subsequently (1715–27), most slave laborers emerged from the Bight of Benin, followed by the Gold Coast and the Congo. Between 1730 and 1738, the order was Gold Coast, Bight of Biafra, followed by Central Africa or Congo; in this era, the Bight of Benin was a distant fourth.

The 153 African captives that Don Juan Ildefonso de Nieva introduced in 1733 offer a poignant example of the varying regional origins of arriving African captives: distinct from earlier groups, this one was composed of 94 Congo, 32 Mina, 14 Zetre, 10 Guaqui, and 3 Chamba (83 men, 30 women, 26 boys, and 14 girls). Because the group is found in another *visita de despacho*, we find details of scarification as well. Of note are the many references to individuals being *picado de viruelas* (smallpox markings), thus calling attention to the disease and death that marked their journey from Central Africa into the heart of the North Andes and its Pacific littoral frontier.[75]

As an endeavor to document these iconic and aesthetic renderings of Old World ethnocultural contexts, this source also betrays the elites' frustration in this effort, as well as the larger limitations they faced—and consequently we face—in attempts to understand "African" ethnic identity. What remains, however, is the fact that Europeans recognized ethnic Africans as members of discrete cultural or political groups whose distinctions mattered, even if those distinctions were found in the nuances of body art and scarification. Whatever these markings meant to Africans, they represented a moving and unknowable target in the colonial effort to possess and police the body. This inability to fix "blackness" (a fundamental mark for all African-descended *castas*) reveals the fundamental anxiety of racial governance and the perplexed look of the emergent "white" gaze throughout the colonial landscape. Ultimately, *bozales* were proto-subjects of foreign lands whose purported origins helped to index them within an order predicated upon capturing, identifying, and utilizing their bodies. In the face of all these conditions, Africans and Afro-Creoles formed relationships and communities through, and in spite of, the constraints of Quito's many slaveries.

The Contraband Passage

It is difficult, of course, to know how many slave traders circumvented royal checkpoints and their corresponding tolls. The contraband trade remained

hidden, making it by its very nature difficult for historians to narrate its processes and patterns. We do know, however, that Panama had long been a conduit for illegal trading activity—both unauthorized trade between the Spanish American colonies and illegal exchanges with the British and the French.[76]
Although other goods and merchandise filled the cargoes of such shipments,
"illegal slaves" were, in fact, a signature feature of this market.[77] Over the course
of the eighteenth century, colonial authorities adjudicated a series of civil and
criminal cases against slaveholders and slave traders for the charge of possessing or exchanging *esclavos de mala entrada*. On September 10, 1710, the governor
and the official judges of Popayán began to investigate Don José Pérez de Vivero for allegedly "introducing clandestinely" eleven slave children (*once negros
muleques*). By the time the officials caught up to Vivero, he had already sold the
slaves to José Sánchez. As in many such cases, officials had learned of these "illegal slaves" through an informant, who noticed that they lacked the brands of
the crown.

By 1711, officials were making great strides in prosecuting the matter against
Vivero, having found seven of the slaves in the Chocó and at least one in the
sugar-producing town of Buga. Ultimately, Vivero was fined 230 patacones for
each of the seven slaves found in the Chocó and 400 patacones for the child
found in Buga.[78] During that same period, officials were hearing another case
involving six slaves *de mala entrada* who were then working in the mines of
Nóvita, deep in the Chocó at the headwaters of the San Juan River. Unfortunately, the extant record stops short of providing the resolution.[79] Nevertheless, it is clear that many individuals, on both sides of the law, were caught up
in this process, and elites were at the heart of it.

In 1723 local officials in Popayán were on the trail of Don Jacinto Mosquera
y Figueroa, one of Popayán's wealthiest slaveholders, for employing African
captives who lacked the crown's "mark" (brand, *esclavos sin marca*) working in
his mines located in the Chocó.[80] Reviews of Mosquera's holdings continued
well into July 1725 and included searches of his mines in Santa Bárbara, a small
mining town. There, officials discovered "los negros de Chure . . . Bombas,
Araras, and Minas" ensconced in one of his holdings near the River Izcuandé.[81]
Despite Mosquera's claims that he acquired the captives legally, officials found
that because the slaves lacked the requisite brandings they could not have entered the Spanish provinces legally.[82]

Popayán's colonial records are replete with cases resembling that of Mosquera. One of the most interesting and perhaps the one most illustrative of
the extensive contraband networks that ran along the Pacific coast of New
Granada, first analyzed and partially edited by historian German de Granda, is

the case against Don Miguel de los Reyes.[83] On March 18, 1730, Reyes obtained clearance from officials in Panama to transport goods (mostly clothing) to Isla del Gallo, Iscuandé, San Buenaventura, and the Bocas de Chirambirá. After paying customs duties totaling 366 patacones and 1 real, Reyes proceeded in the preparations for his trip. Twelve days later, Joseph de Ochoa y Aría, a property holder of Popayán, declared before the royal scribe of Panama that he had purchased fifty slaves from England's South Sea Company. What officials did not know, however, was that forty of these souls belonged to Don Miguel de los Reyes and were the subjects of a series of sales pending throughout the district of Barbacoas. Although Reyes's scheme had gone undetected thus far, a snare awaited him down the Pacific coast.[84]

By September 18 of the same year, officials in Santa Bárbara had apprehended Reyes and confiscated the twenty-three blacks who remained in his custody. Crestfallen, Reyes confessed that five slaves were in a mine owned by Don Gaspar de Estacio, located on the Juajuy River; at least three others could be found in a mine on the Timbiquí River. Although Reyes might have hoped that by cooperating with local officials he would receive mercy, it would soon become clear that Don Joseph de la Guerra and Don Bernardo de Araujo y Bueno, *alcalde ordinario y juece oficial* (magistrate and official judge) of Santa Bárbara, intended to prosecute this matter to the fullest extent of the law.[85] Identifying and capturing the remaining contraband slaves would be their first order of business, both of which were matters that involved "reading" enslaved bodies and European markings of possession.

Arriving at the mine on the Juajuy River, Araujo and de la Guerra set out to inspect the brands of the slaves. Accordingly, they washed the slaves' sores with vinegar, ostensibly to make "the marks they carried" more apparent. While one might assume that brandings would appear clear, reflecting the form of the iron that had burned the flesh of African captives, this was not always the case. People of African descent often suffer from excessive keloids that can morph into indistinguishable scars rather than the clearly recognizable insignia of the crown or licensed trading company. Vinegar was used simply to clean scabbed and still-healing wounds, perhaps helping to render the brand more visible. Ultimately, however, it was the slaves themselves who cleared up the matter for Araujo and de la Guerra.

Shortly after the officials had begun their "inspection," two slaves who had been absent upon their arrival returned to the area. Upon being questioned, they explained that the marks they carried had been burned into their flesh at Chiman, located outside the city of Panama just prior to their departure.[86] The evidence was mounting against Reyes. Officials were beginning to trace his steps and infiltrate his clandestine network. The two slaves continued in their role as informants, explaining that while in the city of Panama, their handlers had kept them hidden in a very small house before their departure in the middle of the night with Reyes and crew. Not only did Araujo and de la Guerra learn that these slaves and several others had been branded "with much fire" (*con mucho fuego*) on the beach of Chiman; they also discovered from two other informants that Reyes had contracts to bring at least seventy slaves into the region.[87]

As news of Reyes's capture spread, individuals associated with his network began to abandon him; several fled Isla del Gallo, where they had awaited his arrival and the African captives he was to bring. Reyes's network had been extensive and had included the mayor of Isla del Gallo, Ypólito de Pinada, who himself had contracted with Reyes to bring seventy slaves into the region, with full knowledge of their illegal status. Noting the corruption in Isla de Gallo, the skipper of the boat the *Jesús, María y San José*, Domingo López, said that Reyes had instructed him to drop the slaves off at Isla del Gallo because "no judges were there" (*allí no había jueces*).[88] Bringing Reyes's scheme into greater relief, an indigenous sailor from the *Jesús, María, y San José* testified that they had extracted the slaves from Panama by moving them through the inlet of San Juan de Dios ("*por el postigo de* San Juan de Dios").[89] With these last details, officials had gained more than enough evidence to prosecute Reyes. On May 4, 1731, Don Bernardo de Araujo ordered the imprisonment of Reyes and the confiscation of all of his property, including thirty-four pounds, six "*castellanos* and four *tomines*" of gold that he had earned through his illicit commerce. The final step in the process was to appraise the slaves and calculate the corresponding taxes that Reyes owed. The question before them then was how much more, if any, would Reyes have to pay the royal treasury?[90]

Officials such as Araujo and de la Guerra, along with those in Quito and Santa Fé, had long been plagued by fraud of various forms. Going back to the late seventeenth century, the *audiencia* of Quito suspected Popayán's treasury of embezzlement.[91] Problems surrounding the collection of the crown's portion of gold mined in the region were endemic. Although the royal fifth (*quinto*) was administered inadequately throughout the colonial era, by the 1690s remittances emerging from the Chocó and Barbacoas had fallen to all-time lows. By and large, clandestine gold fell into a network that featured arrangements between masters and slaves, mine owners and freelancers, and those who transported the untaxed bullion for a commission (*porción*).[92]

In 1730, as Don Bernardo de Araujo and Joseph de la Guerra continued their search for the remaining members of Miguel de los Reyes's clandestine crew, they sought to enter the mines at Timbiquí. There, they encountered a chilly reception. While traveling up the Timbiquí River, de la Guerra and Don Agustín de Germendi, a royal official, encountered resistance from three miners: *el maestro*, Don Manuel de Erazo, a local priest; José Ruíz Bazán; and his mine administrator (*su minero*), Captain Antonio Guerrero.[93] According to de la Guerra and Don Agustín de Germendi, these three men prevented them from entering the mines at Timbiquí, which belonged to presibítero Erazo. Encountering the priest, he yelled, "Long live the King of Spain, death to bad government!" Determined to execute their duties and apprehend the contraband slaves, the officials forged ahead. As they continued up river, at the command of the priest, the three men captured the canoe, forcing crew members into the water to save themselves. Unlike some of their predecessors, Araujo and de la Guerra escaped with their lives. Relentless in their efforts, they then turned their attention to prosecuting their assailants.[94]

The delicate balance of power that characterized Barbacoan politics was evident to all involved. Justice and compliance with royal authority were both conditional and contested matters. As other scholars have shown, in frontier societies justice could often take the form of vigilante action, emerging as it did from within a context of contestation and exchange.[95] In the margins, even priests and colonial officials operated as vigilantes, or at least acted according to the situation. Indeed, the location of judicial authority vis-à-vis mining camps seems to have escalated efforts to circumvent colonial protocols. Regional boundaries and barriers were at once permeable and impenetrable, accessible to those who "belonged" in the region and yet closed off to those who apparently did not. Perhaps in some small way, the margins had become the center. At the very least, regional concerns now threatened to undermine highland efforts to establish royal hegemony within the region. Shifting the tide in the favor of the colonial state would depend largely upon officials' ability to regulate the acquisition of slave labor.

Marking Bodies: Enslavement in Three Acts

Amid the noxious scents of salt water, human excrement, and decaying corpses, the sixty-five African captives, registered by Sebastían Torijano, entered the realm in a manner peculiar to the order that ruled the Spanish-claimed Indies.[96] Upon the ship's arrival at the port of Cartagena, the agent for the French Royal Guinea Company supplied royal officials with the ship's register. It described the captives as "*castas* Congos, Araras, and Minas, between the ages of 20 and 30, . . . marked and countermarked the marks of his majesty."[97] In compliance with Castilian laws, French Royal Guinea Company agents had branded these captives with the company's official seal, marking them within the governing motif through which an emergent Spanish state claimed sovereignty over the ocean sea, ports of entry into American territories, and thereby commerce and markets. From there, slaves were subjected to three public rituals: *bodily inspections* and documentation of valuation for taxation; *branding*, a form of receipt marking legal passage and provenance; and *baptism*, which marked their new status as Christians. These veritable "ceremonies of possession" confirmed the slave's enclosure within the realm, giving a course to their lives within Spain's royal juridical structures. They also bound slaves in specific ways, making them into highly particularized subjects of the king of Spain. Put differently, these three acts ensured that the *bozal*, a foreign-born, enslaved subject and commodity, had been incorporated within the realm in proper juridical fashion.[98]

All vassals had their proper place, conditioned by law and god under the sovereign and his regents. So it would be with entering captive subjects of various polities and sovereigns of Africa. The public spectacle of enclosure observed at the port of arrival served as a vivid and interactive metaphor for slavery in the Spanish realm. Upon arrival, enslaved African captives experienced a level of alienation that even Christian incorporation could not mitigate. Although incorporated as slaves rather than beheaded, and while promised eternal life through Christian salvation, most enslaved foreign subjects could neither speak the Castilian language nor understand the gravity of crown/church power. Forced to live as captives to Spanish colonial governance, these deracinated Africans entered into a world of death. In short, the social death of racial slavery required that enslaved captive subjects of servitude live their lives within the spectacle of colonial power.

Through these first three acts of enslavement, royal and ecclesiastical officials tethered the enslaved body to the body politic and the markets of the realm in explicitly physical ways. First, slave bodies were inspected and "marked" in official ledgers. Viewing the captive bodies already marked by life in Atlantic Africa and the commodification of transatlantic commerce, the scribe took copious notes in the ledger concerning nearly every aspect of the captives' appearance: their hair, eyes, noses, skin, beards, approximate ages, and perceived state of health and mortality. During this process, slaves were appraised and accorded an "intrinsic value," a kind of mark that often dictated the conditions of juridical life for the enslaved.

Once the valuation and payment of all corresponding taxes and tariffs were complete, royal officials branded Africans with the mark of the king above their right breast. They had already been marked according to royal edicts with the insignia of the royally licensed trading company on the left side of their back, where they also carried the insignia of the order that had owned their bodies. The king's brand, on the other hand, signified both their legal entry and the traders' payment of the king's portion of their value. The burning of the royal insignia onto the captive body became an awful reminder of royal power over the lives and affairs of all sovereign subjects. The monarch was the ultimate ruler of all slaves within the realm and the ruler of the realm itself. Through his adjudication of slavery, the sovereign turned the juridical institution of slavery into a royal system of surveillance and power that radiated throughout the realm. The brand—a juridical symbol—served to make use of the enslaved body as an icon of royal power, an emblem of royal law that bound the pater's property rights to the rights and possibilities of the enslaved. Slavery sat at the nexus of civil governance, commerce, and religious discipline. It made for a political economy rife with the tensions of empire—tensions between the governing imperatives of monarchy and colonial vassals with their penchant for dominion as well as truck and barter. It occasioned tensions between the king and paters as well as between paters and slaves.

On and within their bodies, the enslaved carried the fantasies of both slavery and the colonial regime. The ideal slave was a composite of discipline and order governed by a just monarch through a Christian piety. All were bound—master and slave, indigenous and *castas*—before his majesty. Thus, the slave was a key icon of a well-ordered Spanish American society. It should come as no surprise, then, that the adjudication of the kingdom's many slaveries would ultimately prove to be one of the areas that tested the limits of sovereignty for some jurists writing in the eighteenth century. Put differently, slavery was such an elemental aspect of society that even a few slaves could affect every mode of commerce and some of the most fundamental features of political and religious governance. Slaves' very presence in the Americas signified the intrinsic value that tied slavery to claims of authority, status, capital, commerce, and labor. But for all of the fantasies foisted upon the iconic slave, royal and church officials always viewed slaves as objects of colonial governance, people who would act, move, and behave in their own interests and thus required discipline and control. They also assumed that masters might not comply with royal edicts. In short, marking the slave body was an effort to account for the slave's movement across time and space within the society, while shoring up the sovereign's authority over the order, commerce, and all Christian vassals.

In a third act of enslavement, slaves entering Cartagena were baptized, grafted onto the body of Christ, and dispersed into the realm for sale.[99] This act of spiritual redemption completed their enclosure within the realm. The ultimate act of possession and consecration, baptism was yet another royal imposition of the colonial order. Slaves were now free in Christ but bound to spiritual surveillance, culpability, and punishment here on earth. Ultimately, then, enslaved Africans were, as historian Colin Palmer observed, "slaves of the white god" and his earthly kings. Inasmuch as baptism encumbered mastery and afforded slaves with a right to the sacraments, including marriage, it cloaked them within a circumscribed sense of proper moral comportment. Put differently, slaves were conditioned by the predicament and possibilities that resulted from the competing claims of mastery placed upon them and their movements within society. What the enslaved thought of these fonts remains unclear. One imagines that even those moderately autonomous and relatively "free" slaves would have remained mindful of the "ceremonies of possession" that had attended their arrival and, to the extent that they understood them, the macabre implications of these rituals.[100] If the archive of slavery is a mortuary, it is also one filled with fetters, branding irons, and chains that bound both the severely "unfree" slave to the relatively "freer" or "autonomous" slave. For some free blacks, depending upon their rank and location within the kingdom, the stains and chains of slavery may have continued to encumber their freedom, if only owing to the threat of a return to slavery. This was certainly the case for *coartados* (slaves who had fixed the price of the *libertad*). In short, the fetters of slavery were surely entangled with a complement of "freedoms" depending upon where one ended up. Whether circulating as cash-capital or credit, within the moral economies of the realm, or moving about with great personal freedom and physical latitude as spiritual workers or as well-regarded members of spiritual communities, slaves' bodies were marked literally and figuratively with the boundaries of the many forms of slavery possible in Spanish America. Some fetters were simply not as tight as others, but all could be tightened with further binding, as often evidenced through sales. More than a "person with a price," then, the slave was one with live juridical and religious standing within the order. While their price indexed their labor value and implicated them in the market as capital and commodities, those who purchased slaves were, in fact, purchasing the privilege of having authority within the order, that is, of having dominion over other colonial subject peoples within the order. Put differently, for all of the emphasis upon slaves as labor, their numerical market valuations corresponded directly to the political-status culture that constituted order and sovereignty.

Slaves arriving in Quito during the late seventeenth and early eighteenth centuries were of diverse origins. Now, divergent routes would lead into the varied regions of the kingdom. This was a highly randomized process, as various factors, merchants, and traders purchased slaves for Quito's markets through numerous means, some public and legal, others clandestine and illegal. These many routes were part and parcel in the making of slavery for those entering the region and the people they encountered as they labored along the way. Ultimately, the highly randomized and relatively small slave trade to Quito produced highly atomized African subjects, installing peculiar contexts for the ongoing development of slave communities and African-derived subjectivities in the eighteenth century. As Quito's slave population grew incrementally, Africans with varying diasporic experiences and travel knowledge of the region were folded into the expanding and predominantly Afro-Creole slave population.

CHAPTER THREE

Baptism, Marriage, and the Formation of Sacred Communities

In 1648, during his review of the kingdom's religious life and governance, Quito's archbishop, Agustin de Ugarte Sarvia, noted the fruits of Jesuit spiritual labor among those marked as *negros* and *mulatos* within the city of Quito. In this report, he made special mention of two priests, Bastidas and Vergara y Caicedo, who had died serving and instructing the "*negros* and *mulatos*."[1] According to the archbishop, the Jesuit brothers inspired hope with the example of their lives. The archbishop sat at the apex of spiritual and religious governance, and it was his duty to oversee religious compliance and the propagation of the faith among colonial subjects within the imagined Republica de Españoles of Quito.

Religious directives governed vassals by dictating the religious access that masters afforded their enslaved dependents. They were to instruct their slaves in the faith; facilitate their confessional life; allow them free time during holidays, feast days, and Sundays; and respect their rights to the sacrament of marriage in sales involving marked enslaved couples. In the gold camp and rural estates of Popayán, slaveholders were required to pay for the services of itinerant priests, who administered the sacraments to their enslaved flock. In short, the religious governance of slaves and slavery was shaped as the church participated in forging a colonial bureaucracy aimed at marking, corraling, evangelizing, and governing the spiritual lives of those enslaved colonial subjects enclosed and differentiated as "*negros* and *mulatos*." In the cities, parish priests claimed authority over religious compliance, even as regular clergy—Jesuits, Dominicans, Franciscans, and the Mendicants, along with a host of convents—held political and religious authority over slaves, slaveholders, and their intimate affairs. Imperatives of governance included converting and policing the religious lives of the enslaved. The terms under which they were enslaved as well as the conditions of their pasts were of great moral concern to the Catholic religious order. Some priests doubted the moral legality of black slavery on the grounds that they were neither captives of a just war nor any more naturally enslavable than Indians.[2] Others, such as Tomás de Solórzano Pereira, insisted that slavery was their price for spiritual redemption.[3]

Historians have explored the tensions between the possibilities Catholicism afforded enslaved Africans and the ways it imposed colonial religious discipline.[4] Evangelizing, baptizing, marrying, and organizing enslaved blacks into congregations and *cofradías de color* (black religious brotherhoods) created racially constituted and government-orchestrated religious assemblages. These acts and associations obliged the clergy under canon law to perform a series of rites and ritualized performances aimed at harnessing the will and rehabilitating those with non-Christian lineage. It was the priest's pen along with that of the notary that inscribed *casta*, illegitimacy, and other colonial markings for governance and oversight. These localized parish practices were part of the broader institutional imperial practices, such as the Inquisition and the House of Trade. These practices suggest that religious governance was constituted racially through local daily practices of distinguishing between "white/Europeanness" and "non-Europeanness/nonwhiteness" in the development of sacred community, and through everyday practices, such as baptism and marriage, that gave sanction to the development of black social life within a slave-based European colonial horizon.[5]

African congregations, black *cofradias*, African diasporic ethnicities, and godparent relationships not only exemplified colonial black social life, but demonstrated the broader social landscape of colonial governance that defined and differentiated all *castas* (Atlantic and American), Indians, and African non-Europeans. They showcased efforts to maintain and defend Christian sovereignty, situating the clergy and religious authorities within a structure of dominance that governed slavery and, thereby, colonial society. Church leadership, comprised of the powerful, well-connected bishops, archbishops, priests, and nuns, was frequently directly connected to the activities of judges, magistrates, merchants, and propertied individuals through their recording of births. Over time, the church took under its purview the reading, baptizing, and constituting African captives as black within colonial servitude and European-derived religious directions. Priests baptized them as black, mulatto, enslaved, free, or *zambo* and legalized their status as slaves, free people, or *castas*. Each category designated and obligated their operation within particular confines of the law as colonial others, yet culpable confessant Christians. Such sacred acts as baptism and marriage can be recognized as both racializing practices and slaves' attempts to make a life within the predicament of colonial servitude.

Their processions, marriages, and baptisms reveal how the enslaved crafted moments to seize pleasure, repossess their bodies, fix kin, and pool resources as sacred communities.

The church enshrined slavery and racial governance by legislating slave heritage through baptism, policing sex through marriage, and developing black religious orders. Scholars have used these sources to discuss processes of ethnogenesis, or the development of African identity over colonization. This work insists that slave trading, and the associated processes of inspection and marking, baptism, and marriage, exemplified formative practices of racialization. These practices were constitutive of European colonial governance and the non-European racial groupings. In short, far from neat carryovers, African diaspora ethnicities, seen through congregation life, marital unions, and baptismal parties, were in fact productions of the racialized colonial gaze. These assemblages were "symptomatic" of the transoceanic European colonial regimes that installed and governed them. In short, black colonial identities were forged within the purgatory of slavery, a space of colonial captivity, where even those meriting black liberty could never escape racial governance.

These practices suggest the entangled states of social death and racial life under European colonialism. Marriage, baptism, and black sacred communities reproduced slave status and colonial racial heritage, even as they point to Africans' attempts to form meaningful associations, establish kinship unions, and otherwise develop social life. The formation of sacred communities points to religious governance and slavery, insisting that slaves be seen within the iconography of colonial religious life and the spectacle of power. Ultimately, this underscores the ways Africans made social life after suffering the social death and natal alienation of enslavement to the order. The very spiritual redemption that first inscribed racial difference upon those born within captivity became the moral and religious grounds of incorporation for colonial governance and its modes of racial differentiation.

Black Congregants

By the mid-seventeenth century, the Jesuits had a demonstrated commitment to evangelizing among indigenous and African-descended people, efforts they had begun nearly a century earlier in Peru. Two noted Jesuit priests, Alonso de Sandoval and Pedro Claver, made it their life's work to preach, convert, and baptize among slaves arriving in Cartagena from the Atlantic. The Jesuits arrived in Quito in June 1586, preaching in the plazas, markets, and wherever they might find sizable groups of people, including slaves who were already a part of Quito's society. Jesuit father and historian Pedro de Mercado shared the impression that black people were promising evangels and emblems of the gospel. His account suggests that official black religious expression coincided neatly with baroque modes of opulence and ostentation. As a result, Mercado's description of an annual festival showcases how the enslaved were interpolated and compelled to profess in order to be incorporated within the religious colonial order:[6]

> A congregation of *negros y mulatos* who belong to our school each year perform a festival to Jesus, not with the title of this delicious name, but with the one of "Holy Savior," which is the same as Jesus. The day of Transfiguration is the one designated for this celebration, and they do this by showing much adoration with flowers and candles, and [they] seek always for the most desired singers of the *commonwealth* [*república*] to offer the Mass. And in order that this festival be of great enjoyment to the Savior's soul, the *pardo y moreno* congregants are informed that they have been *whitened* by the blood of Christ, which flows in the sacrament of confession; and in the day of the festival they eat as partakers at the holy table of the altar, and this they do with devoted diligence. To the savior enclosed within heaps of bread they make a feast [and] place him on a throne during the Shrovetide [three days preceding Ash Wednesday] in order to prevent [any] disruption due to his presence on those days. During these ceremonies one preaches in the morning and afternoon to a large number of listeners who congregate at our church [La Compañía]. It gives the fervent workers of La Compañía great spiritual pride to see those innumerable men and women who come to the festival of Shrovetide [and] eat the body of Christ; and in gaining this joy they avoid the loss of their *spiritual property* in the snares that the demon hurries to introduce.[7]

Mercado's example opens a window onto official black colonial religious communities and their productions within baroque Quito. For him, blacks— *negros*, *morenos*, *mulatos*, and *pardos*—were among the city's most orthodox Christians, expressing their baroque piety with "devoted diligence." Holding a special festival for Jesus, they took care to revere his "delicious name." The spectacle of the best black vocalists calling up the "Holy Savior" begs the question: What was the liturgical effect of black vocalists (some no doubt slaves) calling upon the power of a *savior*? Was not the passion, the redemptive power that they sought in his blood and bruised body on full display in the bound devotion of the black body? After all, not only were Quito's *negros* and *mulatos* "whitened" through these supplications to God, but they "avoid[ed] the loss of their spiritual property."[8] Their expressions of piety were elemental to the opulence of the baroque. The need for the whiteness of salvation applied to the broader populace of *castas* "blackened" by their impure blood heritage.[9]

The presence of black *cofradías*, their public festivals and processions, suggests fascinating questions regarding the significance of slaves as religious symbols within the context of Catholic evangelism and display. Clearly, both free blacks and slaves alike became Catholic evangelists in Spanish America. For Jesuit priest Mercado, Archbishop de Ugarte Sarvia, and their audiences, black religious compliance signaled effective religious governance and a properly ordered society. While the disciplining and coercive functions of the church are oft considered in the literature of colonial Latin America, it bears remembering that colonial Spanish America was home to a steady struggle to convert and imbue the bodies of society members with the sweet communion of their Holy Spirit. Historian John Leddy Phelan characterized Quito's morality as lying between "the splendor of the cult and the naked contrast of widespread public and private immorality."[10] Falling somewhere between these two poles was a broader dialogue about the spirit world, proper morality, nature, and pleasure. Slaves, then, became emblems within a broader evangelical process that both celebrated and rejuvenated "belief" in the cult. It venerated and reaffirmed the veracity of the cult and its power, compelling a surrender of the will to varying degrees over time. The Catholic calendar was filled with sanctioned and programmed public feasts aimed at both veneration and revival. If slaves participated in these rites with grandeur, we must inquire into their symbolic impact upon society.

The study of religious brotherhoods has guided a great deal of scholarship addressing enslaved black religious life. Researchers suggest, of course, that Catholicism provided a space for the cultivation and extension of communal affinities, social linkages, and forms of kin. Such sources also demonstrate the multiple colonial practices through which enslaved Africans were bound, marked, and recruited into the corporal colonial order. Put differently, slaves' religious practices demonstrate how colonial blackness was also constitutive of colonial religious governance in its various guises. These colonial religious governing motifs, including baptism, confirmation, the Inquisition, marriage, and institutions of devotion such as convents and monasteries, all helped to establish a colonial race relation of governance. Each, in its own way, determined racial status, secured information about its subjects, and otherwise governed the conduct of populations through basic daily behaviors. These were racialized assemblages that marked enslaved black subjects in relation to *naciónes*, *castas*, or geohumoral zones. Memberships in *negro* and *mulato* brotherhoods also served to bind their heritage and imperial status as non-Europeans enslaved and bound within the broader order for governance, even as they allowed the enslaved to collectively marshal resources for mutual benefit. They also allowed racialized subjects to develop local affinities, form associations with specific aspects of Christian veneration, and perform colonial religiosity that naturalized Castilian Christian heritage as normal and sacred.

Mercado's "congregation of *negros* and *mulatos*," for example, helped black subjects form official or institutionalized relationships with the church. In addition to the congregation of La Compañía, the Chapel of Our Lady of the Rosary in the Chapel of Santo Domingo—the Dominican order's church—was home to a religious sodality known simply as the Cofradía de Morenos. This chapel, described as an image of striking beauty, was also the site of festivals and processionals performed by its congregants. In 1589 these congregants petitioned the bishopric for a chapel in the Cathedral for the founding of the Cofradía of Our Lady of Alta Gracia, agreeing to pay annual alms of five hundred pesos. A sum of five hundred pesos strikingly was also the average price of an able-bodied young adult male slave at the time.[11]

During the sixteenth and seventeenth centuries, African and Creole-based sodalities flourished throughout Spanish America in spite of royal efforts to curb their growth. A *cofradía* that developed in Quito's chapel of the Convent of Our Lady of the Rosary was also a convent known for its riches. These riches included slaves donated by its members and other benefactors, rural estates, cattle, and a bevy of handsomely valued jewels found in the chapel.[12] For seventeenth-century Quito, sources are suggestive, but severely limited, regarding sodalities and black congregations.[13] While available accounts reveal the existence of black Catholic communities, they also conceal the processes that helped constitute Mercado's congregants.[14] For example, little can be determined in terms of how their enslaved members were selected, the probable origins of their founding members, or the spiritual or political perspectives they harbored.[15] Neither do they allow for a deeper analysis of the religious understandings that permeated their ranks or their polysemic lingual, ethnic, and political foundations. Similar to the performance of viceregal political cultures in cities such as Lima and Mexico City, Quito's enslaved subjects who fell under the dominion of religious officials were very much alive within the broader culture of religious display that permeated baroque Quito, its architecture, and its choral music.[16] Attempts to make sense of slavery's imprint on society must examine the ways in which the presence of the enslaved proved elemental within the spectacle of power and religious performativity.

Indians and others were cited in celebrations of the Holy Virgin and the saints of the parish (La Compañía).[17] The public nature of these performances suggests that in the cities blacks served as social interlocutors—people who displayed piety, personal discipline, and consent in ways that must have influenced modes of religious embodiment and observance. Through their spiritual and religious interactions with the broader populace, Africans and their descendants affected the tone and texture of Spanish American culture. African memories and intellectual resources (e.g., language and idioms) mattered in Quiteño society, if only as matters of suspicion. In this way, early modern black Catholic devotion must be viewed as offering a powerful commentary upon the righteousness of God, the passion of the Christ, and the promise of salvation. Black bodies were marked, branded, read, baptized, and redeemed through grotesque punishments and crude display. As such, black captives embodied the trope of redemption perhaps more than anyone in the order. They were juridically and spiritually sinners saved by the grace of Castile's prince. In the baroque world, unbridled opulence, communal salvation, mutilated bodies, and scents all served to define the religious, spiritual, and thereby social milieu. Slaves were quite literally emblematic of the macabre symbolism of the passion of a son forced to die in hopes of reuniting the father with his creation. So often, the scholarly concern has been the extent to which people read as "ethnic others" (here the descendants of Africans and Andeans) imbibed and appropriated Catholicism. However, we must also inquire into how enslaved black bodies circulated within the religious symbolism of the bleeding savior, wherein priests and whites also engaged in practices of self-flagellation and gestures of humility. Within this context, black bodies in need of subjection and exemplary discipline were also necessary as physical reminders of the most abject spiritual captives awaiting redemption *and* as representatives of believers' hope in the Christ Jesus.

Quito was rife with examples of self-sacrificing individuals, figures who gave their lives for the greater good of society. In the 1640s, Mariana de Jesus, for example, achieved great prominence as such a religious devotee, laying down her life to end a spate of epidemics and natural disasters that ravaged the highland core. While Mariana de Jesus avoided public adoration, many of Quito's most prominent citizens believed in the power of her sacrificial body and sought her blessings. Although describing the differences between baroque displays of religious observation and private failings, historian John Phelan also effectively describes the extreme and contradictory ways religious symbolism circulated throughout this time: "It was a world of sharp contrasts in which the acts of men seemed to conflict with their professions of belief and in which *gross sensuality coexisted with militant if at times morbid religiosity*" (emphasis added).[18] What was Spanish America, if not an order possessed of a governing motif composed of a series of studies in multiplying contrasts? What were slaves, if not embodiments of grace, objects of a great many sensual desires, and yet fundamentally objects of tremendous scorn? For a great many Spanish Catholics, slaves were quite literally captives saved by grace, whitened in the afterlife. For them, perhaps more than anyone else within the realm, it was imminently necessary to store up timber for a home made without hands in the world to come. While Quito's black spiritual communities reveal the opulence of their holy convocations, they tell us little about the social worlds of kith and kin the enslaved forged. Parish records guide the following analysis of blacks' social networks through a reading of important moments of official black social life.

Sacramental records take us into the intimate lives of the enslaved and offer us rare glimpses, or momentary snapshots, of an enslaved adult's or child's life and the communities within which they lived. Slaves did not stand alone in front of priests at the fonts of baptism and marriage. Instead, people from their daily lives and most personal circles stood with them and corroborated their moral narratives. Consequently, sacramental records index at least a subset of the communities that slaves forged. Examining enslaved people's friends, kin, resource partners, and sexual companions offers powerful clues regarding the context within which Africans and their descendants created cultures and communities under slavery. However, sacramental records are not uncomplicated sources. The ecclesiastical archive is both a product of colonial practices and a reflection of the communal life the enslaved crafted through racial subjugation to the crown. Just as sacramental records reveal moments of African diasporic kinships, political affinities, and religious compliance, they also conceal those whom the enslaved chose as their intimate partners. In other instances, sacramental records suggest the enslaved chose their intimate relationships with little regard for gendered Catholic sexual norms, concerns of "legitimacy," or blood lineage. Using Inquisition records, scholars have shown that slaves engaged the impositions of Christianity in ways that flouted convention.[19] Enslaved blacks married people the church considered their kin. Some took more than one husband or wife, suggesting that slaves, much like others within the society, had individual ways of pleasing the Christian god while continuing to engage in a variety of intimate and sexual partnerships. In short, sacramental records offer important but limited views of enslaved Africans and Afro-Creoles forging communities within bondage. Taken together, these snapshots tell us something very important. Enslaved Africans did not adopt Catholicism wholesale, or even in ways consistent with the colonial fantasy. Indeed, some even formed meaningful relationships without regard for church sanctions. The sacramental records also demonstrate clearly that enslaved conversion and formal adoption of the dominant regime's cultural practices were processes that occurred over time.

Consistent with Quito's small scale of slave imports, Africans do not appear in large numbers within sacramental records. Careful examination of baptismal and marriage records across time suggests that Quito offered distinct New World environments for the making of diasporic subjectivities and affinities. The enslaved made deeply personal choices about who their associates, intimates, and foes were within the contexts of their sites of arrival and subsequent travels. As such, one can glimpse the series of overlapping public and personal networks of affiliation they produced through readings of official moments of communal display and pious religious compliance.

Baptizing a child was a church-mandated, master-sanctioned communal affair. It involved assembling a small cohort of intimates that included the infant's parents and godparents, the temporal and spiritual guides in this life. Godparents were especially important people who would offer the child patronage when needed, as well as spiritual instruction. They were people charged with ensuring the infant would be guided in the faith and developed into a compliant Christian subject. In short, baptism governed and structured parenthood, childhood, and social life in official ways. Theoretically, godparentage might add a layer of oversight to the socialization of children, parenting, and to some degree the dominion of masters. Godparents were people who knew, and would continue to know, the parents throughout the infant's childhood. They were expected to serve as co-parents who might be called upon to offer material support in difficult times. Above all, however, their official role was that of a custodian of the child's religious, social, and cultural development. Still, the process of baptizing did more than structure parenting and childhood. Baptizing slave children called enslaved parents forward along with their godparents, insisting they give an account for how they would raise this child in the fear and admonition of the Lord, the Virgin, and the Catholic faith.[20] Baptism marked more than slave status, racialized heritage, and corporeality. It was aimed at harnessing the will and profession of faith of all colonial subjects while making their godparents responsible for admonishing them in the faith and denouncing those who lived a life of sin.

It was critical, therefore, that those assembled for an infant's baptism at least signal communal bonds, even if these bonds masked—as they could—modes of control and coercion. Ultimately, it was a master's charge to facilitate the religious lives of his slaves and household subordinates, and the fulfillment of this charge could take myriad forms. Consequently, in viewing congregants assembled at the baptismal font, one must ask not if this was a "community" but rather what sort of community each baptism occasioned and how they mapped the interstices of power that formed colonial society. As seen through snapshots of slave associations found in baptismal registries of urban Quito and Guayaquil, one can recognize the material conditions and assembly of personalities within the master's household orbit, including the latitude allowed and taken by dependents therein, that affected lives of bondage.

Similar to baptism registries, slave marriage records disclose the many, varied, and forged communal affinities within an Andean world. In initiating the petition for marriage, the *novios* (bride and groom) appeared before the priest with their godparents and two witnesses, often a party of six. The witnesses were called upon to respond to a series of questions from the priest designed to ascertain the couple's moral availability for marriage and whether they knew each other well enough to make such an important choice. In the process, the witnesses gave information about themselves, their *casta*, and the amount of time and how they had known the *novios*. In short, the small clan presented as a kind of "community," intimates who knew and supported one another morally and religiously and could confirm, therefore, with certainty that the couple were qualified for married life. Following this, the banns were announced three times, calling for other associates, friends, enemies, or anyone with knowledge of the couple's moral behaviors to bear witness to their fitness for marriage. Had either of the two been married before, perhaps in another town? Had the bride or groom had a sexual relation with the other's sibling? Were there any other moral impediments?

Births, Baptisms, and Bound Lives

On November 23, 1607, in the parish church of El Sagrario, Antonio and his wife Madalena (both slaves of Juan Portero) baptized their son, Miguel, in the Catholic faith. Godparents could be assigned by master or priest or chosen by parents. As was customary, in accordance with canon law, the infant received two godparents to assist in the instruction of the faith and to promote his overall well-being. In a move that reflected slave baptismal patterns in Quito city, Miguel was assigned two slaves as godparents: Gaspar and Isabel. Indeed, Miguel's baptism was typical in many ways, reflecting the experiences similar to those of the other eighty-five Afro-Creoles (forty-eight females, thirty-seven males) baptized in El Sagrario parish church between 1606 and 1613.[21] Among the eighty-five Afro-Creoles baptized in Quito's El Sagrario parish between these years, sixty-one fathers were listed, nine of whom were married to the mothers. These data suggest precisely the meaningful relationships not sanctioned by the church. Even though the parents were not married, the father still appeared at the baptism asserting his role and relationship. This also underscores the importance of baptism as the single most important sacrament for most Africans. Some twenty-two infants were left without one or both parents; fourteen lacked both a mother and a father; five were found without their father, and three were without their mother. Accounting for such official absences raises questions about slave compliance and the instability of life within bondage. Baptismal records also offer important perspectives regarding how enslaved women came to understand their sexuality and maternity within the context of sexual violence and the predatory white gaze that imagined them as laborers with reproductive capacity.[22]

The birth of eighty-five Afro-Creole infants in a seven-year period is significant in the context of a small population of approximately four hundred enslaved people. We have already seen that the enslaved population included Afro-Creoles from various regions within the kingdom and beyond. Afro-Creoles, who possessed knowledge of the kingdom's geographies and official bureaucracies, were now producing a second generation of enslaved blacks. They, like their parents, would grow up in the extremely intimate and violent space of baroque Quito. Their broader cultural milieu included the presence of many indigenous Andeans, Europeans, *mestizos*, and other *castas*, as well as Africans who had traveled divergent routes to Quito and spoke various languages. These baptized Afro-Creoles would come of age in a space where bodies were routinely flagellated, chained, dismembered, and read within the broader structures of racial governance.

Their parents' choices of godparents showcase the development of myriad sacred communities among those marked as "black" as well as those considered "indigenous" and, to some degree, "white." How did the small, intimate families who raised these infants shape their children's knowledge of colonial society and its cultures? While their choices suggest more than they reveal, the selection of godparents tells us much about the range of associations that enslaved persons had through their work and living environments. Individual preferences in friends, marital partners, and kin tell us a great deal about the customary practices that connected enslaved blacks in Quito to many different communities and kinship networks. They reveal people living in diverse, intimate, and deeply violent contexts who made a range of choices from day to day through which overlapping communal affiliations developed.

Although Quito's general population growth is attributable in part to immigration and importation, these eighty-five births point to natural growth. They mirror the cumulative growth of Quito's Spanish and Andean populations over the course of the early seventeenth century. Demographic studies of slavery throughout the Americas have shown that the enslaved population's birth and death rates often corresponded to those of the larger society.[23] Quito's enslaved population was experiencing similar growth.[24] Central to that process were enslaved women. Enslaved black women formed a slight majority among the four hundred enslaved blacks who lived in the city of Quito at the turn of the century. They could be seen selling goods, congregating with other poor women of color, and accompanying the entourages of their masters. The population was relatively young and fecund, and pointed to the incremental growth of the Afro-Creole population, a process that had begun in earnest, it seems, in the final two decades of the sixteenth century. Historian Kris Lane notes, for example, that in a sample of 116 women slaves sold in the period between 1580 and 1600, 22 had nursing children, and 1 was pregnant. An additional 22 children were sold separately from their mothers during those decades.[25] The promise of more Creole children may have also been apparent within those sales, as 16 slaves (8 couples) were sold as married couples.[26] The 85 infants born in the first decade of the seventeenth century augmented the enslaved families that made up the blacks in Quito's El Sagrario parish.

In my random sampling of Quito's El Sagrario parish, more than two-thirds of the children baptized were presented to the church by both parents. Moreover, the large number of *compadres* (godparents) standing for these infants underscores the size of the community these infants were entering. Most had at least one godparent; sixteen of the children had both a *padrino* (godfather) and a *madrina* (godmother); forty-six had only a *padrino*; thirty-four had only a *madrina*. At least sixty-two of the godparents are easily identified as enslaved individuals. And since the terms *moreno*, *pardo*, and *negro* had become almost synonymous with "slave," one can rightly assume that most, if not all, whose slave status was not indicated outright were, in fact, slaves as well.

Rarely during this period did slave owners or relatives of slave owners participate in *compadrazgo* by serving as godparents. In this sample, only five elite males served as godfathers of enslaved children. In three of those cases, the children's parents were documented as unknown (*padres no conocidos*); the other two were presented by their mothers. In only one case is it clear that the owner was the godfather (*el amo fue su padrino*). Apparently, this was rare enough that it drew the attention of the priest scribe, who would normally fill in the name of the person along with his appropriate title.[27]

Similarly, only seven cases revealed an elite woman serving as godmother.[28] In one instance the child was a free black; the other six were slaves. At least two lacked both a mother and a father, and of these only one received both godparents.[29] Melchora, baptized on February 3, 1696, illustrates this tendency. Discovered by a free black woman, Melchora had been left at the door of a Jesuit-owned store with no hint as to who her parents were. Like most in her situation, Melchora received only one godparent, an elite—Doña María Vaca de la Cadena, who served as her godmother.

Kris Lane's sample reveals only one instance of free blacks serving as the godparents of the enslaved during this period. In that case, Catalina de Cepeda, described as *morena libre*, served as the godmother for an enslaved boy named Juan.[30] Juan's parents—Madelena (the slave of "Don León") and Cosome (the slave of "Don Juan")—were among those married. Yet even in this instance, the child had only one godparent. It seems that while free blacks occasionally served as the godparents of the enslaved, slaves did not serve as the godparents of free children.

As historians Stephen Gaudeman and Stuart Schwartz found for eighteenth-century Bahia, Brazil, selection of godparents reflected familial and communal affinities and, perhaps to a lesser degree, slaves' aspirations toward upward mobility.[31] However, with the lack of elite and free black *compadres*, it seems more likely that godparent selection in seventeenth-century Quito reflected kinship and communal ties. By and large, Africans and Afro-Creoles (enslaved and free) controlled this aspect of their lives. While there were good reasons to select elites as godparents, particularly for establishing patronage relations that could improve life and opportunities to gain freedom, there were no ecclesiastical impediments to selecting slaves or recently freed persons as the godparents of one's child.

Still, if slaves were seeking to form such alliances with free blacks, there were potential limitations to their accomplishing this goal. In the early decades of the seventeenth century, Quito's free blacks were few in number.[32] Consequently, it is possible that, at times, some free blacks and slaves would have lacked sufficient contact with each other to establish the degree of familiarity and affinity necessary to warrant inclusion in such personal matters as rearing one another's children. Furthermore, one should not assume that those who did find themselves in close proximity enjoyed each other's company or otherwise formed intimate bonds. While some may have been open to the idea of developing such ties, it is also possible that individual idiosyncrasies produced interpersonal differences that precluded such connections.[33] In short, these were extremely personal decisions that individuals—usually mothers and fathers together—made for themselves.

Afro-Indigenous Compadrazgo

Examining indigenous baptismal records in the central Quito parish of El Sagrario, historian Martin Minchom noted a number of people of African descent serving as godparents for indigenous children. Between July and December 1596, eighteen of the ninety-three indigenous children baptized (19.3 percent) featured at least one black godparent. Speculating in regard to the apparent connections between Andeans and blacks, Minchom suggests that these relationships were the result of "the common service role of both Indian and black categories to the Spanish population." Noting that in some instances both the father of the child and the godfather were artisans, Minchom concluded that black persons may have been in a position to "extend a measure of patronage by bringing artisans within the protection of a wealthy Spanish household."[34] They could have also been work associates, friends who came to regard each other as sacred kin within the polysemic ethnocultural worlds of baroque Quito.

Minchom's findings suggest more than a few possibilities regarding black and indigenous interactions in the city. They show, as historian Rachel O'Toole argues, that blacks and indigenous peoples were bound within the intimacies of colonial life, joined through work, proximity, and social discipline.[35] During this typical six-month sample, individuals continued to make choices of kin, and thereby community, that over time produced certain customary norms. An earlier decade had witnessed the very public baptism of the *zambo* lords of Esmeraldas, the pious Afro-Indigenous *caciques* tied to Quito nobility through the sacred communion of godparentage.

Among baptisms of indigenous children between 1606 and 1613, there were eleven cases in which blacks served as the godparents of Andean children.[36] In ten cases, the African-descended godparent was a godmother; only one featured a godfather—Joan Bram, who was, in that instance, the sole godparent.[37] The godparents were ethnic Africans in only five of the instances recorded during this period. On February 5, 1612, for example, an African, Lorenca Biafara, the slave of Don Francisco Lodoño, served as godmother[38] at the baptism of Ponda, the daughter of María de Luis de Pabra and Alberto Xillochu (both *naturales de* Latacunga). Other cases allow us to see these small and intimate sacred communities: María (*Guinea*), Gracía (*morena de* Doña de Ortega), Ana (*morena del* Don Fico y Alauis), and Ana (*negra*) served as godmothers for indigenous children. Africans from the upper Guinea coast, who had been in the region the longest, probably held the greatest standing among the households of the privileged, and thus among the best socialized in Hispano-Catholic mores, making them valued godparents.

The selection of black godmothers may have emerged within the hierarchy of elite households, where enslaved blacks—valued at the price of prime real estate—occupied a position above that of Andean servants. Indeed, if patronage helped indigenous parents select godparents, choosing a "high-ranking" domestic might have served them well. Black women were already serving as caregivers for many of the children within these homes; the idea of formalizing expectations of special care for an indigenous child was likely to have been considered reasonable. Historians Frederick P. Bowser and Martin Minchom have argued that blacks were intermediaries of sorts, who straddled the *república de españoles* and the *república de indios*.[39] The complexity of their colonial designations emerged as blacks lived within the same households, worked together on estates, and occupied the same urban spaces. Straddling these two worlds, black people were integral public performers in the colonial process, even in their most intimate community expressions. Black persons, as members of the *republica de españoles*, were the most suitable colonial lieges to bring subjects of the *republica de indios* into the orbit of Spanish colonial power. As individuals built communities within the structures of work, based on kinship, familiarity, and perhaps aspirations of upward mobility, these often transcended perceived racial boundaries even as they continued to constitute categories of racialization. Blacks and Andeans supported one another in life's most intimate and important moments. These were, of course, extremely personal matters, which varied from person to person, family to family, community to community, and, perhaps more importantly, across time.

Africans and Afro-Creoles created communities and families that apparently fit their desires, degrees, and durations of familiarity, kinship ties, and geographic proximity. These communities were filled with Afro-*mestizos* (*pardos*, *mulatos*, and *zambos*), Afro-Creoles, and ethnic Africans (some *bozales* and *ladinos*).[40] Afro-Creoles constituted the clear majority; fifty-two of the couples featured two Afro-Creoles, while nine featured an Afro-Creole and an ethnic African. But even here, diversity was the rule. Among the ethnic monikers assigned, one finds Angola, Bañon, Biafara, Bram, and Conga. Only two unions featured two ethnic Africans: Palonía Biafara and Juan Biafara, who baptized their daughter, Melchora in 1610; and Juliana Angola and Francisco Biarfora, who baptized their son Antonio.

To the extent that Palonía Biafara and Juan Biafara were looking for others of the Biafara caste to serve as Melchora's godparents, they would have found a good number of them in Quito. Of the fifteen Africans listed among the baptisms, six of them carried the moniker Biafara. But ethnic origin would not have been the sole reason for individuals to form unions, engage in friendships, and serve as godparents. Simón Biafara and Catalina Biafara, as godparents for Angola and Francisco Biarfora's son Antonio, may have reflected patterns of kinships forged in the diaspora.

Unfortunately, baptismal registries—simple lists detailing dates, the names of individuals present at the baptism, and their role or position in the child's life—conceal the thoughts and motivations of those participating in the ceremony. In the sole instance of apparent endogamy, for example, Palonía Biafara and Juan Biafara secured only one godparent for young Melchora—an Afro-Creole named [Do]mingo. Was there a kinship (biological or fictive) tie that was silenced in the process that produced this source? Could this have signaled the limitations of Palonía and Juan's communal connections? Perhaps they were relatively new to the city and knew only Domingo and a few other individuals. It is also possible, of course, that they were simply choosy parents who had difficulty reaching agreement regarding who would serve as young Melchora's godmother.[41]

The web of colonial power and terror that enclosed both Africans and Andeans also produced a Quiteño society wherein Afro-Andean kinship, social ties, and communities overlapped, shifted, and were reimagined. Individual trends in Afro-Indigenous godparentage continued into the seventeenth century. On October 10, 1610, a woman described as "Gorbala *India*" served as the sole godparent of the enslaved child Manuel (*natural de* Angola). Apparently, Manuel's owner, Pedro Pinto, brought him to be baptized, as the scribe documented his parents as "unknown."[42] Judging from the lack of other such cases and the absence of Manuel's parents, it seems that during this period black people rarely chose Andeans as their godparents in Quito. In contrast, it appears that Andeans lacked the same degree of latitude to make such decisions—or simply chose to be more flexible than their African and Afro-Creole counterparts in this matter. Thus, the selection of black godparents for indigenous children should come as no surprise. Godparentage in Quito city seems to have rarely moved in the opposite direction.[43] Yet it is worth mentioning that plebeians made their lives together in large measure because the system was both fluid and doggedly hierarchical. While baptism sometimes afforded well-resourced godparents to offer patronage, the space of elite homes and the strictures within which many "choices" were made must also be considered. Historian Thavolia Glymph has showcased compellingly just how violent the space of the plantation household was for enslaved women who labored under white mistresses.[44] Why would Spanish America's hierarchical homes enclosing indigenous, black, and plebian subordinates be any more peaceful or less cruel or repressive? In short, power must not be read out of these documents or the acts they disclose. Contests for dominance, including slavery, shaped Quito's sociocultural milieu.

Baptism in Eighteenth-Century Quito

Similar to the fonts of incorporation applied to Africans upon entry, baptism became a legal marking. Many slave owners diligently baptized their slaves, some twice. On February 4, 1696, for example, Monseñor Dr. Juan Gonzalez Gordillo from Latacunga presented the young infant María for baptism in the parish church of El Sagrario. Fray Gonzalez had already baptized little María in the presence of her mother, Ariana Cidana, and her indigenous midwife, Angelina Yndio. Young María's first baptism was more of a spiritual observance, "en caso de necesidad (durante) el mes que nació," meant to protect her soul if she died before the formal baptism. The logic of original sin left all humans in need of salvation. Amazingly, sin existed even within the souls of suckling babes. Baptizing her in Quito, however, served two purposes: religious compliance and legal documentation.

Individuals of African descent made similar choices in eighteenth-century Quito as their predecessors had in times past.[45] Ethnic Africans and free blacks appear infrequently in eighteenth-century Quito baptismal registries. In only one instance is it clear the child in question is the "legitimate" child of two ethnic Africans, in this case Francisco Angola and Dominga Congo, who baptized their child on March 23, 1701. Among eighty-one baptisms occurring between 1700 and 1760, only thirty-nine included free black parents. In most of these cases, the godparent was also a free black person.

Rarely did colonial elites serve as slave godparents, and when they did, it was usually only during moments of necessity when one or more biological parent was absent. Among the eighty-one children baptized between 1700 and 1760, forty-two were slaves. Of these, eleven had an elite male—usually the owner—as their sole godparent, and eight female slaveholders served as the sole godparent. In almost every instance, the reason for this arrangement was the absence of biological parents.[46] For slaveholders, baptizing the offspring of female captives offered additional evidence of their legal entitlement to the enslaved infant. Illegitimacy rates were high. Between 1695 and 1760, El Sagrario's parish priest baptized 115 children of African descent. On seventy-seven occasions, the father was not present, and in at least thirty-seven instances the mother was absent, too.[47] Overall, El Sagrario's priest documented only sixteen legitimate births.

Marriage and Community in the Cities
Quito

A sampling of marriage records reveals some trends similar to those found in baptismal records: the presence of numerous Afro-Creoles, a small yet diverse group of ethnic Africans, and few marriages between ethnic Africans generally, and even fewer of perceived endogamy. Among the records consulted, only a few contained marriages from the 1650s to the 1680s. Fifty-three marriages make up my sample, only four of which featured ethnic Africans marrying one another, and only two of which feature endogamous unions (unions between Africans with the same ethnic or country moniker). In one marriage, both witnesses carried the ethnic moniker Angola. In the other, however, the witnesses were apparently not of Angolan descent. In what was perhaps an indication of the size of the enslaved population, both wedding parties fell short of the requisite four witnesses, featuring only two.

The extent to which ethnic Africans sought endogamous unions is unclear. In one of the unions, occurring in 1688, the *novios* (bride and groom) were described simply as *ambos bozales* (both *bozales*). Further, the union of Manuel Bran and María Josepha Conga in 1704 obviously lacked any hint of endogamy. Neither of these unions featured ethnic Africans as the sponsors. Individuals married people whom they had known for some time, lived near, or knew through an acquaintance or relative. In like manner, they chose sponsors they had known for some years, as such sponsors could testify to the fact there were no impediments that might make the betrothed ineligible for marriage.

Reflecting the character of the population, most marriages featured Afro-Creoles. Nine of the fifty-three unions featured free blacks; two of these cases involved free black men marrying indigenous women. In the other seven, both *novios* were Afro-Creole (most described as *pardo*); only one featured the union of an enslaved black man to a free black woman. In at least seventeen of these unions, the scribe failed to document clearly the status of the individuals getting married. Since the scribe cites the race of at least sixteen of the thirty-four *novios* featured in these unions, the impression is that at least one of the *novios* in these instances was enslaved. Eight of them carried the label *pardo* or *parda*, two were cited as "Angolans," two *mulatos*, three *moreno*, and one *negra*. Because only the scribe's notations remain, without any reference to the words the bride and groom spoke, it is nearly impossible to ascertain how these individuals perceived themselves. Had they taken on these racial or *casta* labels themselves? Or had the priest assigned these labels on the basis of potentially changeable perceptions of what they meant? While these are worthy questions that merit our best efforts and our most imaginative intellectual engagement, sources that might provide clearer direction continue to elude this scholar's grasp.

The marriage of Manuel Balensuela to Magdalena Balensuela (both *de casta* Congo) on April 1, 1761, was atypical.[48] First, inventories and marriage registries from the region revealed that, much as in the seventeenth century, ethnic Africans of this period were not typically in a position to allow ethnicity to be the overriding determinant in their selection of spouses. Obviously, as Manuel and Magdalena demonstrate, some managed to marry endogamously; most did not, however. Still, the marriage of Manuel and Magdalena was unique in yet another way: they were among the few ethnic Africans who appeared in the marriage and baptismal registries of the parish. In fact, ethnic Africans appear only in the unions of Manuel Bran and María Joseph Cruz (1704), Thomás Colisto (*negro* Congo) and Josepha Grijolba (1766), and Luis de villa Rocha (Congo) and María Antonio Sanches (*color parda*) in 1766.[49]

While this might suggest that ethnic Africans had discarded ethnic monikers as they sought to formalize their relations, taking on Spanish surnames instead, the prevalent use of ethnic monikers such as Popó, Arará, Lucumí, Congo, Mina, and the occasional Zetre all suggest otherwise.[50] Even as late as 1731, records show that elites, such as Don Alberto Mathías del Pradeo, were purchasing ethnic Africans.[51] Dropping ethnic labels, in fact, would have offered ethnic Africans almost no advantage when appearing before church *provisors*. According to historian Herman Bennett, for ethnic Africans residing in seventeenth-century Mexico City, the use of these labels allowed them to represent themselves in a manner that resonated with colonial church officials. That is, the intentional self-aggregation of discrete cultural groups from Central Africa, for example, facilitated the legitimacy of marital petitions. Slave laborers who claimed to have known one another while in the region of "Angola" appeared usually with four witnesses who testified that they knew the couple while in the same "land." Long-term familiarity underscored the credibility of a couple's claim.

Formalizing intimate relationships with the help of the church became a costly endeavor as many ethnic Africans who arrived in the region lived and worked on estates scattered over the north-central highlands. Given that they had such little contact with the urban center, many who chose to marry did so within these estates or the parishes of the corresponding towns. Still, in eighteenth-century Quito, church marriages seem to have been largely the preserve of free black congregants. The marriage registries of Quito's central parish church reveal 181 marriages involving people of African descent between 1700 and 1816. Among these, thirty-five free black women were involved. Of the free black men who married, eleven married free black women, one married a *mestiza*, and twelve married Andeans. Apparently, enslaved men also preferred women with free status. At least nine slave men married indigenous women during the period. Marriage helped cement upward mobility by signaling that increased status and freedom had been achieved. *Parda* women, for example, were more likely to marry free black males or men with higher-status claims. Similarly, six *pardas* married *montañes* men, while at least two enslaved *pardas* married *montañes* men. (The term *montañes* signified a *mestizo* born of legitimate marriage in Quito at this time.) Only one *montañes* woman, Joaquina Carabajal, married an enslaved man—Josef (1802). The records also indicate that free men marked as *pardo* tended to marry women of a higher *casta* status. Eleven enslaved men married *montañes* women. Only two *montañes* men married enslaved women, both of whom were described as *pardas*.[52]

Marriage and the Challenge of Bondage

Joachin and Ysabel Congo serve as an excellent example of the struggles that enslaved people faced in protecting their marriage rights. In 1749 they appeared before colonial authorities in search of new owners in order to protect their conjugal rights.[53] Joachin stated that after looking for a new master, he had identified one who was willing to pay 750 pesos for him and his wife, but current master Don Estevan de Cuesta (the sheriff) had raised their price to 1,200 pesos, which according to Joachin was against the kingdom's overarching sense of justice, or *comun equidad*. The extra 450 pesos were to defray the cost of items that Joachin had allegedly stolen from his master. According to Joachin, however, he had taken only some books that he sold for 15 pesos because he and his wife had nearly starved to death owing to the inhumane treatment they had received at the hands of Don Estevan. He claimed he had no choice but to resort to taking the books, given that his master was so merciless that he had given them only two reales and a half a lamb or sheep. As a result of a cruel master who had failed to "feed, clothe, and educate them in the faith," Joachin and Isabel suffered. Estevan's decision to raise their price constituted yet another injustice.

Estevan insisted that he had not mistreated the captives, and he demanded his right to sell them for a just price. While he might be forced to sell them, he insisted that he could not be forced to sell them below their value, which according to him was at least one thousand pesos, given that Joachin had stolen from him. Insisting upon his property rights and his authority in this matter, Estevan sought to bolster his argument further by stating that he could get a good price for the two captives in the mines of Barbacoas. Joachin's efforts underscore ethnic Africans' attempts to enjoy the privileges of church-sanctioned married life. The case suggests that ethnic Africans married those with similar ethnoregional backgrounds whenever possible. Not surprisingly, along the way they learned to defend those unions against the threat of sale.

Guayaquil

Guayaquil offers a counterpoint to social and cultural life in colonial Quito. Far more slaves lived and worked there, including a greater number of ethnic Africans who apparently forged bonds in relation to their ethnoregional origins. On March 27, 1702, the parish priest of Guayaquil's El Sagrario had completed the banns to solemnize the marital union of two enslaved West Central Africans: Francisco, who was described as "*de Casta* Congo," and Ana Conga.[54] Their godparents, Antonio de Salvador and Lorensa Nabay, did not carry ethnoregional designations in this record. It is likely they were Afro-Criollos born in Guayaquil or some other town within the Spanish Pacific/Andean realm.[55] But if Francisco and Ana did not constitute a wedding party comprising exclusively West Central Africans, as so many had managed to do in New Spain, their marriage showcases a similar process of community building, or the formation of "diasporic ethnicities" that had taken place among West Central Africans in Guayaquil.[56] In this sense, Guayaquil was distinct from its highland neighbor and *audiencia* seat, Quito, being more similar to urban sites connected more closely to the Atlantic, where enslaved Africans could find marriage partners with whom they had long-standing connections and affinities based on ethnoregional origins. Amid a sample of forty-five marriages, seven featured enslaved Afro-Creoles and at least one African married to free blacks, five featured unions between Africans that we might call "endogamous," five featured blacks marrying indigenous people, and fourteen were between free blacks. The remaining fourteen featured enslaved blacks of varying *casta* designations.[57] In at least one case, an enslaved "mina" married a freed "mina" woman. On February 11, 1719, Antonio Nabarro, described as "negro de casta mina y esclavo de Don Juan Nabarro," married Ana mina, described as "negra libre." Ana had been the slave of María de Lasaro. While the names of their *padrinos* (godparents), Domingo Hadaleta y Juana de Bargal, offered no indication of African origin, at least one of their three witnesses—Juan Mina—was of similar origin.[58]

Marriage and Community in the Mines

Frontier regions usually featured missions, but this was not the case in the Pacific lowlands. Consequently, the church's presence was not particularly strong in the region of Barbacoas, or the Chocó for that matter. Historian and Jesuit Pedro de Mercado noted that when Fray Francisco de Fuentes visited the mines of Jelima, he encountered three Spaniards who, driven by their insatiable desire for gold, were especially cruel to their slaves. Fuentes claimed that their obsession with gold caused them to force their slaves "with the rigor of the lash," working them from sunrise to sunset without allowing them the "treasures of heaven." For Mercado's part, the mission was not to be abandoned. While many enslaved were ignorant of the faith, Mercado's reports confirmed for him that they were eager to learn. Over the course of two nights, enslaved laborers from the small *ranchería* (mining camp) received religious training and the sacrament of communion. In Anserma, similar success was reported when Father Juan de Rivera relayed that, when he arrived, he was received properly as an emblem of the church. Rivera had also entered slave mining camps to evangelize, baptize, and marry enslaved couples living in "illicit friendship" (*mala Amistad*), or concubinage.[59]

Over the years, many more enslaved people received religious instruction, baptized their children, and were otherwise afforded church-sanctioned marriages. Since the 1590s, the synods, or bishops' councils, had ordered that the sacraments be administered to slaves, requiring that masters pay itinerant priests to provide for the spiritual needs of those held in captivity on their estates and in their mining settlements. The solemnity of these matrimonies was of great concern to both slaveholders and the enslaved because slaves were entitled to a conjugal life. Masters wished to know the earnestness of their slaves' marriages, and slaves longed for their unions to be kept whole. The solemnity of the matrimony, however, was largely tied to the announcement of the bann. The limited proclamations of the bann, the announcement of the opportunity for anyone to object to an intended marriage, produced a range of disciplinary sanctions on the enslaved. While the bann in a parish church was disclosed on three successive Sundays, itinerant priests, quickly passing through towns, estates, and mining camps, often disclosed the upcoming banns only once. As such, rumors denouncing the moral impediments of the enslaved couple spread quickly to the mining gang captain, who subsequently disclosed the information to church authorities. These matters normally came to light during the archbishop's review, or *vista* of the spiritual health of the bishopric. The conditional issuing of the banns for enslaved couples and the potential hardships that could ensue underscore the mechanisms of religious governance, policing, and disciplining in the most intimate worlds of the enslaved, even in the most remote regions of the kingdom.[60]

Given the tenuous and ongoing engagement with church authorities, it is likely that many of the household unions listed in inventories simply as *hombre* and *su mujer* were unions sanctioned at some point by a priest. Notably, listed after couples' names were "their children." Other children of the man or the woman from outside the marriage were listed later, along with the names of their parents. Single men and women were also listed in these inventories, as were widows.[61] Slave owners also resented being required to pay a per capita fee to itinerant priests each year, approximately eight pesos during the 1680s. Discord among clergy and slave owners regarding such remittances and religious issues on their estates prompted some estate owners to install chapels on their own estates.

Although we lack marriage registries for the region of Barbacoas, mining inventories reveal two patterns. The first pattern that emerges are marriages between Africans and Afro-Creoles, or interethnic marriages that feature exogamous marriages between Africans. The second pattern reveals births of most of the children from within such unions. Although there were moments when the aggregate *bozal* population could claim, in general terms, a specific region in West Africa or specific ethnic groups, it appears that most chose not to formalize such affinities through their marital arrangements. While scholars have taken marital unions and the relationships among the African-descended population to imply African-derived ethnogenesis, these mining inventories suggest otherwise. Instead, most marital unions were not constituted predominantly with regard for Atlantic *casta* monikers. Even in mining camps like Don Jacinto de Arboleda's Quintamayó, where two African "ethnics" appeared to dominate, ethnic African slaves were often outnumbered by Afro-Creoles. When Quintamayó was inventoried in 1699, the total population numbered forty-five slave laborers, of whom thirteen were ethnic Africans (six Conga, one Mina, one Bram, and five Luango)—a clear Central African majority—while the remaining thirty-two captives were Afro-Creoles.[62] While Calavarís, Arara, Minas, Congos, and Zetre all appear quite commonly, most of those carrying these monikers were married to someone who fell outside of their ethnic group.

During the eighteenth century, 24 percent of all children were born to a union featuring an African and an Afro-Creole, 32 percent of children were born to unions of two Afro-Creoles, 20 percent were born to single Afro-Creole women, and only 4 percent were born to unions featuring two ethnic Africans who carried the same ethnic moniker or hailed from the same culture zone. While 2 percent were born to Africans from distinct culture zones, 10 percent were born to single African women, and 9 percent were baptized with single

African fathers. These findings underscore that despite large importations of African slave laborers, Afro-Creoles formed a clear majority in most mining communities throughout Barbacoas.

When the mine of Sezego was inventoried in 1767, the scribe recorded some fascinating ethnographic material. In addition to assigning ethnic monikers like Caravalí, Nongó, Pompo, and Zetre, he recorded titles associated with work and, in some cases, more common or communal names and aliases. Pío Quinto, for example, a young boy of seven years, was possibly a humorous or pious reference to his namesake, sixteenth-century pope Pius V.[63] Pío—a rare enough name by itself—was listed along with his sister, Petrona, and their mother, María Caravalí. Her ethnic moniker—Caravalí, Carabalí—is a misappropriation of Calabar, which suggests someone from the Bight of Biafra. Given María Caravalí's age, it is likely that she was taken from the region sometime in the mid-1740s and was Igbo.[64] In addition to young Pío Quinto, Juan Criollo, whose alias was "Bishop" (Obizpo), was also listed shortly after Manuel Obache.[65] Were these Afro-Creoles the spiritual leaders of the entire mining population, or had they formed their own spiritual community apart from others in the population? In either case, it is clear that ethnic Africans drawn from discrete culture groups throughout West and West Central Africa were developing communities and cultures that were complex and based on a range of ethnic affinities.

Four likely participants in this process were Manuel Criollo, Francisco Arara Bobo, and Bobo's wife and daughter, María Zetre and Francisca. Manuel Criollo, one of the gang captains and a canoeist, was a *curandero de viboras* (curer of vipers). In the next dwelling lived Francisco Arara Bobo and his family.[66] Manuel's eminence as cocaptain, canoeist, and curer suggests the prominent role that Afro-Creoles might have played in ethnogenic processes. Whether his knowledge had come from local Amerindians, various African ethnies, or some mixture of both, it seems clear that people within the community—presumably Africans and Afro-Creoles—saw Manuel as possessing curative powers. Also, Francisco Arara's name, Arara, was associated with people from the region of Dahomey in the Bight of Benin. "Bobo" was likely a descriptive reference—a *tacha* or citation of a defect—suggesting that he was mute.[67]

Ultimately, the slave trade produced a dispersal effect in the region of Barbacoas. What people made of these realities surely changed over time. Life in the sweltering mines of eighteenth-century Barbacoas had been hard, even if talk of freedom filled the air. And though connected to and reflective of the slave experience throughout Quito, life in the north-central highlands was sure to have taken on a different pattern and texture. In eighteenth-century Barbacoas, slavery and slave life evolved within the context of two fierce struggles: mine owners' battles with colonial officials for the right to determine theirs and the region's economic destiny and colonial inhabitants' battle to define the sociocultural characteristics of the region. Although slaveholders and court officials ultimately reduced African and Afro-descended captives to personal property, power was negotiated. Spanish colonial law (civil and canon), masters' conflicts with the state, and the availability of gold increased slaves' chances at self-purchase and shaped evolving legal parameters of racial identity and racial slavery. Maroon communities, the presence of free blacks living among slave laborers, and the terror that marauding rebels and fugitives represented created a context where slaveholders had little choice but to form arrangements with slaves regarding their freedom or that of a loved one. Consequently, not only did slaves hope for freedom; they came to expect it.

But while regional geopolitics and slave resistance created a context for elaborate freedom arrangements, the contours of slave life were also marked by regional changes in ethnic diversity. In the early eighteenth century, African slaves (drawn from a broad cross section of locations throughout West Africa) entered the region in unprecedented numbers. From 1705 to 1713, most came into the region from Africa's Gold Coast, the Bight of Benin, Senegambia, and Central Africa. However, between 1715 and 1722, they emerged from the Bight of Benin, the Gold Coast, and the Congo. Finally, between 1730 and 1738, they emerged from the Gold Coast, Central Africa, and the Bight of Benin. In the end, Cartagena's position as a secondary trading port in the circum-Caribbean drew human cargo from a range of trading partners (Dutch, English, and French).

At the close of the eighteenth century, as gold production sustained the high levels reached in the 1780s, three realities remained: slaves continued their long-standing resistance struggles, masters continued to place greater pressure upon slaves to produce gold and provide for themselves, and Africans and Afro-Creoles continued to draw creatively upon varying ethnocultural traditions as they produced and reproduced their culture within a highly diverse slave population.

"In the Days of Our Keepers": Holding On to Community on Jesuit Estates

On December 1, 1757, Doña Ysabel Yepe undertook a legally required but seldom observed action: she gave legal notice that her bondwoman, Antonía, had fled her jurisdiction (*a echo fuga huir*). Striking were her choice of words, as she described Antonia's husband as "a slave of her religion." Doña Ysabel alleged that Antonía had fled to and found asylum within the hacienda of Pusír, where she remained with her husband, a slave laborer on this Jesuit-owned estate. Ysabel Yepe had made "repeated requests" to be allowed entrance into the hacienda to confirm her worst suspicions, but to no avail. Now she was calling upon her no doubt estranged husband (given that she was a *recogida* of the Limipía Concepción Convent) to assist in the execution of her legal claim.[68]

Similar to the experience of many slave laborers in Quito's north-central highlands, Antonía's love and life existed within the world that was a Jesuit-owned and operated agropastoral estate complex. Pusír, a farming enterprise, fell within the jurisdiction of the Colegio de Ibarra and was connected directly to at least two sugar-producing estates (*trapiches*): La Concepción, which by this time possessed close to 380 slave laborers, and Caldera, where the enslaved population was approximately 95 individuals (see table 3.1).

By 1780, each Jesuit-owned sugar-producing estate held an average of 165 slaves and the order held lands stretching from the Chillos Valley to Ibarra.[69] In this region, Amerindian population figures had fallen into severe decline, opening the way for widespread use of ethnic African and Afro-Creole slave laborers. The region's warm temperatures and proximity to the Chota and Mira Rivers made it ideal for agricultural endeavors, especially sugarcane cultivation. Nevertheless, only 44 percent of Ibarra's Amerindian population lived on Spanish estates. Situated in and around the town of Otavalo, there were large numbers of Amerindian laborers who produced foodstuffs and worked within the corresponding Jesuit-owned *obrajes*.[70] The Jesuits tied textile mills to agropastoral estates, which held sizable pools of laborers who could be rotated when needed to disparate estates to address agricultural, transport, or cane production and refining demands. These were self-sufficient enterprises that "allowed the Jesuits to control land and water resources across different ecological zones, recruit needed laborers, and dominate many local markets for rural produce."[71] Stretching from Ibarra to Latacunga, the Jesuit system supported its thirteen colleges and missions. Textile and food production in the Chillos Valley served the needs of slave laborers working the *trapiches* of Ibarra. Not only was food production connected to *trapiches*; *trapiches* were in turn connected to livestock ranches, thus completing the systematic circle.[72]

By 1776, in the *trapiches* of Santiago, Carpuela, Chaluayaca, and Caldera alone, 398 slave laborers along with large numbers of Amerindians were producing *aguardiente* and sugarcane on more than five hundred cuadras, which were small blocks of land approximately 83.5 meters each, roughly equivalent to one city block.[73] While the mines were booming in Barbacoas, Jesuit

Table 3.1. Jesuit Sugar Haciendas and Slave Holdings in Quito, ca. 1779

Haciendas	Number of Slaves
Concepción	380
Cuajara	268
Chamanal	152
Tumbaviro	126
Santiago	123
Caldera	95
Carpuela	93
Chalguayacu	87
TOTAL	1,324

Source: Coronel Feijóo, El valle sangriento, 88.

production remained strong in the north-central highlands as well. This production, along with extensive landholdings, enabled the Jesuits to leverage the capital needed to develop their "pastoral enterprise." The order's total revenues during its final years in the region ranged from 222,896 pesos in 1765 to 168,975 in 1766, with profits rising as high as 60,000 pesos.[74] Although their enterprise was far more elaborate, with greater overhead costs than that of a large mining operation, they also generated revenues (and at times turned profits) that eclipsed regional gold outputs. Sound fiscal management combined with highly efficient operations predicated upon strict control of laborers produced profitable results.

Examining inventories emerging from the records of Administración de Temporalidades in 1780, Coronel shows that there were 1,037 cuadras of sugarcane and 1,271 slaves, 508 *borriqueros* (mule loaders or drivers), 181 *conductores* (drivers), 94 *viejos* (seniors) and *liciados* (handicapped), and 488 children below the age of ten.[75] Although these figures were taken more than a decade after the expulsion of the Society of Jesus, it is plausible that at the very least, the Jesuits had maintained this number of slaves throughout their time in the valley, including their last major land acquisition in 1692. According to Andrien, Carpuela, Chaluayaca, and Caldera, "an inventory of the estates in 1776 listed more than five hundred cuadras of sugarcane, tended by 398 slaves and numerous part-time Andean laborers."[76] Hence, Coronel's assertion that the eight slaveholding haciendas possessed a total of 2,615 slaves throughout the Jesuits' tenure in this region, is probably accurate.[77] Several *padrones* (census records) taken in the jurisdiction of Ibarra, during the years 1779, 1780, 1784, and 1786 reveal that there was an average of 1,203 slaves in this area, approximately 50 percent of them married. The other 50 percent were single males, females, and children. Their sexual ratio was almost always balanced 1:1.[78] These numbers further underscore the existence of a significant Afro-Quiteño community, a people who, although subjected to the onerous tasks of sugar cultivation, created families and communities that persisted over several generations.

According to the Jesuit plantation operation manual *Instrucciones a los hermanos jesuitas*, Jesuits were to firmly establish the spiritual and temporal viability of their estates. When managing slave laborers, barracks were to be enclosed by a fence and be locked at night. A *mandadero* (male captain) was to be selected from among the slaves whose duty was to watch for possible disorder and remedy disagreements. It was the captain who gave slave laborers their daily instructions. In addition to the *mandadero*, the manual instructed that a *mandadera de las mujeres* be assigned to watch over the women and, most importantly, administer lashes to wayward women. And although the manual indicated that leaders were not to punish slaves at will, justice was to be harsh and swift. Above all, the manual admonished that slave laborers be fed, clothed, and instructed in the faith. In connection with religious instruction, each estate was to have its own chapel, and managers were expected to provide laborers with time off on Sundays and holidays.

For most of the eighteenth century, life on Jesuit haciendas must have resembled that described in the manual. Enslaved men and women lived and worked within the estate complex. Yet they also formed relationships and fought to maintain love, affection, and even intimacy in spite of their containment at the Jesuit estates. The brutal, backbreaking work that defined enslaved life produced the highly efficient "management" of the Jesuit estate complex. As one slave leader from the Quaxara hacienda wrote in 1789, "in the days of our keepers" slave laborers received time for rest on Sundays, and time to observe various *días de festival* (religious holidays). While slaves did not live in barracks, as prescribed by the instruction manual, they did have houses made of straw and bamboo. The Chalmanal estate, inventoried in 1786, had 162 slave laborers organized by household, most often nuclear or extended family units. Solitaires were grouped and placed in homes together, while barracks were created for the single, widowed, or otherwise detached members of the community.[79] Much like the slave trade to the region, the hacienda inventory revealed a range of ethnic monikers, including Congo, Mina, Caravalí, Arara, and Mondongo, all of whom lived with and married Afro-Creoles, who by this time formed an overwhelming majority. Nevertheless, these monikers had now emerged as surnames for even Afro-Creoles, who passed them on to their progeny.

Children under the age of ten accounted for 35.2 percent of the overall population (fourteen were in fact infants), whereas adults over the age of fifty-two constituted 6.79 percent. Rather remarkable for this period, one-half of the slaves were over the age of sixty, and two—Ignacio Indungui (82 years) and Francisco Congo (72 years)—were above the age of seventy. In keeping with the manual and the mines of Barbacoas, the hacienda was led by a captain and several older community members, no doubt Ignacio and Francisco. Whereas mine owners often referred to senior community members as "useless," the Jesuits placed them in an advisory position to assist young captains, such as Josef Bonifacio, who was only thirty-six years of age but had been selected "due to his intelligence and government."[80] Bonifacio, a married man (the husband of Vicenta de Larrea), who was thirty-two years old and the father of six, was not flanked with a female captain. It was his charge to motivate and maintain order among the thirty-two families represented within the plantation. Life as described on the pages of this eighteenth-century inventory looked relatively stable. But in 1786, the year of the inventory, it had been nineteen years since the crown had expelled the Jesuits from all its American provinces, sequestering their properties and extant documentation. The expulsion created a new set of challenges for those living and working within the estate complex.

The state made a good faith attempt at maintaining the Jesuits' massive operation, but it failed to execute their strategic management processes. According to historian Kenneth J. Andrien, the state was hampered in four ways: through the hiring of "corrupt or inefficient administrators, the lack of warehouses, market connections, and capital reserves."[81] Ultimately, however, it seems that the state did not understand the inner workings of the Jesuit system. To increase profits, for example, the state often sold livestock, ignored much-needed maintenance projects and improvements, and fired workers.[82] The failure to comprehend the objectives and roles of each *obraje*, *trapiche*, and *hato* (ranch) undermined the state's ability to manage the entire system effectively.

In the 1780s, the state undertook a different approach to the challenges of the Jesuit properties and began selling them to the highest bidder, thereby undercutting the reciprocal relationships that had existed between the various estates. Now one estate would be called upon to undertake what three or more had handled in the past. At this time, *trapiches* in the north would be cut off from agricultural estates in the south, leaving slave laborers with the burden of feeding and clothing themselves. Indeed, new pressures befell the enslaved as the state and subsequent estate owners pressured them to produce at a level exceeding what they had previously achieved. Whereas the Jesuits had been careful not to disrupt estate communities through the sale of its members, leaving them intact for several generations, new owners would move almost immediately to either relocate or sell members of these communities.

As of 1778, slave laborers like Pedro Pascual Lucumín of the Concepción estate were petitioning colonial officials concerning the mistreatment they were receiving, largely in the form of neglect.[83] For Pascual and others, the question quickly became, Who does a slave petition when the state is the abusive master in question? Operating with little regard for the slave laborers, the state sold all of these properties several times. Most often, the sale was in the form of credit and was followed by default. Consequently, the estates changed hands several times in the remainder of the colonial period. Chamanal, when inventoried in 1786, was on its way to a third owner Gomez de la Torres. Torres would soon sell the property to Carlos Araujo, an unscrupulous itinerant merchant, who amassed several properties in a reckless fashion and then began to divide the slave community through a series of sales.

On November 9, 1784, Doña María Ana Nava filed a civil lawsuit against her brother-in-law, Don Antonio de Peña, then owner of one of the largest sugar plantations, Santiago. Don Antonio, who was deceased by this time, had charged her with the duty of giving oversight to his plantation. While managing the property, she heard the outcry of slaves in "extreme necessity." Having pity on them, she gave them flour and honey and in short order initiated a legal claim against de Peña's estate. After Doña María's attorney, Francisco de Xavier Barbara, filed his deposition, the high court justices commissioned a lengthy investigation. While the case is replete with testimony that addresses the contract between Doña María and her brother-in-law, the conditions and experiences faced by the slaves whom Don Antonio left to starve on the Santiago plantation are almost entirely ignored. Indeed, the slave laborers were incidental, as the principal concerns of investigators were whether Doña Maria had given the food to the slave laborers, whether she had authority to do so, and finally whether she would be compensated for her gesture.

By the time Doña Ana Nava received payment for her services in December 1788, the property had changed owners at least twice.[84] Unfortunately, the extant record relates nothing of how the enslaved fared during this period or thereafter. It is clear, however, that their lives had changed for the worse since the "days of [their] keepers." Snatched from the bowels of a brutal yet functioning estate complex system, slave laborers who might have wondered previously if things could get any worse while ruled by the Jesuits encountered a form of extreme cruelty they had never known. The irony, however, was that this cruelty came from the state and courts, the entities ostensibly designed to protect them.

By the end of the century, the state's role in the growth and administration of slavery in the north-central highlands had come full circle. At the beginning of the century, state policies had dealt a mortal blow to the *obraje* complex, prompting new waves of Andean migrations and provoking elites to turn to African slave labor as they searched for a cash crop. During this era, the state served as the mediator in struggles between slaveholders and the enslaved, according mercy to those found undeserving of extreme cruelty. Over the course of the century, the state had admonished masters to treat their slaves fairly in justice and in accordance to the law. The high court had honored the marriage vows of the few slaves who found their way to Quito's central parish church, issuing judgments that protected slave families and their avenues to freedom. But by the end of the century, the state took on a more ambiguous role as it became the single largest slaveholder in all of the *audiencia*.

Reckless in its management of the formerly Jesuit-owned estate complex, the state dismantled what had been an efficient, albeit cruel, agropastoral enterprise and broke apart long-standing slave families and communal formations. Yet, once more, slave laborers resisted their conditions of bondage and drew upon their shared knowledge to challenge Bourbon officials and unscrupulous merchants undermining the constitutions of their households, families, and communities. Now, in a changing world, these contexts and concerns continued to shape their actions and embolden their resolve.

CHAPTER FOUR

Enslaved Rebels, Fugitives, and Litigants

On May 7, 1640, in the town of Popayán, Francisco, an enslaved Afro-Criollo, filed a lawsuit against his master, Fray Diego Revelo de Chaves, a priest in the local Augustinian monastery. Francisco explained that Fray Chaves was a harsh taskmaster who punished him daily with extreme cruelty. Referring to his master's influence and perhaps also to his lack of confidence in a system that tended to prefer elite interests, Francisco said, "[Although] one flees, neither is this effective, and [now] they have me in the jail [*carsel*] to return me to his command."[1] Theoretically, in such instances the *cárcel pública* served as a locus for *deposito* (a form of protective custody), as masters were required to pay one real per day to cover the costs associated with the slave's stay while the authorities investigated the veracity of the charges.[2] But according to Francisco, officials were holding him there only to return him to the abusive Augustinian friar. Unfortunately for the historian, the documentary trail ends with these eight handwritten pages; missing are the resolution of the case, as well as precious details of Francisco's experience before Popayán's judicial authorities. Consequently, it is difficult to know for certain if Fray Chaves had in fact "mistreated" Francisco or if Francisco was simply seeking to evade punishment by filing a *sevicia* (mistreatment) claim. Francisco's basic argument, however, is certainly plausible, and it reflects, moreover, the phenomenon of legal action by the enslaved, a resistance strategy that African and Afro-Criollo captives would carry to its full extent throughout the colonial era and beyond. Fundamentally, Francisco's case illustrates both master abuses and the ways that slaves challenged the master's brutality, whether the master was an exacting secular figure or an Augustinian friar. Specifically, it provides evidence of early legal action by the enslaved, a juridical strategy that slaves—marked Christian vassals—would push to its limits long before Europeans began to engage Lockean notions of liberty and freedom. Royal governance had allowed slaves an "audience" before the crown through its representatives in the Indies. Indeed, all subjects had varying degrees of standing before the crown. Slaves, like other vassals, pursued their legal opportunities, developing customary legal norms that might later become legal rights and, in the process, help precipitate an emergent crisis within royal governance. Although Francisco's claim was early, he was not the first enslaved subject of the realm to make such claims.

In Quito, as in many other areas of Spanish America, slaves had been suing their masters since the early 1590s. As the 1596 freedom suit of Duarte González (native of Angola) demonstrates, slave petitions involving everything from mistreatment to the right to *reclamaciones* (*libertad* or freedom lawsuits), underscore Africans' and Afro-Criollos' early acquired legal savvy, along with their keen awareness of their rights as persons, though they were described as property. Baptism and branding had placed slaves squarely within the sociopolitical fabric of colonial societies.

By now, it should not be news that Africans and their descendants were major players in the making of colonial Latin American societies. Just as elites claimed land and created hidden commercial networks and settlements away from the official channels of colonial jurisprudence, fugitives forged territorial claims that were marked in the juridical landscape as *palenques*, or unauthorized maroon settlements in mountains and brush-laden riverways. Enslaved subjects, like other colonial inhabitants, flouted the colonial authorities and lived pious public lives that sometimes hide more "subversive" private aspirations. Appearances before magistrates, ecclesiastical courts, and royal justices of the *audiencia* could also at times reveal piety, compliance, and conformity with the edicts of majesty, even as such representations might also conceal more sinister private transcripts and longings. The enslaved were not just participants in Quito's highly litigious colonial world; they were constitutive of colonial jurisprudence and foundational to legal understandings of sovereignty and royal authority over the Indies.

In going to court, slaves' immediate goals varied considerably. An enslaved woman might seek to stop the sale of a husband or father of her children, while others sought to enforce the terms of agreements made with their master regarding their freedom or the freedom of their offspring. Still others sued to change masters, hoping that their new master might provide more acceptable conditions of servitude.

This was a small and intimate world. By the early eighteenth century, the tributary population of the entire *corregimiento* of Quito was approximately 8,500 people, with no more than 500 enslaved blacks residing in Quito city. Poverty had set in within the north-central core, and status was tenuous.

Slaves lived in a world where their value was extremely fungible. They were therefore in a thoroughly determined space. Still, the intimacies of daily life also brought slaves within the reach of circuits of information within the legal culture of the Spanish realm. Their status as colonial subjects and emblems of royal power made it so.

The right to sue a master was initially set forth in medieval codes that Spaniards transferred to the Indies and further endorsed within New World legislation found in both the civil and canonical codices.[3] While both sets of laws contain what at first glance appear to be paternalistic measures, the central concern for both crown and clergy was controlling potentially restive souls and maintaining the empire.[4] Royal edicts ordering masters to Christianize, Hispanize, feed, and clothe their slaves were fundamentally pragmatic concerns *and* consistent with just governance and proper order. These measures were designed to control an errant population through the harnessing of the will. Ultimately, the society was ordered properly, thus ensuring the public peace. Even so, such edicts constituted legal mandates that, when applied, could pressure slave owners to manage their captives with a degree of benevolence. They served to remind slaveholders of their Christian duty to temper justice with mercy. Perhaps more importantly, "paternalistic" slave codes signaled that even masters were subject to God and the crown. They signaled that slavery was an elemental feature of governance, bringing even the paters' claim to property under the scrutiny of royal oversight.[5] The question of exactly when enslaved Africans began to take consistent advantage of the Spanish legalistic tradition has recently drawn scholarly attention.[6]

Highlighting the foundations of black legal action, Herman Bennett finds that as early as 1572, ethnic Africans in New Spain had obtained the "cultural, if not linguistic, dexterity" needed to petition *provisors* for marriage licenses, and they often sought ecclesiastical intervention when masters threatened to separate them from spouses.[7] Bennett finds, moreover, that by 1579 the enslaved were suing unscrupulous masters who sought to deny them their conjugal rights.[8] The work reminds us of the ways that Spanish America was governed within a culture of legal pluralism, where canon law and religious discourse structured the would-be "civil" or "secular" domain. This was a Christian Spanish monarchical order. Laws and royal edicts emanating from the metropolis encroached upon the master's domain, while the clergy's determination to have exclusive authority in the administration of sacraments such as marriage further eroded masters' authority over human chattel. In this way, slavery offers a microcosm of Spanish American juridical norms and the overlapping regimes or technologies of governance.[9] The enslaved took careful note of their position within this apparent dichotomy, exploiting every loophole (real and theoretical) available to them. They did this, as historian Bianca Premo shows, with the assistance of broader legal discussions about *buen gobierno*.[10] Lawyers, judges, magistrates, clergy, slave owners, and slaves all contributed to a larger dialogue about both justice and the just limits of sovereignty. Ultimately, however, it was enslaved men and women who turned their private daily struggles into a public spectacle in order to temper their owners' mastery and control the terms of their existence. It was their outcry that kept the question of the just limits of mastery and proper paths to increased social rank and status on the docket of the *audiencia*.

Despite the fact that slaves in early colonial Quito used the law astutely and politically, most historians examining the region have paid scant attention to the early cases, leaving the field with an imbalanced, if not incomplete, treatment of the phenomenon.[11] Most scholars have suggested that earlier cases were inherently different from and less political than those of the later period, based on the premise that earlier enslaved litigants were seeking mercy, not change. By the mid-eighteenth century, they argue, slaves awoke and began to employ the legal tradition "in more radical ways."[12] And although enslaved men and women had imbued their legal arguments with the gendered discourse of honor since the early colonial era, some have argued that it was the context of the Bourbon and Independence eras that allowed slave women to employ the discourse of honor when challenging their masters.[13] In short, scholars have heralded the post-1750 era as the watershed moment of black radical discourse in colonial Spanish America.[14] According to Peter Blanchard, "The wars of independence had given the black population of Spanish South America an unprecedented opportunity to give voice to their feelings," and thus, they "fervently adopted the catchword of the period, freedom."[15] Consequently, the enslaved, having found a "liberating language," could move more deliberately toward the complete destruction of the peculiar institution.[16]

Despite their imbalanced characterizations, however, scholars have shown the critical importance of consulting colonial court records in order to see how slaves developed an understanding of the juridical landscape and fashioned strategies to give voice to their grievances with master abuses and lack of access to self-purchase. María Eugenia Chaves and Camilla Townsend, for example, have employed civil court cases to highlight the ingenuity, courage, and complex networks that enslaved women drew upon in their fight for the legal recognition of their honor and control over their lives in a radicalizing world.[17] Carlos Aguirre has emphasized the far-reaching implications of legal action by slaves, arguing that as the enslaved continued to participate in the

Spanish legalistic tradition of early republican Peru, they helped to dismantle the system of slavery by insisting that judiciaries issue rulings that went far beyond the scope of contemporary law.[18] And as Peter Blanchard's recent work suggests, Independence leaders' adoption of slaves' "lexicon" of liberation and social inclusion must have emboldened slaves' resolve to fight ever more fervently for freedom.[19]

Slaves apparently brought more civil suits during the late colonial period than in any other era. In Quito and Lima, the extant record contains far more civil cases after 1750 than before, especially those addressing masters' mistreatment of slaves (*sevicia*).[20] Of the one hundred cases appealed before Quito's high court, only twenty-three were heard before 1750, with the number of civil cases rising yet again after the turn of the century.[21] Moreover, this period appears to constitute what several scholars have referred to as a "discursive opening."[22] The language of the Enlightenment, Bourbon policies, and the independence movements must have helped to maintain a juridical space for slaves and provided a language that resonated with blacks' long-standing discourse on freedom and improved treatment.[23] Further, during this period Bourbon kings, hoping to regain control in the Indies, issued edicts like the Real Cédula de 1789, encroaching yet again upon the master's domain by reinforcing slaves' rights to just treatment and a day in court.[24] But while it is true that the Bourbon reforms, the Enlightenment, and the independence movements gave litigants particular political opportunities, the notion that earlier lawsuits brought by slaves were inherently different from—less radical than—those of the later period is simply not accurate. Moreover, the notion is inconsistent with broad patterns and processes of slave resistance in Quito and throughout the Americas more generally.

Throughout the *audiencia* of Quito, enslaved rebels and fugitives consistently contributed to white fears and to white law making from the very earliest moments of the colonial enterprise, and these slaves at times actively played upon white fears (directly and indirectly) in order to obtain desired outcomes. Not only did slaves use the courts in deeply political and radical ways from very early in the colonial period; existing documentary evidence from Quito's courts reveals a continuum, not a break, between earlier cases and those emanating from the late colonial era. Although this continuum may be difficult to document— principally because slaves' most successful tactic in the pre-Bourbon era was to claim to be divorced from the politics of rebellion and to be seeking individual mercy—we can identify early legal precedents reflected in civil court cases heard by the *audiencia* of Quito over the course of the colonial era. Reading slave actions as a continuum of strategies aimed at influencing the conditions of daily life affords a more detailed rendering of the material conditions that defined Quito's slave regime, a deeper look at how slaves' strategies to control the terms of bare life interacted with royal efforts to discipline all colonial subjects, and a reading of the gendered challenges that enslaved men and women faced in litigating and living life within the circuits of bondage.

Therefore, it is within the context of the potential for radical resistance that we must place the cases of Francisco and other enslaved litigants in our effort to understand how, when, and why they were able to take advantage of openings within the system.

The slaves' ability to bring suit was almost always connected to—and enhanced by—other, more radical, forms of resistance employed by the enslaved. Indeed, one of the primary reasons why this process worked as well as it did was because Africans and Afro-Quiteños acted not only as litigants but also as rebels and fugitives, motivating judicial authorities to consider seriously the concerns of the peaceful. While colonial authorities consciously sought to uphold both *leyes* (laws) and *derecho* (legal principles), it is also probable that they were motivated by their anxieties about captives who might choose more radical forms of resistance, such as rebelling, absconding, and joining maroon settlements. The specter of maroon settlements coupled with well-known incidents of flight, confrontation, and outright rebellion would have provided jurists and magistrates with an added incentive to take the pleas of the enslaved seriously. Through their roles as rebels, fugitives, and litigants, the enslaved carved out autonomy for themselves even as they suffered under the onslaught of brutal masters and institutional realities. By claiming their rights under the law while others functioned as rebels and fugitives, they forced the system to work as well as it did. The legal system thus served as a safety valve, allowing an avenue for redress so they did not have to resort to more violent, extralegal measures.

By understanding the ways that rebels and fugitives contributed to elites' anxieties concerning the control of the slave population, scholars can provide a more precise description of the context of enslaved legal action, its possibilities, and its challenges. Rebels and fugitives threatened the social order, occupying the position of "outsiders." As such, the law prescribed that they be treated with all harshness. Slave litigants desiring fairness and mercy thus had to assume a posture of subservience and, in effect, distance themselves from the antisocial behavior of their seemingly more rebellious counterparts. Slave litigants faced the challenge of presenting and re-presenting themselves as "insiders," subjects of the king who deserved royal mercy instead of the harsh punishments dealt to their more radical brethren.

But even as so-called rebels and fugitives helped to create a context where legal action remained a possibility, litigants must have realized that the legal system had its limits. Often the process and the judgments rendered served only to underscore the chattel status of the enslaved. Francisco was not the only one to doubt the objectivity of the system. The legal system in effect confirmed that the enslaved was a subjugated being, vulnerable to the lash of another individual and to a system built to control and exploit slave bodies. In many instances, the enslaved lost their cases or witnessed them being tied up in months or even years of legal maneuvering. Their motive for suing was therefore not that their counterparts had experienced overwhelming success in winning the judgments they sought. Rather, the enslaved had different motives for suing, as well as varying definitions of what constituted success. The challenge, then, is to explore the various definitions of success that might have motivated the enslaved, realizing that at times they must have determined that they would fight despite the potential outcome.[25] Even those who failed were educating themselves, speaking out, and illuminating other captives in the ways of the system. The process demanded, at the very least, that they develop their legal and performance skills. Acting, speaking, and merely appearing in the courtroom required a complex performance that evoked specific ideas or feelings in the minds of whites, including not only pity but also fear of rebellions and attitudes about judicial fairness.

From the 1550s to the 1640s, restive blacks, along with "unruly" and "disruptive" citizens more generally, found themselves within a shifting imperial context. Royal attempts at absolutism coincided with a renewed emphasis on an "imperial" de jure order to circumscribe the lives of all subjects while promoting an increasingly racialized discourse that cast all persons of color into the context of things wild and potentially subversive. The need for various forms of regulation had spawned strict controls aimed at all potentially disruptive subjects.[26] In the case of the enslaved, conciliatory slave codes—rights to marriage, property ownership, inheritance, and merciful treatment—rewarded complicity in hopes of quelling all potential for violence. On the other hand, restrictive legislation, with its corresponding punishments—whippings, castrations, and lynching—served to encode the hopes and fears of the crown and its American surrogates. Regulatory responses, therefore, signaled the pervasiveness of actual imperial threats, providing a twofold approach to social control. Complicity would be rewarded by inclusion, providing one with access to the law; flouting royal authority, however, rendered one worthy of the most brutal aspects of the Reconquista.[27]

By the early seventeenth century, the juridical context had been established with great certainty. Imperial and municipal slave codes had emerged over the course of the early colonial period as responses to the cumulative effects of slave flight and rebellion. Though functioning within *derecho*, and while extending the boundaries of the royal court, royal edicts and municipal ordinances constituted judicial reactions to radical resistance by the enslaved—reactions that were predicated upon elite fears and assumptions about blacks, both enslaved and free. The crown and its representatives in the New World had articulated a legal discourse that sought to be both conciliatory and restrictive in an effort to achieve and sustain social order. The dividing lines were clear, as all were cast as either "insiders" or "outsiders" of an expanding imperial order. Those who conformed and performed the duties of the loyal subjects would be accorded certain conciliatory measures; those who failed to comply would suffer the harsher side of the law. In this way, sixteenth-century and early seventeenth-century antecedents laid the groundwork for managing colonial Spanish America and controlling errant slaves.

But even if laws were in part about extending the reach of the church and crown, the fear that rebels of all stripes invoked was real to those who lived in the Indies. News of contentious encounters between whites and the enslaved continued to strike fear in the hearts and minds of whites, both poor and elite. In eighteenth-century Quito, so-called radicals continued to undermine the delicate balance of hegemony, frustrating the efforts of elites while seizing moments and claiming all sorts of spaces within the colonial milieu. Retracting the much-coveted rights and privileges enjoyed by the slaving ranks promised to fracture the already fragile constitution of public order. Above all, however, slaves were Christian vassals, subjects imagined within the order. As such, they were entitled to a hearing before the prince and his regents. Enslaved rebels must have reminded judiciaries and the crown of its tenuous hold on regions in the Americas, particularly those gold-laden margins that they had worked so tirelessly to claim and inhabit.

The Challenge of Rebels and Fugitives in Eighteenth-Century Quito

In 1727 Friar Augustín Melén from the town of La Cruz in the valley of Patía came forth to verify the existence of a maroon settlement called "El Castigo" near the river Bajo. Melén stated that runaways "live[d] outside of the service and jurisdiction of their masters, and there others—free blacks [*libres de colores pardos*] . . . live also."[28] Other individuals addressed the court with Fray Melén, expressing their concern that several masters were losing their slaves to this area. They sought to bolster their case, stating that these blacks "[went] without the Mass and without confessing their sins and some [were] even murderers." Witnesses explained, "If one tries to go into this *palenque*, they are even killed." Fray Melén concluded that those living in this area were indeed "living outside of the precepts of the holy mother church," in part, he argued, because they lacked a judge. In other words, Patía was an area that local officials had not adequately pacified. Both crown and clergy needed an official presence in this area to check the rogue, pagan element that threatened the order of the colony. These statements echoed those of enslaved plaintiffs like Francisco and others who used affiliation with the church as a way of differentiating between legitimate and illegitimate behavior—that is, a way of situating themselves within—or, in this case, outside of—the expected norms of society.

In response to this complaint, on January 28, 1729, the high court in Quito dispatched a group of soldiers to the region to apprehend all slaves and "suspicious persons" (*personas sospechozas*). Local officials and their soldiers failed at this and subsequent attempts, leaving the maroons of Patía in place throughout much of the colonial period and well into the Independence period. In 1732 the town council of Popayán was still pondering how to deal with the maroon problem in Patía.[29]

The fear generated by reports of maroons in Esmeraldas and Patía, along with reports of runaway slaves throughout the kingdom, heightened elite concerns about daily interactions with blacks. One only needs to review notary records of the period to find that numerous enslaved Africans and Afro-Criollos chose to abscond, if only for a matter of days, as one of their methods of resistance in their negotiations with masters.[30] In addition to the problem of flight, colonials had to "manage" those black persons whose actions continued to be read as aggressive. This task would prove to be one that required an undying resolve, as blacks challenged the status quo and aggravated existing tensions and power struggles among elites throughout Quito. One notable example reveals two slaves who found themselves at the center of a 1739 dispute involving Captain Don Xavier de Mosquera Figueoa, his friend Don Francisco Arboleda, and the bishop of Popayán, Don Diego Fermin de Vergara.[31] According to Don Xavier, while visiting the home of his friend Arboleda, he had encountered a slave attempting to enter the city of Popayán mounted on a horse and armed with a sword and lance. When he instructed the slave to disarm, the slave responded that he would not unless instructed by his own master, a cleric named Jacinto Sánchez. He then insisted that he intended to travel on to his master's house, spear in hand. Arboleda instructed one of his own slaves to attack the rebel from behind. He did so, dislodging the spear from his hand. When Don Xavier pulled a gun and shot, both slaves attempted to flee. He misfired, drew another gun, and fired again. Fortunately for the slaves, he missed, allowing them to escape, allegedly into the confines of the local monastery.

At times the enslaved verbalized the threat of violence and flight in order to motivate their masters to accord them measures of freedom and autonomy. New, inexperienced, and otherwise cash-strapped slave owners such as Carlos Araujo experienced violent confrontations when they threatened the sociocultural constitution of slave communities.[32] Araujo, a long-distance merchant, took possession of Quajara, a sugar plantation that had previously been part of a larger Jesuit-owned complex of sugar plantations located nearby.[33] In March 1783 the plantation held some 266 slaves from fifty-five families. When Araujo officially took possession of the plantation, he prohibited the slaves from leaving the premises or working on other nearby estates. He then transferred six to eight young slaves to work in the city of Quito. Shortly thereafter, the entire enslaved community confronted Araujo, threatening that unless they were allowed to live together and practice their customs, they would kill all his indigenous workers and flee to the mountains.[34] Araujo had a serious problem. Even the few slaves that he had sent to work in other places had fled those sites to return to their Quajara community. Araujo needed only two-thirds of the existing slave community to complete the work at Quajara and could not afford to maintain even one more slave than he required. Consequently in May 1785, Araujo requested a small cadre of soldiers from the government to assist him in removing the slaves so that he could sell them. Apparently the specter of slaves as thieves or robbers hiding along roads convinced the officials of the *audiencia* to get involved. *Audiencia* members must have understood that, at a minimum, Araujo was forced to either sell off some of the slaves or employ them on other plantations. Thus, in 1786 soldiers assisted in the sale and removal of eighty-eight captives. These souls were dispersed in two groups. The first comprised sixty individuals who were sold to Don Gregorio Larrea, the owner of other haciendas in the Ibarra region, while the remaining twenty-eight were sold to Doctor Don Martín de Chiriboga, a parish priest from Urcuquí. Ultimately, the judicial authorities must have registered these slaves' actions as an affront to both the authority of the master class as well as that of royal officials. Although masters were required to provide the enslaved with adequate care and education in the Christian faith, they also had the right to dispose of them as property.

The Politics of Mercy: Fealty, Obeisance, and Bodies of Evidence

Throughout the colonial era, notorious incidents such as Araujo's challenges with the Quajara slave population would have been impossible for crown officials to forget. From the outset, it was apparent to royal officials that controlling restive blacks would demand concurrent approaches as indicated by rebel actions in Esmeradas, Patía, and throughout the Americas. Absolute authority on the part of the crown was an elusive goal, and the maintenance of an orderly society seemed to require a delicate balance between domination and the application of an abbreviated policy of fairness and mercy.

From the earliest era, however, in an effort to garner royal mercy, the enslaved had to present and "perform" their cases in a manner that was consistent with conceptions of royal power. They had to perform as if they were vassals who understood the implied royal authority of the crown and its representative in the Indies, the *audiencia*. Historian Kris Lane suggests that, like the church, the courts' mediating role in the colonial hierarchy rested on a shared belief in, or at least shared acceptance of, a central mystery—in this case, the divine right of kings rather than divinity itself.[35] Nevertheless, "shared belief and acceptance" did not mean "uniform understanding or experience" across lines of color, gender, and so on, but could often play out as parallel interpretations that appear on the surface to have been uniform. Thus, scholars must question the extent to which slaves' and *mestizos*' expectations of "royal mercy" might have differed, and why. Ultimately, although Africans and Andeans alike came to the courts with culturally specific notions of regalism and how it functioned, the success of their pleas hinged upon their ability to perform within what was a European-derived and European-ordered spectacle.[36]

Mercy had to be won by declarations of fealty, penitent pleas, and bodies of evidence, for even posture and physical condition could affect one's experience before royal judicial officials, whether a scribe, magistrate, or judge. When petitioning, the enslaved almost always included a plea for mercy along with declarations of fealty aimed at the Christian God, the church, and even the crown of Spain. Careful to depict themselves as observant Christians and humble subjects, they often bowed before the scribe, prostrating themselves with their heads in their hands. Several who found themselves badly bruised, beaten, and scarred entered their bodies as evidence of the brutality of their current owners. All of this was a part of what appears on the surface to be ritualized behavior that individuals at all levels of society participated in to some degree. Yet for the enslaved and other members of the lower classes, this was far more than ritualized behavior: these were necessary performances aimed at ingratiating themselves to court officials in hopes of eliciting royal mercy.[37]

Slaves, in fact, manipulated a variety of norms and postures in their attempts to gain their ends. Early conflicts among slaves hint specifically at a subaltern belief in the effectiveness of articulations of honor—and perhaps also at the internal code of ethics that informed slave interaction.[38] Evidence of both is found in one notable case against five slave women: Barbola; her mother, María; Sabrina (all slaves of Doña Mariana de Porteros); Beatriz (a *mulatta* deposited with Juan Ortiz); and an unnamed female servant. In 1615, officials from the town of Popayán initiated criminal proceedings against the women for attacking, "in word and deed" (*de palabra y obra*), Catalina, who was the slave of Diego de Salazar, chief magistrate of Popayán.[39] Officials charged and convicted the women for attacking Catalina while at a local river mill.

Catalina had suffered serious injuries. Perhaps she had been permanently injured; one cannot be sure. Given the description of the crime as *descalabrada*, which referred normally to the act of smashing one over the head, it is clear that Catalina's condition was critical. In all likelihood, she was still bleeding (externally and perhaps internally) and was quite possibly at death's door. Lurking behind the matter of her physical injuries was the allegation that her assailants had also "*insulted* [her] with intimidating words," thereby impugning her honor.[40] Though no outright claim of honor was made—the case is perhaps more appropriately assigned to the rubric of assault—the use of the verb *insultar* is quite suggestive. It had the dual effect of suggesting that Beatriz held a level of honor that her violent, unladylike comrades lacked, while criminalizing both the actions and the personas of her alleged assailants. The justification for Catalina's belief in her own honor remains unclear. Perhaps she felt she derived a level of honor and status from that of her owner, insisting upon some superiority to the other women. This certainly would have been plausible in a society bound by concepts of honor and shame such as early colonial Quito.[41] On the other hand, she might have assumed a level of honor based on her observance of elite honorific norms and well-established standards of piety and virtue. In either case, slaves were in possession of codes of conduct—indeed, notions of honorable behavior—which they used in court. Whether derived from elite notions of honor and virtue or found within the heart of the emerging Afro-Criollo culture, or both, it is clear that, like slaves in colonial New Spain and the eastern Andes, Quito's bondmen and bondwomen were developing the discursive tools needed to maneuver colonial courts long before the mid-eighteenth century. As they dialogued with attorneys, argued and negotiated with masters, overheard debates about the law and legal rights, and interfaced with other royal subjects in search of a juridical *audience* for specific outcomes, slaves developed the knowledge that subsequent generations would inherit as a kind of cultural arsenal. When the time and context was right, they would argue for increased control over the terms and conditions of bare life and self-ownership, as well as increased sociopolitical standing. These learned everyday tactics later became distinct political strategies.

The source of slaves' increased legal acumen is found not only in their interactions with attorneys and elite whites but also in their associations with free blacks. By the last quarter of the seventeenth century, free blacks like Adán Pardo were turning to the courts with increasing frequency to adjudicate in matters concerning their honor. On July 12, 1675, for example, Adán Pardo presented a case against Captain Juán Larra de los Archos y Ríos, the *alcalde ordinario* of Cali. Adán alleged that Juan had forced his sons, two married daughters, and his one engaged virgin daughter to serve him.[42] While the colonial record does not reveal with certainty if the court upheld Adán's claims, it is certain that he vigorously defended the honor of his family, and thus his own honor. All who fell within Adán's orbit (enslaved and free) would have been aware of his concern for family honor. Slaves who took notice must have gained a valuable education in the nuances of Spanish American jurisprudence.

Early enslaved and free black litigants were—perhaps unintentionally—establishing a pattern of legal precedents, a corpus of case law, as it were.[43] They sought change for themselves and their loved ones, employing tactics that foreshadowed those used by litigants of the late colonial period. Individuals like Francisco, the captive cited at the beginning of this chapter, labored to radically alter their circumstances, costing their masters time, lost wages, and legal fees. Rather than see his case thwarted by patronage politics, Francisco implicated local officials in the crime of his suffering, charged the local priest with malfeasance, and questioned the integrity of the local magistrate.

Gradually informed by a body of legal precedents, and emboldened by their knowledge of the possibilities that legal action afforded, slave litigants forged ahead in some notable cases. On September 6, 1690, in the city of Quito, Pedro de Silva, a free black man, initiated a lawsuit against Don Thomás and Doña Geronima Reymundo for the freedom of his wife, Phelipa del Castillo.[44] Pedro declared that the four hundred pesos he had offered Doña Geronima ought to have been sufficient to secure the freedom of his thirty-two-year-old enslaved wife, Phelipa. Moreover, Doña Geronima had refused to submit to them the portion of Phelipa's *jornales* (day wages) the law prescribed for slave owners. Don Thomás countered, insisting that Pedro de Silva was seeking more than his and Phelipa's fair share of the day wages. He argued that Phelipa had run away earlier, and that despite having knowledge of this, Pedro continued to charge Thomás and Geronima four reales per day as a stipend to care for Phelipa. By Thomás's reckoning, Pedro and Phelipa owed him one thousand pesos. The case, however, pivoted upon the testimony of two elite whites, an enslaved black woman, and a free black man. Perhaps more importantly, their success hinged upon the ability to cast themselves as loyal, trustworthy subjects who deserved a most merciful judgment.

Pedro and his wife endeavored to showcase their honorable, law-abiding behavior while highlighting the deplorable actions and disposition of Phelipa's master. Not only was Don Thomás in violation of the agreement he had entered into with Phelipa and Pedro, but his actions undermined the realization of the very legal principle that allowed for such master-slave arrangements—the idea that slavery was inherently transitory. Extorting potentially endless amounts of money from Phelipa prevented her from realizing her dream of freedom. But if Don Thomás was to be believed, Phelipa was a thieving runaway who had joined forces with an opportunistic free black whose integrity was questionable at best. And while Pedro and Phelipa might have felt an overwhelming sense of anger and frustration over such allegations, they had to suppress such emotions before judiciaries, for lack of composure would surely have undermined their credibility while simultaneously upholding that of Thomás. In such instances, performing the role of loyal subject with great humility proved both useful and necessary.

Yet humility and restraint were not the only performance techniques deployed by slaves before the courts. When Juana Rica and her two daughters appeared, along with her grandchildren and great-grandchildren, before the high court of Quito in 1703 to present their *libertad* petition, they brought with them a certain dramatic appeal that could not have been achieved through the mere presence of the matriarch Juana and her attorney.[45] On that day, the court witnessed the gestures, physical resemblances, and familial affinities that legal discourse could not convey. The spectacle of four generations of would-be free blacks emphasized the importance of the court's verdict. Such appearances were, in fact, rare, and might therefore have added credence to the case they sought to present.

Juana and her family argued that they were all free, claiming to be descendants of a free black woman by the name of Ana Rica who had lived in the village of Zaruma. According to the plaintiffs, Ana Rica had been a free woman who lived with a *mestiza* by the name of Francisca Calderón. They argued that although she lived and worked in the home of Francisca, she had not been Francisca's slave. As time passed, Ana Rica gave birth to a daughter—Magdalena Rica—who also lived in the home with Ana and Francisca until she was about eight or nine years of age. Around this time, Pedro Pesantes arrived and asked to take Magdalena to the town of Cuenca. She was not to be his slave but his maid. According to these plaintiffs, Ana Rica agreed and sometime later had occasion to travel to the town of Cuenca. There, she found her daughter in the home of Doña Magdalena de Espinosa. In the course of their conversation and visit, she decided that this woman was treating her daughter well. She was well dressed, fed, and appeared to be in a good situation. But over the years, the descendants of Magdalena—Juana and her children—somehow came to be understood as the property of Doña María de Zúniga and Doña Juliana Espinosa Montero.

According to the white women, Doñas María and Juliana, the claims of the Rica family were absurd. They argued that they had owned Juana and her family for years and that recently they had sold some of their relatives, including a *mulato* named Bernardo to Cristoval de Raíz of Cuenca and a *mulata* named Gregoría to Don Diego Ruíz de Roxas of Latacunga. They had also sold another *mulata* named Augustina to Maestro Benito Montero, their brother, who was a priest in the city of Quito. One of these purported slaves, Bernardo, had returned to the city of Cuenca and was ultimately resold to the aforementioned Doña María de Zúniga. They went on to argue that their uncle, Maestro Antonio Espinosa de las Monteros, had indeed freed some of his slaves upon his death but had left others in slavery and still others as church donations. At this point in the case, Doña María and Doña Juliana requested that the slaves be placed in *depósito* while an investigation and trial took place.

The Rica family argued that they had lived in freedom and had not received any day wages as slaves, nor had they received any sort of maintenance from Doñas María, Juliana, or their family. Furthermore, the family argued, "We have tended our own gardens in order to feed and maintain ourselves and our children."[46] While they stopped short of invoking the term "honor," the Rica family members clearly sought to demonstrate that they were not only free but honorable and industrious subjects. By extension, the Rica family also asserted that the doñas were dishonorable owners who had failed to provide for their would-be slaves. The might-be slaves brought several witnesses to help substantiate their claims, ranging from other blacks, both slave and free, to whites and Indians. Each verified various aspects of the history, as told by this family. Several of the witnesses even asserted that the ancestor, Ana Rica, was the daughter of an indigenous woman.

The defendants, Doñas María and Juliana, continued to bring forth evidence in support of their case. During the course of the trial, they produced bills of sale documenting that they had indeed sold some of Juana's family members; the will and testament of their brother, to whom they had sold a couple of the relatives; the will of their mother, which left slaves to them by the names of Magdalena and Ana; and a statement from the Zaruma parish that claimed Magdelena had been born the daughter of Ana, who was the slave of Beatriz (not Francisca) Calderón.

Nevertheless, Juana and her family members pressed ahead, basing their claims not only on the corroboration of their account of their lineage but also on the very constitution and viability of their union. Mother testified for daughter, while husband testified for wife and mother-in-law. Ultimately, however, they sought to convey a larger, and perhaps more notable, picture. Even if their story was to be viewed as mere family folklore supported only by a barrage of hearsay, their larger message was undeniable. They were the meritous free black family that Justice Auncibay had fantasized about in his 1592 treatise that opens this book. They loved and supported one another, adhering doggedly to the laws of the land. They were an honorable family whose members had inherited and earned their freedom. After all, they had not lived as slaves; nor had they received support from their alleged owners. Rather, they were victims of generational wrongs, and now it was up to the high court to correct the injustices of a bygone era.

The extant record does not provide the outcome of this case. By the time the documentary trail ends, Ana and her descendants had been assigned a new lawyer, and the case was further hindered by delays from the opposing side. Nevertheless, the dramatic effect of the presence of not just an entire family but several generations and the considerable degree of tenacity in securing evidence to propel the case forward demonstrate their resourcefulness in securing their freedom. Their saga offers an undeniable indication of the long and protracted process of legal action and suggests the radical implications of the enslaved legal culture being crafted in early eighteenth-century Quito. Families like the Rica family drew upon the same technologies and knowledge that had enslaved them to also set them free. The case foreshadows legal actions that would emerge in the late colonial and Independence eras and points to the enslaved, and the cases they lodged, as critical catalysts in slave jurisprudence.

Prudencio Correa, an enslaved *pardo* from Quito, demonstrated that he, too, possessed a sense that performing submissiveness was key to resisting via the courts. Prostrating himself before the scribes, Prudencio petitioned for his freedom, claiming his parents had been free and "had baptized him in the faith."[47] Prudencio availed himself to members of the court as an insider by bolstering his bona fide claim as a Christian and a legitimate member of society. Prudencio sought to nullify the recent sale of his person on two accounts: his true *liberto* status and the cruelties that he had suffered at the hands of the purchaser. According to Prudencio, the priest Sebastián de Araujo had falsely stated that he was a slave, forging documents that said his father and mother had not presented him to the faith in baptism.[48] His would-be owners, Doñas Bernarda de Ariniga y Margarita de Sambrano, argued, however, that not only was Prudencio their slave but that he had been "born and raised" in their home as the son of Gerónima Correa, an enslaved woman who had another child, a daughter named Getrudis. According to these two elite women, his mother had sought her freedom some years earlier but could not find anyone to help in the matter. They were also careful to point out that they had inherited this family as the heirs of Barnada Pérez, the daughter of their great-grandmother, Magdalena Pérez, arguing, moreover, that their great-grandmother had owned both Prudencio's grandmother and his great-grandmother.[49]

Prudencio continued to appeal to the justices, complaining that Don Jaime Ortiz had information about his freedom that would nullify the sale "of his person." Prudencio explained: "Proceeding maliciously he [Fray Sebastián] turned over [a false] writ of sale to don Jaime Ortiz, architect of this city [Quito], who has committed a grave crime because he has sold a free person which is against one to give attention to such evil and grant the said sale without bringing in someone who could protest this falsely placed slavery, and without bringing in anything [such as] information that has not been considered [which might] resolve my case [or demonstrating that] I am free, and as I have been as such in the city of Loja and in [my] travels to this city."[50] Citing the bodily harm that he had endured at the hands of Ortiz, he stated:

> Yesterday, Thursday, which makes 14 days of the current [month] around seven at night, the *mayordomo* of the house of Don Jaime Joseph de Ortiz requested to keep me inside the *obraje*, dragging me into it, I leaned against a staff which I had, and for this the said, Don Joseph, knocked the staff out of my hand. He gave me many blows to the body and luckily I am [not] totally crushed, after which he took a strip of leather and gave me cruel lashes, leaving me defenseless and at risk [of losing] my life because my chest, arms, and back are swollen with marks so prominent and in order to use my right as it suits me . . . I ask and plead [that you] circulate [this] petition [in order] that an attorney might receive my case, for heaven's sake given the beating, marks, and the swelling place me in the *carsel real de cuerpo* [public jail] while you determine the case of my freedom I will be in [the] said *carsel*, and moreover, [because] he has assaulted me and will [assault me], and nevertheless the said has in times past knocked my wife down as she carried the petitions to the Real Audiencia de Cruz, don't be malicious.[51]

Prudencio's case highlights both the technical sophistication of slave petitions and the great lengths petitioners took in order to characterize themselves as "insiders" who were not only royal subjects but plaintiffs who deserved justice and mercy. Like Francisco (the slave cited at the beginning of this discussion), Prudencio paid obeisance to royal authorities and called for justice and mercy. Even captives who related testimony as compelling as that of Prudencio could not be strident in their claims. Rather, they had to draw upon their position as subjects of the king when imploring the court not to be malicious in its verdict. This phrase, "don't be malicious," found throughout court petitions, reflects the petitioners' final attempt to impress upon the court the critical importance of its decision. Not only did Prudencio seek to ingratiate himself to the court by insisting on his upstanding Christianity, having been "baptized in the faith," but his body became evidence of the cruelties he had endured at the hands of a master to whom he did not belong. These cruelties are further augmented when Prudencio mentions the abuses his wife, a defenseless woman, had suffered in her attempts to aid his just cause. Simply put, the court could either accord them mercy and end the past and current injustices or become complicit in a slave master's cruelties.

The investigation of Prudencio's case continued until August 3, 1703, when the justices of the *audiencia* ruled in favor of the alleged masters. And while Prudencio filed appeals, protesting his malicious mistreatment, he was no closer to his freedom at the end of the documentary trail than he had been at the beginning.

For enslaved women, the process of seeking freedom could be a double-edged sword. Those single women who earned enough money to purchase their freedom were assumed to be prostitutes or thieves, while those in loving relationships with men who desired to purchase their freedom also risked being viewed as prostitutes, inherently dishonored, and untrustworthy. Because the master-slave relationship was fundamentally coercive, the very nature of the relationship meant that anytime a woman entered into an agreement with a man to "purchase her freedom" (which in fact meant purchasing the slave, male or female), she remained vulnerable to her new owner's advances and demands (sexual or otherwise).

This is the picture that Juana Antonía Márquez painted when giving her deposition in the lawsuit she filed against her owner, Francisco Antonio de Abeldebeas. On August 8, 1754, Juana testified that she had just received word that Francisco was leaving for Guayaquil "early in the morning of the following day." His departure would disrupt and perhaps jeopardize her pending lawsuit aimed at acquiring her freedom.[52] Juana testified that she and Francisco had begun an arrangement, or more precisely a relationship, five years earlier. In 1749 she had agreed to enter into *amistad ilisita* (concubinage) with Francisco if he purchased her "freedom" from Captain Don Juachin DeSoto Mayor for

370 pesos. While Francisco had indeed purchased her, five years had passed in which he had not granted Juana her freedom. Juana contended:

> It has been my obligation, without giving him my hand [marrying him], the affliction [or forced sex continually] until he impregnated me with his baby boy, who lives [and is] four years of age, and as in all that I have reported as I said, I have served [him] not only in this city [Quito] but as far as the city of Guayaquil with my person and my mother per the contract that I made owing me the writ of freedom, and in the city of Guayaquil, there [were] many potential purchasers, not only as a servant but also in order to take me, or enter with me into the holy state of matrimony, and in such cases Don Francisco prevented me, saying many times that I did not have the freedom to marry [in this case that she was not free to marry, insinuating that she was married or possessed some other moral impediment] to make such an arrangement, and these proposals were not two or three times, but many more, thus in the city of Guayaquil, las Bodegas de Babahoyo y Guaranda, but also in the city of Quito.[53]

She stated, moreover, that throughout their illicit affair, Francisco had mistreated her: "Not only with blows but with an instrument in his hand as in all that I demonstrate I have only endured all of this to obtain my freedom, and not all of the abuses that I [have endured] have been solely [at the hand] of my master, but also his brother-in-law, Don Juan Romero, who tried to kill me when I had been violated [in order] to extract the aforementioned for which I add also that [he caused] me to miscarry another child—also the result of the *maltratos* [rapes] of Don Francisco—of one month and fifteen days pregnant."[54] According to Juana, she had paid an exorbitant price for her freedom, a price that included her body; her time; opportunities for a meaningful, desirable, and church-sanctioned relationship; the death of an unborn fetus; and her own mother's time. Juana entered into this arrangement expecting to give of herself and her resources for a limited time in exchange for her freedom. Her owner, Francisco, claimed, however, that he had not purchased Juana under any such pretenses, nor had he committed any of the alleged crimes. Rather, he claimed that his sister—Juana Abeldebeas—had requested that he purchase Juana, and he had obliged. His attorney, Carlos de Larrayos, insisted that the claims brought by the enslaved woman were unfair and constituted a misrepresentation of the truth, and he implored the court to seek the truth by investigating these claims.[55]

In an apparent effort to neutralize Juana, they requested that she be placed in *depósito*. Once Juana was placed in the custody of the Santa Catherina

Monastery, Larrayos moved to have the case thrown out based on two claims. He claimed that around the time when Juana would have conceived Juachin Phelipe (the living child), Francisco was in Panama, and therefore the young child could not be his. Furthermore, because he had never made such an agreement, he argued the case lacked merit and therefore was unworthy of the court's time and the defendant's resources.

Much to the chagrin of Larrayos, the justices found that the case warranted a trial and ordered both sides to develop and present their cases. While Juana was *depositada* in the Santa Chatherina Monastery, her lawyer, Phelipe Victorio de Miranda, *procurador de los pobres*, continued to build and argue her case, insisting among other things that shortly after Juana gave birth to Juachin Phelipe, Francisco went to Panama city, leaving her in the care of Dominican priest Fray Santiago de Jesús for several weeks while he traveled. Miranda argued, moreover, that the "illicit friendship" between Juana and Francisco continued upon Francisco's return in the home of Francisco's aunt. The couple had made one trip to the coastal city of Guayaquil alone, but upon their second, Francisco transported Juana's mother, Getrudis de la Cruz (*morena libre*), to serve him and assist with laundry and other household chores in the city of Guayaquil, the Bodega de Babahoyo, and in the town of Guaranda. Thereafter, Francisco placed Juana in the house of his brother-in-law. It was "known publicly" that he could no longer keep her in the city of Guayaquil because his wife had learned of the relationship and of the "excesses that he had committed with his own slave." "If he brought her there," they argued, "that would cause a scandal."[56] His brother-in-law, they argued, had also abused Juana.

Juana and her attorney developed a considerable cadre of witnesses, many of them women of all classes and hues. María Petrona Sotomayor, for example, testified on Juana's behalf, stating that she had met Juana when she and Francisco were occupying a rented room in the home of Miguel Sotomayor. She testified that Francisco did not treat Juana like his slave, but "like his lady" (*sino como su dama*) with whom he had "business" (*con quien tenia comercio*). According to María, he had Juana stay in the same room where he slept. On various occasions, she noticed that in the mornings and in the evenings Juana Antonia got out of the same bed as Don Francisco, "with whom she slept and recognized with much love."[57]

Several other witnesses came forth testifying essentially to the same account, many of them arguing that the relationship between Juana and Francisco was "public and notorious in the city of Guayaquil" (*público y notorio en oha ciudad de Guayaquil*).[58] One witness, Juan Bezerra Chabarria, said that Juana sojourned at his house in the parish of San Marcos on various occasions.

He also claimed to have witnessed Francisco de Abeldebeas come searching for Juana. Upon finding her, Chabarria stated that Francisco "mistreated her with words, and actions, and the witness did not know what the motive was." Later, he learned from a conversation with Juana Antonio that she was the slave of the said Don Francisco, was his lover, and had a son by him while in concubinage. Further, Chabarria had heard that Don Francisco wanted to take her to the city of Guayaquil and had promised to give her fifty pesos to stay with him. With these earnings, Don Francisco claimed "she could work and find her own life, increase her freedom and move out of the *esclavitud* that she possessed."[59]

Another witness, Bernarda Muños Chamorro, testified that she and Juana Antonia worked in the home of one Señora Leonora. According to Barnarda, Francisco proposed that she hold Juana hostage in the room where Juana and Francisco had lived together previously. While she never agreed to this, she testified that Juana and Francisco did share a room, explaining that Francisco had Juana "for his friend which has been public and notorious just like it is also known that he had offered her freedom like this witness has heard on various occasions from his mouth." In addition, Bernarda noted that Juana suffered because she lacked "various necessities, enduring hunger and many bouts of mistreatment."[60] As a result, Juana hid in the home of one Señor Thobar. When this occurred, Bernada noted, Don Francisco sent Doña Luisa Amaya to look for Juana and to promise her that she would receive her freedom in exchange for returning. But rather than return with Doña Amaya, Juana caused a scene, recounting openly the escapades of she and Francisco, all while screaming through the door of the house where she hid. Bernarda alleged that during this exchange Juana insisted that she would not return until Francisco provided her with a *carta de libertad* and fifty pesos. Several other witnesses affirmed Bernarda's claims, each testifying to having witnessed or heard about Juana's now infamous performance.

As the trial went on, Francisco's lawyer came forth on several occasions to complain that Juana should be confined to the Recogimiento de Santa Martha, insisting that it was not legal for her to be walking the streets and plazas while in *depósito*.[61] He continued to prolong the case, filing complaints that stated, among other things, that he had not received all of the "*autos*"—evidence, testimonies, and the like—in order that he might review them before the trial.

Entering her body and physical state as evidence, Juana and her lawyer called upon the testimony of Fray Jasinto Gauisandes, a local priest who had cared for Juana at the behest of her master Francisco. Fray Jasinto claimed that Juana fell into his care because of the abuses she had suffered at the hand of her master. He explained: "[Juana] suffered from pain in her body as a result of an object that her master used to beat her because the night before he had been in a bar . . . enjoying himself with some of his acquaintances, but he needed the said *mulata* to be treated in order that she might travel to Quito as he did the third day of my having the confessed [Juana]; and I did not receive notice that she had another accident; neither that she might miscarry from this bout of sickness."[62]

Francisco and his attorney countered that the case lacked merit and should be thrown out, and they sought to demonstrate the absurdity of Juana's claims by denying the sexual relationship, the paternity of Juana's child (or children), and the alleged pretenses under which Francisco had purchased Juana. Calling upon several witnesses, they argued that Francisco had never engaged in such an illicit affair. It was impossible: Francisco had been traveling in Panama at the time of the child's conception and could not have impregnated Juana. Evidence of this fact lay in their view that the child did not resemble Francisco (*ni en color, ni en fisonomia*) but rather had the likeness of one Manuel Nicolas, a free black tailor from Quito, whom witnesses claimed to have seen leaving Juana's quarters on several mornings.

The defense continued its simultaneous attack upon Juana's reputation and the validity of her claims, charging that she had a pattern of making outlandish accusations against former masters. Francisco had purchased Juana, he claimed, while she was in *depósito*, looking for a new master after having leveled similar claims against her former owner. Her reputation as an incorrigible, bellicose prostitute was so notorious that when Francisco tried to sell her, he found that no one wanted to purchase her, even from as far away as Guayaquil.

Eventually, the president of the *audiencia* rendered a verdict: "I find that the said María Juana Antonia has not proven the said promise [*como probar le convino*] and that her master proved in great form [*en bastante forma*] his exception and defense. And in conformity I must [therefore] order that the said *mulata* be returned [*restituida*] to the dominion and *esclavitud* of her master understanding that only for the effect because she is not to be returned to his service, not to his house, neither to his custody due to the danger . . . and for the scandal that he had caused, the said Don Francisco Antonio de Aveldebeas with the said concubinage with his own slave to whom he was obligated to give good doctrine and example, I apply the fine of 50 pesos."[63]

Although Juana failed to receive her freedom, the court granted her thirty days to secure a new owner. While this was hardly the verdict she sought, the justices had accorded her with a measure of mercy, a signal to the merits of her case, and an acknowledgment of her ability to present herself as an insider, as opposed to the rebellious harlot Francisco had alleged. She continued to appeal her case to the justices' sense of fairness and compassion, requesting three additional months to find a new master or the money to purchase her freedom. By the end of the extant record, it is clear that things were not moving in Juana's favor. Her owner's fine of fifty pesos had been forgiven, and her appeals largely ignored.

Juana had done all she could in her quest for freedom. Like many others in search of freedom, she relied upon the concept of *sevicia* (gross mistreatment) while reifying the extralegal contract she had created with her owner. Following the pattern and process of her predecessors, Juana also relied upon the art of performing submissiveness to present herself as a mercy-worthy *esclava*, one whose last opportunity for just treatment lay in the hands of the court. Juana's case demonstrates how black women, awash in a sea of subjugation and despair, displayed fortitude, legal savvy, and social awareness. In addition to epitomizing the struggle of enslaved black Quiteñas, her lawsuit forms a chronological bridge spanning from cases presented in the early colonial era to those of the late colonial and early national periods. Over the course of the second half of the eighteenth century, many more slave women would follow Juana's course, employing a strikingly similar pattern of legal and performative techniques when appearing before the court. By century's end, the salience of Juana's techniques would have been obvious to enslaved litigants throughout the *audiencia*. Consequently, women like María Chiquinquirá Díaz and Angela Batallas would present cases in 1794 and 1823 strongly resembling those brought by Juana and her predecessors.

Like Juana, María Chiquinquirá Díaz entered into a legal battle with her alleged owner, Presbyter Afonso Cepedas de Arizcum Elizondo, in the city of Guayaquil in May 1794.[64] María Chiquinquirá demanded legal confirmation of her freedom and that of her daughter, María del Carmen Espinzo, based on the fact that she had secured "compulsory manumission" prior to María del Carmen's birth, a legal action sparked by Cepedas's treatment of her daughter. Retreating from earlier days of generosity, Cepedas characterized María del Carmen as "a filthy bitch . . . worse than a whore, a prostitute and lascivious."[65] For María Chiquinquirá's part, such an insult was an affront to the family's honor and constituted grounds for severing all ties to Cepedas. María, in turn, challenged the presbyter's honor, charging him with taking sexual liberties with his slave women and fathering children by some. These alleged improprieties led to further investigation by the court.[66]

For historian María Eugenía Chaves, the first to publish an analysis of the María Chiquinquirá Díaz case and a pioneer in the study of enslaved women in Guayaquil, María Chiquinquirá's use of the discourse of honor constituted a new tactic for enslaved women, one peculiar to the late colonial era.[67] Bourbon reform policies reified notions of race and honor in gendered terms, Chaves argues, providing enslaved women with a normative discourse that made it possible for female slaves to put forth claims of honor in the waning years of the eighteenth century.[68] However, enslaved men and women had employed honorific language in lawsuits dating back to the early seventeenth century. Many proclaimed, for example, that they had been tormented in "word and deed," and they in turn attacked and disparaged their master's honor, recounting dishonorable acts, including siring children with slave women, requiring work on Sundays, withholding time for Mass, and failing to provide instruction in the faith.

Although the Díaz case displays subtle differences from those of earlier generations, her use of the language of honor was not as unique as Chaves suggests. Rather, it typified slaves' well-established pattern and process of combining "compulsory manumission" or special contractual arrangements with charges of *sevicia*. Prior to Chiquinquirá, many others had merged *sevicia* claims with any number of infractions, including the denial of conjugal rights, neglect, harsh words, disparaging comments, and extreme physical cruelty. In *Juana v. Juachin DeSoto Mayor*, for example, the verdict was based not only on her mistreatment but also on the court's desire to condemn Juachin's dishonorable conduct. Juana had successfully combined her claim to freedom with charges of *sevicia* and shameful actions. During the colonial period, *sevicia* had become the touchstone for slave lawsuits, as slaves sought to extend this category to include all possible discomforts and disquietudes experienced at the master's hand.

The cases studied by historian Camilla Townsend illustrate that even when slaves deviated from this norm, they continued to rely upon well-established arguments from previous generations—arguments that often concerned feminine honor and masters' deplorable behavior. Townsend finds that in 1823, when Angela Batallas sued her master, Ildefonso Coronel, a prominent citizen of Guayaquil and leader in the independence movement, she did not put forth any evidence of *sevicia*.[69] Rather, she argued that her master had fallen in love with her, promised her freedom, purchased her a house, visited her regularly, and had fathered her child. To Angela's mind, Ildefonso had "become one with her," consummating a symbolic marriage that manifested itself in uniting his freedom with her bondage, thereby redeeming her from the yoke of servitude.

Ildefonso had a different perspective, however. His explanation was simple: Angela was lying. The child was not his, but rather the offspring of a free

Afro-Guayaquileño and known friend of Angela. Seeking to characterize her as a knavish whore, Ildefonso suggested also that the child might well belong to Angela's attorney, a typical accusation leveled at women's sexual comportment in the hope of discrediting them and their testimony. This trial, like Juana's, was inherently about honor, as questions of paternity implied the maligning of either the owner's or the enslaved woman's character. But try as he did to muster a formidable defense, Ildefonso had already made a colossal mistake. At the time of the child's baptism, Ildefonso had given Angela's *parda* midwife a note to take to the priest stating that the child was his, making no mention of the status of the mother. Whether Ildefonso meant this gesture as acknowledgment of the agreement he had made with Angela or as a basic step in securing the free status of his offspring is unclear. In either case, the note became a critical piece of evidence as the trial unfolded.

Uncertain as to whether her well-articulated case, supported by the baptismal note, would be enough to secure her freedom, Angela visited Simón Bolívar, the liberator himself. We may never know if the liberator was truly impressed with the merits of Angela's case or if he merely perceived an opportunity to make an important political statement regarding the values of the new regime as well as garner the support of a frustrated segment of the population. Townsend tells us that Bolívar supported Angela, sending a note to the court in recommendation of "justice for this unhappy slave."[70] While Bolívar's support held obvious significance, Ildefonso's baptismal note to the priest determined the outcome. Whereas Juana, the enslaved woman cited earlier, failed to "prove the said promise," Ildefonso's note offered material evidence demonstrating beyond a reasonable doubt his promise to free Angela. Angela must have benefited greatly from the politically radical moment of independence, but above all, she had presented key evidence while emphasizing her master's dishonorable behavior—using the well-worn tactics and techniques of her ancestors.

Conclusion

By the end of the eighteenth century, enslaved rebels and fugitives had helped create a context in which judges and officials could not ignore the larger implications of their rulings. The laws and judicial processes reflected a sort of pragmatism born of elites' long history with slavery and the human reaction to bondage: resistance. At the close of the eighteenth century, slaves like Claudio Delgado and Bonfacio Isidro Caravalí continued to remind colonial officials of this perspective, providing judges with a range of factors to consider when rendering a verdict.

On July 4, 1798, Claudio and Bonfacio appeared before the scribe of the high court to protest the ill treatment they and their wives had received at the hands of their overseer, Captain Onorio Estopiñan.[71] Onorio had whipped Claudio's wife relentlessly, lashing her torn flesh one hundred times in the morning and evening for two straight days, then reducing the amount to fifty lashes and then to twenty-five. After the whippings, Captain Onorio demanded she cure pieces of meat, denying her rest and recuperation. Despite the lacerations of her flesh, Onorio had proceeded to commit other "abuses" but stopped abruptly, leaving her to die in an inconspicuous area near the mining camp. Fortunately for her, family members heard her crying and rescued her, treating her wounds with *aguardiente* and cascarilla. Claudio had suffered the castigation of many lashes as well, enduring whippings to the point that large pieces of flesh tore and hung from his buttocks. Underscoring the gravity of their circumstances, he lamented, "It would have been better to receive a bolt of fire than to suffer such punishments. Only infidels should suffer in this manner." Claudio's reference to infidels suggested a particular understanding and reading of slave law; only people who were blasphemous, unbelieving, or socially and religiously belligerent were worthy of such treatment. Claudio's "infidels" could have been among the indigenous communities who lived within the region, including Singdaguas, Chupas, Boyas, Nulpes, and Guapíes. Perhaps he also considered the recently arrived enslaved Africans, some no doubt ensconced in the runaway slave communities that dotted the intermountain valleys and the lowlands.

Despite the fact that their wives had been using "dust" to cure foot injuries and were guilty, by their own admission, of engaging in "superstition," Claudio and Bonfacio displayed confidence in their case, advising the court: "Now we are not in any state to return to the said mine. Therefore, we supplicate with major submission, [that you] order that the said master provide us [with a] license to look for [a] new master. And when he gives it to us [it can be] for wherever he wishes, since none will intimidate [us] to see the similar barbarous experience [again]. This liberty the laws give us for having all been born free since the beginning of the world. And if other slaves have obtained such with less cruelty, we will expect given [our] more just causes to obtain this justice from Your Excellency."

The message was clear: they were not moving until the justices awarded them their desired judgment. While it is impossible to peer into the thoughts of the judges, the potential implications of this case must have been obvious. Standing before the *audiencia* were two men whose court appearance signified their last attempt at redress. Failure to grant their reasonable request might have motivated these slaves, their wives, and extended family members to run away or, worse still, revolt. Long-standing maroon settlements, including Esmeraldas and Patía, dotted the South Pacific littoral, the location of Claudio and Bonfacio's mining camp.

The justices must have found themselves in an even greater dilemma as these types of complaints were becoming more frequent. The previously booming gold economy centered in Barbacoas was in decline. Masters were selling off slaves in large numbers, separating entire slave communities that had lived together for generations. Similar problems were occurring in the north-central highlands on former Jesuit-owned sugar estates. As already mentioned, ten years before Claudio and Bonfacio's case, officials had dispatched a small contingent of soldiers to assist Carlos Araujo in dismantling a generations-old slave community. Members of the community had threatened his life and the lives of his Amerindian workers precisely because he mistreated them, denying them time off on festival days, adequate food and supplies, and the opportunity to maintain their own households. Similar concerns filled the docket of the high court, such that some slaves might have known about the pending claims of the others. Justices were now faced with the challenge and legal obligation of sending an official message to all parties: Slavery would be upheld, but excessive lashings and mistreatment by masters were unacceptable.

Consistent with long-held legalistic and performance techniques, Claudio and Bonfacio represented themselves as insiders. At the outset of their deposition, they stated their knowledge of the laws of "the heavens" and royal law. Both legal codes demanded "humane treatment." If references to the heavens were not enough, they also made striking reference to the damnation and destruction that infidels should suffer. While appearing somewhat strident in their claims, they had been careful to address the court with all the honorific trappings, gestures, and codes required for proper consideration in Spanish American courts. Even admission of their wives' sociocultural activities was made in a manner that would distance them from their wives' behavior, seemingly to discredit the system and draw attention to the greater, more damning crime of their master: the failure to restrain a sadistic overseer.

Whether Claudio and Bonfacio believed in the power of their wives' spiritual activities evades our comprehension, as do the motivations of the judges before whom they stood. In this instance, what seems to have mattered more than beliefs and motivations was the extent to which they were convincing in their role before the court. Had they placed enough distance between their claims and their wives' questionable activities? Would the overseer seem just in having stamped out such ruinous behavior in the context of the moment? Given the fact that they won their desired judgment, one might accurately assume that they were convincing in their role. Nevertheless, for Claudio and Bonfacio, the question would quickly become, What was the educational value of this process? What had they learned en route to Quito, as they maneuvered in the city, and in their interactions with court officials? These lessons were likely to serve them well as they returned to Barbacoas to exercise the rights and privileges they had received from the high court on January 15, 1799. As judiciaries transferred the case to officials in Barbacoas for oversight and enforcement, Claudio and Bonfacio's quest to receive good treatment and protection for their family seemed to have just begun. They faced the challenge of locating a new master and working with the local court that, from the beginning, had denied them their legal rights. If the behavior of other masters is any indication, Claudio and Bonfacio were sure to face a series of setbacks as they continued their fight to enjoy the rights granted them by the law and enforced by Quito's high court. They would have to face the fact that, in colonial Quito, legal entitlements and opportunities to engage in justified acts of resistance always seemed to be weakened due to the limitations of bondage. Legal struggles of the enslaved were old; their battle for a degree of autonomy had a long life, too. And while the republican era would usher in a new sociopolitical context, the war for freedom and justice was far from over.

CONCLUSION

In Ecuador's contemporary social imaginary, the story of blackness is seldom considered through the lens of racial slavery. This is certainly true of a number of countries in the Western Hemisphere. Indeed, not only is slavery pushed to the margins within the contemporary Andean imaginary, but it is often eclipsed by discourses of *mestizaje* (race mixture) and stories of relative freedom. Ecuador's preferred national narrative of blackness begins in the province of Esmeraldas, known in the popular imagination as a free black and indigenous enclave that came about following the wreckage of a single ship along the coast of Ecuador. In the popular retelling of this story, the enslaved blacks overtook their captors and absconded into the Esmeraldas interior. There, they formed strategic marriage alliances with local Amerindian chieftains, thus becoming the emblematic mulatto gentlemen depicted in a 1599 print by the indigenous Quiteño artist Andrés Sánchez Gallque. In this commonly held national mythology, Ecuador narrowly escaped a history of slavery through a single shipwreck carrying would-be slaves turned freed Afro-Amerindians.

Truth in this instance is not stranger than fiction. In fact, at least three shipwrecks occurred near Atacames beach beginning in the 1540s. These events resulted in the emergence of two distinct groups of African-descended clans, both of which took up refuge among and married into key regional chieftaincies. In so doing, they became veritable native lords of what some colonists deemed an "*indio mulatto*" territory, an area that became recognized by colonial authorities in Quito as governed by their Afro-Andean colonial vassals. Contemporary descriptions of the Afro-Ecuadorean past differ dramatically from the historical descriptions and portraits found in documentary evidence from the period. In this social imaginary slavery is largely forgotten, absolving the national consciousness of any recognition regarding the colonial presence, contributions, and suffering in bondage of its black populace.[1] Consequently, slavery and the early modern African diaspora have been whitewashed from the region's history, subsumed under the rubric of *mestizaje* and otherwise rendered illegible.[2]

Deeper readings of the Esmeraldas episode and other early conquest campaigns reveal a colonial society formed in relation to African slavery and

Andrés Sánchez Gallque, *Los mulatos de Esmeraldas* (Quito, 1599).
Museo de America, Madrid.

struggles over access to indigenous subjects, labor reserves, and land. Through such readings, we discover a story of slavery resisted but not disavowed or absent. Contrary to its contemporary telling, the foundational history of colonial Esmeraldas is, in fact, a complex tale of would-be slaves who escaped perpetual servitude—first physically and then by becoming cultural and political brokers who marshaled religious and Spanish royal discourses to mediate between the royal state and its local Afro-Amerindian and Indian subjects. In the process, they transformed themselves from *esclavos negros* to *indios mulattos.* Along the way, they secured titles as "lords" of a strategically positioned province along the pirate-infested Pacific coast of what was then an emerging and vulnerable kingdom. These were long and arduous processes that required blood, sacrifice, and skillful diplomacy. The development of Quito's free Afro-Amerindian province was, therefore, not the natural outgrowth of a single shipwreck. Esmeraldas did not develop because slavery was benign, unimportant, or otherwise marginal to the local colonial project. Indeed, the lords of Esmeraldas *were* fugitives for nearly half a century. In this sense, and certainly in the broader sense of governance, during the period of their fugitivity, they were surely considered slaves and vulnerable to re-enslavement during that period. For decades the colonial authorities in Quito sent campaigns to the region aimed at subduing the fugitives and reducing local chiefdoms to colonial service. Ultimately, the fugitives' successful escape from racial slavery was the result of their ability to capitalize on a series of fortuitous events—shipwrecks, strategic marriages, and military alliances. In short, it was their ability to serve the aims of regional chieftancies that allowed for their escape. In the end, however, although they freed themselves of the fetters of colonial race bondage, they could not escape the predicaments of race governance.[3]

This book began in the context of such denials, misrecognitions, and elisions. By and large, African-descended people have only come to figure prominently in the historiography of Latin America in the last quarter century as new scholarship on black life in colonial settings such as Lima, Mizque, Trujillo, Mexico City, Cartagena, and Costa Rica has come to the fore.[4] Recent scholarship has focused on the social, economic, and, increasingly, cultural history of slavery and black life. The questions and contextualization of such studies have concerned the kind of labor slaves performed, the commodities they produced, their lived experiences, and the dynamism between life lived under the colonial gaze and the lives slaves forged apart from, against, and within the confines of mastery. But as historian Christopher L. Brown states, "The history of slavery, with a few crucial exceptions, has been served less well."[5] Latin Americanists have treated the politics of slavery largely through examinations of law, order, social control, and slaves' participation in social and religious life.[6] In many ways the political history of slavery remains under development. And although Latin American postcolonial scholarship has conceptualized the coloniality of power as constituted through colonial governance and mercantile practices, the ways in which slavery proved foundational to these modes of thinking, archiving, and being remain undertheorized.[7]

Rivers of Gold has sought to address both the political history of slavery in the Andes and the ways in which slavery, and race for that matter, continues to evade the grasp of postcolonial theoretical innovations concerning and coming out of Latin America. It has insisted that the colonization, enslavement, and race governance of sub-Saharan Africans occurred through a series of royal impositions. Castilians deemed sub-Saharan Africans *black* in their *naturaleza* (a geohumoral reference to landscapes of birth and formation), a people of varying non-European *naciónes* (distinct collectives, polities), and inherently deficient and immoral in their *calidades* (physical and moral qualities). *Naturaleza* marked belonging in a physical and physiognomic way—one of color, mapped onto landscapes that Europeans considered uninhabitable and damning to the character and physiognomy of the person; *nación* was an imagined corporate community or polity with its own laws and privileges or reprehensible vices (e.g., cannibalism)—collectivities inhabiting territories, provinces, countries, or kingdoms. Although color was not a sign of fixed biological or cultural traits of people, it marked individuals with traits and status that mapped onto the context, demography, and territorialities of slavery. In short, landscapes and territories had a way of inducing these traits such that people were viewed and governed as products of the territories they "naturally" inhabited. By the turn of the sixteenth century, Castile was using these practices to read, mark, constitute, and govern colonial subjects through notions of *casta*, *calidad*, nation, and color. *Rivers of Gold* has argued, therefore, that these emerging practices of governance slowly over time came to produce race, not as an ideology or system of thought but as a set of colonial practices of rule. And slavery was chief among them.

Reading the vast colonial archive that slavery produced in Quito, this work insists that slavery and race governance were quintessential to Spanish rule in the Andes. Enslaved blacks vividly displayed the powerful advance of Christian sovereignty emerging out of the Kingdoms of Castile and Aragon at the end of the fifteenth century. Although the intrinsic nature of slavery in Iberia was not immediately equated to bodies read as "black," over time, slave status was indexed increasingly through the geopolitical frame of color, especially "blackness," which Castile used to deem them enslavable. These processes reached their fullest expression as the enslavement and dispersal of Africans were applied in the Americas. The Andes were not exceptional to these patterns and practices. In Quito and throughout Spanish America, the bodies that Europeans read and constituted as black became emblematic of prestige, wealth, royal power, and majesty.

As African captives were converted into saltwater slaves, they entered the world of the socially dead, bereft of family, community, legitimacy, and social standing. Leaving behind any semblance of social standing they may have enjoyed, they were reduced legally and commercially to the status of chattel. They were "mobile capital," people who circulated marked with a condition and a predicament. Already priced as and reduced to a kind of corporeal body of people defined as property, the enslaved were inaugurated into the life of bondage (within a realm, not merely in an economic system) through a similar series of ritualized acts or "ceremonies of possession."[8] These included cargo inspections, annotations of bodily conditions (markings, such as scars from illnesses, scarification, and Atlantic branding), and a series of rituals, markings, and modes of commodification. In this sense, they were commodified, not only in relation to emerging markets and economic networks but also as a kind of royal good. In short, slavery was an expression of sovereign power and a disciplining force radiating throughout the commonwealth. Passages into the kingdom marked journeys into a new life in bondage within Castile's imperial order.

Throughout the Kingdom of Quito, enslaved people and the broader symbolism of slavery were very much alive. Slavery was both a productive force and a conduit through which the power of the sovereign might be said to reside and flow within the kingdom. Slaves' lives were marked by a *visible* or *seen* condition. They were enslaved, racialized others whose sociopolitical and estate rights as a corporate body within society were severely limited and ruled through sovereign acts *and* a predicament that had to be negotiated, resisted, and restructured inside of the monotheistic, Catholic sovereign community where they were both chattel and racialized "others" outside of their communities of origin—localized, ethnolinguistic polities where they might have enjoyed some level of legitimate "social life" or political standing within the power grid of official authority. This formulation seeks to account for how slaves were viewed or seen within a society or what they represented; what they reflected and occasioned within the monarchy; and how their presence must have affected any and all notions of personage, the body, and power within the order. Simultaneously, it calls attention to how enslaved Africans and their descendants negotiated the dual impositions of racial slavery *and* Spanish Catholic monarchy across time and space. Ultimately, this requires conceptualizations of slavery before and apart from an economic rationale of governance, before the rise of modern states and capitalist economies in the wake of the industrial and bourgeois revolutions—that is, before the ascendancy of the plantation complex.

This is not to suggest that labor and commercial investments did not drive slavery's demand in Quito. To be sure, slaves and slavery had real implications for commerce throughout the kingdom. Slaves circulated as cash and credit, and they were mobile capital—people with monetary value against which owners could borrow, even while assigning them to labor that produced cash that could in turn pay off previous notes and build wealth. Even in instances, such as the case of slavery in Quito, where slaves were often too expensive to be incorporated as laborers on a grand scale, they had a significant impact on the economy because of slavery's adaptability to temporal and physical circumstances. As luxury items, enslaved Africans occasioned the ostentatious display of wealth and status. Nevertheless, *Rivers of Gold* has insisted that also contributing to slaves' value were the ways in which they conferred *majesty*, the circulation of power within the realm, and their juridical importance as a way to govern all subjects.[9] This formulation recalls the ways in which slavery informed how everyday colonial subjects understood themselves in relation not only to slavery but also to the enslaved—living, breathing people who were the most unfree subjects in the realm and therefore the most vulnerable to sovereign acts.

Unlike Amerindians, enslaved blacks were not protected minors with legal representatives. Consequently, they were in the greatest need of royal mercy. Their branded, baptized, claimed, and valued bodies were emblematic of both the wages of sin and the hope of salvation. The brand of the crown, received at Cartagena, the port of entry, signified the slave's juridical standing as royal vassal and the king's territorial claims and duty. The governance of slaves, the disciplining of them physically, sexually, and politically, was emblematic of the kind of sovereignty that all vassals were ultimately subject to and pointed to the kind of fealty they were therefore expected to render. The presence of the marked, policed, claimed, punished, and redeemed slave body was a crucial aspect of the work of slavery within Spanish American societies—and may indeed be part of the answer to the question of how sovereignty was achieved or shored up throughout the realm. How much fealty the presence of slaves preserved is difficult to determine. Still, the sights, scenes, and sounds of slavery should remind us that, where slavery existed, everyone lived with its horrors. It is worth contemplating the kinds of self-governing impulses that such a spectacle might have produced.

In short, this reconceptualization of slavery points to its relationship to Spanish colonialism *and* monarchy. It was not a mere mode of organizing labor. It was the baseline against which all other social relations were measured. This raises pressing questions for studies of slave societies. From what perspective do we inquire into slave societies or societies with slaves? How would royal officials have understood their societies? How would slaveholders or aspiring slaveholders have understood their societies? Or is the very notion of slave society one grounded in more contemporary concerns with monetary capital? What did the average *indio*, *mestizo*, or Español see when he saw a slave, however seldom or frequently this might have been? What did it mean to live in a society where one saw, however infrequently, the brands or Atlantic scars that marked enslaved bodies? What did it mean to hear a slave wearing an iron collar with bells before actually seeing him? What did it mean to hear the lash? How did that impact or discipline others in relation to ecclesiastical and civil authority? How did such sights and sounds affect the way they related to their own bodies?[10]

These are difficult and thorny historical questions. But while it may be hard to measure precisely how these sights and sounds mattered, when placed in the context of other ceremonies—the auto-da-fé, the arrival of the viceroy, processionals, and displays of power and glory in Spanish America—one should be able to understand the work of slavery in its many guises. At base, slavery showcased the blunt force of colonial sovereignty and the violence of law. In cities where the Holy Office of the Inquisition resided and functioned, people marked as black, who were often enslaved, fell disproportionately under the eye and discipline of the office—a powerful reminder of the broad reach of the king.[11] Slaves receiving juridical redress from the church and the civil authorities also offered a powerful signal from whence justice came, thereby reinforcing the legitimacy of both slavery and sovereignty. In the end, the enslaved body, reclaimed from the disorienting Atlantic, inspected, baptized, and branded with the king's brand, served as a vivid and gripping reminder of the ways that power *ordered* society and, therefore, the ways that society must order itself. It shows the conditions under which alienated African captives confronted a world of death and forged social life.

If "social death was a receding horizon," as historian Vincent Brown insists, this was because slavery—the thing that social death defined—was so dependent upon people *living in bondage* to their masters *and* to the realm or the king. This state of affairs put sovereignty and mastery in direct conflict with human volition—thoughts, aspirations, urges, desires, beliefs. As Brown puts it, sovereignty extended "even into the most elemental realms: birth, hunger, health, fellowship, sex, death, and time."[12] This book has narrated precisely this struggle and the dialogues it produced. It is, therefore, a history of a slave society, an insistent one that hopes to force us to *see* the enslaved as they would have been seen in society, to look at *the slave* in our attempts to define and describe the life cycle of colonial Quito.

We are accustomed to the economic and demographic majesty of slavery within the context of plantation agriculture. But how does slavery fit within the political culture of a society without plantations? This work contributes to a growing body of literature on legal cultures and colonial society, and on slavery and the law, in three fundamental ways. First, it looks at slave legal action across time to understand how slaves' engagement with the law evolved. Second, it uses court cases as a window into the lived experiences of slaves, rather than seeing the court and legal systems as mere battlegrounds where slaves claimed rights and contested mastery. Third, and perhaps most radically, it insists that law penetrated society and slave life beyond the urban centers, where most historians have insisted slaves needed to reside in order to feel the law's mediating influence. While the high courts of Quito were more difficult for the enslaved in the goldfields of Popayán to access than for those in the urban centers, there are a number of cases that document the courts' interventions in rural affairs. A case of child murder attracted the attention of the high court in faraway Quito, as did cases filed by slaves who traveled from Barbacoas to Quito to register grievances on behalf of an entire community and claims filed by masters relating to the legitimacy of slave marriages in the gold-mining camps and Popayán's landed estates.[13] All of these cases point to nonurban slaves' engagement with the legal system, even from the most remote corners of Quito's northern frontier.

Slave suits from the Kingdom of Quito offer glimpses of slave life and display the ongoing struggles between slaves and slaveholders for mastery, autonomy, and rights. What emerges from a reading of more than five hundred civil, criminal, and ecclesiastical court cases is an expansive dialogue between slaves and slaveholders about slavery and slave life in the Spanish American slave society of Quito. Because most enslaved litigants were women, such sources also open a window into the gendered realities of slavery in colonial Quito. While several historians have employed some of these sources in the past, most have used them to discuss resistance or slave women's efforts to gain freedom in the late colonial and early Independence eras. Through their limited legal access we see slaves' small victories, as well as the heinous nature of slavery in Spanish America.

Spanish American laws governing slavery did indeed afford slaves legal redress in the face of abusive masters, the possibility of self-purchase, and access to the sacraments. But as this work shows, redress was often slow in coming. Here we see both what was at stake for slave laborers who sought legal action and the ways that the law and colonial jurisprudence occasioned (albeit unintentionally) the ability of the enslaved to argue with slaveholders about the just limitations of mastery. Yet the outcome of these processes and dialogues was a bit more pernicious than may be apparent at first glance. Legal redress, though it sometimes benefited the enslaved, served to further enshrine slavery and legitimate colonial authority, even as the creation of slave rights through case law over time slowly eroded the slavery ideal—absolute power of the master over his human property. Ultimately, if court cases between slaves and slaveholders are to be viewed as one locus of struggle or a space of resistance, the colonial state was the supreme victor. As historian Cynthia Milton argues, colonialism was forged precisely through processes of "tacit consent, voluntary appeals, and ideological hegemony"—the very stuff of slave legal action, as well as requests from all sides for courts to adjudicate the daily matters of slavery.[14]

Up close, *Rivers of Gold* has explored the many forms of slavery that developed in Quito and the ways they changed, eroded, and were maintained across time. It is about how enslaved Africans and Afro-Creoles helped to provoke such change, their limited access to freedom, and the way that slavery endured even as the colonial regime and economy faltered at the end of the eighteenth century.

NOTES

Abbreviations

ACC Archivo Central del Cauca, Popayán, Colombia
AHG Archivo Histórico del Guayas, Guayaquil, Ecuador
AMG Archivo Municipal de Guayaquil, Guayaquil, Ecuador
AMQ Archivo Municipal de Quito, Quito, Ecuador
ANHQ Archivo Nacional de Historia, Quito, Ecuador
APG Archivo de la Paroquia, El Sagrario, Guayaquil, Ecuador
APQ Archivo de la Paroquia, El Sagrario, Quito, Ecuador
EP/P Expedición de Escrituras Públicas
NP Notaria Primera
PN Protocolos Notaria
RHGQ *Relaciones Historico-Geograficas de La Audiencia de Quito*

Introduction

1. *RHGQ*, 1:550, 567, 518–25; "Informe sobre de la poblacion indigena de la gober-nacion de Popayán y sobre la necesidad de importar negros para la explotacion de sus minas." Auncibay was one of three *oidores* (justices), who along with one *fiscal* (crown attorney) served on Quito's Real Audiencia (Royal Audience or High Court). These three judges, along with the crown's attorney (*fiscal*), literally represented the embodiment of the king as his royal audience (*real audiencia*). The *audiencia* sat at the apex of the Span-ish colonial bureaucracy that attempted to rule over the territories that Spain deemed the Kingdom of Quito. Apart from edicts emanating from the king and the Council of the Indies, their rulings were second only to those of the viceroy, or vice king, who resided in Lima. The royal audience they afforded colonial subjects throughout the land represented the voice and governing aims of King Philip II. They also advised his high-ness in matters of good governance, order, and commerce, all of which constituted royal concerns or matters upon which sovereignty and order rested. See Andrien, "Legal and Administrative," and Herzog, *Upholding Justice.*

2. There were at least three other such petitions to the crown prior and after the 1592 petition. One, sent in 1615, was sent by the members of the Popayán town council to the Council of the Indies. One such petition penned by Auncibay pertained to mining operations in the south-central highlands of Quito near Zamora and Zaruma. These petitions concerned royal efforts to limit the use of indigenous peoples in the mines and thus reflected prevailing norms around colonial labor status and vassalage at that time. See Lane, *Quito 1599*; Marzahl, *Town in the Empire*; and Bryant, "Finding Gold, Forming Slavery," for discussions of similar petitions for labor subsidies. See also O'Toole, *Bound Lives*, for similar petitions from northern Peru.

3. Auncibay actually penned two proposals. Together they argued for installing four thousand enslaved Africans in the region's two chief gold-mining centers: Popayán and Zaruma. See *RHGQ*, 1:84–89, 550, 567–68, 518–26.

4. Throughout this book I will refer to "governance" as a set of practices, protocols, laws, and customs aimed at conducting social practice, economic exchange, and comportment. I will at times use the term interchangeably with "governing." By "government" I mean to suggest more than bureaucracy and state formation, thus situating governance, government, and governing within the broader sociocultural power matrix.

5. More, *Utopia*, Book 2, 168–69.

6. *RHGQ*, 1:550, 567, 518–26.

7. Morgan, *Laboring Women*.

8. O'Toole, *Bound Lives*.

9. Auncibay's petition suggests the ways in which free black subjection was constituted through labor tribute as well. F. Bowser, *The African Slave*, 17–18; Lockhart, *Spanish Peru*, 191–92. On Indian slavery and the prevalence of slaveholding across every stratum of society, see ibid., 179–80.

10. Herzog, *Upholding Justice*; Black, *The Limits of Gender Domination*; Lane, "Captivity and Redemption"; Gauderman, *Women's Lives*.

11. J. Miller, *The Problem of Slavery*, 1–35.

12. V. Brown, "Social Death."

13. J. Miller, *The Problem of Slavery*, 6.

14. Restall, *The Black Middle*, 281–82, 402 (n. 7). It is important and appropriate to cite Frank Tannenbaum's words here: "Slavery changed the form of the state, the nature of property, the system of law, the organization of labor, the role of the church as well as its character, the notions of justice, ethics, ideas of right and wrong. Slavery influenced the architecture, the cooking, the politics, the literature, the morals of the entire group— white and black, men and women, old and young. . . . Nothing escaped . . . nothing and no one." *Slave & Citizen*, 117. Tannenbaum was not speaking here of large-scale slavery, small-scale slavery, or mere economic outputs—the primary variables driving Restall's interpretation regarding the Yucatan and his responses to Bennett regarding Mexico City or to my own work regarding Quito. Rather, Tannenbaum was concerned with social order, mores, practices, and the way that any amount of slavery (large or small) served to impact social practice, as I argue, and thereby constituted a slave society. In short, we need approaches to slavery that are not overdetermined by economic rationales. See Berlin, *Many Thousands Gone*, for his conceptualization of slave societies. See also Herman Bennett, *Africans in Colonial Mexico*, and Sherwin K. Bryant, "Finding Gold, Forming Slavery." On the need to rethink slavery, see J. Miller, *The Problem of Slavery*, and C. Brown, *Moral Capital*.

15. Lane, *Quito 1599*, xiii.

16. For a broader discussion of this historiography, see Vinson, "African (Black) Diaspora History," and Bryant, O'Toole, and Vinson, "Introduction." On a history of "A Black Andes," see O'Toole, *Bound Lives*, 161–64.

17. Early colonial laws governing the travel of Spanish vassals initially allowed them to bring enslaved subjects and household servants prior to Castile's legal development of the slave trade beginning in 1513.

18. In spite of the fact that the crown would be the chief financier in the importation of these slaves, Auncibay's proposed slaves were not to be "royal slaves" per se, that is, slaves owned outright by the crown. The crown would hold a stake in Auncibay's proposed shipments and thereby placed serious limitations on such matters as the conditions under which the slaves would be sold, when masters would assume title of the slaves, the conditions of resale of the slaves, and the possibilities for mobility within the order. Ideally, these enslaved captives would be sold and held privately, if continually governed by the strictures of this royally subsidized installation. As principal shareholder, the crown stipulated the terms and conditions of sale, manumission, and daily regulation. If the proposal failed, however, the slaves and the territories into which they were introduced could be confiscated and held indefinitely as royal slaves. In this sense, Auncibay's proposal was structured in ways that suggested that at least for a term these captives would be royal slaves. Royal slavery was a particular form of slavery in the Spanish transoceanic empire, offering the crown sole dominion and access to royal slaves. The practice developed usually in places where the crown found it necessary for the purposes of colonial development and use in public works, garrisons, fortifications, or circumstances wherein the colonial state confiscated slave-operated mines and estates. In distinguishing between royal slaves and other enslaved subjects, however, this study insists that the crown held a juridical stake in the circulation of all slaves and governed their owners in part through the regulation of slavery. All slavery occurred with leave of the king in accordance with Christian norms of honor and the exercise of proper dominion. For a discussion of "royal" or "state" slavery, see Díaz, *The Virgin, the King, and the Royal Slaves*, and Jennings, "War as the 'Forcing House of Change.'"

19. For these principles, see *Las siete partidas*; Solórzano Pereira, *Política Indiana*; and *Recopilación de leyes*. See also MacLachan, *Spain's Empire*. Circa 1615, Felipe Guaman Poma de Ayala placed slavery and the proper governance of enslaved blacks squarely on the royal docket with his *El primer nueva corónica y buen gobierno*.

20. Agamben, *The Kingdom and the Glory*; Cañeque, *The King's Living Image*; Andrien, *Crisis in Decline*; Herzog, *Upholding Justice*; Grafe, *Distant Tyranny*.

21. J. Miller, *Problem of Slavery*, 16–22.

22. Burns, *Into the Archive*, 1–15.

23. Seed, *Ceremonies of Possession*.

24. Ibid. For a discussion of writing as violence and possession, see Rabasa, *Writing Violence*, and Rappaport and Salomon, *Beyond the Lettered City*.

25. Lane, *Quito 1599*.

26. Benton, *Law and Colonial Cultures*; Owensby, *Empire of Law and Indian Justice*; Grafe, *Distant Tyranny* and "A Stakeholder Empire."

27. Black, *Limits of Gender Domination*; Haring, *The Spanish Empire*; Phelan, *The People and the King* and "Authority and Flexibility in the Spanish Imperial Bureaucracy"; Kagan, *Lawsuits and Litigants*; Cutter, *The Legal Culture of Northern New Spain*; MacKay, *The Limits of Royal Authority*; Nader, *Liberty in Absolutist Spain*; Owens, *"By My Absolute Royal Authority"*; Gauderman, *Women's Lives in Colonial Quito*; Cañeque, *The King's Living Image*; Irigoin and Grafe, "Bargaining for Absolutism"; Premo, *Children of the Father King*.

28. R. Scott, "Paper Thin" and "Slavery and Law"; Fuente, "Slaves and the Creation of Legal Rights in Cuba"; Fuente and Gross, "Comparative Studies of Law"; Grinberg, "Freedom Suits and Civil Law"; Gross, "Race, Law and Comparative History."

29. Bryant, "Enslaved Rebels, Fugitives and Litigants"; Echeverri, "Enraged to the Limits of Despair"; Fuente, "Slaves and the Creation of Legal Rights"; Premo, *Children of the Father King* and "An Equity against the Law"; Owensby, *Empire of Law and Indian Justice.*

30. McKinley "Till Death Do Us Part"; O'Toole, *Bound Lives.*

31. McKinley, "Till Death Do Us Part," 389.

32. Hesse, "Forgotten Like a Bad Dream"; Beckles, "Sex and Gender in the Historiography of Caribbean Slavery"; V. Brown, "Social Death and Political Life"; Camp, *Closer to Freedom*; Young, *Rituals of Resistance*; O'Toole, *Bound Lives*; Echeverri; "Enraged to the Limits of Despair"; Hahn, *A Nation under Our Feet*, 163–215.

33. McKinley, "Till Death Do Us Part," 389.

34. Mumford, *Vertical Empire*; O'Toole, *Bound Lives*; Stern, *Peru's Indian Peoples*; Ramírez, *The World Upside Down*; Spaulding, *Huarochirí.*

35. This study contributes to the vibrant literature that uses slave-trading nomenclature as a guide back in time to ethno-cultural zones. In a similar vein, I use slave-trading monikers to contextualize African social practice in the Andes. This study insists, however, that scholars look beyond the ethnographic promise of the slave trade's archive to expose the colonial practices of race governance these monikers indexed, mapped, and constituted over time. I argue that the very practices embedded within slave trading—branding, baptizing, and binding slaves for the development and sustaining of the trade, its markets, valuations, and currents—were all constitutive practices of race governance. In this sense, the work of race and *casta* was not to index thought or biological fixity upon bodies but to forge differentiated subject status upon Africans for subordinated governance within the colony. The work of early modern race governance (including *casta* and other methods of marking and ruling non-Europeans) was, therefore, the work of constituting white, Christian, European authority and dominion, not biological thought. The work of *casta* was, in this sense, the work of race governance, which thereby constituted race over time through governing norms within the broader social order. On the "work of race and the work of casta," see O'Toole, *Bound Lives*, 164–67. This is to suggest that race was less a unified system of thought concerned always and already with fixity, or even a social construction regarding identification, and more a series of colonial practices aimed at constituting non-Europeanness for differentiated and subordinated rule within Europe's expanding monarchical orders.

36. Hesse, "Racialized Modernity."

37. Hesse, "Self-Fulfilling Prophecy," and "Racialized Modernity."

38. Again, it is important to note that this "difference" was not bodily or biological but an imposition of the gaze and European governance. See also Jennifer Morgan, *Laboring Women.*

39. Bennett, "Sons of Adam"; van Deusen, "Seeing *Indios.*"

40. Many notions and images of blacks and blackness were in circulation at the turn of the fifteenth century and well into the sixteenth. See Larissa Brewer Garcia's discussion of the varying images and notions of blackness in circulation in "Beyond Babel,"

19–36. Indeed, even as some subjects who were deemed "black" were allowed a modicum of shared governance, this moment of conjuncture was characterized by emergent practices of inscribing blackness through slaving norms of marking, binding, and governing the social, spiritual, and commercial lives of enslaved black subjects of varying monikers as non-European subjects, abject, and undeserving of self-governance. These were aimed to situate them geopolitically in relation to Castile for governing and ruling to the good of the order. Bennett, "Sons of Adam."

41. Van Deusen, "Seeing *Indios*"; Bennett, *Africans in Colonial Mexico.*

42. Blumenthal, *Enemies and Familiars*, 1–6.

43. This moment saw the encroachment of Christians and Muslims upon the domains of sub-Saharan Africans who were deracinated, described, marked, and governed as *black and slave*. While slavery existed in Africa and sub-Saharan Africans were traded as slaves throughout the Mediterranean and to the East, the scale and increasing association of slavery with notions of *blackness* proved elemental to the development of Christian-Ibero monarchies and their claiming of the Americas. This is to write conquest, exploration, Christian colonization of the Americas, and the expansion of the abodes of Christendom and Islam as coterminus processes within the epoch of early modernity. Blackness as a mode of governing and constituting "Africans" and "Africa" was made, inscribed, and developed within "coloniality" beginning in the fifteenth century. Ware, "Slavery in Islamic Africa"; Robinson, *Black Marxism*. On coloniality and diaspora, see Iton, "Still Life," 28.

44. Blumenthal, *Enemies and Familiars.*

45. Cedric Robinson delineates beautifully how Genoese capital provided the funding for Iberian transoceanic expansion and the early development of the Atlantic slave trade and African labor through racial subjugation. Embedded in his narration of the development of what he terms "racial capital," however, are the governments and governing practices of early modernity. See Robinson, *Black Marxism*, 101–20.

46. Blumenthal, *Enemies and Familiars*, 1–6.

47. Rout, *The African Experience*; Robinson, *Black Marxism*; Williams, *Capitalism and Slavery*; Bennett, *Colonial Blackness.*

48. The early modern Atlantic practice of constituting enslavable blackness was applied within sub-Saharan Africa, imported to the Caribbean, and applied to the landscapes and peoples there. On matters of *casta*, color, and Castilian adjudication of slave status, see van Deusen, "Seeing *Indios*." On early modern Atlantic associations with Africanity and enslavability, see Green, "Building Slavery in the Atlantic World." For a discussion of the expanding association of blackness and slavery in Islamic West Africa between the years 1400 and 1800, see Ware, "Slavery in Islamic Africa." Finally, on mapping and Aristotelian notions of difference, natural law, and the right to dispossess, see Wey-Gómez, *Tropics of Empire*, and Huffine, *Producing Christians from Half-Men and Beasts.*

49. Ware, "Slavery in Islamic Africa"; van Deusen, "Seeing *Indios*"; Wey-Gomez, *Tropics of Empire*; Torres, Martínez, and Nirenberg, *Race and Blood.*

50. On politics as the absence of a proper foundation, see Rancière, *Dis-agreement.* On politics as provocation and the rule of governance as a project, see Li, *Will to Improve*, 10–12.

51. Burns, *Into the Archive*, 1–3.

52. Thomas, *Rivers*.

53. Grafe, *Distant Tyranny*.

54. Thomas, *Rivers*, 155.

55. The Islamic imperial vision also had a long history that inscribed blackness upon sub-Saharan African territories and peoples through slaving. Constructing the abode of Islam increasingly vis-à-vis blackness, unbelief, and slavery, between 1400 and 1800 Muslims came to enslave sub-Saharan Africans on an unprecedented scale. Yet the link between blackness and slavery under Islam remains underconsidered. Still, the full weight of current historiography points to old linkages between blackness and slave status proliferating in the context of Christian and Muslim imperial advances into Atlantic Africa and the Americas. Governing practices deployed by Christians, Muslims, and those in the New World constituted Africa as a non-European, unbelieving, and enslavable colonial frontier. See Ware, "Slavery in Islamic Africa," for one of the most current and insightful treatments of the question of slavery, blackness, and Islam. See also Green, "Building Slavery in the Atlantic World."

56. Van Deusen, "Seeing *Indios*," 207.

57. Ibid.

58. Thomas, *Rivers*, 155. On the theme of legitimacy in late medieval Valencia and the tremendous diversity of slave origins, see Blumenthal, *Enemies and Familiars*, 20.

59. Van Deusen, "Seeing *Indios*," 205–6. See also "Instrucción al comendador fray Nicolás de Ovando," Granada, 16/IX/1501, in Konetzke, *Colección de documentos*, 4–6, and Pacheco, Cárdenas, and Torres de Mendoza, *Colección de documentos inéditos, relativos al descubrimiento, conquista y colonización*, 21:209.

60. *RHGQ*, 1:550, 567, 518–26.

61. Mumford, *Vertical Empire*; O'Toole, *Bound Lives*.

62. Rout, *The African*; Robinson, *Black Marxism*.

63. Rout, *African Experience in Spanish America*, 22.

64. See Susan Buck-Morss's treatment of paintings by Franz Hals to showcase the sociocultural importance of black slavery in the formation of Dutchness and Dutch imperialism in "Hegel and Haiti," 824–27.

65. Ibid.

66. Andrien, *The Kingdom of Quito*, 36; Visita de la Gobernación de Popayán (1797), in Diego Antonio Nieto, ed., *Cespedia*, nos. 45–46, suppl. 4 (January–June 1983). See also Egardo Pérez Morales, "Naturaleza, paisaje y memoria: Alturas y Ciudades del Reino de Quito en la experiencia del siglo XVIII," in *Procesos Revista Ecuatoriana de Historia* 28 (II semestre, 2008, Quito): 5–28.

67. For examples of this, see Lane, *Quito 1599*; Gauderman, *Women's Lives in Colonial Quito*; and Milton, *The Many Meanings of Poverty*.

68. For a useful synthesis of these practices in Brazil, see Robinson, *Black Marxism*, 149–50.

69. Walker, "'He Outfitted His Family.'"

70. Cañeque, *The King's Living Image*.

71. Foucault, *Power-Knowledge*, 116.

72. Lane, *Quito 1599*, 122–29.

73. By the end of the century, Popayán was producing 90 percent of all gold smelted in Quito. Indeed, the 42,000 kilograms of gold the mines produced between 1535 and 1639 were far from insignificant since they accounted for a full 23 percent of all gold registered in Seville during this period. Ibid., 171–72.

74. Although Almaguer was home to 3,520 Amerindians, only 636 were employed in mining by the late sixteenth century. *RHGQ*, 1:26–29.

75. *RHGQ*, 1:84–89.

76. Lane, *Quito 1599*, 58.

77. *RHGQ*, 1:15–24.

78. Ibid.

79. *RHGQ*, 1:531.

80. By this date there were approximately 250–300 enslaved blacks in Quito city, 350 in Guayaquil, 2,000 in the district of Popayán, 300 in Cuenca and Loja, and 150 in Zaruma; an additional 150 were dispersed throughout the central coastal and highland Corregimientos. See *RHGQ*, vols. 1 and 2; Lane, *Quito 1599*, 58; and West, *Colonial Placer Mining in Colombia*. In Cuenca alone, at least thirty wills, inventories, and land sales from 1587 to 1620 feature slaves. In addition, upward of one thousand documents pertaining to slavery and freedom for 1587 to 1748 are located in the provincial Archivo Histórico Nacional del Cuenca. I thank Debbie Truhan for sharing these citations with me by personal correspondence, October 16, 2000.

81. V. Brown, "Social Death," 1248.

82. Camp, *Closer to Freedom*.

83. This is not an attempt to return voyeuristically to the scene of the grotesque, but rather an effort to showcase the ways in which the legal archive actually reveals the violence of slavery and law as enacted upon the body as modes of subjection and racial rule. See Hartman, *Scenes of Subjection*, and Moten, *In the Break*, for an expansive dialogue regarding violence and the recuperation of the black past.

Chapter One

1. Van Deusen, "Diaspora, Bondage, and Intimacy in Lima, 1535-1555"; Salomon and Schwartz, *Encyclopedia of Native Peoples*.

2. The war within the Inka Empire began shortly after the death of the Sapa Inca Huana Capac in 1527 most likely from a smallpox or measles epidemic that spread from new Spanish settlements to the north and along the Pacific coast near Túmbez and Atacames. See Andrien, *Andean Worlds*, and Cook, *Born to Die*.

3. On slaves as military auxiliaries, see Lockhart, *Spanish Peru*, 171-72; Bowser, *The African Slave*, 3-7; and Restall, "Slave Conquistador." The arming of slaves remains an undertheorized aspect of early colonial government, sovereignty, and jurisprudence. Useful and recent exceptions include Vinson and Restall, "Black Soldiers, Native Soldiers"; and Brown and Morgan, *Arming Slaves*.

4. As Rudolph Ware states, "There are three major components of any system of slavery: reduction of human beings to servitude, distribution of the enslaved within and between societies, and the nature of servitude within a society. These categories are utilitarian, not absolute. Biological reproduction of slaves belongs in categories one

and three. Category three implies the continuous reproduction of the meanings of category one without the initial act of capture or birth. Examples could be multiplied. The categories are heuristic aids, not precise hermeneutical tools." Ware, "Slavery in Islamic Africa."

5. Van Deusen, "Diasporas, Bondage, and Intimacy" and "The Intimacies of Bondage"; Salomon, *Native Lords*; Powers, *Andean Journeys*; Ramirez, *The World Upside Down*.

6. "An encomienda is generally described as a royal grant, in reward for meritorious service at arms, of the right to enjoy the tributes of Indians within a certain boundary, with the duty of protecting them and seeing to their religious welfare. An encomienda was not a grant of land. In Peru the grant came from the governor or viceroy, the crown taking no active part in the process, and particularly in the first years after conquest, the terms of the grant went beyond the right to collect tributes, specifically entitling the encomendero or grantee to use the Indians in mines or agricultural enterprises. In practice grants were assigned not only to reward service at arms, though that was usually a prerequisite, but also for social and political considerations. And the encomenderos, leaping over technicalities, made their encomiendas the basis of great estates even if they did not legally own the land. Historically, the encomienda is situated on a line of development leading from the march lord domain of the European Middle Ages to the Spanish American hacienda or large estate of the seventeenth century and later." Lockhart, *Spanish Peru*, 11.

7. Andrien, *Andean Worlds*, 44–45.

8. Bowser, *The African Slave*, 8.

9. Andrien, *Andean Worlds*, 44–45.

10. Saco, *Historia de la esclavitud*, 4:205; Tardieu, *El Negro*, 19–25.

11. On the matter of personalistic power, see J. Miller, *The Problem of Slavery*; Bowser, *The African Slave*, 8; and Lockhart, *Spanish Peru*, 180–81, esp. 192.

12. Bowser, *The African Slave*, 15–17; Andrien, *Andean Worlds*, 45.

13. Bowser, *The African Slave*, 4–8.

14. Ibid.; Lockhart, *Spanish Peru*, 179.

15. On *fueros*, see Grafe, *Distant Tyranny*; Ben Vinson III, *Bearing Arms*; and Nader, *Liberty in Absolutist Spain*.

16. Bowser, *The African Slave*, 9–11; Tardieu, *El Negro*, 25–26.

17. Bowser, *The African Slave*, 9–10.

18. Ibid., 10.

19. Ibid., 10; Tardieu, *El Negro*, 25–26.

20. This was a concern that would continue to plague town councils and efforts to govern slaveholders. In 1665, the Guayaquil town council restated this prohibition against arming enslaved subjects or allowing them to mount horses. See AMG, tomo XII, *Actas del Cabildo Colonial de Guayaquil*, folio 25.

21. Tardieu, *El Negro*, 25–26.

22. On "moral economies"—systems of credit wherein religious entities such as convents served as local lenders—see Kathryn Burns, *Colonial Habits*. On slavery, captivity, and redemption in Quito, see Lane, "Captivity and Redemption." On slaveholding convents and monasteries, particularly those with ties to Quito's gold-mining sector as well as agro-pastoral estates in the Cauca Valley, see Bryant, "Finding Gold, Forming

Slavery." On Jesuit slaveholding as tied to *obrajes* and agro-pastoral enterprises, see Cushner, *Farm and Factory*; Andrien, *The Kingdom of Quito*; Coronel, *El valle sangriento*; and Lavalle, *Amor y opresion*.

23. Tardieu, *El Negro*, 20. On the importance of canon law in governing colonial life and slavery, see Bennett, *Africans*, and Tannenbaum, *Slave and Citizen*.

24. Herzog, *Upholding Justice*, 21.

25. Ibid.

26. Gonzalez Rumazo, *Libro Segundo*, 18.

27. Ibid., 19–34; Jurado Noboa, "Algunos reflexiones," 93–101.

28. For evidence that such punishments were indeed enforced, see Lane, "Captivity and Redemption," 242 (n. 50). See also Carlos Aguirre, *Agentes*. See also the proscriptions of Justice Auncibay in *RHGQ*, 1:518–26.

29. *Recopilación*, tomo ii, libro vii, titulo v, ley xxiij, folio 289v. Still, the crown endorsed the penalty of death by hanging for those who committed the gravest of crimes in colonial society. Ibid., folio 288.

30. *RHGQ*, 1:518–26.

31. *Recopilación*, tomo ii, libro vii, titulo v, ley xij, folio 286v.

32. The term "delinquent" here suggests the continuum between marronage and petite marronage, or the practice of slaves absenting themselves for periods of days for respite and to see loved ones as opposed to attempts at permanent escape. Ibid., ley xxj, folio 288.

33. "En la provincia de Tierra Firme (Panama) han sucedido muchas muertes, robos, danos, hecho por los negros cimarrones algados, y ocultos en los terminas, y arcabacas." Ibid.

34. Royal admonishments to American courts also commanded that judiciaries ensure that free blacks who adhered to the rule of law were not molested or provoked to unruly behavior. The Real Cédula of 1540, for example, ordered American courts to "hear and provide justice to those [blacks] that proclaim free status . . . and do justice, and rule, that in this they are not mistreated by their masters." Ibid.

35. See Andrien, *Andean Worlds*, 49–50, and Mumford, *Vertical Empire*, 1–71.

36. Davidson, "Slave Control," 85–86.

37. On the absolutist colonial state, see Cañeque, *The King's Living Image*; Bennett, *Africans in Colonial Mexico*; and Osorio, "The King in Lima." See also Grafe, *Distant Tyranny*.

38. Nancy E. van Deusen, for example, charts the increased policing that *beatas* (pious lay women with informal religious vows, often black or some other *casta*) experienced in late sixteenth- and early seventeenth-century Lima. See *Between the Sacred and the Worldly*.

39. *Recopilación*, tomo ii, libro vii, titulo v, ley xxij, folios 288v–289v; tomo ii, libro vii, titulo xviij, ley vij, folio 88; tomo ii, libro vii, titulo v, ley xxv, folio 289v–290; tomo ii, libro vii, titulo v, ley xxij, folio 288v; and tomo ii, libro vii, titulo v, ley xix, folio 287v; Hall, *Social Control*, 74–78. See also Jane Landers, *Black Society* and "Cimarrón Ethnicity and Cultural Adaptation."

40. For a discussion of the Dutch slave trade to the region during this period of depression, see O'Toole, *Bound Lives*, and McKinley, "Till Death Do Us Part."

41. AMG, tomo III, 1650–59, *Actas del Cabildo Ciudad de Guayaquil*, folios 7–10.

42. Ibid., folios 99–100. See also Clayton, *Caulkers and Carpenters*, 148.

43. AMG, tomo III, 1650–57, *Actas del Cabildo Ciudad de Guayaquil*, folios 24v, 25, 26.

44. Ibid., folio 35, Antonio Hidalgo.

45. Ibid., folios 141–142.

46. This study insists that the label that followed enslaved people had value as a juridical category that shaped legal possibilities of slavery as well as the limitations of mastery. As "*esclavo cautivo subjecto de servidumbre* [enslaved captive subjects of servitude]," the enslaved had no corporate "protected" status but were rather subject to a life of servitude, surveillance, and Christian service within the order. They occasioned, however, a particular kind of colonial status and authority for the vassals who claimed dominion over them. It was their governance by slaveholding vassals and authority figures that slavery served to enclose and occasion.

47. Mangan, *Trading Roles*; Andrien and Adorno, *Transatlantic Encounters*; Brockington, *Blacks, Indians, and Spaniards*.

48. Andrien, *The Kingdom of Quito*.

49. Ibid., 15–16.

50. Powers, *Andean Journeys*; Alchon, *Native Disease*.

51. Restall, *The Black Middle*, 280–82, 402 (n. 7).

52. Lane, "Captivity and Redemption"; Gauderman, *Women's Lives in Colonial Quito*, 59, 64, 74, 76, 79, 81.

53. For a highly original and informed discussion of the ways the crown sought to govern these practices as well as the ways the enslaved made use of material resources for self-fashioning, see Walker, "'He Outfitted His Family.'"

54. See Lane, "Captivity and Redemption," 61, and Tardieu, *El negro*.

55. Palmer, *Slaves of the White God*; Villa-Flores, *Dangerous Speech* and "'To Lose One's Soul'"; Bennett, *Africans in Colonial Mexico*; Proctor, "Gender and the Manumission of Slaves in New Spain"; Bristol, *Christians, Blasphemers*; von Germeten, *Black Blood Brotherhoods*.

56. *RHGQ*, 2:203–7.

57. Andagoya, *Narrative of the Proceedings*.

58. Williams, "Resistance and Rebellion"; Lane, *Quito 1599*, 215–25, "Taming the Master," and "Transition from *Encomienda*."

59. West, *The Pacific Lowlands of Colombia*.

60. *RHGQ*, 2:203–7.

61. Calero, *Chiefdoms under Siege*, 152–53.

62. Lane, "Transition from *Encomienda*."

63. Lane, "Mining the Margins," 104.

64. Another Barbacoan elite purchased an entire mining operation in 1676, an enterprise that included twenty-eight slaves, water rights, plantation groves, and other items. See Lane, "Transition from *Encomienda*," 84. Juan Philupo de los Rios was likely to have come from the Fulupo Kingdom situated along the Casamance River in West Africa. See Colmenares, *Popayán*, 48–54, and Thornton, *Africa and Africans*, 184–205. While Colmenares argues that "most" of Popayán's slaves (after 1680) embarked from the coasts of West Africa that surround the mouth of the Niger and Congo Rivers in

the south, chapter 2 of this study shows that Popayán's slave market was characterized consistently by heterogeneity. Lane, "Transition from *Encomienda*," 85.

65. Lane, "Mining the Margins"; Bryant, "Finding Gold, Forming Slavery."

66. Lane, "Taming the Master," 481. See also Twinam, *Miners, Merchants, and Farmers*, which notes that Antioquia was registering an average of 22,485 castellanos of gold per year from 1670 to 1749.

67. Zulugua, "Clientelismo y guerrillas."

Chapter Two

1. Stephanie Smallwood's concept of "saltwater slavery" allows for a conceptualization of an enslaved life caught within the currents of diaspora. These currents and diasporic conditions continued into and were constitutive of the Afro-Andes. See her *Saltwater Slavery*, 3–6.

2. ACC, NP, tomo 19, folios 275v–277. Torijano and Captain Juan Gonzalez (Honda property holder), for whom he registered the slaves, were a part of a growing network of slave traders who brought increasingly diverse cargoes of ethnic Africans into the region.

3. Torijano sold or donated the majority of these individuals within a few days. It was unusual for factors to waste time dispensing with their caches of human cargoes; they usually sold the majority of them within a month or two of their arrival. Ibid., 301, 304, 305, 308, 308v, 319, 320, 321, 322.

4. Hesse, "Racialized Modernity" and "Creolizing the Political."

5. Martínez, *Genealogical Fictions*; Silverblatt, *Modern Inquisitions*; Bennett, *Colonial Blackness*; Cope, *The Limits*; O'Toole, *Bound Lives*; Burns, "Unfixing Race"; O'Hara et al., *Imperial Subjects*.

6. Early modern monarchs and colonial officials deployed racial slavery within an overlapping set of colonial technologies that conferred elite status, honor, and prestige. Slavery, of course, promoted and policed commerce even as enslaved subjects presented a range of concerns for masters and colonial officials alike around the managing and conditioning of the social order. The bureaucracies that slavery and slave trading produced and promoted allowed the colonial state to gain meaningful intelligence on all subjects. In claiming slaves as royal subjects, the king did not displace slave masters. He did not undermine their dominion or remove their ability to derive personalistic power, acquire real estate, or perform honor and prestige through the public display of the enslaved black bodies they claimed as their New World possessions. As Rachel O'Toole has remarked, "slave masters ruled." After all, colonial elites sought to rule conquered Indians even as the crown treated them as corporate vassals. Slave masters and *encomenderos* alike (often one and the same) were entitled to rule, but always in the interest of the kingdom and the overall public peace. Just as the notion of "I obey but do not comply" was law (Cañeque and Grafe), so too was the notion that a slave master just like an unjust prince could be justly dispossessed of his dominion. This suggests that enslaved blacks were indeed "more than chattel," that more was commodified than a price or personal proprietary claims. Indeed, as historian Christopher Brown has remarked, "not all interests are economic" interests. The multiple values and interests

that slaves and slavery embodied proved elemental to the economy and government in the colonial north Andes. As objects of royal governance and oversight, slaves, along with the household estates they forged and the markets and networks their marked bodies constituted, proved to be critical subjects of the empire—people whose bodily subjection, souls, and territorial contexts conditioned colonial commerce and governing norms. Installing foreign subjects by leave of the crown had the effect of claiming regions, creating fractured sovereignty, and forging market economies within distant regions throughout the Americas. Notions of just rule were extended to slaveholders and royal officials in the New World, yet under the sovereign claims of the crown of Castile. This is why masters could be dispossessed. But not in a way that undermined slavery other colonial honorifics. Marking the enslaved as royal subjects did not challenge slavery, nor did it add value to black life. Rather, it marked slaves as the most dispossessed and subjugated people, abject human subjects through which the crown and its surrogates (slaveholders and royal officials) claimed and harnessed natural resources and established rule over vast and distant territories of the Americas. Merchants and indigenous caciques all sought dominion over African conscripts to racial modernity as an avenue to wield the accoutrements of European power, prestige, and market-based "racial capital" (Cedric Robinson, *Black Marxism*).

7. Van Deusen, "Seeing *Indios*"; Floyd-Wilson, *English Ethnicity and Race*.

8. Li, *Will to Improve*, 10–12.

9. Hesse, "Self-Fulfilling Prophecy," 164. To understand Castilian-designed slavery, we must break with the labor metaphor of slavery as well as the biological and ideological notions scholars have established about race. Recognizing slavery as an installation of governance predicated on race relations allows us to consider an alternative colonial history of race and slavery. Although marked upon, and in part through, physical bodies, race was "historically and geographically constructed by European colonial-derived regimes as a governing practice to distinguish between 'whiteness/Europeanness' and 'non-Europeanness/nonwhiteness' in terms of regulations, affinities, spaces, and discourses in modernity's colonies." On "race thinking," see Arendt, *Origins*, and Silverblatt, *Modern Inquisitions*. For a critical reading of these formulations around race and ideology, see Hesse, "Racialized Modernity."

10. Van Deusen, "Seeing *Indios*," 213–14; Rappaport, "'Asi lo paresçe por su aspeto,'" 601–31; Herzog, "Identities and Process of Identification."

11. Bennett, "Sons of Adam."

12. Van Deusen, "Seeing *Indios*," 212–14; Rappaport, "'Asi lo paresçe por su aspeto.'"

13. Smallwood, *Saltwater Slavery*.

14. O'Toole, "From the Rivers of Guinea"; van Deusen, "Seeing *Indios*."

15. Recall that the crown initially desired *ladinos* in its territories, a preference soon abandoned for *bozales*, with special provisions meant to limit the acceptance of enslaved Africans from Muslim kingdoms into the Americas. The Portuguese crown mandated slaves be baptized before departing the shores of Atlantic Africa. See Newson and Minchim, *From Capture to Sale*.

16. AHG, EP/P Santiago de Guayaquil, November 28, 1712, p. 85, entry 137.133, folios 186v–198.

17. See Sandoval, *Un tratado sobre la esclavitud*, 1647.

18. Newson and Minchim, *From Capture to Sale*.

19. See the series of sales registered by notaries in eighteenth-century Guayaquil, noting the official licensed shipping company and the comment *sin bautizar* (without baptism).

20. ACC, Protocolos, NP, tomo 19.

21. ACC, Protocolos, NP, tomo 19, folios 17–19v, 28–29, 77–78.

22. While they had arrived in Cartagena de Indias in 1698, it was not until 1700 that they made their way into the Gobernación de Popayán through the river port of Honda. This seems odd, even when allowing for time spent in Cartagena and travel to Popayán, and even when one considers that river travel was suspended for approximately five months during the rainy season. Chandler, "Health and Slavery," 48–95.

23. The complete Spanish phrase is *como huesos en costal y alma en boca*. One also finds the phrase *por huesos en costal*, or, as in this instance, simply *casi muriendo*. Normally, however, the latter did not constitute a disclaimer such as those found in typical sales transactions but was a phrase commonly found in registries of new arrivals. See Bowser's *African Slave in Colonial Peru*, 84, which credits Fernando Ortiz for making sense of the term in Spanish. See also Lane, *Quito 1599*, 65, 244 (n. 22).

24. On seasoning, see Chandler, "Health and Slavery," and Palmer, *Human Cargoes*, 59, 61–62.

25. Chandler, "Health and Slavery," 73–75.

26. He discounted the group by the price of two slaves, or three *piesas de indias*.

27. Colmenares, *Historia económica y social*.

28. Ibid., 41. Among the more prominent slaveholders one finds La Marqueesa Dionisa Pérez Marique, daughter of the president of the *audiencia*, upon whose death the slaves passed to the Society of Jesus, as well as Don Christóbal de Mosquera Figueroa, who held at least forty-five slaves; Don Francisco José de Arboleda, who held forty-two; Don Pedro de Valencia, who held twenty-eight; and Don Fernando Baca de Ortega, who held twenty. Ibid.

29. While the document does not cite perceived ethnicity, it includes a general description of each captive. Much like the *despacho* cited in chapter 4, careful attention was paid to scarification, wounds, and blemishes due to smallpox. ANHQ, Protocolos, NP, act. 250, folios 289v–291.

30. ANHQ, Esclavos, caja 2, exp. January 1, 1713.

31. ANHQ, Esclavos, caja 1, exp. September 28, 1700, folio 1.

32. María de la Cruz—whose moniker *Guinea* betrays only that she was an ethnic African, since the Upper Guinea was by this time almost completely out of the slave trading business—had been the slave of Rosa de Solarte, who had purchased the woman from Doña Ignasia de Texada in 1715. ANHQ, Esclavos, caja 2, exp. November 4, 1722, folios 1–3.

33. ANHQ, Protocolos, NP, act. 330, folio 238.

34. ANHQ, Protocolos, NP, DOL, act. 304, folios 143–45.

35. Purchased by the Reverend Padre of the Order de los Predicadores from Doña Theresa de Panto la Española, who in turn had purchased her from Captain Don Antonio de Falabarria, *vezino de la ciudad de Guayaquil*, in 1702 for 525 pesos. See ANHQ, Protocolos, NP, GL, act. 302, folios 999v–1002v. The Dominicans provide a useful example

of the extent to which slave laborers helped fuel Quito's moral economy, as well as trade in the city more generally. Note their purchase of an enslaved *mulato* boy named Manuel in 1704. Valued at three hundred pesos, the Dominicans exchanged the boy for one hundred mules. See ANHQ, Protocolos, NP, OM, act. 250, folios 125v–126.

36. Entering Guayaquil in 1703, these captives were traded for a total of 910 pesos de ocho reales. See ANHQ, Protocolos, NP, OM, act. 250, folio 287.

37. This group arrived in the context of a subsequent shipment of African captives from the Caribbean port of Cartagena, purchased by Joan de Corral and sold in Popayán in November 1702. They were sent to Quito by power of attorney for sale shortly thereafter. Ibid., folios 303–303v.

38. ANHQ, Protocolos.

39. For a cogent discussion of the various routes leading to slavery in the eastern Andes with hints regarding slaves from La Plata, see Brockington, *Blacks, Indians, and Spaniards*, 259–65.

40. ANHQ, NP, act. 250 (1702–5), folios 177–178v.

41. See the sales of Luis *de nación* Portugues in 1713, María *de casta* Conga (thirty years old) from a master in Riobamba in 1717; Rossa de Casta Mina (twenty-three years of age) from the "city" of Puerto Viejo in 1718; Baltassera, a native of the "city" of Puerto Viejo (fourteen years of age); Francisco Criollo in the city of Santa Fee (twenty-four years of age). ANHQ, Protocolos, NP, GL, act. 302, folios 947v–949; ANHQ, Protocolos, NP, no. act. 250 (July 31, 1703), folios 177–178v; ANHQ, Protocolos, NP, act. 313 (December 18, 1717), folio 524v; ANHQ, Protocolos, Notaria Tercera, no. act. 29 (April 6, 1710), folio 31.

42. ANHQ, Protocolos, NP, MFC, act. 269 (1692–1701), folio 14; ANHQ, Protocolos, NP, ALU, act. 272 (1694–95), folios 136v–138, 140–41, 145–47, 150–150v. Additional citations from Archivo Histórico del Guayas re: Lanzagorta.

43. Ibid.

44. As Linda Heywood has argued, Central Africans maintained a formidable presence in the enslaved population of Quito. See Heywood, *Central Africans*. Nevertheless, the late seventeenth century brought a sizable contingent of slave laborers from the Gold Coast, Bight of Benin, and, to a lesser degree, the Bight of Biafra. See, for example, ANHQ, Protocolos, NP, DOL, act. 304 (1709–11), folios 143–45, wherein Captain Don Marcos de Arugillo (*vecino de la ciudad de Popayán*) sells a family of slaves to Doña Mariana Guerrero de Jelazar. The sale was completed for 1,150 pesos de ocho reales.

45. Eltis, Behrendt, Richardson, and Klein, *Transatlantic Slave Trade*. See also the work of Mariana Restrepo, who charts ethnoregional origins for seventeenth-century Cartagena. Tardieu's most recent work is also quite suggestive for Panama. See Tardieu, *Cimarrones de Panamá*. See also and Restrepo, *Brujeria y reconstrucción*.

46. See Tardieu, *El Negro*, who says that Quito city constituted an "emporium" of slaves. See his sample of seventeenth-century sales, 170–71.

47. On enslaved women and nursing, see Premo, *Children of the Father King*; McKinley, "Till Death Do Us Part," 14–16; and van Deusen, "Intimacies of Bondage."

48. Before the 1760s, when Bourbon governance come to Quito in earnest, Hapsburg monarchical rule operated to govern the varying forms of slavery and slaves within what historian Chad Black calls an "ethos of decentralism, contingency, and negotiation through a matrix of competing jurisdictions, contradictory laws, and special privileges."

For many scholars of colonial Spanish American legal culture, the notion of an absolutist monarch did not adhere through forms of coercive force or a hierarchical state apparatus—at least not before the eighteenth century. Instead, localism, customary law, and negotiation were the rule, on the one hand, while kings claimed absolute royal authority—largely in name only—on the other. The reading of colonial legal culture deployed here suggests something a bit more dialectical—in short, that Hapsburg absolutism adhered both in spite of and due to the lack of coercive force or a reliable state apparatus. Indeed, the point is not that the royal bureaucracies in the Americas were corrupt, but that the dialectic of rule through diffusion, negotiation, and consent maintained royal authority. And while coercive force was not present in the form of a standing army, coercive symbols and structures were in place, such as the Inquisition, ecclesiastical courts, and the proliferation and governance of masters through the marking and arbitration of many of the most fundamental and quotidian matters relating to enslaved people and their bodies. These were among the ways that royal power was maintained and radiated throughout the body politic. See Black, *Limits of Gender Domination*, 7; Foucault, *Power/Knowledge*; and Cañeque, *The King's Living Image*.

49. Seed, *Ceremonies of Possession*. Ironically, Africa and Africans, two of the principal "sites" of European "marking" and "possession"—arguably most emblematic of Iberian claims to sovereignty and empire—are completely absent from this work. See also Bennett, *Colonial Blackness*; Morgan, *Laboring Women*; and Hartman, *Scenes of Subjection*.

50. W. Johnson, *Soul by Soul*, 21.

51. For varying perspectives within this debate, see Chambers, "Ethnicity in the Diaspora" and "The Significance of Igbo"; Northrup, "Igbo and Myth Igbo"; Kolapo, "Igbo and Their Neighbors"; Thornton, *Africa and Africans*; Gomez, *Exchanging Our Country Marks*; Bennett, *Africans in Colonial Mexico*; and Lovejoy, *Identity in the Shadow of Slavery*. See also Mann, "Shifting Paradigms."

52. See also Gomez, *Exchanging Our Country Marks*.

53. See, for example, Sandoval, *De instuaranda aethiopum salute*, and Thornton, *Africa and Africans*.

54. Chambers, "Ethnicity in the Diaspora," 27–28. See also Hutchinson and Smith, *Ethnicity*, esp. 3–14, and Nash, "Core Elements of Ethnicity," 24–28. Relying upon the work of Ernest Geller, Douglas suggested that "shared amnesias" allow people to suppress subethnic differences. Gellner, *Culture, Identity, and Politics*, 6–10. See also Hastings, *Construction of Nationhood*, 14, and Anderson, *Imagined Communities*, 204.

55. Hutchinson and Smith, *Ethnicity*, 6–7, quoted in Chambers, "Ethnicity in the Diaspora," 27.

56. Chambers, "Ethnicity in the Diaspora," 27. See also Gomez, *Exchanging Our Country Marks*.

57. Chambers, "Ethnicity in the Diaspora," 25–39, esp. 27–28.

58. See Vilar, *Hispanoamérica y el comercio de esclavos*, 169–79. It is no small wonder, then, that Mexico held a much higher proportion of "Angolans" (75.4 percent), while in Lima they accounted for just over 20 percent of the overall ethnic African enslaved population between 1560 and 1650. Historian Colin A. Palmer sampled some 402 sales and exchanges of all those registered in Mexico City during the seventeenth century and found that 303 of the 402 had embarked from West Central Africa and that 271 carried

the ethnic monikers "Angola," 24 Congo, 1 Loango, 2 Anchico, and 1 Luanga. Among the other 91 sales examined by Palmer were the following: 22 Guineau, 3 Golofs, 2 Cabo Verde, 1 Berbesi, 8 Bran, 2 Bañol, 1 Xoxo, 6 Arara, 1 Mina, 1 Bioho, 14 São Tomé, 9 Arda, 6 Carabalí, 1 Terra Nova, 2 Zape, 7 Cafre, 7 Mozambique, and 1 Zozo. See Palmer, *Slaves of a White God*, 20–23. Historian Frederick Bowser's work on Peru is particularly insightful, since Quito drew a good number of its enslaved population from the port of Callao. Out of all existing slave sales and exchanges in Lima for the period spanning 1560 and 1650, Bowser sampled 5,278, finding that 1,355 Angolans, 849 Brans, 594 Biafrans, 316 Bañols, 284 Mandinga, 267 Congo, 237 Folupos, 214 Zape, 180 Guinea (unspecified), 143 Terranovos, 128 Jolofos, and 103 Nalus had entered Peru—and these are merely those groups whose numbers registered more than 100 individuals. See Bowser, *African Slave in Colonial Peru*, 40–44, 79.

59. This was especially true in the late seventeenth century, when traders sought to "season" ethnic Africans by stopping in the Caribbean to allow their African captives, and themselves, rest and refreshment before traveling on to Cartagena and Panama. Subsequent shipments might carry a more diverse group of slave laborers, as many contained slave laborers who had been purchased or traded previously within the Caribbean.

60. Antonio Minas (thirty-five years old), Polina (no "nation" given, probably a *criolla*) (thirty years old); two black girls, daughters of the aforementioned Polina (Laura, two years old, and the other an unnamed infant of three months); Manuel Congo (thirty years old) and his wife, María Popo (twenty-five years old); Juana, daughter of the aforementioned (three years old); Antonio Golofo (forty years old) and Llina, his wife of the same *nación*; Miguel Mina (sixty years old); Bernardo Criollo (eighteen years old); Marta Criolla (sixteen years old); Gaspar Criollo (forty years old), and Francisco Mina (forty-five years old). ACC, Sig. 8736 (Col.-Jl-22su), 1694–95, folios, 47v–48.

61. ACC, Protocolos, PN, tomo 22, folios 63–71v.

62. ACC, Protocolos, PN, tomo 22, 1712–13, folios 63–71v.

63. Ibid.

64. Ibid.

65. Ibid., 63.

66. See Drewal, "Art or Accident," and Drewal and Mason, "Ogun and Body/Mind Potentiality," 333.

67. See Hall, *Africans in Colonial Louisiana*, and Karash, *Slave Life in Rio*.

68. Chandler, "Health and Slavery," 64.

69. Ibid., 66–67.

70. Ibid.

71. Alonso de Sandoval took care to pay some attention to African scarification and interviewed Africans for what modern scholars would call ethnographic details of their African pasts in an attempt to document their *casta* or *nación*. Though knowledgeable of West and West Central Africa, Sandoval was also often guilty of collapsing regional and linguistic distinctions.

72. Smallwood, *Saltwater Slavery*, 15–60; Law, *Slave Coast of West Africa*; Davies, *Royal African Company*.

73. ACC, Protocolos, PN, tomo 19 (18-hernero-1700), folios 17–19.

74. Curtin, *Atlantic Slave Trade*, 129. It was Minas and Popos who figured prominently within the mining camp of Santa María de los Remedios, numbering five of
twenty-eight and one of twenty-eight, respectively. Among the twelve who made up
the Señora de la Soledad gang (situated along the Raposo River as well) were three Arara
and one Mina. See ACC, Colonia, C-I-21mn, Sig. 2834, folios 6–9.

75. ACC, Protocolos, PN, tomo 28, 1733, folios 16–22. For a sense of the extremely high
local demand, follow the rapid dispersal of these captives in ibid., 28–48v, 50, 65–70v,
72, 75v, 80–80v, 83v, 86–87v, 98v–100, 176v, 179, 198–201, 204v, 207, 213v, and 206–8.

76. According to historian Colin A. Palmer, the slave trade connecting the islands
of Jamaica and Barbados to the Spanish ports of Cartagena and Porto Bello functioned
in many ways as a cover for illegal trading activities between the nations. While Cartagena had been the primary slave trading port leading to South America, Porto Bello and
Panama (notorious for its centuries-old contraband activity) came to rival Cartagena in
the early years of the eighteenth century, as English slave traders adopted the trend of
refreshing slaves in the Caribbean (principally in Jamaica and Barbados) before trans-
shipping them directly to Porto Bello. During this period, Porto Bello also received ships
directly from Africa. Palmer, *Human Cargoes*, 136–37.

77. Apparently, some slaves entered through the ports within the district of Barbacoas legally, as customs records note the arrival of captives not classified as *de mala
entrada*. Historian Kris Lane found one such record as early as 1678, a contract to import *bozales* from Panama to Barbacoas. There is also the citation of the Royal Guinea
Company bringing five slaves—three men and two women—directly from Panamá into
Playa de Amaral, a port town situated near Iscuandé in the district of Barbacoas. See
Lane, "Transition from *Encomienda*," 85, 93 (n. 32), and ANHQ, Esclavos, caja 2 (1716). A
similar record emerges for the year 1788, documenting the entrance of two thousand
bozales de Panamá into Barbacoas. See ACC, Sig. 6041 (Col.-CIII-2h), 1788. This is interesting, however, given that Colmenares notes that few *bozales* appear in the notary
protocols of Popayán after 1780. Apparently, there were two processes running concur-
rently: as the mining camps of the Chocó declined during the 1780s, mine owners were
moving south into the district of Barbacoas, thereby supplying any continuing demand
in the region. In addition, the secondary and illegal slave-trading network that operated
between Panamá and Barbacoas continued in concert with other, "legal" market activity
occurring between Panamá and Barbacoas.

78. ACC, Sig. 2758 (Col.-CI-22h), Popayán, July 14–September 10, 1710, folios 1–12;
ACC, Sig. 2762 (Col.-CI-22h), December 19, 1710–March 13, 1711, folios 1–10.

79. ACC, Sig. 2761 (Col.-CI-22h), Nóvita–Popayán, October 6–December 11, 1710,
folios 1–10. There was a good deal of money to be had in prosecuting such cases; usually,
officials confiscated the slaves, fined the owners, and auctioned the slaves off. In addition, those who had sold the "illegal slaves" were often fined. In one case that reached
officials in Bogotá (signaling the bureaucratic overlap within the Spanish north Andes
at this time), the trafficker was fined thirty-three patacones for each slave introduced
de mala entrada. In this case, the slaves had the "marks" of the South Sea Company but
lacked those of the Spanish crown. ACC, Sig. 3104 (Col.-CI-22h), October 31, 1722.

80. ACC, Sig. 3124 (Col.-CII-2h), June 21, 1723–October 24, 1724. Most of these cases
were discovered when individuals tried to make good on the slaves—legalize them—or

when someone related the fact that such slaves lacked the necessary brands to officials. This was the case with one slave named Antonio, who claimed that his master "Eduardo Bolton" from Jamaica (where he had a mother and siblings) had brought him to Cartagena "con las tropes de Vernón y fué herido y preso en la acción de San Lázaro . . . se adjudicó a don Manuel Castrellón por 300 patacones" in Popayán. See ACC, Sig. 4173 (Col.-CII-6h), June 6–July 18, 1748, folios 1–10.

81. ACC, Sig. 3144 (Col.-CII-2h), June 11–July 1, 1725, folios 1–3. See also ACC, Sig. 4150 (Col.-CII-6h), which features the denunciation of an enslaved man named José Congo, who had been introduced illegally by his first master, Manuel González, who was then deceased. González had purchased José from one Juan de Orejuela and made an attempt to send him to Raposo with *una negra de Miguel Cortés*, to whom José was married. Fortunately for the couple, José was "deposited" in the home of Miguel Cortés while officials sought to resolve the case. Unfortunately for the modern scholar, like many such cases, the resolution for this case remains unavailable.

82. A similar case, adjudicated in Buga, against Don Miguel Nagle Alvarez de Toledo, featured two female African captives (*negras bozales*) named Petrona la Colarada y Poloni. The two were appraised at a value of 400 patacones each, giving officials license to auction them off for 710 *patacones* to Doña Ana de Becerra. Don Miguel Nagel Alvarez de Toledo protested, insisting upon his right to the slaves, but officials found that they were in fact "contraband," because they lacked the necessary marks indicating legal entry into the provinces. In this instance, officials were a bit lenient; the slaves would be returned to Toledo if he paid Doña Becerra the 710 patacones. ACC, Sig. 3319 (Col.-JI-4cv), May 7, 1721–March 4, 1728, folios 1–46.

83. See Granda, "Una ruta maritima." Focusing upon the contraband trade between Barbacoas and Panana, Granda based his analysis upon the first fourteen pages of this forty-nine-page document (ACC, Sig. 3607 [Col.-JI-2cr], March 30, 1730–December 23, 1734, folios 1–49), transcribing critical portions of the central facts in and the turn of events surrounding the capture of Reyes. Those fourteen pages contained the details that allowed him to reconstruct the clandestine trade route and the network of individuals who drove it. The remaining thirty-five pages are unedited and in their original form in the Archivo Central del Cauca (Popayán, Colombia). Although of lesser concern to Granda, they contain important information regarding the contraband slaves in question, the local economy, and the region's relationship with the *audiencia* and its regional subsidiary, the Gobernación de Popayán.

84. Granda, "Una ruta maritima," 127.

85. Ibid., 127–28.

86. Granda, "Una ruta maritima," 128.

87. Ibid.

88. Ibid., 128–29.

89. Granda makes it clear that this was a little-patrolled area within the province of Darién, located along Panama's Pacific coast. It is uncertain, however, if "el postigo" is meant to refer to an inlet or an actual doorway or gate. Ibid., 130, esp. n. 19. Slaves were also introduced illegally through the Atrato River that flowed into the heart of the Chocó and the northernmost portions of the Gobernación de Popayán. In 1705, for example, officials were investigating Vazquez León for having introduced five slave

men and three women to mines in Raposo by way of the Río Atrato. In this case, officials confiscated them and placed them in the custody of Carlos Camacho—a miner of Raposo—while an investigation took place. See ACC, Sig. 2657 (Col.-Jl-3cv), September 4, 1705, folios 1–15.

90. Lane, "Mining the Margins," 1:129.

91. Ibid., 149–50.

92. Ibid., 186.

93. ACC, Sig. 3607 (Col.-Jl-2cr), March 30, 1730–December 23, 1734, folios 15–49. Subsequent documents suggest that Don Miguel de los Reyes was not going down without a fight, as he is found requesting copies of the case against him in order to petition officials in Popayán. What happened beyond these maneuvers escapes us for the moment. For these legal actions, see ACC, Sig. 3530 (Col.-CII-2h), September 14, 1734, folios 1–9; and ACC, Sig. 3531 (Col.-CII-2h), November 17, 1734, folios 1–36.

94. ACC, Sig. 3607 (Col.-Jl-2cr), March 30, 1730–December 23, 1734, folios 15–49.

95. See Usner, *Indians, Settlers, and Slaves*, and Brooks, *Captives and Cousins*.

96. ACC, NP, tomo 19, folios 275v–277.

97. ACC, NP, tomo 19, folio 275v.

98. By the eighteenth century, many had endured a second passage involving transshipment from Jamaica after "seasoning." Death—their constant attendant in the initial passage, on land in Jamaica, and in the second passage of the Caribbean Sea—now accompanied them to Cartagena.

99. All slaves entering Quito did not experience all fonts of incorporation equally. Some, for example, arrived without having been baptized, such as an enslaved *bozal* woman sold in Guayaquil by Don Roque García Salgado (AHG, EP/P Santiago de Guayaquil, November 28, 1712, p. 85, entry 137.133, folios 186v–198) or the *bozal* man of *casta no conocida* sold for 475 pesos. These were, after all, juridical fonts. Slaves arriving illegally would have missed these or been subjected to attempts of counterfeit branding. Notably, slaves could be imported legally without having been baptized. Baptism was almost always mentioned, however, in the bill of sale or other sales papers that accompanied slaves' arrival at ports like Guayaquil. Scribes and merchants usually took care to note when slaves had not been baptized. In some instances, these could have been contraband slaves they were trying to pass off as legal. It certainly begs the question of how regular baptism was for slaves passing legally through Panama or even Cartagena during the eighteenth century. We know Sandoval and his agents, many of them enslaved multilingual Africans involved in conversion and baptismal rituals in Cartagena during the early seventeenth century (Sandoval, *Un tratado sobre la esclavitud*, 1647). It was clearly a royal mandate going back to the sixteenth century that *bozales* be baptized upon arrival. The Portuguese crown, for example, mandated that all slaves entering the slave trade be baptized (Newson and Minchin, *From Capture to Sale*). Some were. In either case, the act or lack thereof conditioned the legal incorporation of slaves. They could shore up their master's proprietary claims or invite inquiry from royal officials, revealing the contested nature of majesty in Spanish America and simultaneously the enslaved body as text. See the series of sales registered by notaries in eighteenth-century Guayaquil, noted earlier, with the official licensed shipping company but *sin bautizar* (without baptism).

100. V. Brown, "Social Death." See especially the case of Fermin, a slave in 1712 Guayaquil who refused to work until his partial freedom, or the terms under which he might secure his freedom, were acknowledged in the sale and conditions of his enslavement to a new master in Guayaquil. Santiago de Guayaquil, 1712-VIII-26. Venta real-esclavos. Thomas Gonzáles de Fuentes y Juan Gonzáles de Fuentes a don Thomas Carbo un zambo nombrado Fermín en 300 pesos de contado. AHG, EP/P 137, p. 70, entry .100, folios 110–11.

Chapter Three

1. *RHGQ*, 2:259–76. "Relación and visita ordered by don Agustin de Ugarte Sarvia, Diego Rodriguez DoCampo, Presidente secretario del venerable dean and cabildo de Aquiella Catadral." See Tardieu, *El Negro*, 217.

2. See Sandoval's *De instauranda Aethiopum salute*, published initially in 1627, and later in an expanded edition in 1647. This expanded edition added a fourth and final book to the work, detailing the work of the Jesuits among black peoples of the world, Sandoval's "etíopes." See also Olsen, *Slavery and Salvation*. And for a useful English translation of selected portions of Sandoval's text, see von Germeten, *Sandoval Treatise on Slavery*.

3. Black compliance with Christian discipline and the joy with which they received the Catholic faith caused some to question if they should be subject to enslavement any more naturally than Indians. Las Casas recanted his position on black slavery, having learned that they were not just war captives; Mexico's archbishop argued in 1560 that blacks should not be captives any more than Indians because they received faith so joyfully and did not make war against Christians; Alonso de Sandoval questioned if enslaved captives coming out of Luanda were obtained morally through just war. Others such as Tomás Mercado and Luis de Molina questioned or rejected the notion of a just war. See Rout, *African Experience*, 33–35.

4. Bennett, *Africans in Colonial Mexico*; Bristol, *Christians, Blasphemers, and Witches*; van Deusen, "God Lives."

5. Silverblatt, *Modern Inquisitions*; Martínez, *Genealogical Fictions*; Hesse, "Self-Fulfilling."

6. Phelan, *Kingdom of Quito*; Voekel, *Alone before God*.

7. The interchangeable use of *negro* and *esclavo* in seventeenth-century Quito suggests that among these were enslaved blacks (African and Creole). Mercado, *Historia de la Provincia del Nuevo Reino y Quito*, 3:13–14. This was likely the "cofradía de los naturales y los morenos y morenas" documented as late as April 30, 1619, by historian J. Jouanen, who also refers to a *congregación* of "morenos e indios chonotales"—blacks and brutish Indians—in 1635. Both, whom Tardieu speculates are one in the same, were found in La Compañía. Tardieu, *El Negro*, 217. Apparently a congregation of Negros developed within the Jesuit Colegio of Guayaquil similar to those in Quito. While this was likely the case, Tardieu is following Jouanen, who offered no citations. Ibid., 262, 266 (n. 60) (emphasis added).

8. Historian Jean-Pierre Tardieu conveys the local preoccupation that blacks would adopt the customs of indigenous peoples in Quito, as found in the synods redacted

by Archbishop Fray Luis López de Solis in 1594, which dictated instructing slaves in the faith. An anonymous report from the year 1570 describes Sundays and festival days when a Mass was held for blacks and Indians. In the evenings they received doctrinal instruction. Tardieu, *El negro*, 217. Whatever blacks represented within the liturgy—the pomp and circumstance of baroque piety and evangelism—their racialized religious performativity, however orthodox outwardly, often concealed a logic of its own. There was a vibrant conversation within society about the spirit world, what held atrocities at bay or brought them near, how to heal the land and ways of having personal power over another. Magic was real for *everyone*. And enslaved blacks spoke loudly in a range of ways within that milieu. Sweet, *Recreating Africa*; Bristol, *Christians, Blasphemers, and Witches*.

9. Martínez, *Genealogical Fictions*. See also Lewis, *Hall of Mirrors*, and Bennett, *Colonial Blackness*.

10. Phelan, *Kingdom of Quito*, 175–77.

11. See Tardieu, *El Negro*, 218.

12. For a layered study of black congregants in Mexico, see Bristol, *Christians, Blasphemers, and Witches*, and "Afro-Mexican Saintly Devotion." According to legend, a "Mandinga" royal shipyard carpenter named Jacú brought a painting of Our Lady of the Rosary from Spain and installed it in the chapel. Mysteriously, it caught afire, from which Jacú saved the painting. Considering the events a miracle, a cult developed among the blacks of the *cofradía* of the chapel. Over time, they came to venerate Jacú and the painting. Ultimately, this image achieved cultlike devotion, wherein black devotees controlled the dogma and liturgy of its veneration. Tardieu, *El Negro*, compares this to the image of the black Christ in the little hermit of Pachacamilla in Lima, who soon came to be called the Lord of Miracles. See also Bristol, "Afro-Mexican Saintly Devotion," 262. See also Rostworowski de Diez, *Pachacámac y el Señor de los Milagros*. For a discussion of confraternities and the emergence of "Afro-Peruvian ethnicities," see Graubart, "'So color de una cofradía.'" Select studies exist on black and indigenous sodalities and mutual aid societies. On Peru, see Varón, "Cofradías de indios." On African corporate identity in the circum-Caribbean, see Landers "Cimarrón and Citizen." On Brazil, see Nishida, "From Ethnicity to Race and Gender," and Kiddy, *Blacks of the Rosary*. On Mexico, see von Germeten, *Black Blood Brothers*. And on Colombia and the Dominican Republic, see Soulodre-La France, "Socially Not So Dead," and Sáez, *La iglesia y el esclavo negro*.

13. Sodality records proved unavailable to me during the research that went into this writing. Marriage petitions were also unavailable. Church officials governing archives allowed me access to only sacramental lists—*libros de bautismos* and *libros de matrimonios*. In addition, mining and estate inventories proved useful in helping to construct this reading of the intimate worlds of the enslaved and the communities they developed within bondage.

14. Describing the piety and potential for religious instruction, Sandoval relayed the story of an elite Quiteño, Diego de Calderón. Calderón's elderly slaves had been rude, rustic, and uncultured during their early years. When encountered initially, he had barely developed facility with the Spanish language. Over the years, however, he proved himself through tests of "sanity and virtue." Ultimately, he received his freedom

in order to serve with the habit of a humble *donado* of the religious Convent of San Francisco. Tardieu, *El Negro*, 218.

15. For a first-rate meditation on black Christian devotive subjectivity, see De Jesús, *Souls of Purgatory*, and von Deusen, "God Lives." For a nuanced reading of witchcraft and the "reconstruction" of identities, see Restrepo, *Brujeria y reconstrucción*. For a look at one of the royal religious worlds that produced many of eighteenth-century Spanish America's enslaved Africans, see Thornton, *Kongolese Saint Anthony*.

16. Cañeque, *The King's Living Image*.

17. Mercado, *Historia de la Provincia*, 14–17.

18. See Phelan, *Kingdom of Quito*, 177.

19. Colin A. Palmer pioneered the use of Inquisition records to read enslaved peoples' efforts at maintaining what he termed "folk Catholicism" in colonial New Spain. See Palmer, *Slaves of the White God*; Villa-Flores, *Dangerous Speech*; Bennett, *Africans in Colonial Mexico* and *Colonial Blackness*; and Sweet, *Recreating Africa* and *Domingos Álvares*. The Inquisition was active in the Kingdom of Quito, but only to a very limited degree. Religious crimes were handled locally within the parish and bishopric. More egregious claims of religious offense were passed along to the tribunal in Lima and later Santa Fé de Bogota. Visitas, or bureaucratic reviews, of parishes reveal that a number of slave marriages were called into question and annulled on grounds of consanguinity due to prior sexual relations between one of the *novios* and their would-be sister- or brother-in law. See, for example, the annulment of Eugenio and Juana, "the black slaves of María Manuela Pelaez vezina de la ciudad de Cali," Arquidiocesis de Popayán, Archivo Histórico, Rollo 219; Legajo 3170 (1720–21).

20. Masters were responsible for ensuring their slaves were properly fed, clothed, and instructed in the faith. Legally, slave children fell under the patriarchal authority of their father and their master, if not also the crown. Consequently, masters owed their enslaved dependents the dual obligation of care and instruction. Critically, they were to instruct enslaved subjects in the faith, insuring that they attended Mass and baptized their children, all while offering instruction, correction, and reproof in the faith. After all, they needed colonial discipline. See Premo, *Children of the Father King*, 211–42.

21. El Sagrario Parish Church, Libro de Bautismos de niños de toda clase: Montañeces, Mestizos, Indios, Negros y Mulatos (Quito, April 1, 1606–October 7, 1613). Ninety-six individuals compose my sample of baptisms, of whom eighty-two were clearly identifiable as enslaved children (with one adult—María in 1611), and two were free black children. Eleven of the ninety-six baptisms featured Andean children.

22. Morgan, *Laboring Women*, 69–143. On the "anomalous intimacies of slave cargo," see Smallwood, *Saltwater Slavery*, 101–21. See also Hartman, *Scenes of Subjection*.

23. Africans and Afro-Creoles throughout New Spain were reproducing themselves at considerable rates. While historian Frederick P. Bowser found high death rates among Lima's slave population (a full 10 percent annually), the work of Tardieu reveals a striking number of Afro-Creoles for Cusco. It seems that Lima suffered from a number of setbacks, chief among them a markedly different environment from Quito; as a coastal city vulnerable to the spread of infectious diseases, Lima received large imports of infirm *bozales* annually. Many had enjoyed little rest in Cartagena before being forced on to Lima, adding longer times at sea to their journey. Those arriving in Veracruz,

however, had spent less time at sea and, perhaps for this reason, fared better. And while Quito was not exempt from epidemics and natural disasters, it was not a distribution point of slaves for the entire viceroyalty. Compounding Lima's death rate was the fact that one-third of all slaves arriving in Lima was subsequently shipped throughout the viceroyalty. No doubt, at times Lima lost many of its healthier slaves to this intracolonial trade, leaving a good many sick and emaciated souls to die in the slave pens of the city. See Bowser, *African Slave in Colonial Peru*, 75.

24. Caution is needed here due to the inconsistency of sales records and birth and death records for these years. Nevertheless, existing sales, discussed below, provide suggestive data that lean in favor of this hypothesis.

25. African-descended populations were reproducing themselves in New Spain during this time as well. Between 1570 and 1646, the Creole population of New Spain had increased by 50 percent (from 2,437 to 116,529). By this time, Africans constituted only 30 percent of the total population of African descent. In short, black reproduction was not the preserve of British North America. See Bennett, *Africans in Colonial Mexico*, 23, 202 (n. 29). See also the work of Laird W. Bergad, who found that slaves in eighteenth-century Minas Gerais reproduced themselves by similar margins. Bergad, *Slavery and the Demographic and Economic History of Minas Gerais*.

26. Lane, *Quito 1599*, 58–59.

27. These cases occur in my second sample that stretches from 1653 to 1707.

28. All seven of these instances appear in the later period, corresponding to an apparent increase in this phenomenon. More on this below.

29. El Sagrario Parish Church, APQ, Libro de Bautismos.

30. Ibid., September 2, 1610.

31. Gaudeman and Schwartz, "Cleansing Original Sin."

32. It is difficult to estimate population figures during this period, but there were probably no more than fifty to seventy-five free blacks in the city at this time.

33. For works that address the theme of class construction among free blacks, see Hanger, *Bounded Lives, Bounded Places*; Vinson, *Bearing Arms for His Majesty*; and Landers, *African in Spanish Florida*. See also O'Toole, "To Be Free and *Lucumí*."

34. Minchom, *People of Quito*, 54–55.

35. O'Toole, *Bound Lives*.

36. El Sagrario Parish Church, APQ, Libro de Bautismos, April 12, 1611; February 5, 1612; September 28, 1607; December 4, 1606; May 24, 1611; May 25, 1611; September 11, 1612; May 20, 1610; June 6, 1610; May 23, 1610; July 29, 1612; and December 4, 1606.

37. On April 4, 1606, Joan Bram served as the *padrino* for an indigenous boy named Juan, son of Catalina Quiniana and Guoeci Chiconieu, described simply as *naturales*.

38. Apparently, Lorenca served as the godmother for at least two indigenous children. In the first instance, Lorenca is merely a *morena*—a geohumoral referent related to *negro*. In the second she is described as "morena Biafara," noting her geohumoral marker and national or Atlantic *casta*. She was one among the less than 250 Africans sold in Quito city between 1586 and 1660. Of those only 13 (eight women and five men) were ascribed the *nación* or Atlantic moniker "Biafara."

39. Frederick P. Bowser and James Lockhart were two of the first scholars to suggest this to have been the case for colonial Peru. See Bowser, *The African Slave*, and Lockhart,

Spanish Peru. See also Minchom, *People of Quito*, 55. For more recent appraisals of the black intermediary thesis, see Beatty-Medina, "Between the Cross and the Sword," and Restall, *Black Middle*.

40. For discussions of Afro-Mestizo as a *casta* category, see Bennett, *Africans in Colonial Mexico*, and Vinson, *Bearing Arms for His Majesty*.

41. In other instances, ethnic Africans served as godparents for the children of apparent Afro-Creoles. See, for example, the baptism of Leonor on September 24, 1609. Her parents were Ines negra and Gernabe negro; serving as godfather was Juan Mandingo. Similarly, in 1609, for Santiago, the son of María Bran and Leonar[do] de Olmedo (two married slaves), Alonso Angola served as godfather. Finally, in the baptism of Simón, the adult slave of Sebastián Francisco, Agustín, described as "moreno Congo," served as godfather. See APQ, Libro de Bautismos, 1606–13.

42. El Sagrario Parish Church, APQ, Libro de Bautismos, 10-x-1610.

43. O'Toole shows indigenous women and men serving as godparents for Araras, finding that this was at times a mutually beneficial practice to solidify social ties forged between ethnic Africans and indigenous migrants to the Chicama Valley, as local Andean communities could sometimes prove hostile to Andean migrants. O'Toole, *Bound Lives*, 56–57. On conflict and affinity among enslaved Bran men, see O'Toole, "From the Rivers of Guinea."

44. Glymph, *Out of the House of Bondage*.

45. El Sagrario Parish Church, APQ, Libro de Bautismos.

46. Ibid.

47. Ibid.

48. Ibid.

49. Ibid.

50. In addition, there was Doña Juana María's purchase of Michaela Nieva, a fifteen-year-old girl described as "de casta Cetra." ANHQ, Protocolos, Notaria Tercera, no. act. 41, folio 276.

51. ANHQ, Protocolos, NP, DO, act. 334 (tomo 2), folios 643v–644v.

52. El Sagrario Parish Church, APQ, Libro de Matrimonios.

53. ANHQ, Esclavos, caja 4, exp. October 7, 1749.

54. Here "de casta Congo" and "Conga" stand as indicators of ethnoregional origin but might also indicate emergent social, political, or diasporan ethnic identities. See O'Toole and Proctor's essays in Bryant, O'Toole, and Vinson, *Africans to Spanish America*.

55. APG, Libros de Matrimonios, 1701–25, folio 7v. The extant record mentions nothing of the free or enslaved status of the godparents or witnesses. Throughout the registries, one does find individuals carrying the titles "don" and "doña" serving as godparents, but more often as witnesses to slave unions.

56. Bennett, *Africans in Colonial Mexico*; Palmer, "From Africa to the Americas," 223–35; Proctor, "African Diasporic Ethnicity."

57. APG, Libros de Matrimonios, folio 7v, 27 de Marzo de 1702 . . . segun orden Francisco de Casta Congo con Ana conga sus padrinos: Antonio de Salvador y Lorensa Nabay . . . Testigos: Nicolas de Martin y Juan de Castro, Joseph de Navarino; folio 69, 29 de henero de 1716 . . . Julian de Montalban yndio natural de asiento de Hanbato con leonor Miranda negra esclava de Doña Ana de Robles y fueron sus padrinos el Capp.

Don Juan de Robles y Doña Leonor de robles, testigos Don Felis de Mesa, y Agustin de Billacreses . . . ; folio 69v, 24 de junio de 1716 . . . Lucas Canpurano mulato libre natural de esta ciudad con Francisca, dume Yndia, natural del Pueblo de Daule y fueron sus padrinos Diego domingo de orosco y Gregoria Peres testigos, don Felis Mesa y Don Juan de Honura, Agustin Billacreses . . . ; p. 87 . . . 31 de Agosto de 1718 . . . Miguel Sandobal de escurra Zambo libre natural de Lambayeque con Leonor Ballesteros mestiza natural de esta ciudad aviendo precedido lo dispuesto por el santo con cilo de trento fueron sus padrinos Joseph Duarte y Francisca Duarte su muger de que fueron testigos Pasqual Alvarez y Jus. de la Cruz y Andres . . . ; p. 87 . . . 4 de septiembre de 1718 . . . Christobal Duarte mulato libre natural de esta ciuadad, y a Nicolasa de Leon, mulato libre natural tanbien de esta ciudad; a viendo los cassdo y con licencia; por palabras de presente que hazen verdadero Matrimonio en tiempo prohibido de velaciones a siete de abril del ano de mil setecientos y diez y seis . . . y fueron padrinos de ocho casamiento; Anttonio de Salvatierra y Getrudis Gonsales de que fueron testigos Francisco Gogonet Andrian de Arriola y Juan de la Cruz por verdad. . . . ; p. 88 . . . 29 de Nobiembre de 1718 . . . segun orden de . . . a Pedro Dias Negro de casta Mina esclavo del cap. don thomas Coello del Castro con Juana Romulada nagra de la misma casta Mina esclava de Juana Romualda besina de esta ciudad fueron sus padrinos el Cap. don Joseph Abiles y Doña Ygnana Goyonete, de que fueron testigos don Pedro Sandoy a Felis de Canales negro casta mina y Juan Antonio Ynostra negro de casta Chala y por que. . . .

58. APG, Libros de Matrimonios, 90.

59. Mercado, *Historia de la Provincia*, 4:22, 28–30.

60. Archivo General de la Nación, Arquidiocesis de Popayán, Archivo Histórico, Rollo 19, Legajo 3170 (1720–21); Rollo 220, Legajo 3213 (1741–42).

61. ACC, Col.-JII-18su, Sig. 10.362 (1767), folios 37–44; ACC, Col.-JII-15su, Sig. 10.282, folios 10v–16v; ACC, Col.-CI-21mn, 2834, folios 6–12, 14v–17v; and ACC, Colonia Judicia su, 1699–1727, Sig. 8742, folios 4, 18–19.

62. ACC, Col.-CI-21mn, Sig. 8742, 1699, folio 4.

63. Antonio Cufi (meaning Friday or sixth), a thirty-year-old, was listed also in the mines of Caloto, inventoried in 1757. See ACC, Col.-JII-15su, Sig. 10.282, folio 11.

64. Igbo has become a vexed category, ethnic moniker, and "identity" within scholarship on the early modern African Diaspora. Selected works on Igbo include Gomez, *Exchanging Our Country Marks*; Byrd, *Captives and Voyagers*; Chambers, "My Own Nation"; Northrup, "Igbo and Myth Igbo" and "Significance of Igbo"; Hall, *Slavery and African Ethnicities*; and Carretta, *Equiano*, xiv–xv. See also Carretta, "Olaudah Equiano or Gustavus Vassa?"; Sweet, "Mistaken Identities?"; and Sidbury, *Becoming African in America*.

65. ACC, Col.-JII-18, Sig. 10.362 (1767), folios 41v–42.

66. Ibid., folio 38v.

67. "Bobo" is also a term associated with people north of the Asante state and is thought to have entered the slave trade by way of the Gold Coast.

68. ANHQ, Esclavos, caja 5, exp. December 1, 1757.

69. According to historian Rosario Coronel, the Jesuits purchased a "determined" number of slave laborers between 1680 and 1750 but turned thereafter to depend upon the growth of fourth-generation *criollos*. Coronel, *El valle sangriento*, 93–94.

70. Andrien, *Kingdom of Quito*, 84–85.

71. Ibid., 102.

72. Ibid., 103.

73. Ibid. See also Cushner, *Farm and Factory*, 193.

74. Ibid., 104.

75. Coronel, *El valle sangriento*, 104. See also ANHQ, Temporalidades, caja 18 (años 1782, 1783) and 25, exp. August 18, 1786 and exp. March 3, 1785.

76. Andrien, *Kingdom of Quito*, 103. See also ANHQ, Temporalidades, caja 18, November 22, 1782.

77. Coronel, *El valle sangriento*, 89.

78. Andrien notes an average slave population of 1,203. Andrien, *Kingdom of Quito*, 36. For documentation of the number of married slaves and singles, including children, see ANHQ, Empadronamientos, caja 15, Padrones de Ibarra, 1779, 1780, 1784, 1786.

79. ANHQ, Temporalidades, caja 25, exp. 4, August 18, 1786.

80. Ibid.

81. Andrien, *Kingdom of Quito*, 106–7.

82. Ibid.

83. ANHQ, Esclavos, caja 8, exp. January 26, 1778.

84. ANHQ, Temporalidades, caja 25, exp. November 9, 1784.

Chapter Four

1. ACC, Sig. 108, Col.-JI-1cv, 1640.

2. For a more in-depth understanding of the judicial system and how civil courts functioned in Spanish America, see Andrien, "Legal Texts"; Cutter, *Legal Culture of Northern New Spain*; Herzog, *La adminstración*; and Taylor, *Drinking, Homicide, and Rebellion*. For discussions concerning *procuradores* (attorneys, public defenders), see Bonnett, *El Protector de naturales*, and Uribe-Uran, *Honorable Lives*. Susan Kellogg's *Law and the Transformation of Aztec Culture* provides an excellent analysis of how Spanish rule of law transformed Aztec society in the early colonial period. And for greater detail regarding the implications of *depósito*, its connection to the phenomenon of *recogimiento*, and women's (enslaved and free, white and other) ability to employ this process on their behalf, see van Deusen's *Between the Sacred and the Worldly*.

3. For Castilian civil laws regarding slaveholding, see *Las Siete Partidas*. For American codices, see *Recopilación*. A number of royal codes that were left out of the *Recopilación* may be found in collections such as *Documentos*. For an excellent commentary on laws and the Spanish legal tradition, see Solórzano Pereira, *Política Indiana*, esp. vols. 252, 253. See also Salmoral, *Los códigos*, and Watson, *Slave Law*.

4. Davidson, "Negro Slave Control"; Palmer, *Slaves of the White God*.

5. Bennett, *Africans in Colonial Mexico*.

6. Ibid.; Brockington, "African Diaspora in the Eastern Andes."

7. Bennett, *Africans in Colonial Mexico*.

8. Lolita G. Brockington has shown also that in the area of Mizque, in the Audiencia de Charcas, the enslaved sued for their freedom as early as the 1580s. Noting that the Audiencia de Charcas "heard dozens" of such cases, Brockington points to the "fugitive overtones" of this process. Rightly, she notes, the enslaved had to flee their place

of employment in order to engage the judicial process. The early political implications of this phenomenon are not lost on Brockington. Compellingly, she asserts, "It can be argued that the *reclamaciones*, appearing earlier than expected, harkened to something far more deeply ingrained than political independence from colonial rule" See Brockington, "African Diaspora in the Eastern Andes," 223.

9. Bennett, *Africans in Colonial Mexico*.

10. Premo, "An Equity against the Law."

11. King, "Negro History," and Davidson, "Negro Slave Control," are two of the earliest works to examine this phenomenon for Latin America. Both argued, as does Palmer, "Slaves of a White God," that the law ultimately had little substantive effect in the lives of the enslaved. While the right to sue was available, they asserted, few cases existed, and hence the law had limited effect. Chandler, "Slave over Master," and Meiklejohn, "Implementation of Slave Legislation," examine enslaved legal action for late eighteenth-century New Granada, an area whose juridical authority encompassed the Kingdom of Quito, or modern-day Ecuador and southern Colombia. Chandler highlighted New World legislation and its bearing upon how the process functioned, emphasizing laws passed as late as 1775 as the key to enslaved legal action. Meiklejohn, on the other hand, was one of the few to question why this system worked. Yet he often overstated the importance of attorneys and magistrates, arguing that they were so dedicated to implementing colonial legislation that they "made the slave institution more humane." Meiklejohn argued that places like New Granada, which were geographically and economically on the margins of the Spanish empire, constituted colonies with cultures wherein "medieval Iberian attitudes and practices regarding slaves were able to survive and eventually to evolve" (p. 182). While this is certainly part of the answer, slaves used the law throughout Spanish America and were allowed and even encouraged to do so by civil and clerical officials as early as the sixteenth century. Furthermore, such an argument bent toward economic determinism overlooks slave action within the legal channels and beyond.

12. Aguirre, *Agentes de su propia libertad*; Aguirre, "Working the System"; Chandler, "Slave over Master"; Lavallé, "Lógica esclavista y resistencia negra"; Townsend, "Half My Body Free"; Villegas, *Negros y mulatos esclavos*.

13. Chaves, *María Chiquinquirá Díaz*; Chaves, "Slave Women's Strategies"; Chaves, *Honor y libertad*.

14. Driving this perspective has been scholars' overwhelming interest in the ways that slave litigation corresponded to Bourbon- and Independence-era politics and the subsequent abolition of slavery. See Aguirre, *Agentes de su propria libertad* and "Working the System"; Chaves, *Honor y libertad* and "Slave Women's Strategies"; Hünefeldt, *Paying the Price*; Soulodre-La France, "Socially Not So Dead!"; and Townsend, "Half My Body Free." It would appear that this preoccupation has led many scholars to focus almost exclusively on this later period, understating, if not overlooking, slaves' long history of using the courts in deeply political ways. As the work of Bennett (*Africans in Colonial Mexico*) shows, yet another possible reason for scholars' failure to address early cases of enslaved legal action lies in the fact that scholars have overlooked (particularly in the case of the North Andes) the importance of canon law and the cases generated by ecclesiastical courts in Latin America. Although slave experiences before church courts

in Quito fall outside of the scope of this volume, a comprehensive analysis of slave resistance and legal action must include captives' experiences before ecclesiastical courts
and tribunals. Colin A. Palmer (*Slaves of the White God*) was one of the first to demonstrate the importance of these records. In so doing, he highlighted slaves' early radical
critique of Catholicism and canon law. Most recently, the works of Paul Lokken ("Marriage as Slave Emancipation"), Kathryn Joy McKnight ("En Su Tierra Lo Aprendió"), and
Javier Villa-Flores ("To Lose One's Soul") have also underscored the critical importance
of "church as strategy" in the lives of the enslaved. For Peru, see the works of Jean-Pierre
Tardieu (*Los Negros*). For an examination of the ways that royal slaves employed colonial
courts, see Díaz, *The Virgin, the King*, 285–313.

15. Blanchard, "Language of Liberation," 522.

16. Ibid., 523.

17. Chaves, "Slave Women's Strategies," 2000; Townsend, "En busca de la libertad,"
73–86, and "Half My Body Free." Christine Hünefeldt was one of the first to publish
analysis of court cases to examine the ways that families deployed the force of civil
law to gain freedom in early republican Lima. Highlighting the overwhelmingly female
presence among Afro-Limeño litigants, Hünefeldt demonstrated also the ways that female litigants invoked the discourse of honor in their efforts to gain emancipation via
the courts. Although pathbreaking, Hünefeldt's work focuses on the nineteenth century, thereby eliding the early colonial foundations and formations of this slave-led
phenomenon. See Hünefeldt, *Paying the Price*.

18. Aguirre, *Agentes de su propia libertad*.

19. Blanchard, "Language of Liberty."

20. Premo, "An Equity against the Law," 500–502.

21. ANHQ, Esclavos, cajas 1–54.

22. Aguirre, "Working the System"; Chaves, "Slave Women's Strategies"; Townsend,
"Half My Body Free"; Lavallé, "Logica esclavista."

23. Blanchard, "Language of Liberty."

24. ANHQ, Esclavos, caja 16 (1790–94), folios 214–23.

25. Aguirre, "Working the System."

26. Van Deusen, *Between the Sacred and the Worldly*, for example, charts the increased
policing that *beatas* (pious lay women with informal religious vows) experienced in late
sixteenth- and early seventeenth-century Lima.

27. Suggestive of a just war, royal language included declarations of "war on maroons" and "campaign to search out maroons." See Ponce Leiva, *Recopilación*, tomo 2,
libro 7, titulo 5, ley xxij, folios 288v–289v; titulo 18, ley vij, folio 88; and titulo 5, ley 25,
folio 289v–290. The crown went to great lengths to administer it, prescribing in 1624
that those who worked in this service in Cartagena receive six reales for each maroon
they apprehended. The crown also provided incentives for slaves who returned voluntarily and even better incentives for those willing to bring in other runaways. Governing
slavery was governing the Indies. *Recopilación*, tomo 2, libro 7, titulo 5, ley xxij, folio
288v. On the island of Cuba, for example, officials sent out armed militias accompanied
by dogs (*perras de busca*) to seek out and apprehend runaways. Apparently this measure
caused just as much confusion as it sought to quell. These bands often forced free blacks
into slavery and/or extorted cash, goods, and services from them. This became such a

problem that in 1623 the crown demanded that these bands not "molest" free blacks ("que los rancheadores no molesten a los morenos libres, que estuvieren pacificos"). *Recopilación*, tomo 2, libro 7, titulo 5, ley 19, folio 287v; Hall, *Social Control*, 74–78. See also Landers, *Black Society in Spanish Florida*, and "Cimarrón Ethnicity."

28. ANHQ, Popayán, caja 51, exp. January 28, 1729, folios 1–3.

29. Popayán *cabildo* proceedings reveal steady streams of correspondence between the town councils of Popayán, Cali, and the high court in Quito regarding this matter. ACC, Libros de los Cabildos Popayán, no. 11, May 28, 1732. Similar to that of Esmeraldas and other *palenques*, Patía's geographic location—in a valley, near riverways, and laden with thick brush—provided its inhabitants with considerable defenses. Escalante, "Palenques in Colombia," 76–77.

30. In addition to Lane's findings and other examples found in the notary records of Quito, cimarrones (runaways) are documented in civil and criminal court cases, including Juan de San Martin of Cuenca, Pasqual, and Antonia who was reputed to be a repeat or chronic runaway. See ANHQ, Esclavos, caja 1, exp. September 15, 1702; caja 3, exp. September 29, 1740; and caja 5, exp. December 1, 1757, respectively. For documentation of runaways and delinquents in sixteenth-century Quito, see Lane, *Quito 1599*, 67.

31. ACC, Libros de los Cabildos Popayán, no. 11, May 28, 1732. See also the Cabildo records of Guayaquil.

32. Exploring the "nature" of maroonage in late colonial Colombia, Anthony MacFarlane states, "At times, rebellion and the threat of flight was used to bring pressure on the slave owner, while stopping short of actual escape to a palenque." MacFarlane, "Cimarrones and Palenques," 158. For examples of other confrontations between formerly Jesuit-owned slaves and new masters, see Souledre-La France, "Socially Not So Dead." For additional treatments of flight, rebellion, and the Araujo saga, see also Lavallé, *Amor y opresión*, 205–64, and Tardieu, *El negro*, 317–58.

33. Borchart de Moreno, "Capital comercial y producción agrícola."

34. ANHQ, Temporalidades, caja 18, 1782–83; ANHQ, Esclavos, caja 10, exp. March 19, 1783. See also ibid., caja 12, exp. December 16, 1788. Araujo had similar problems with enslaved Afro-Criollos from the haciendas of Puchimbuela and San Joseph. See ibid., exp. July 30, 1789, February 26, 1790, April 13, 1790, and August 23, 1790. For another example of enslaved Afro-Criollos who chose direct confrontation on yet another formerly Jesuit-owned plantation—La Concepción—see ANHQ, Esclavos, caja 15, exp. July 25, 1798. Christiana Borchart de Moreno ("Capital comercial y producción agrícola") was one of the first to publish an analysis of this incident and the post-expulsion fate of formerly Jesuit-owned enslaved women, children, and men. Rosario Coronel Feijóo (*El valle sangriento*) provided an excellent discussion of Jesuit land acquisition and management processes. Bernard Lavallé ("Lógica esclavista y resistencia negra") used the aforementioned case in developing his argument that slave resistance increased in the latter half of the eighteenth century. For discussions of the Jesuits and their agropastoral slaveholding enterprises throughout Quito, see Andrien, *Kingdom of Quito*, and Cushner, *Farm and Factory*.

35. In his work on enslaved legal action in nineteenth-century Peru, Carlos Aguirre points also to courts' mediating role in society, arguing, "The courts are not only arenas

for the contention between different sets of actors but, in addition, they are also scenarios for the deployment, reshaping, and dissemination of social and political ideas, cultural values, and different forms of representation." Aguirre, "Working the System," 204. See also Phelan, *Kingdom of Quito*.

36. I thank Kris Lane for encouraging me to further consider the ways that colonial courts were not merely instruments of domination and resistance but were also connected to the crown and its "central mystery," the divine right of kings. Personal communication, September 25, 2001.

37. My theoretical approach to reading slave postures, declarations, and carriage as political performances is informed by scholars of performance studies. See Conquergood, *Performance Studies* and "Ethnography, Rhetoric and Performance"; Schechner, *Between Theater and Anthropology*; and Drewal, *Yoruba Ritual*. When I refer to "performances," while identifying a common thread or trope used by petitioners—requests for mercy and honorific comportment—I do not intend to suggest that slaves' [re]presentations before the courts were rigid, stoic, or uniform. To be sure, the legal process imposed its conventions and protocols. Nevertheless, litigants improvised, transforming each court appearance into a dramatization that became their very own. Other works influential to this reading include Kelley, "We Are Not What We Seem," and J. Scott, *Weapons of the Weak* and *Domination and the Arts of Resistance*.

38. Lauderdale-Graham, "Honor among Slaves."

39. ACC, Sig. 1407, Col.-Jl-2Cr, 1615.

40. For a more in-depth discussion of competing notions of honor in Latin America, see Lipsett-Rivera and Johnson, *Faces of Honor*. In the same volume, see especially Lyman L. Johnson's entry on the importance of words and gestures (127–51). For a discussion of notions of honor among plebeians and the enslaved, see Boyer, "Honor among Plebeians," 152–78, and Lauderdale-Graham, "Honor among Slaves," 201–28, both in Lipsett-Rivera and Johnson, *Faces of Honor*. And for more in-depth discussions of the ways that honor functioned in colonial Latin America, see Gutiérrez, *When Jesus Came*; Martin, *Governance and Society*; Seed, *To Love, Honor, and Obey*; Socolow, *Women of Colonial Latin America*; Twinam, *Public Lives, Private Secrets*; and van Deusen, "Determining the Boundaries of Virtue" and *Between the Sacred and the Worldly*.

41. The desire to assert and defend one's honor was the likely catalyst in the 1580 incident where *audiencia* judge Diego de Ortegón's slave was murdered by the master of another enslaved Afro-Quiteña in the city plaza for having questioned his authority to settle an argument. Lane, *Quito 1599*, 67.

42. ACC, Sig. 2010, Col.-Jl-2cv, 1675.

43. See de la Fuente, "Slaves and the Creation of Legal Rights," and Premo, "Equity against the Law." Premo showcases the ways that while the Spanish American system was not based upon precedent outright, prior rulings were referenced, studied, and written about and could have some impact upon how a particular case might be ruled upon, for better or worse. The legal system was dynamic, and as an elemental function of good governance, the implications of how the court (the royal audience, the king's representative) ruled mattered greatly in how justice radiated throughout the body politic, and therefore mattered in shoring up or undermining the legitimacy of the prince. Slaves catalyzed these processes through direct action.

44. ANHQ, Esclavos, caja 1, exp. November 9, 1690.

45. Ibid., exp. December 2, 1706.

46. Ibid., folios 1–2.

47. ANHQ, Esclavos, caja 1, exp. October 5, 1702, folios 1–3.

48. For examples of similar cases, see Augustín Menza, ANHQ, Esclavos, caja 2, exp. December 15, 1716; María Josepha Guerro and Inés Guerro—mother and daughter captives, exp. July 29, 1718; Manuel de Adarbe exp. June 18, 1720; exp. May 13, 1722; exp. March 27, 1726; Francisca Montero, exp. January 13, 1730; Andres Dominguez with Phelipa Thomero, ANHQ, Esclavos, caja 3, exp. May 5, 1730; Josepha Porto Carrero, exp. May 26, 1732; María de Losas and her children, exp. November 9, 1737; exp. October 8, 1744; Cazetaro de Guerra with wife and child, exp. November 3, 1744; María Nicolasa along with children and cousins, caja 4, exp. December 12, 1746; and several others, including caja 4, exp. May 9, 1750; exp. August 3, 1750; exp. August 25, 1750; exp. February 6, 1751; and Geronima Nates's case in caja 5, exp. March 22, 1753.

49. ANHQ, Esclavos, caja 1, exp. October 5, 1702, folios 10–17.

50. Ibid., folio 32.

51. Ibid., folios 38–38v.

52. ANHQ, Esclavos, caja 5, exp. August 5, 1754, folios 1–1v.

53. Ibid., folios 38–38v.

54. Ibid., folio 38v.

55. Ibid., folios 2–3v.

56. Ibid., folio 16.

57. Ibid., folio 17.

58. For discussions of the critical implications of what was "público y notorio," see Herzog, *La administración*, 96–100, 201–2.

59. Ibid., folio 18.

60. Ibid., folio 21.

61. Recall that Juana's owner complained of her movement while in *deposito*. This is not a mere coincidence but rather a pattern that reflects gendered norms. Nancy E. van Deusen has found, for example, that men commonly sought to control the mobility of their wives during divorce proceedings. They often sought to restrict the woman's ability to communicate with their family members, holding that such interactions would allow for negative influence. Moreover, men insisted that their wives' mobility and freedom to communicate with relatives was "a male prerogative." Van Deusen, *Between the Sacred and the Worldly*, 93–94. In a real sense, Juana's case reveals the kind of patriarchy of ownership all enslaved subjects endured.

62. ANHQ, Esclavos, caja 5, exp. August 5, 1754, folio 45.

63. Ibid., folio 74v.

64. Chaves, *Maria Chiquinquirá Diaz*; Chaves, "Slave Women's Strategies."

65. Quoted in Chaves, "Slave Women's Strategies," 114.

66. Ibid., 115.

67. Chaves, *Maria Chiquinquirá Diaz*; Chaves, "Slave Women's Strategies."

68. Chaves, "Slave Women's Strategies," 109–11.

69. Townsend, "Half My Body Free."

70. Ibid., 117.

71. ANHQ, Esclavos, caja 15, exp. July 4, 1798.

Conclusion

1. On the forgetting of slavery, see Hesse, "Forgotten Like a Bad Dream." On European colonial sovereignty as founding violence and Iberian monarchical claims to the sole power to judge laws and to ensure this authority's maintenance, spread, and permanence, see Mbembe, *On the Postcolony*, 66–103.

2. This recalls the ongoing need for black narratives of recuperation and reinsertion, as well as the need for a broadening of our conceptions of black subjectivity. Bennett, *Colonial Blackness*, xii–xiii. On Esmeraldas, see Beatty-Medina, "Rebels and Conquerors," "Fray Alonso de Espinosa's Report," and "Between the Cross and the Sword." See also Lane, *Quito 1599*, and Tardieu, *El Negro*, 29–133.

3. D. Scott, *Conscripts of Modernity*.

4. See Bryant, Vinson, and O'Toole, "Introduction," for an overview of these developments.

5. C. Brown, "British Slavery and British Politics, 275.

6. Aguirre, *Agentes*; Premo, *Children of the Father King*; Proctor, *"Damned Notions of Liberty"*; Bristol, *Christians, Blasphemers, and Witches*; von Germeten, *Black Blood Brotherhoods*; O'Toole, *Bound Lives*; Bennett, *Africans in Colonial Mexico*; Brockington, *Blacks, Indians, and Spaniards*; R. Scott, *Slave Emancipation in Cuba*; Villa-Flores, *Dangerous Speech*.

7. For more on this critique and a useful attempt to address this omission, see Bennett, *Colonial Blackness*.

8. Seed, *Ceremonies of Possession*.

9. On the colonial importance of majesty, see Alejandro Cañeque, *The King's Living Image*.

10. This is not a voyeuristic attempt to return students of slavery to scenes of the grotesque. Nor does it overlook the quotidian acts of domination found in the granting of pleasure. Rather, it is meant to point to a need to further conceptualize the political importance of the grotesque as well as the ways these forms of exemplary violence conditioned colonial subjection and the constitution of race. See Hartman, *Scenes of Subjection*.

11. Bennett, *Africans*; Restrepo, *Brujería*.

12. V. Brown, "Social Death."

13. Marcela Echiverrí, "Enraged to the Limit of Despair."

14. Milton, *The Many Meanings of Poverty*, 1–16.

BIBLIOGRAPHY

Archival Sources
Colombia

Archivo Central del Cauca, Popayán
    Colonia—Judiciales
    Protocolos
Archivo General de la Nación, Bogotá
    Arquidiocesis de Popayán, Archivo Histórico (microfilmed collection)
    Fondos de Negros y Esclavos

Ecuador

Archivo de la Paroquia, El Sagrario, Guayaquil
    Libros de Bautismos
    Libros de Matrimonios
Archivo de la Paroquia, El Sagrario, Quito
    Libros de Bautismos
    Libros de Matrimonios
Archivo Histórico del Guayas, Guayaquil
Archivo Municipal de Guayaquil, Guayaquil
    Libros de los Cabildos
Archivo Municipal de Quito, Quito
    Libro de los Cabildos
Archivo Nacional de Historia, Quito
    Carnicerias y pulperias
    Criminales
    Esclavos
    Indigenas
    Popayán
    Protocolos
    Temporalidades

Spain

Archivo General de Indias, Seville (Via Pares)
    Contaduría
    Contratación
    Escribanía

United States

John Carter Brown Library, Brown University, Providence, Rhode Island
John Hay Library, Brown University, Providence, Rhode Island
Newberry Library, Chicago, Illinois
    Ayer Collection

Printed Primary Sources

Acosta, José de. *Historia natural y moral de las Indias*. 1590. Edited by Fermín del Pino-Díaz. Madrid: CSIC, 2008.

Cabello Balboa, Miguel. "Verdadera descripción y relación larga de la provincia y tierra de Las Esmeraldas, contenida desde el cabo comúnmente llamado Pasao, hasta la Bahía de la Buena Ventura, que es en la Costa del Mar del Sur del Reino del Piru; Dirigida al muy Illustre Señor Licenciado Jhoan López de Cepeda de el Concejo de su Majestad y su Presidente en la provincia de los Charcas, Reinos del Piru; Hecha por Miguel Cabello Balboa, clérigo; dónde se Contiene una breve suma del alzamiento y rebelión de los indios de la provincia de los Quixios y de la entrada del Inglés en el Mar del Sur." In Miguel Cabello Balboa, *Obras*, vol. 1, edited by Jacinto Jijón y Camaño, 7–76. Quito: Editorial Ecuatoriana, 1945.

Canons and Decrees of the Council of Trent. Translated by H. J. Schroeder. St. Louis: B. Herder Books, 1941.

Casas, Bartolomé de las. *Brevísima relación de la destrvycion de las Indias*. 1552.

———. *Apologética historia sumaria*. Edited by Edmundo O'Gorman. Mexico, 1967.

———. *En defense de los indios*. Seville: Editoriales Andaluzas Unidas, 1985.

Castel Blanco, Manoel de Andrada. *To Defend Your Empire and the Faith: Advice on a Global Strategy Offered c. 1590 to Philip, King of Spain and Portugal, by Manoel de Andrada Castel Blanco*. Translated and edited by P. E. H. Hair. Liverpool: Liverpool University Press, 1990.

Cieza de Léon, Pedro de. *The Travels of Pedro de Cieza de Léon*. 1553. London: Hakluyt Society, 1864.

Cook, Noble David, comp. *Numeración general de todas las personas de ambos sexos, edades y calidades [que] se ha [h]echo en esta Ciudad de Lima, año de 1700*. Facsimile ed. Lima: COFIDE, 1985.

Cooke, Edward. *A Voyage to the South Sea, and Round the World, Performed in the Years 1708, 1709, 1710, and 1711*. London: Printed by H.M. for B. Lintot and R. Gosling, 1712.

Covarrubias Orozco, Sebastián de. *Tesoro de la lengua castellana o española*. 1611. Edited by Felipe C. R. Maldonado. Revised by Manuel Camarero. Madrid: Editorial Castalia, 1995.

de Jesus, Ursula. *The Souls of Purgatory: The Spiritual Diary of a Seventeenth-Century Peruvian Mystic, Ursula de Jesus*. Translated by Nancy E. van Deusen. Albuquerque: University of New Mexico Press, 2004.

de Vargas Machuca, Bernardo. *The Indian Militia and Description of the Indies: An English Translation of the Original Spanish Published in Madrid, 1599*. Edited with an introduction by Kris E. Lane. Translated by Timothy F. Johnson. Durham: Duke University Press, 2008.

———. *Defending the Conquest: Bernardo de Vargas Machuca's Defense and Discourse of the Western Conquests.* Latin American Originals, vol. 4. Edited by Kris Lane. Translated by Timothy F. Johnson. University Park: Penn State University Press, 2010.

Escriche y Martín, Joaquín. *Diccionario razonado de legislación y jurisprudencia.* Paris: Librería de Rósa, Bouret y Cia., 1851.

Ferrer Benimeli, José Antonio. *Masonería, iglesia e ilustración.* Vol. 1, *Las bases de un conflicto (1700–1739).* Vol. 2, *Inquisición: Procesos históricos (1739–1750).* Madrid: Publicaciones de la Fundación Universitaria Española, 1976.

Freile-Granizo, Juan. *Actas del cabildo colonial de Guayaquil*, vol. 6, *1682–1689.* Guayaquil: Archivo Histórico del Guayas, 1980.

Gauderman, Kimberly. *Women's Lives in Colonial Quito: Gender, Law, and Economy in Spanish America.* Austin: University of Texas Press, 2003.

Gómez de Silva, Domingo. *Practica, y instrvcion para albaceas, tvtores, y cvradores, que administran bienes de menores.* Lima: Pedro de Cabrera, 1640. John Hay Library, Brown University.

Guamán Poma de Ayala, Felipe. *El primer nueva corónica y buen gobierno.* 1615. Edited by John V. Murra, Rolena Adorno, and Jorge L. Urioste. 3 vols. Colección América Nuestra, no. 31. Mexico: Siglo Veintiuno, 1980.

Herrera, Antonio de. *Historia general de los hechos de los castellanos en las islas y tierra firme del Mar Oceana.* 1601. Madrid: Oficina Real de Nicolás Rodriguez Franco, 1730.

Illescas, Alonso de. "Maroon Chief Alonso de Illescas' Letter to the Crown, 1586." In *Afro-Latino Voices: Narratives from the Early Modern Ibero-Atlantic World, 1550–1812*, edited by Kathryn Joy McKnight and Leo J. Garofalo; translated by Charles Beatty-Medina, 30–37. Indianapolis: Hackett Publishing Company, 2009.

"Individual y verdadera relación de la extrema ruyna que padeció la Ciudad de los Reyes Lima . . . (Lima, 1746)." In *Noticias del Perú*, 714. John Carter Brown Library, Brown University.

Jopling, Carol F., ed. *Indios y negros en Panamá en los siglos XVI y XVII: Selecciones de los documentos del Archivo General de Indias.* Antigua: Centro de Investigaciones Regionales de Mesoamérica, 1994.

Juan, Jorge, and Antonio de Ulloa. *Noticias secretas de América, sobre el estado naval, military y politico de los reinos del Perú y provincias de Quito, coastas de Nueva Granaday Chile.* 1826. Vol. 2. Facsimile edition. Bogotá: Biblioteca Banco Popular, 1983.

Konetzke, Richard, ed. *Colección de documentos para la história de la formación social de hispanoamérica, 1493–1810.* 3 vols. Madrid: Consejo Superior de Investigaciones Científicas, 1953–63.

Lanuzo y Sotelo, Eugenio. *Viaje ilustrada a los reinos de Perú.* 1738. Lima: Pontificia Universidad Católica del Perú, 1995.

Las siete partidas del sabio rev D. Alfonso el nono. 1555. Madrid: Boletín Offícial del Estado, 2003.

Leyes de toro. 1505. Madrid: Ministerio de Educación y Ciencia, 1977.

Muro Orejón, Antonio, trans. and ed. *Las Leyes Nuevas de 1542–1543: Ordenanzas para la gobernación de las Indias y buen tratamiento y conservación de los indios.* Seville: Escuela de Estudios Hispano-Americanos de la Universidad de Sevilla, 1945.

Pacheco, Joaquin Francisco, Francisco de Cárdenas, and Luis Torres de Mendoza, eds. *Colección de documentos inéditos relativos al descubrimiento, conquista y colonización de las posesiones españolas en América y Oceanía, sacados, en su mayor parte del Real Archivo de Indias.* Vol. 2. Madrid: Imprenta Española, 1864.

Ponce Leiva, Pilar, ed. *Relaciones histórico-geográficas de la audiencia de Quito, siglo XVI–XIX.* 2 vols. Quito: Instituto de Historia y Antropología Andina, 1994.

Ordoñez de Zevallos, Pedro. *Historia, y del mundo del clérigo agradecido don Pedro Ordoñez de Zevallos, natural de la insigne civdad de Jaen, á las cinco partes de la Europa, Africa, Asia, América y Magalanica, con el Itinerario de todo él.* 1614. Madrid: Juan Garcia Infancon, 1691.

Ortiz de la Tabla Ducasse, Javier, Montserrat Fernandez Martinez, and Agueda Rivera Garrido, eds. *Cartas de cabildos hispanoamericanos: Audiencia de Quito (siglos XVI–XIX).* Seville: Consejo Superior de Investigaciones Científicas, 1991.

Real Díaz, José Joaquin, ed. *Recopilación de leyes de los reynos de las Indias.* 1681. 4 vols. Madrid: Ediciones Cultura Hispánica, 1973.

Rogers, Woodes. *A Cruising Voyage Round the World: First to the South-Sea, Thence to the East-Indies, and Homewards by the Cape of Good Hope. Begun in 1708, and Finish'd in 1711.* 2nd ed. 1712. London: Bell & Lintot, 1718.

Rumazo González, José. *Libro segundo de cabildos de Quito.* 1548. Quito: Archivo Municipal, 1934.

———. *Colección de documentos para la historia de la audiencia de Quito.* 8 vols. Madrid: Afrodisio Aguado, 1948–50.

Sabio, Alfonso X el. *Las siete partidas.* 1555. Edited by Robert I. Burns, S.J. Translated by Samuel Parsons Scott. Vol. 1, *The Medieval Church: The World of Clerics and Laymen.* Vol. 2, *Medieval Government: The Worlds of Kings and Warriors.* Vol. 3, *Medieval Law: Lawyers and Their Work.* Vol. 4, *Family Commerce and the Sea: The Worlds of Women and Merchants.* Vol. 5, *Underworlds: The Dead, the Criminal, and the Marginalized.* Philadelphia: University of Pennsylvania Press, 2001.

Saco, José Antonio. *Historia de la esclavitud desde los tiempos más remotos hasta nuestros días.* Habana: Editorial "Alfa," 1937.

Sánchez, Santos. *Colección de todas las pragmáticas, cédulas, provisiones, circulares, autos acordados, vandos y otras providencias publicadas en el actual reynados del Señor Don Carlos IV.* Vol. 1. Madrid: Viuda e Hijo de Marím, 1794.

Sánchez, Tomás. *Disputaciones de sacro matrimonium sacramentum.* 3 vols. Madrid, 1602–3.

Sandoval, Alonso de. *De instauranda aethiopum salute: El mundo de la esclavitud negra en América.* Bogotá: Empresa Nacional de Publicaciones, 1956.

———. *Un tratado sobre la esclavitud.* 1627. Edited by Enriqueta Vila Vilar. Madrid: Alianza, 1987.

———. *Treatise on Slavery: Selections from De instauranda Aethiopum salute.* Edited and translated with an introduction by Nicole von Germeten. Indianapolis: Hackett, 2008.

Santos, Sánchez, ed. "Relación de algunos puntos de consultas de Indias." In *Colección de todas las pragmáticas, cédulas, provisiones, circulares, autos acordados, vandos y otras providencias publicadas en el actual reynados del Señor Don Carlos IV.* Vol. 1. Madrid: Viuda e Hijo de Marím, 1794.

Snelgrave, William. *A New Account of Some Parts of Guinea and the Slave Trade.* 1734. London: Frank Cass, 1971.

Solórzano Pereira, Juan de. *Política Indiana.* 1629. Vols. 252–56, *Biblioteca de Autores Españoles.* Madrid: Editorial Atlas, 1972.

Sylvestre, Don Manuel. *Librería de jueces, utilísima, y universal para toda clase de personas.* Madrid: Imprenta de la Viuda de Eliseo Sánchez, 1765.

Valero, Juan Bernardo. "Relación del exemplar castigo que acaba de executarse en esta Ciudad de los Reyes en una Quadrilla de Ladrones el día 13 de agosto de este año de 1772 de órden del Exmo. Señor Virey D. Manuel de Amat y Juniet." John Carter Brown Library, Brown University.

Vélez, Diana Bonnett. *La Sección Indígenas del Archivo Histórico de Quito, siglos XVI–XVIII: Documento.* Quito: Editorial Abya-Yala, 1992.

"Voyages: The Trans-Atlantic Slave Trade Database." Emory University. http://www .slavevoyages.org/tast/index.faces (accessed July 19, 2009).

Printed Secondary Sources

Abercrombie, Thomas A. *Pathways of Memory and Power: Ethnography and History among an Andean People.* Madison: University of Wisconsin Press, 1998.

Acosta Saignes, Miguel. *Vida de los esclavos negros en Venezuela.* Caracas: Hespérides, 1967.

Adderley, Rosanne Marion. *"New Negroes from Africa": Slave Trade Abolition and Free African Settlement in the Nineteenth-Century Caribbean.* Bloomington: Indiana University Press, 2006.

Adelman, Jeremy. *Sovereignty and Revolution in the Iberian Atlantic.* Princeton: Princeton University Press, 2006.

Adorno, Rolena. "Images of Indios Ladinos in Early Colonial Peru." In *Transatlantic Encounters: Europeans and Andeans in the Sixteenth Century,* edited by Kenneth J. Andrien and Rolena Adorno, 232–70. Berkeley: University of California Press, 1991.

———. "Reconsidering Colonial Discourse for Sixteenth- and Seventeenth-Century Spanish America." *Latin American Research Review* 28, no. 3 (1993): 135–45.

———. "The Indigenous Ethnographer: The 'Indio Ladino' as Historian and Cultural Mediation." In *Implicit Understandings: Observing, Reporting, and Reflecting on the Encounters between Europeans and Other Peoples in the Early Modern Era,* edited by Stuart B. Schwartz, 378–402. New York: Cambridge University Press, 1994.

———. "Estevancio's Legacy: Methodological, Historiographic, and Philosophical Problems in the Comparative Study of the Early Americas." Conference paper, annual meeting of the Early Ibero/Anglo Americanist Summit, Tucson, Ariz., May 16–19, 2002.

———. *The Polemics of Possession in Spanish American Narrative.* New Haven: Yale University Press, 2007.

Agamben, Giorgio. *Homo Sacer: Sovereign Power and Bare Life*. Stanford, Calif.: Stanford University Press, 1995.

———. *The Kingdom and the Glory: For a Theological Genealogy of Economy and Government*. Stanford, Calif.: Stanford University Press, 2011.

Aguirre, Carlos. *Agentes de su propia libertad: Los esclavos de Lima y la desintegración de la esclavitud, 1821–1854*. Lima: Fondo Editorial Universidad Católica, 1993.

———. "Working the System: Black Slaves in the Courts in Lima, Peru, 1821–1854." In *Crossing Boundaries: Comparative History of Black People in Diaspora*, edited by Darlene Clark Hine and Jacqueline McLeod, 202–22. Bloomington: Indiana University Press, 1999.

Alchon, Suzanne Austin. *Native Society and Disease in Colonial Ecuador*. Cambridge: Cambridge University Press, 1992.

Alexander, Leslie M. *African or American?: Black Identity and Political Activism in New York City, 1784–1861*. Urbana: University of Illinois Press, 2012.

Alier-Martínez, Verena. *Marriage, Class and Colour in Nineteenth-Century Cuba: A Study of Racial Attitudes and Sexual Values in a Slave Society*. Cambridge: Cambridge University Press, 1974.

Anda Aguirre, Alfonso. *Indios y negros bajo el dominio español en Loja*. Quito: Abya-Yala, 1993.

Andrews, George Reid. *Afro-Latin America, 1800–2000*. Oxford: Oxford University Press, 2004.

Andrien, Kenneth J. *Crisis and Decline: The Viceroyalty of Peru in the Seventeenth Century*. Albuquerque: University of New Mexico Press, 1985.

———. "Economic Crisis, Taxes and the Quito Insurrection of 1765." *Past & Present* 129 (1990): 104–31.

———. *The Kingdom of Quito, 1690–1830: The State and Regional Development*. Cambridge: Cambridge University Press, 1995.

———. *Andean Worlds: Indigenous History, Culture, and Consciousness under Spanish Rule, 1532–1825*. Albuquerque: University of New Mexico Press, 2001.

———. "Legal and Administrative Documents." In *Guide to Documentary Sources for Andean Studies, 1530–1900*, vol. 1, edited by Joanne Pillsbury, 107–19. Washington, D.C.: Center for Advanced Study in the Visual Arts, 2008.

Andrien, Kenneth J., and Rolena Adorno, eds. *Transatlantic Encounters: Europeans and Andeans in the Sixteenth Century*. Berkeley: University of California Press, 1991.

Aptheker, Herbert. *American Negro Slave Revolts*. New York: Columbia University Press, 1943.

Aráuz, Maritza. *Pueblos indios en la costa ecuatoriana: Jipijapa y Montecristi en la segunda mitad del siglo XVIII*. 2nd ed. Quito: Ediciones Abya-Yala, 2000.

Arrom, Silvia Marina. *The Women of Mexico City, 1790–1857*. Stanford, Calif.: Stanford University Press, 1985.

Asad, Talal. *Genealogies of Religion: Discipline and Reasons of Power in Christianity and Islam*. Baltimore: Johns Hopkins University Press, 1993.

Asher, Kiran. *Black and Green: Afro-Colombians, Development, and Nature in the Pacific Lowlands*. Durham: Duke University Press, 2009.

Baber, Jovita. "Categories, Self-Representation and the Construction of *Indios*." *Journal of Spanish Cultural Studies* 10, no. 1 (2009): 27–41.

Bailyn, Bernard. *Atlantic History: Concept and Contours*. Cambridge, Mass.: Harvard University Press, 2005.

Bakewell, Peter John. *Miners of the Red Mountain: Indian Labor in Potosí, 1545–1650*. Albuquerque: University of New Mexico Press, 1984.

———. "Conquest after the Conquest: The Rise of Spanish Domination in America." In *Spain, Europe and the Atlantic World: Essays in Honour of John H. Elliot*, edited by Richard Kagan and Geoffrey Parker, 296–315. Cambridge: Cambridge University Press, 1995.

Baptist, Edward E., and Stephanie M. H. Camp, eds. *New Studies in the History of American Slavery*. Athens: University of Georgia Press, 2006.

Barcia, Manuel. "Fighting with the Enemy's Weapons: The Usage of the Colonial Legal Framework by Nineteenth-Century Cuban Slaves." *Atlantic Studies* 3, no. 2 (2006): 159–81.

Barickman, B. J. *A Bahian Counterpoint: Sugar, Tobacco, Cassava, and Slavery in the Recôncavo, 1780–1860*. Stanford, Calif.: Stanford University Press, 1998.

Barona, Guido B. "Estructura de la producción de oro en las minas de la real corona: Chiquio (Cauca) en el siglo XVII." *Anuario Colombiano de Historia Social y de la Cultura* 11 (1983): 5–42.

———. *La maldición de midas: En una región del mundo colonial, Popayán, 1730–1830*. Cali: Universidad del Valle, 1995.

Baum, Robert M. *Shrines of the Slave Trade: Diola Religion and Society in Precolonial Senegambia*. New York: Oxford University Press, 1999.

Bay, Edna G. *Asen: Iron Altars of the Fon People of Benin*. Atlanta, Ga.: Emory University Museum of Art and Archaeology, 1985.

———. *Wives of the Leopard: Gender, Politics, and Culture in the Kingdom of Dahomey*. Charlottesville: University of Virginia Press, 1998.

———. *Asen, Ancestors, and Vodun: Tracing Change in African Art*. Urbana: University of Illinois Press, 2008.

Beatty-Medina, Charles. "Rebels and Conquerors: African Slaves, Spanish Authority, and the Domination of Esmeraldas, 1563–1621 (Ecuador)." Ph.D. diss., Brown University, 2002.

———. "Caught between Rivals: The Spanish-African Maroon Competition for Captive Indian Labor in the Region of Esmeraldas during the Late Sixteenth and Early Seventeenth Centuries." *The Americas* 63, no. 1 (2006): 113–36.

———. "Alonso de Illescas (1530s–1590s): African, Ladino, and Maroon Leader in Colonial Ecuador." In *The Human Tradition in the Black Atlantic, 1500–2000*, edited by Beatriz G. Mamigonian and Karen Racine, 9–22. Lanham: Rowman & Littlefield Publishers, 2010.

———. "Fray Alonso de Espinosa's Report on Pacifying the Fugitive Slaves of the Pacific Coast." In *Documenting Latin America: Gender, Race, and Empire*, vol. 1, edited by Erin E. O'Connor and Leo J. Garofalo, 69–74. New York: Prentice-Hall, 2010.

———. "Between the Cross and the Sword: Religious Conquest and Maroon Legitimacy in Colonial Esmeraldas." In *Africans to Spanish America: Expanding the*

Diaspora, edited by Sherwin K. Bryant, Rachel Sarah O'Toole, and Ben Vinson III, 95–113. Urbana: University of Illinois Press, 2012.

Beckles, Hillary. "Caribbean Anti-Slavery: The Self-Liberation Ethos of Enslaved Blacks." *Journal of Caribbean History* 22, no. 1 (1988): 1–19.

———. *Natural Rebels: A Social History of Enslaved Black Women in Barbados*. New Brunswick, N.J.: Rutgers University Press, 1989.

———. "Sex and Gender in the Historiography of Caribbean Slavery." In *Engendering History: Caribbean Women in Historical Perspective*, edited by Verene Sheperd, Bridget Brereton, and Barbara Bush, 125–40. New York: St. Martin's Press, 1995.

Behar, Ruth. "Sex and Sin, Witchcraft and the Devil in Late-Colonial Mexico." *American Ethnologist* 14, no. 1 (1987): 34–53.

Behrendt, Stephen D. "Crew Mortality in the Transatlantic Slave Trade in the Eighteenth Century." *Slavery and Abolition* 18, no. 1 (1997): 49–71.

Bennett, Herman L. "Lovers, Family and Friends: The Formation of Afro-Mexico, 1580–1810." Ph.D. diss., Duke University, 1993.

———. "The Subject in the Plot: National Boundaries and the 'History' of the Black Atlantic." *African Studies Review* 43, no. 1 (2000): 101–24.

———. *Africans in Colonial Mexico: Absolutism, Christianity, and Afro-Creole Consciousness*. Bloomington: Indiana University Press, 2003.

———. "'Sons of Adam': Text, Context, and the Early Modern African Subject." *Representations* 92, no. 1 (2005): 16–41.

———. "Writing into a Void: Representing Slavery and Freedom in the Narrative of Colonial Spanish America." *Social Text* 25, no. 4 (Winter 2007): 67–89.

———. *Colonial Blackness: A History of Afro-Mexico*. Indianapolis: Indiana University Press, 2009.

Benton, Lauren. *Law and Colonial Cultures: Legal Regimes in World History, 1400–1900*. Cambridge: Cambridge University Press, 2002.

Benton, Lauren, and Benjamin Straumann. "Acquiring Empire by Law: From Roman Doctrine to Early Modern European Practice." *Law and History Review* 28, no. 1 (February 2010): 1–38.

Bergad, Laird W. *Cuban Rural Society in the Nineteenth Century: The Social and Economic History of Monoculture in Matanzas*. Princeton: Princeton University Press, 1990.

———. *Slavery and the Demographic and Economic History of Minas Gerais, Brazil, 1720–1888*. Cambridge: Cambridge University Press, 1999.

Berlin, Ira. "From Creole to African: Atlantic Creoles and the Origins of African-American Society in Mainland North America." *William and Mary Quarterly*, 3rd ser., 53, no. 2 (1996): 251–88.

———. *Many Thousands Gone: The First Two Centuries of Slavery in North America*. Cambridge, Mass.: Harvard University Press, 1997.

Bhabha, Homi K. *The Location of Culture*. New York: Routledge, 1994.

Black, Chad Thomas. *The Limits of Gender Domination: Women, the Law, and Political Crisis in Quito, 1765–1830*. Albuquerque: University of New Mexico Press, 2010.

Blackburn, Robin. *The Overthrow of Colonial Slavery, 1776–1848*. New York: Verso Books, 1988.

———. "The Old World Background to European Colonial Slavery." *William and Mary Quarterly* 54, no. 1 (January 1997): 65–102.

———. *The Making of New World Slavery: From the Baroque to the Modern, 1492–1800*. New York: Verso Books, 1998.

Blanchard, Peter. *Slavery and Abolition in Early Republican Peru*. Wilmington, Del.: Scholarly Resources Books, 1992.

———. "The Language of Liberation: Slave Voices in the Wars of Independence." *Hispanic American Historical Review* 82, no. 3 (2002): 499–523.

———. *Under the Flags of Freedom: Slave Soldiers and the Wars of Independence in Spanish South America*. Pittsburgh: University of Pittsburgh Press, 2008.

Blassingame, John W. *Slave Testimony: Two Centuries of Letters, Speeches, Interviews, and Autobiographies*. Baton Rouge: Louisiana State University Press, 1977.

———. *The Slave Community: Plantation Life in the Antebellum South*. New York: Oxford University Press, 1979.

Blumenthal, Debra. *Enemies and Familiars: Slavery and Mastery in Fifteenth-Century Valencia*. Ithaca, N.Y.: Cornell University Press, 2009.

———. "The Promise of Freedom in Late Medieval Valencia." In *Paths to Freedom: Manumission in the Atlantic World*, edited by Rosemary Brana-Shute and Randy J. Sparks, 51–68. Columbia: University of South Carolina Press, 2009.

Boisson, Emmanuelle. "Esclavos de la tierra: Los campesinos negros del Chota-Mira, siglos XVII–XX." *Procesos: Revista Ecuatoriana de Historia*, no. 11 (1997): 45–67.

Bonnett V., Diana. *El Protector de Naturales en la audiencia de Quito, siglos XVII y XVIII*. Quito: FLACSO, 1992.

Borchart de Moreno, Christiana. *La audiencia de Quito: Aspectos económicos y sociales (siglos XVI–XVIII)*. Quito: Abya-Yala, 1982.

———. "Capital comercial y producción agrícola: Nueva España y la audiencia de Quito en el siglo XVIII." *Anuario de Estudios Americanos* 46 (1989): 131–72.

———. "La imbecilidad y el coraje: La participación femenina en la economía colonial (Quito, 1780–1830)." *Revista Complutense de Historia de América* 17 (1991): 167–82.

———. "Words and Wounds: Gender Relations, Violence, and the State in Late Colonial and Early Republican Ecuador." *Colonial Latin American Review* 13, no. 1 (2004): 129–44.

Bourdieu, Pierre. *An Outline of a Theory of Practice*. Chicago: University of Chicago Press, 1991.

———. "Structures, Habitus, Power: Basis for a Theory of Symbolic Power." In *Culture/Power/History: A Reader in Contemporary Social Theory*, edited by Nicholas B. Dirks, Geoff Eley, and Sherry B. Ortner, 155–99. Princeton: Princeton University Press, 1994.

Bowser, Frederick. "The African Experience in Colonial Spanish America: Reflections on Research Achievements and Priorities." *Latin American Historical Review* 7, no. 1 (1972): 77–94.

———. *The African Slave in Colonial Peru, 1524–1650*. Stanford, Calif.: Stanford University Press, 1974.

Boxer, C. R. *The Church Militant and Iberian Expansion, 1440–1770*. Baltimore: Johns Hopkins University Press, 1978.

Boyer, Richard E. *Lives of the Bigamists: Marriage, Family, and Community in Colonial Mexico*. Albuquerque: University of New Mexico Press, 1995.

———. "Honor among Plebeians." In *The Faces of Honor: Sex, Shame, and Violence in Colonial Latin America*, edited by Sonya Lipsett-Rivera and Lyman L. Johnson, 179–200. Albuquerque: University of New Mexico Press, 1998.

Boyer, Richard E., and Geoffrey Spurling. *Colonial Lives: Documents on Latin American History, 1550–1850*. New York: Oxford University Press, 2000.

Brading, David A. *The First America: The Spanish Monarchy, Creole Patriots, and the Liberal State, 1492–1867*. Cambridge: Cambridge University Press, 1991.

———. *Church and State in Bourbon Mexico: The Dioceses of Michoacán, 1749–1810*. Cambridge: Cambridge University Press, 1994.

Braude, Benjamin. "The Sons of Noah and the Construction of Ethnic and Geographical Identities in the Medieval and Early Modern Periods." *William and Mary Quarterly* 54, no. 1 (January 1997): 103–42.

Bristol, Joan C. "'Although I Am Black, I Am Beautiful': Juana Esperanza de San Alberto, Black Carmelite of Puebla." In *Gender, Race and Religion in the Colonization of the Americas*, edited by Nora E. Jaffary, 67–80. Burlington, Vt.: Ashgate Publishing, 2007.

———. *Christians, Blasphemers, and Witches: Afro-Mexican Ritual Practice in the Seventeenth Century*. Albuquerque: University of New Mexico Press, 2007.

———. "Afro-Mexican Saintly Devotion in a Mexico City Alley." In *Africans to Spanish America: Expanding the Diaspora*, edited by Sherwin K. Bryant, Rachel Sarah O'Toole, and Ben Vinson III, 114–35. Urbana: University of Illinois Press, 2012.

Brockington, Lolita Gutiérrez. *The Leverage of Labor: Managing the Cortés Haciendas in Tehuantepec, 1588–1688*. Durham: Duke University Press, 1989.

———. "The African Diaspora in the Eastern Andes: Adaptation, Agency, and Fugitive Action, 1573–1677." *The Americas* 57, no. 2 (2000): 207–44.

———. *Blacks, Indians, and Spaniards in the Eastern Andes: Reclaiming the Forgotten in Colonial Mizque, 1550–1782*. Lincoln: University of Nebraska Press, 2006.

Brooks, James F. *Captives and Cousins: Slavery, Kinship, and Community in the Southwest Borderlands*. Chapel Hill: University of North Carolina Press, 2002.

Brown, Christopher Leslie. "British Slavery and British Politics: A Perspective and a Prospectus." In *New Studies in the History of American Slavery*, edited by Edward E. Baptist and Stephanie M. H. Camp, 275–94. Athens: University of Georgia Press, 2006.

———. *Moral Capital: Foundations of British Abolitionism*. Chapel Hill: University of North Carolina Press, 2006.

Brown, Christopher Leslie, and Philip D. Morgan, eds. *Arming Slaves: From Classical Times to the Modern Age*. New Haven: Yale University Press, 2006.

Brown, Kathleen M. *Good Wives, Nasty Wenches, and Anxious Patriarchs: Gender, Race, and Power in Colonial Virginia*. Chapel Hill: Published for the Institute of Early American History and Culture by the University of North Carolina Press, 1996.

Brown, Kendal. *Bourbons and Brandy: Imperial Reform in Eighteenth-Century Arequipa*. Albuquerque: University of New Mexico Press, 1985.

Brown, Vincent. *The Reaper's Garden: Death and Power in the World of Atlantic Slavery*. Cambridge, Mass.: Harvard University Press, 2008.

———. "Social Death and Political Life in the Study of Slavery." *American Historical Review* 114, no. 5 (2009): 1231–49.

———. "History Attends to the Dead." *Small Axé* 14, no. 1 (2010): 219–27.

Bryant, Sherwin K. "Enslaved Rebels, Fugitives, and Litigants: The Resistance Continuum in Colonial Quito." *Colonial Latin American Review* 13, no. 1 (2004): 7–46.

———. "Slavery and the Context of Ethnogenesis: Africans, Afro-Creoles and the Realities of Slavery in the Kingdom of Quito, 1600–1800." Ph.D. diss., Ohio State University, 2005.

———. "Finding Gold, Forming Slavery: The Creation of a Classic Slave Society, Popayán, 1600–1700." *The Americas* 63 (2006): 81–112.

———. "Finding Freedom: Slavery in Colonial Ecuador." In *The Ecuador Reader: History, Culture, Politics*, edited by Carlos de la Torre and Steve Striffler, 52–67. Durham: Duke University Press, 2008.

Bryant, Sherwin K., Rachel Sarah O'Toole, and Ben Vinson III. "Introduction." In *Africans to Spanish America: Expanding the Diaspora*, edited by Sherwin K. Bryant, Rachel Sarah O'Toole, and Ben Vinson III, 1–23. Urbana: University of Illinois Press, 2012.

———, eds. *Africans to Spanish America: Expanding the Diaspora*. Urbana: University of Illinois Press, 2012.

Buck-Morss, Susan. "Hegel and Haiti." *Critical Inquiry* 26, no. 4 (2000): 821–65.

———. *Hegel, Haiti, and Universal History*. Pittsburgh: University of Pittsburgh Press, 2009.

Burkholder, Mark A., and D. S. Chandler. *From Impotence to Authority: The Spanish Crown and the American Audiencias, 1678–1808*. Columbia: University of Missouri Press, 1977.

Burnard, Trevor. *Mastery, Tyranny, and Desire: Thomas Thistlewood and His Slaves in the Anglo-Jamaican World*. Chapel Hill: University of North Carolina Press, 2004.

Burns, Kathryn. *Colonial Habits: Convents and the Spiritual Economy of Cuzco, Peru*. Durham: Duke University Press, 1999.

———. "Unfixing Race." In *Rereading the Black Legend: The Discourses of Religious and Racial Difference in the Renaissance Empires*, edited by Margaret R. Greer, Walter D. Mignolo, and Maureen Quilligan, 188–204. Chicago: University of Chicago Press, 2007.

———. *Into the Archive: Writing and Power in Colonial Peru*. Durham: Duke University Press, 2010.

Butler, Judith. *Gender Trouble*. New York: Routledge, 1990.

Butler, Kim D. *Freedoms Given, Freedoms Won: Afro-Brazilians in Post-Abolition São Paulo and Salvador*. New Brunswick, N.J.: Rutgers University Press, 1998.

———. "From Black History to Diasporan History: Brazilian Abolition in Afro-Atlantic Context." In *Africa's Diaspora*, edited by Ralph Faulkingam and Mitzi Goheen, special issue of *African Studies Review* 43, no. 1 (April 2000): 125–39.

———. "Africa in the Reinvention of Nineteenth Century Afro-Bahian Identity." *Slavery and Abolition* 22, no. 1 (2001): 135–54.

———. "Defining Diaspora, Refining a Discourse." *Diaspora: A Journal of Transnational Studies* 10, no. 2 (2001): 189–219.

Byrd, Alexander X. "Eboe, Country, Nation, and Gustavus Vassa's 'Interesting Narrative.'" *William and Mary Quarterly* (2006): 123–48.

———. *Captives and Voyagers: Black Migrants across the Eighteenth-Century British Atlantic World*. Baton Rouge: Louisiana State University Press, 2010.

Cáceres, Rina. "Mandingas, congos, y zapes: Las primeras estrategias de libertad en la frontera commercial del Cartagena. Panamá, siglo XVI." In *Afrodescendientes en las Américas: Trayectorias sociales e identitatarias*, edited by Claudia Mosquera, Maricio Pardo, and Odile Hoffman, 143–68. Bogotá: Universidad Nacional de Colombia, 2002.

Cahill, David. "Colour by Numbers: Racial and Ethnic Categories in the Viceroyalty of Peru, 1532–1821." *Journal of Latin American Studies* 26, no. 2 (1994): 325–46.

Camp, Stephanie M. H. *Closer to Freedom: Enslaved Women and Everyday Resistance in the Plantation South*. Chapel Hill: University of North Carolina Press, 2004.

Cândido, Mariana. "Merchants and the Business of the Slave Trade in Benguela, 1750–1850." *African Economic History* 35 (2007): 1–30.

———. "African Freedom Suits and Portuguese Vassal Status: Legal Mechanisms for Fighting Enslavement in Benguela, Angola, 1800–1830." *Slavery and Abolition* 32, no. 3 (2011): 447–59.

———. *An African Slaving Port and the Atlantic World: Benguela and Its Hinterland*. Cambridge: Cambridge University Press, 2013.

Cañeque, Alejandro. *The King's Living Image: The Culture and Politics of Viceregal Power in Colonial Mexico*. New York: Routledge, 2004.

Cañizares-Esguerra, Jorge. *How to Write the History of the New World: Histories, Epistemologies, and Identities in the Eighteenth-Century Atlantic World*. Stanford, Calif.: Stanford University Press, 2001.

Cantor, Erik. *Ni aniquilados, ni vencidos: Los emberá y la gente negra del Atrato bajo el domino español, siglo XVIII*. Bogotá: Instituto Colombiano de Antropología e Historia, 2000.

Carney, Judith Ann. *Black Rice: The African Origins of Rice Cultivation in the Americas*. Cambridge, Mass.: Harvard University Press, 2009.

Carretta, Vincent. "Olaudah Equiano or Gustavus Vassa? New Light on an Eighteenth-Century Question of Identity." *Slavery and Abolition* 20, no. 3 (1999): 96–105.

———. *Equiano, the African: Biography of a Self-Made Man*. Athens: University of Georgia Press, 2005.

Carroll, Patrick J. *Blacks in Colonial Veracruz: Race, Ethnicity, and Regional Development*. Austin: University of Texas Press, 1991.

Castellanos, Jorge. *La abolición de la esclavitud en Popayán, 1832–1852*. Cali: Universidad del Valle, 1980.

Castillo Mathieu, Nicolás del. *Esclavos negros en Cartagena y sus aportes léxicos*. Bogotá: Instituto Caro y Cuervo, 1982.

Chakrabaty, Dipesh. *Provincializing Europe: Postcolonial Thought and Historical Difference*. Princeton: Princeton University Press, 2000.

———. "The Climate of History: Four Theses." *Critical Inquiry* 35 (Winter 2009): 197–222.

Chambers, Douglas B. "'My Own Nation': Igbo Exiles in the Diaspora." *Slavery and Abolition* 18, no. 1 (1997): 72–97.

———. "Ethnicity in the Diaspora: The Slave-Trade and the Creation of African 'Nations' in the Americas." *Slavery and Abolition* 22, no. 3 (2001): 25–39.

———. "The Significance of Igbo in the Bight of Biafra Slave-Trade: A Rejoinder to Northrup's 'Myth Igbo.'" *Slavery and Abolition* 23, no. 1 (2002): 101–20.

Chambers, Sarah C. *From Subjects to Citizens: Honor, Gender, and Politics in Arequipa, Peru, 1780–1854.* University Park: Pennsylvania State University Press, 1999.

Chance, John K. *Race and Class in Colonial Oaxaca.* Stanford, Calif.: Stanford University Press, 1978.

Chandler, David L. "Health and Slavery in Colonial Colombia." Ph.D. diss., Tulane University, 1972.

———. "Slave over Master in Colonial Colombia and Ecuador." *The Americas* 38, no. 3 (1982): 315–26.

Chaplin, Joyce E. "Natural Philosophy and an Early Racial Idiom in North America: Comparing English and Indian Bodies." *William and Mary Quarterly* 54, no. 1 (January 1997): 229–52.

Chaves, María Eugenia. *María Chiquinquirá Díaz una esclava del siglo VIII: Acerca de las identidades de amo y esclavo en el puerto colonial de Guayaquil.* Guayaquil: Archivo Histórico del Guayas, 1998.

———. "Slave Women's Strategies for Freedom and the Late Spanish Colonial State." In *Hidden Histories of Gender and the State in Latin America*, edited by Elizabeth Dore and Maxine Molyneux, 108–26. Durham: Duke University Press, 2000.

———. *Honor y libertad: Discursos y recursos en la estrategia de libertad de una mujer esclava (Guayaquil a fines del período colonial).* Gothenburg, Sweden: Departamento de Historia/Instituto Iberoamericano de la Universidad de Gotemburgo, 2001.

———. "Race and Caste: Other Words and Other Worlds." In *Race and Blood in the Iberian World*, vol. 3, edited by Max S. Hering Torres, María Elena Martínez, and David Nirenberg, 39–60. Münster: LIT Verlag, 2012.

Christopher, Emma. *Slave Ship Sailors and Their Captive Cargoes, 1730–1807.* Cambridge: Cambridge University Press, 2006.

Clayton, Lawrence A. *Los astilleros de Guayaquil colonial.* Guayaquil: Archivo Histórico del Guayas, 1978.

Clendinnen, Inga. *Ambivalent Conquests: Maya and Spaniard in Yucatan, 1517–1570.* 1987. Cambridge Latin American Series, no. 61. Cambridge: Cambridge University Press, 2003.

Colmenares, Germán. *Las haciendas de los Jesuitas en el Nuevo Reino de Granada.* Bogotá: Universidad Nacional de Colombia, 1969.

———. *Historia económica y social de Colombia, 1537–1719.* Cali: Universidad del Valle, 1973.

———. *Popayán: Una sociedad esclavista, 1680–1800.* Vol. 2. 1979. Reprint, Santafé de Bogotá: Tercer Mundo, 1997.

Conquergood, Dwight. "Ethnography, Rhetoric and Performance." *Quarterly Journal of Speech* 78 (1992): 80–123.

———. "Performance Studies: Interventions and Radical Research." *Drama Review* 46, no. 2 (2002): 145–56.

Conrad, Robert Edgar. *Children of God's Fire: A Documentary History of Black Slavery in Brazil.* Princeton: Princeton University Press, 1983.

Cook, Alexandra Parma, and David Noble Cook. *Good Faith and Truthful Ignorance: A Case of Transatlantic Bigamy*. Durham: Duke University Press, 1991.

Cook, Karoline P. "'Moro de Linaje y Nación': Religious Identity, Race, and Status in New Granada." In *Race and Blood in the Iberian World*, edited by Max S. Hering Torres, María Elena Martínez, and David Nirenberg, 81–98. Münster: LIT Verlag, 2012.

Cook, Noble David. *Born to Die: Disease and New World Conquest, 1492–1650*. Cambridge: Cambridge University Press, 1998.

Cooper, Frederick, and Ann Laura Stoler, eds. *Tensions of Empire: Colonial Cultures in a Bourgeois World*. Berkeley: University of California Press, 1997.

Cope, Douglas R. *The Limits of Racial Domination: Plebeian Society in Colonial Mexico City, 1660–1720*. Madison: University of Wisconsin Press, 1994.

Coronado, Jorge. *The Andes Imagined: Indigenismo, Society, and Modernity*. Pittsburgh: University of Pittsburgh Press, 2009.

Coronel Feijóo, Rosario. *El valle sangriento: De los indígenas de la coca y el algodón la hacienda cañera jesuita, 1580–1700*. Quito: FLACSO, 1991.

Coronil, Fernando. "Towards a Critique of Globalcentrism: Speculations on Capitalism's Nature." *Public Culture* 12, no. 2 (2000): 351–74.

Cummins, Thomas B. F., and William B. Taylor. "The Mulatto Gentlemen of Esmeraldas, Ecuador." In *Colonial Spanish America: A Documentary History*, edited by Kenneth Mills and William B. Taylor, 147–49. Wilmington, Del.: Scholarly Resources Press, 1998.

Curtin, Philip D. *The Atlantic Slave Trade: A Census*. Madison: University of Wisconsin Press, 1969.

———. *Economic Change in Precolonial Africa: Senegambia in the Era of the Slave Trade*. Madison: University of Wisconsin Press, 1975.

Cushner, Nicholas P. *Lords of the Land: Sugar, Wine, and the Jesuit Estates of Coastal Peru*. Albany: State University of New York Press, 1980.

———. *Farm and Factory: The Jesuits and the Development of Agrarian Capitalism in Colonial Quito, 1600–1767*. Albany: State University of New York Press, 1982.

———. *Soldiers of God: The Jesuits in Colonial America (1567–1767)*. Buffalo, N.Y.: Language Communications, 2002.

Cutter, Charles R. *The Legal Culture of Northern New Spain, 1700–1800*. Albuquerque: University of New Mexico Press, 1995.

Da Costa, Emilia Viotti. *Brazilian Empire: Myths and Histories*. Chicago: University of Chicago Press, 1986.

———. *Crowns of Glory, Tears of Blood: The Demerara Slave Rebellion of 1823*. New York: Oxford University Press, 1994.

Davidson, David M. "Negro Slave Control and Resistance in Colonial Mexico, 1519–1650." In *Maroon Societies: Rebel Slave Communities in the Americas*, edited by Richard Price, 82–104. 1966. Reprint, Baltimore: Johns Hopkins University Press, 1996.

Davies, Kenneth Gordon. *The Royal African Company*. New York: Atheneum, 1970.

Davis, David Brion. *The Problem of Slavery in Western Culture*. New York: Oxford University Press, 1966.

————. "Constructing Race: A Reflection." *William and Mary Quarterly* 54, no. 1 (January 1997): 7–18.

————. *The Problem of Slavery in the Age of Revolution, 1770–1823*. New York: Oxford University Press, 1999.

Davis, Natalie Zemon. *Fiction in the Archives: Pardon Tales and Their Tellers in Sixteenth Century France*. Stanford, Calif.: Stanford University Press, 1987.

————. "Judges, Masters, Diviners: Slaves' Experience of Criminal Justice in Colonial Suriname." *Law and History Review* 29, no. 4 (2011): 925–84.

Dawdy, Shannon Lee. *Building the Devil's Empire: French Colonial New Orleans*. Chicago: University of Chicago Press, 2009.

Dean, Mitchell. *Governing Societies: Political Perspectives on Domestic and International Rule*. New York: Open University Press, 2007.

————. *Governmentality: Power and Rule in Modern Society*. 2nd ed. Los Angeles: Sage, 2010.

De Certeau, Michel. *The Practice of Everyday Life*. Berkeley: University of California Press, 1984.

De Friedemann, Nina S. "Cabildos negros refugios de Africanía en Colombia." *Caribbean Studies* 23, nos. 1–2 (1990): 83–97.

De Friedemann, Nina S., and Carlos Patiño Rosselli. *Lengua y sociedad en el Palenque de San Basilio*. Vol. 66. Bogotá: Instituto Caro y Cuervo, 1983.

De Granda, Germán. "Una ruta marítima de contrabando de esclavos negros entre Panamá y Barbacoas durante el asiento inglés." *Revista de Indias*, nos. 134–44 (1976): 123–42.

Derrida, Jacques. "Racism's Last Word." Translated by Peggy Kamuf. *Critical Inquiry* 12 (Autumn 1985): 290–99.

Devisse, Jean. "The Black and His Color: From Symbols to Realities." In *The Image of the Black in Western Art*, vol. 2, *From Early Christianity to the "Age of Discovery," Part 1: From the Demonic Threat to the Incarnation of Sainthood*, edited by David Bindman and Henry Louis Gates Jr., 73–138. Cambridge, Mass.: Harvard University Press, 2010.

————. "Christians and Black." In *Image of the Black in Western Art*, vol. 2, *From Early Christianity to the "Age of Discovery," Part 1: From the Demonic Threat to the Incarnation of Sainthood*, edited by David Bindman and Henry Louis Gates Jr., 31–72. Cambridge, Mass.: Harvard University Press, 2010.

Diamond, Jared M. *Guns, Germs, and Steel: The Fates of Human Societies*. New York: Norton, 1998.

Díaz, María Aguilera, and Adolfo Meisel Roca. *Tres siglos de historia demográfica de Cartagena de Indias*. Cartagena: Banco de la República, 2009.

Díaz, María Elena. *The Virgin, the King, and the Royal Slaves of El Cobre: Negotiating Freedom in Colonial Cuba, 1670–1780*. Stanford, Calif.: Stanford University Press, 2000.

Díaz, Zamira. *Oro, sociedad, y economía: El sistema colonial en la gobernación de Popayán, 1533–1733*. Bogotá: Banco de la República, 1994.

Díaz Díaz, Rafael Antonio. *Esclavitud, región y ciudad: El sistema esclavista urbano-regional en Santafé de Bogotá, 1700–1750*. Bogotá: Centro Editorial Javeriano, 2001.

Diouf, Sylviane. *Servants of Allah: African Muslims Enslaved in the New World*. New York: New York University Press, 1998.

Dodds, Jerrilynn D., María Rosa Menocal, and Abigail Krasner Balbale. *The Arts of Intimacy: Christians, Jews, and Muslims in the Making of Castilian Culture*. New Haven: Yale University Press, 2008.

dos Santos Gomes, Flávio. "A 'Safe Haven': Runaway Slaves, *Mocambos*, and Borders in Colonial Amazonia, Brazil." *Hispanic American Historical Review* 82, no. 3 (2002): 469–98.

Drewal, Henry John. "Art or Accident? Yoruba Body Artists and Their Deity Ogun." In *Africa's Ogun: Old World and New*, edited by Sandra T. Barnes, 235–60. Bloomington: Indiana University Press, 1997.

———. "Senses in Understandings of Art." *African Arts* 38, no. 2 (Summer 2005): 1, 4, 6, 88, 96.

Drewal, Henry John, and John Mason. "Ogun and Body/Mind Potentiality: Yoruba Scarification and Painting Traditions in Africa and the Americas." In *Africa's Ogun: Old World and New*, edited by Sandra T. Barnes, 332–52. Bloomington: Indiana University Press, 1997.

Drewal, Margaret Thompson. *Yoruba Ritual: Performers, Play, Agency*. Bloomington: Indiana University Press, 1992.

Dubois, Laurent. *Avengers of the New World: The Story of the Haitian Revolution*. Cambridge, Mass.: Belknap Press of Harvard University Press, 2004.

———. *A Colony of Citizens: Revolution and Slave Emancipation in the French Caribbean, 1787–1804*. Chapel Hill: University of North Carolina Press, 2004.

Dubois, Laurent, and Julius S. Scott, eds. *Origins of the Black Atlantic*. New York: Routledge, 2010.

Dueñas, Alcira. *Indians and Mestizos in the "Lettered City": Reshaping Justice, Social Hierarchy, and Political Culture in Colonial Peru*. Boulder: University of Colorado Press, 2010.

Dunn, Richard S. *Sugar and Slaves: The Rise of the Planter Class in the English West Indies, 1624–1713*. New York: Norton, 1972.

Echeverri, Marcela. "Conflicto y hegemonía en el suroccidente de la Nueva Granada, 1780–1800." *Fronteras de la Historia* 11 (2006): 343–76.

———. "Los derechos de indios y esclavos realistas y la transformación política en Popayán, Nueva Granada (1808–1820)." *Revista de Indias* 69, no. 246 (2009): 45–72.

———. "'Enraged to the Limit of Despair': Infanticide and Slave Judicial Strategies in Barbacoas, 1788–98." *Slavery and Abolition* 30, no. 3 (2009): 403–26.

———. "Popular Royalists, Empire, and Politics in Southwestern New Granada, 1809–1819." *Hispanic American Historical Review* 91, no. 2 (2011): 237–69.

Elliott, J. H. *The Old World and the New, 1492–1650*. Cambridge: Cambridge University Press, 1970.

Elliott, John H. *Empires of the Atlantic World: Britain and Spain in America, 1492–1830*. New Haven: Yale University Press, 2006.

Eltis, David, Stephen D. Behrendt, David Richardson, and Herbert S. Klein. *The Trans-Atlantic Slave Trade: A Database on CD-ROM*. Cambridge: Cambridge University Press, 1999.

Eltis, David, Paul E. Lovejoy, and David Richardson. "Slave-Trading Ports: Towards an Atlantic-Wide Perspective, 1676–1832." In *Ports of the Slave Trade (Bights of Benin and Biafra): Papers from a Conference of the Centre of Commonwealth Studies, University of Stirling, June 1998*, edited by Robin Law and Silke Strickrodt, 12–34. Stirling: Centre of Commonwealth Studies, University of Stirling, 1999.

Enríquez, Eliecer Bermeo, ed. *Quito a través de los siglos*. Vol. 2. Quito: Imprenta Municipal, 1942.

Epstein, Steven A. *Speaking of Slavery: Color, Ethnicity, and Human Bondage in Italy*. Ithaca, N.Y.: Cornell University Press, 2001.

Escalante, Aquiles. "Palenques in Colombia." In *Maroon Societies: Rebel Slave Communities in the Americas*, edited by Richard Price, 74–81. 1954. Reprint, Baltimore: Johns Hopkins University Press, 1996.

Escobar, Arturo. *Encountering Development: The Making and Unmaking of the Third World*. Princeton: Princeton University Press, 1995.

———. *Territories of Difference: Place, Movements, Life, Redes*. Durham: Duke University Press, 2008.

———. "Postconstructivist Political Ecologies." In *The International Handbook of Environmental Sociology*, edited by Michael R. Redclift and Graham Woodgate, 91–105. Northampton, Mass.: Edward Elgar, 2010.

Escudero, Grecia Vasco de, ed. *Boletin del Archivo Nacional*. No. 22. Quito: Sistema Nacional de Archivos, 1992.

Falola, Toyin, and Matt D. Childs, eds. *The Changing Worlds of Atlantic Africa: Essays in Honor of Robin Law*. Durham: Carolina Academic Press, 2009.

Farriss, Nancy M. *Maya Society under Colonial Rule: The Collective Enterprise of Survival*. Princeton: Princeton University Press, 1984.

Feierman, Steven. *Pleasant Intellectuals: Anthropology and History in Tanzania*. Madison: University of Wisconsin Press, 1990.

Ferreira da Silva, Denise. *Toward a Global Idea of Race*. Minneapolis: University of Minnesota Press, 2007.

Fields, Barbara J. "Ideology and Race in American History." In *Region, Race, and Reconstruction: Essays in Honor of C. Vann Woodward*, edited by J. Morgan Kousser and James M. McPherson, 143–77. New York: Oxford University Press, 1982.

Fischer, Brodwyn. "Quaese Pretos de Tao Pobres? Race and Social Discrimination in Rio de Janeiro's Twentieth-Century Criminal Courts." *Latin American Research Review* 39, no. 1 (2004): 31–59.

———. *A Poverty of Rights: Citizenship and Inequality in Twentieth-Century Rio de Janeiro*. Stanford, Calif.: Stanford University Press, 2008.

Fisher, Andrew B., and Mathew D. O'Hara, eds. *Imperial Subjects: Race and Identity in Colonial Latin America*. Durham: Duke University Press, 2009.

Fisher, John R. *Government and Society in Colonial Peru: The Intendant System, 1784–1814*. London: Athlone Press, 1970.

Floyd, Troy S. *The Columbus Dynasty in the Caribbean, 1492–1526*. Albuquerque: University of New Mexico Press, 1973.

Floyd-Wilson, Mary. *English Ethnicity and Race in Early Modern Drama*. Cambridge: Cambridge University Press, 2003.

Foucault, Michel. *Power/Knowledge: Selected Interviews and Other Writings, 1972–1977*. New York: Vintage Books, 1977.

———. *Discipline and Punish: The Birth of the Prison*. New York: Vintage Books, 1995.

———. "What Is Critique?" In *The Politics of Truth*, edited by Sylvère Lotringer; translated by Lysa Hochroth and Catherine Porter, 41–81. New York: Semiotext(e), 1997.

Fox-Genovese, Elizabeth. *Within the Plantation Household: Black and White Women of the Old South*. Chapel Hill: University of North Carolina Press, 1988.

Fracchia, Carmen. "Constructing the Black Slave in Early Modern Spanish Painting." In *Others and Outcasts in Early Modern Europe: Picturing the Social Margins*, edited by Tom Nichols, 179–93. Aldershot: Ashgate, 2007.

Franch, José Alcina. "El problema de las poblaciones negroides de Esmeraldas, Ecuador." *Anuário de Estudios Americanos*, no. 31 (1974): 33–46.

Franch, José Alcina, Encarnación Moreno, and Remedios de la Peña. "Penetración española en Esmeraldas (Ecuador): Tipología del descubrimiento." *Revista de Indias* 37, nos. 143–44.

Frank, Zephyr L. *Dutra's World: Wealth and Family in Nineteenth-Century Rio de Janeiro*. Albuquerque: University of New Mexico Press, 2004.

Fuente, Alejandro de la. "Esclavos africanos en La Habana: Zonas de procedencia y denominaciones étnicas, 1570–1699." *Revista Española de Antropología Americana* 20 (1990): 135–60.

———. "Slaves and the Creation of Legal Rights in Cuba: *Coartación* and *Papel*." *Hispanic American Historical Review* 87, no. 4 (2007): 659–92.

———. *Havana and the Atlantic in the Sixteenth Century*. Chapel Hill: University of North Carolina Press, 2008.

Fuente, Alejandro de la, and Ariela J. Gross. "Comparative Studies of Law, Slavery and Race in the Americas." *Annual Review of Law and Social Science* 6 (2010): 469–85.

Furtado, Júnia Ferreira. *Chica da Silva: A Brazilian Slave of the Eighteenth Century*. Cambridge: Cambridge University Press, 2009.

Games, Alison. "Atlantic History: Definitions, Challenges, and Opportunities." *American Historical Review* 111, no. 3 (2006): 741–57.

———. *The Web of Empire: English Cosmopolitans in an Age of Expansion, 1560–1660*. New York: Oxford University Press, 2008.

Garcia, Guadalupe. "Urban Guajiros: Colonial Reconcentracion, Rural Displacement, and Criminalization in Western Cuba, 1895–1902." *Journal of Latin American Studies* 43, no. 2 (2011): 209–35.

Garofalo, Leo J. "Conjuring with Coca and the Inca: The Andeanization of Lima's Afro-Peruvian Ritual Specialists, 1580–1690. *The Americas* 63, no. 1 (July 2006): 53–80.

———. "Afro-Iberian Sailors, Soldiers, Traders, and Thieves on the Spanish Main." In *Documenting Latin America: Gender, Race, and Empire*, vol. 1, edited by Erin E. O'Connor and Leo J. Garofalo, 25–34. New York: Prentice-Hall, 2010.

———. "The Shape of a Diaspora: The Movement of Afro-Iberians to Colonial Spanish America." In *Africans to Spanish America: Expanding the Diaspora*, edited by Sherwin K. Bryant, Rachel Sarah O'Toole, and Ben Vinson III, 27–49. Urbana: University of Illinois Press, 2012.

Garraway, Doris. *The Libertine Colony: Creolization in the Early French Caribbean*. Durham: Duke University Press, 2005.

Gaspar, David Barry. *Bondsmen and Rebels: A Study of Master-Slave Relations in Antigua with Implications for Colonial British America*. Baltimore: Johns Hopkins University Press, 1985.

———. "Sugar Cultivation and Slave Life in Antigua before 1800." In *Cultivation and Culture: Labour and the Shaping of Slave Life in the Americas*, edited by Ira Berlin and Philip D. Morgan, 101–23. Charlottesville: University Press of Virginia, 1993.

Gauderman, Kimberly. *Women's Lives in Colonial Quito: Gender, Law, and Economy in Spanish America*. Austin: University of Texas Press, 2003.

Geggus, David P. "Slave and Free Colored Women in Saint Domingue." In *More Than Chattel: Black Women and Slavery in the Americas*, edited by David Barry Gaspar and Darlene Clark Hine, 257–78. Bloomington: Indiana University Press, 1996.

Genovese, Eugene D. *The Political Economy of Slavery: Studies in the Economy and Society of the Slave South*. New York: Vintage Books, 1965.

———. *The World the Slaveholders Made: Two Essays in Interpretation*. New York: Vintage, 1971.

———. *Roll, Jordan, Roll: The World the Slaves Made*. 1972. Reprint, New York: Vintage, 1974.

———. *From Rebellion to Revolution: Afro-American Slave Revolts in the Making of the Modern World*. Baton Rouge: Louisiana State University Press, 1979.

Gerhard, Peter. "A Black Conquistador in Mexico." *Hispanic American Historical Review* 58, no. 3 (1968): 451–59.

Gibson, Charles. *Tlaxcala in the Sixteenth Century*. New Haven: Yale University Press, 1952.

———. *The Aztecs under Spanish Rule: A History of the Indians of the Valley of Mexico, 1519–1810*. Stanford, Calif.: Stanford University Press, 1964.

Gilroy, Paul. *The Black Atlantic: Modernity and Double Consciousness*. Cambridge, Mass.: Harvard University Press, 1993.

Ginzburg, Carlo. *The Cheese and the Worms: The Cosmos of the Sixteenth-Century Miller*. Baltimore: Johns Hopkins University Press, 2012.

Glassman, Jonathon. *Feast and Riot: Revelry, Rebellion, and Popular Consciousness on the Swahili Coast, 1856–1888*. Portsmouth, N.H.: Heinemann and James Currey, 1985.

Glymph, Thavolia. *Out of the House of Bondage: The Transformation of the Plantation Household*. Cambridge: Cambridge University Press, 2008.

Gomez, Michael A. *Exchanging Our Country Marks: The Transformation of African Identities in the Colonial and Antebellum South*. Chapel Hill: University of North Carolina Press, 1998.

Gómez, Nicolás Wey. *The Tropics of Empire: Why Columbus Sailed South to the Indies*. Cambridge: MIT Press, 2008.

González, Gerardo Andrade. "Economía y esclavitud en la colonia." *Estudios Colombianos* (1976): 1–22.

Grafe, Regina. *Distant Tyranny: Markets, Power, and Backwardness in Spain, 1650–1800*. Princeton: Princeton University Press, 2012.

———. "A Stakeholder Empire: The Political Economy of Spanish Imperial Rule in America." *Economic History Review* 65, no. 2 (2012): 609–51.

Graubart, Karen B. *With Our Labor and Sweat: Indigenous Women and the Formation of Colonial Society in Peru, 1550–1700*. Stanford, Calif.: Stanford University Press, 2007.

———. "'So Color de Una Cofradía': Catholic Confraternities and the Development of Afro-Peruvian Ethnicities in Early Colonial Peru." *Slavery and Abolition* 33, no. 1 (2012): 43–64.

Gray, Lewis Cecil. *History of Agriculture in the Southern United States to 1860*. 2 vols. Washington, D.C.: Carnegie Institute, 1932.

Green, Toby. "Building Slavery in the Atlantic World: Atlantic Connections and the Changing Institution of Slavery in Cabo Verde, Fifteenth–Sixteenth Centuries." *Slavery and Abolition* 32, no. 2 (2011): 227–45.

Greenblatt, Stephen. *Marvelous Possessions: The Wonder of the New World*. New York: Oxford University Press, 1991.

Greene, Sandra E. *Gender, Ethnicity, and Social Change on the Upper Slave Coast: A History of the Anlo-Ewe*. Portsmouth, N.H.: Heinemann, 1996.

———. "Cultural Zones in the Era of the Slave Trade: Exploring the Yoruba Connection with the Anlo-Ewe." In *Identity in the Shadow of Slavery*, edited by Paul E. Lovejoy, 86–101. New York: Continuum, 2000.

Greer, Margaret R., Walter D. Mignolo, and Maureen Quilligan, eds. *Rereading the Black Legend: The Discourses of Religious and Racial Differences in the Renaissance Empire*. Chicago: University of Chicago Press, 2008.

Grinberg, Keila. "Freedom Suits and Civil Law in Brazil and the United States." *Slavery and Abolition* 22, no. 3 (2001): 66–82.

Gross, Ariela J. "Race, Law and Comparative History." *Law and History Review* 29, no. 2 (May 2011): 549–65.

Gudeman, Stephen, and Stuart B. Schwartz. "Cleansing Original Sin: Godparenthood and the Baptism of Slaves in Eighteenth-Century Bahia." In *Kinship Ideology and Practice in Latin America*, edited by Raymond T. Smith, 35–58. Chapel Hill: University of North Carolina Press, 1984.

Gudmundson, Lowell, and Justin Wolfe, eds. *Blacks and Blackness in Central America: Between Race and Place*. Durham: Duke University Press, 2010.

Guha, Ranajit. *Dominance without Hegemony: History and Power in Colonial India*. Cambridge, Mass.: Harvard University Press, 1997.

Gutiérrez, Ramón A. *When Jesus Came, the Corn Mothers Went Away: Marriage, Sexuality, and Power in New Mexico, 1500–1846*. Stanford, Calif.: Stanford University Press, 1991.

Guyer, Jane I. "Wealth in People, Wealth in Things—Introduction." *Journal of African History* 36, no. 1 (1995): 83–90.

Guyer, Jane I., and Samuel M. Eno Belinga. "Wealth in People as Wealth in Knowledge: Accumulation and Composition in Equatorial Africa." *Journal of African History* 36, no. 1 (1995): 91–120.

Hahn, Steven. *A Nation under Our Feet: Black Political Struggles in the Rural South from Slavery to the Great Migration*. Cambridge, Mass.: Belknap Press, 2003.

Hall, Gwendolyn Midlo. *Social Control in Slave Plantation Societies: A Comparison of St. Domingue and Cuba*. Baltimore: Johns Hopkins University Press, 1971.

———. *Africans in Colonial Louisiana: The Development of Afro-Creole Culture in the Eighteenth Century*. Baton Rouge: Louisiana State University Press, 1992.

———. *Slavery and African Ethnicities in the Americas: Restoring the Links*. Chapel Hill: University of North Carolina Press, 2009.

Hamerly, Michael T. *El comercio de cacao de Guayaquil durante el período colonial: Un studio cuantitativo*. Quito: Comandancia General de Marina, 1976.

———. *Historia social y económica de la antigua provincia de Guayaquil, 1763–1842*. Quito: Banco Central del Ecuador, 1987.

Hanger, Kimberly S. *Bounded Lives, Bounded Places: Free Black Society in Colonial New Orleans, 1769–1803*. Durham: Duke University Press, 1997.

Hank, Lewis. *The Spanish Struggle for Justice in the Conquest of America*. Philadelphia: University of Pennsylvania Press, 1949.

———. *Aristotle and the American Indians*. Bloomington: Indiana University Press, 1959.

Haring, Clarence Henry. *The Spanish Empire in America*. 1947. Reprint, New York: Oxford University Press, 1957.

Harris, Leslie M. *In the Shadow of Slavery: African Americans in New York City, 1626–1863*. Chicago: University of Chicago Press, 2004.

Hartman, Saidiya V. *Scenes of Subjection: Terror, Slavery, and Self-Making in Nineteenth-Century America*. New York: Oxford University Press, 1997.

———. *Lose Your Mother: A Journey along the Atlantic Slave Route*. New York: Farrar, Straus and Giroux, 2007.

———. "Venus in Two Acts." *Small Axe* 12, no. 2 (June 2008): 1–14.

Hauser, Mark W. "Between Rural and Urban: The Archaeology of Slavery and Informal Markets in Eighteenth-Century Jamaica." In *Archaeology of Atlantic Africa and African Diaspora*, edited by Akinwumi Ogundiron and Toyin Falola, 292–310. Bloomington: University of Indiana Press, 2007.

———. *An Archaeology of Black Markets: Local Ceramics and Economies in Eighteenth-Century Jamaica*. Gainesville: University Press of Florida, 2008.

Hawthorne, Walter. *Planting Rice, Harvesting Slaves: Transformation along the Guinea-Bissau Coast, 1400–1900*. Portsmouth, N.H.: Heinemann, 2003.

———. "Being Now, as It Were, One Family: Shipmate Bonding on the Slave Vessel *Emilia*, in Rio de Janeiro and throughout the Atlantic World." *Luso-Brazilian Review* 45 (2008): 53–77.

Heiner, Brady Thomas. "Foucault and the Black Panthers." *City: Analysis of Urban Trends, Culture, Theory, Policy, Action* 11, no. 3 (2008): 313–56.

Helg, Aline. *Our Rightful Share: The Afro-Cuban Struggle for Equality, 1886–1912*. Chapel Hill: University of North Carolina Press, 1995.

———. *Liberty and Equality in Caribbean Colombia, 1770–1835*. Chapel Hill: University of North Carolina Press, 2004.

Heng, Geraldine. *Empire of Magic: Medieval Romance and the Politics of Cultural Fantasy*. New York: Columbia University Press, 2003.

Herskovits, Melville J. *The Myth of the Negro Past*. Boston: Beacon Press, 1958.

Herzog, Tamar. *La administración como un fenómeno social: La justicia penal de la ciudad de Quito (1650–1750)*. Madrid: Centro de Estudios Constitucionales, 1993.

———. *Los ministros de la audiencia de Quito (1650–1750)*. Quito: Ediciones Libri Mundi, 1995.

———. *Defining Nations: Immigrants and Citizens in Early Modern Spain and Spanish America*. New Haven: Yale University Press, 2003.

———. *Upholding Justice: Society, State, and the Penal System in Quito (1650–1750)*. Ann Arbor: University of Michigan Press, 2004.

———. "Identities and Processes of Identification in the Atlantic World." In *The Oxford Handbook of the Atlantic World*, edited by Nicholas Canny and Philip Morgan, 480–95. New York: Oxford University Press, 2011.

———. "Beyond Race: Exclusion in Early Modern Spain and Spanish America." In *Race and Blood in the Iberian World*, vol. 3, edited by Max S. Hering Torres, María Elena Martínez, and David Nirenberg, 151–68. Münster: LIT Verlag, 2012.

Hesse, Barnor. "Forgotten Like a Bad Dream: Atlantic Slavery and the Ethics of Post-colonial Memory." In *Relocating Postcolonialism*, edited by David Theo Goldberg and Ato Quayson, 143–73. Malden: Blackwell Publishers, 2002.

———. "Racialized Modernity: An Analytics of White Mythologies." *Ethnic and Racial Studies* 30, no. 4 (2007): 643–63.

———. "Self-fulfilling Prophecy: The Postracial Horizon." *South Atlantic Quarterly* 110, no. 1 (2011): 155–78.

———. "Symptomatically Black: A Creolization of the Political." In *The Creolization of Theory*, edited by Françoise Lionnet and Shu-Mei Shih, 37–61. Durham: Duke University Press, 2011.

Heuman, Gad J., and Trevor G. Burnard. *The Routledge History of Slavery*. London: Routledge, 2011.

Heywood, Linda M., ed. *Central Africans and Cultural Transformations in the American Diaspora*. Cambridge: Cambridge University Press, 2002.

———. "Queen Njinga Mbandi Ana de Sousa of Ndongo/Matamba: African Leadership, Diplomacy, and Ideology, 1620s–1650s." In *Afro-Latino Voices: Narratives from the Early Modern Ibero-Atlantic World, 1550–1812*, edited by Kathryn Joy McKnight and Leo J. Garofalo, 38–51. Indianapolis: Hackett Publishing Company, 2009.

Heywood, Linda M., and John K. Thornton, eds. *Central Africans, Atlantic Creoles, and the Foundation of the Americas, 1585–1660*. New York: Cambridge University Press, 2007.

Higgins, Kathleen J. *"Licentious Liberty" in a Brazilian Gold-Mining Region: Slavery, Gender, and Social Control in Eighteenth-Century Sabará, Minas Gerais*. University Park: Pennsylvania State University Press, 1999.

Hilton, Anne. *The Kingdom of Kongo*. Oxford: Clarendon Press, 1985.

Hine, Darlene Clark. "Rape and the Inner Lives of Black Women in the Middle-West: Preliminary Thoughts on the Culture of Dissemblance." *Signs* 14 (Summer 1989): 912–20.

———. *Hine Sight: Black Women and the Re-construction of American History*. Brooklyn, N.Y.: Carlson Publishing, 1994.

Hine, Darlene Clark, Trica Danielle Keaton, and Stephen Small, eds. *Black Europe and the African Diaspora*. Urbana: University of Illinois Press, 2009.

Hine, Darlene Clark, and Jacqueline McLeod, eds. *Crossing Boundaries: Compara-tive History of Black People in Diaspora*. Bloomington: Indiana University Press, 1999.

Hine, Darlene Clark, and Kate Wittenstein. "Female Slave Resistance: The Economics of Sex." In *The Black Woman Cross Culturally*, edited by Filomena Steady, 289–91. Cambridge, Mass.: Schenkman, 1981.

Hobsbawm, Eric, and Terence Ranger, eds. *The Invention of Tradition*. Cambridge: Cambridge University Press, 1983.

Hoetink, H. *Slavery and Race Relations in the Americas: Comparative Notes on Their Nature and Nexus*. New York: Harper and Row, 1973.

Holt, Thomas C. "Slavery and Freedom in the Atlantic World: Reflections on the Diasporan Framework." In *Crossing Boundaries: Comparative History of Black People in Diaspora*, edited by Darlene Clark Hine and Jacqueline McLeod, 33–44. Bloom-ington: Indiana University Press, 1999.

Huffine, Kristin. *Producing Christians from Half-Men and Beasts: Jesuit Ethnography and Guarani Response in Colonial Rio de la Plata*. Pittsburgh: University of Pittsburgh, forthcoming.

Hünefeldt, Christine. *Paying the Price of Freedom: Family and Labor among Lima's Slaves, 1800–1854*. Translated by Alexandra Stern. Berkeley: University of California Press, 1994.

Irigoin, Alejandra, and Regina Grafe. "Bargaining for Absolutism: A Spanish Path to Nation-State and Empire Building." *Hispanic American Historical Review* 88, no. 2 (2008): 173–209.

Iton, Richard. *In Search of the Black Fantastic: Politics and Popular Culture in the Post–Civil Rights Era*. New York: Oxford University Press, 2008.

———. "Still Life." *Small Axe* 17, no. 1 (2013): 22–39.

Jaramillo Uribe, Jaime. "Esclavos y señores en la sociedad colombiana del siglo XVIII." *Anuario Colombiano de Historia y de la Cultura* 1, no. 1 (1963): 5–76.

———. "Los estudios afroamericanos y afrocolombianos: Balance y perspectivas." *Ensayos de historia social* 2 (1989): 203–24.

Jennings, Evelyn Powell. "The Atlantic Economy in an Era of Revolution." *William and Mary Quarterly* 62, no. 3 (2005): 411–40.

———. "War as the 'Forcing House of Change': State Slavery in Late-Eighteenth-Century Cuba." *William and Mary Quarterly* (2005): 411–40.

Johnson, Lyman L. "Manumission in Colonial Buenos Aires, 1776–1810." *Hispanic American Historical Review* 59, no. 2 (1979): 258–79.

———. "'A Lack of Legitimate Obedience and Respect': Slaves and Their Masters in the Courts of Late Colonial Buenos Aires." *Hispanic American Historical Review* 87, no. 4 (2007): 631–57.

Johnson, Sylvester. *The Myth of Ham in Nineteenth-Century American Christianity: Race, Heathens, and the People of God*. New York: Palgrave Macmillan, 2004.

Johnson, Walter. *Soul by Soul: Life Inside the Antebellum Slave Market*. Cambridge, Mass.: Harvard University Press, 2001.

———. "On Agency." *Journal of Social History* 37, no. 1 (2003): 113–24.

———. "Resetting the Legal History of Slavery: Divination, Torture, Poisoning, Murder, Revolution, Emancipation, and Re-enslavement." *Law and History Review* 29, no. 4 (2011): 1089–95.

Jones, Martha S. "Time, Space, and Jurisdiction in Atlantic World Slavery: The Volunbrun Household in Gradual Emancipation New York." *Law and History Review* 29, no. 4 (2011): 1031–60.

Jouve-Martín, José Ramón. *Esclavos de la ciudad letrada: Esclavitud, escritura y colonialismo en Lima (1650–1700)*. Lima: Instituto de Estudios Peruanos, 2005.

———. "Death, Gender and Writing." In *Afro-Latino Voices: Narratives from the Eary Modern Ibero-Atlantic World, 1550–1812*, edited by Kathryn J. McKnight and Leo Garofalo, 105–25. Indianapolis: Hackett, 2009.

Joyner, Charles. *Down by the Riverside: A South Carolina Slave Community*. Urbana: University of Illinois Press, 1986.

———. *Remember Me: Slave Life in Coastal Georgia*. Atlanta: Georgia Humanities Council, 1989.

Jung, Moon. *Coolies and Cane: Race, Labor, and Sugar in the Age of Emancipation*. Baltimore: Johns Hopkins University Press, 2006.

Jurado Noboa, Fernando. "Esmeraldas en los siglos XVI, XVII y XVIII, sus tres afluentes negros coloniales." In *El Negro en la historia: Aportes para el conocimiento de las raíces en América Latina*, edited by Rafael Savoia, 31–41. Quito: Centro Cultural Afro-Ecuatoriano, 1987.

———. *Esclavitud en la costa pacífica: Iscuandé, Barbacoas, Tumaco y Esmeraldas siglos XVI al XIX*. Quito: Ediciones Abya-Yala, 1990.

———. "Algunos reflexiones sobre la tenencia de los esclavos en la colonia, 1525–1826." *Boletín del Archivo Nacional* (August 1992): 93–101.

———. *Historia social de Esmeraldas: Indios, negros, zambos, españoles, y mestizos del siglo XVI al XX*. Esmeraldas: Sociedad de Amigos de la Genealogía, 1995.

Kagan, Richard. *Lawsuits and Litigants in Castile, 1500–1700*. Chapel Hill: University of North Carolina Press, 1981.

Kagan, Richard, and Geoffrey Parker, ed. *Spain, Europe and the Atlantic World: Essays in Honour of John H. Elliot*. Cambridge: Cambridge University Press, 1995.

Kamen, Henry. *The Spanish Inquisition: A Historical Revision*. New Haven: Yale University Press, 1998.

Karasch, Mary C. *Slave Life in Rio de Janeiro, 1808–1850*. Princeton: Princeton University Press, 1987.

Katzew, Ilona. *Casta Paintings: Images of Race in Eighteenth-Century Mexico*. New Haven: Yale University Press, 2004.

Katzew, Ilona, and Susan Deans-Smith, eds. *Race and Classification: The Case of Mexican America*. Stanford, Calif.: Stanford University Press, 2009.

Kelley, Robin D. G. "'We Are Not What We Seem': Rethinking Black Working-Class Opposition in the Jim Crow South." *Journal of American History* 80, no. 1 (June 1993): 75–112.

———. *Hammer and Hoe: Alabama Communists during the Great Depression*. Chapel Hill: University of North Carolina Press, 1990.

———. *Yo' Mama's Dysfunktional! Fighting the Culture Wars in Urban America*. Boston: Beacon Press, 1998.

Kellogg, Susan. *Law and the Transformation of Aztec Culture, 1500–1700.* Norman: University of Oklahoma Press, 1995.

———. "Depicting *Mestizaje*: Gendered Images of Ethnorace in Colonial Mexican Texts." *Journal of Women's History* 12, no. 3 (2000): 69–92.

Kiddy, Elizabeth W. *Blacks of the Rosary: Memory and History in Minas Gerais, Brazil.* University Park: Pennsylvania State University Press, 2005.

King, James F. "Negro History in Continental Spanish America." *Journal of Negro History* 29 (1944): 7–23.

Klein, Herbert S. "The Colored Militia of Cuba, 1568–1868." *Caribbean Studies* 6, no. 2 (1966): 17–27.

———. *Slavery in the Americas: A Comparative Study of Virginia and Cuba.* Chicago: University of Chicago Press, 1967.

———. *The Middle Passage: Comparative Studies in the Atlantic Slave Trade.* Princeton: Princeton University Press, 1978.

———. *The Atlantic Slave Trade.* Cambridge: Cambridge University Press, 1999.

———. "The African American Experience in Comparative Perspective: The Current Question of the Debate." In *Africans to Spanish America: Expanding the Diaspora,* edited by Sherwin K. Bryant, Rachel Sarah O'Toole, and Ben Vinson III, 206–22. Urbana: University of Illinois Press, 2012.

Klein, Herbert S., and Francisco Vidal Luna. *Slavery in Brazil.* Cambridge: Cambridge University Press, 2009.

Klein, Herbert S., and Ben Vinson III. *African Slavery in Latin America and the Caribbean.* 1986. Reprint, New York: Oxford University Press, 2007.

Knight, Franklin. *Slave Society in Cuba during the Nineteenth Century.* Madison: University of Wisconsin Press, 1970.

Kolapo, Femi J. "The Igbo and Their Neighbours during the Era of the Atlantic Slave-Trade." *Slavery and Abolition* 25, no. 1 (2004): 114–33.

Kolchin, Peter. *Unfree Labor: American Slavery and Russian Serfdom.* Cambridge, Mass.: Harvard University Press, 1987.

Kupperman, Karen Ordahl. "Presentment of Civility: English Reading of American Self-Presentation in the Early Years of Colonization." *William and Mary Quarterly* 54, no. 1 (January 1997): 193–228.

Kuznesof, Elizabeth A. "Ethnic and Gender Influences on 'Spanish' Creole Society in Colonial Spanish America." *Colonial Latin American Review* 4, no. 1 (1995): 153–76.

Lamana, Gonzalo. *Domination without Dominance: Inca-Spanish Encounters in Early Colonial Peru.* Durham: Duke University Press, 2008.

Lamb, Jonathan. *Preserving the Self in the South Seas, 1680–1840.* Chicago: University of Chicago Press, 2000.

Landers, Jane. *Black Society in Spanish Florida.* Urbana: University of Illinois Press, 1999.

———. "*Cimarrón* Ethnicity and Cultural Adaptation in the Spanish Domains of the Circum-Caribbean, 1503–1763." In *Identity in the Shadow of Slavery,* edited by Paul E. Lovejoy, 30–54. London: Continuum, 2000.

———. "*Cimarrón* and Citizen: African Ethnicity, Corporate Identity, and the Evolution of Free Black Towns in the Spanish Circum-Caribbean." In *Slaves, Subjects, and*

Subversives: Blacks in Colonial Latin America, edited by Jane G. Landers and Barry M. Robinson, 111–46. Albuquerque: University of New Mexico Press, 2006.

———. *Atlantic Creoles in the Age of Revolutions*. Cambridge, Mass.: Harvard University Press, 2010.

Landers, Jane, and Barry Robinson, eds. *Slaves, Subjects, and Subversives: Blacks in Colonial Latin America*. Albuquerque: University of New Mexico Press, 2006.

Lane, Kris E. "Mining the Margins: Precious Metals Extraction and Forced Labor Regimes in the Audiencia of Quito, 1534–1821." 2 vols. Ph.D. diss., University of Minnesota, 1996.

———. *Pillaging the Empire: Piracy in the Americas, 1500–1750*. Armonk, N.Y.: M. E. Sharpe, 1998.

———. "Taming the Master: *Brujería*, Slavery, and the *Encomienda* in Barbacoas at the Turn of the Eighteenth Century." *Ethnohistory* (1998): 477–507.

———. "Captivity and Redemption: Aspects of Slave Life in Early Colonial Quito and Popayán." *The Americas* 57, no. 2 (2000): 225–46.

———. "The Transition from *Encomienda* to Slavery in Seventeenth-Century Barbacoas (Colombia)." *Slavery and Abolition* 21, no. 1 (2000): 73–95.

———. *Quito 1599: City and Colony in Transition*. Albuquerque: University of New Mexico Press, 2002.

———. "Slaves, Rebels, Apprentices: The Captivity Gradient in Early Colonial Quito." Conference paper, annual meeting of the American Historical Association and Conference on Latin American History, Chicago, January 2–5, 2003.

———. *Colour of Paradise: The Emerald in the Age of Gunpowder Empires*. New Haven: Yale University Press, 2010.

———. "Gone Platinum: Contraband and Chemistry in Eighteenth-Century Colombia." *Colonial Latin American Review* 20, no. 1 (2011): 61–79.

Larson, Brooke. *Cochabamba, 1550–1900: Colonialism and Agrarian Transformation in Bolivia*. Expanded ed. Durham: Duke University Press, 1998.

Larson, Brooke, Olivia Harris, and Enrique Tandeter, eds. *Ethnicity, Markets, and Migration in the Andes: At the Crossroads of History and Anthropology*. Durham: Duke University Press, 1995.

Lasso, Marixa. "Race War and Nation in Caribbean Gran Colombia, Cartagena, 1810–1832." *American Historical Review* 111, no. 2 (2006): 336–61.

———. *Myths of Harmony: Race and Republicanism during the Age of the Revolution, Colombia, 1795–1831*. Pittsburgh: University of Pittsburgh Press, 2007.

Laurent, Muriel. "Nueva Francia y Nueva Granada frente al contrabando: Reflexiones sobre el comercio ilícito en el contexto colonial." *Historia Crítica* 25 (2003): 137–63.

Lavallé, Bernard. "Lógica esclavista y resistencia negra en los Andes ecuatorianos a finales del siglo XVIII." *Revista de Indias* 53, no. 199 (1993): 699–722.

———. "'Aquella ignominiosa herida que se hizo a la humanidad': El cuestionamiento de la esclavitud en Quito a finales de la época colonial (Estudios)." *Revista Ecuatoriana de Historia*, no. 6 (1994): 23–48.

———. *Amor y opresión en los Andes coloniales*. Lima: Instituto de Estudios Peruanos, 1999.

Laviana Cuentos, María Luisa. *Guayaquil en el siglo XVIII: Recursos naturales y desarrollo económico*. Seville: Escuela de Estudios Hispano-Americanos, 1987.

Law, Robin. "'My Head Belongs to the King': On the Political and Ritual Significance of Decapitation in Pre-colonial Dahomey." *Journal of African History* 30 (1989): 399–415.

———. "Further Light on Bulfinch Lambe and the Emperor 'Pawpaw': King Agaja of Dahomey's Letter to King George I of England, 1726." *History in Africa* 17 (1990): 211–26.

———. "King Agaja of Dahomey, the Slave Trade, and the Question of West African Plantations: The Mission of Bulfinch Lambe and Adomo Tomo to England, 1726–32." *Journal of Imperial and Commonwealth History* 19 (1991): 137–63.

———. *The Oyo Empire, c. 1600–c. 1836: A West African Imperialism in the Era of the Atlantic Slave Trade on an African Society.* Oxford: Clarendon Press, 1991.

———. *The Slave Coast of West Africa, 1550–1750: The Impact of the Atlantic Slave Trade on an African Society.* Oxford: Clarendon Press, 1991.

———. "Ethnicity and the Slave Trade: 'Lucumi' and 'Nago' as Ethnonyms in West Africa." *History in Africa* 24 (1997): 205–19.

———. *The Kingdom of Allada.* Leiden: Research School CNWS, School of Asian, African and Amerindian Studies, 1997.

———. *Ouidah: The Social History of a West African Slaving "Port," 1727–1892.* Athens: Ohio University Press, 2004.

Law, Robin, Toyin Falola, and Matt D. Childs. *The Changing Worlds of Atlantic Africa: Essays in Honor of Robin Law.* Durham: Carolina Academic Press, 2009.

Law, Robin, and Paul E. Lovejoy, eds. *The Biography of Mahommah Gardo Baquaqua: His Passage from Slavery to Freedom in Africa and America.* Princeton: Markus Wiener Publishers, 2001.

Lewin, Linda. "Natural and Spurious Children in Brazilian Inheritance Law from Colony to Empire: A Methodological Essay." *The Americas* 48, no. 3 (1992): 351–96.

———. *Surprise Heirs.* Vol. 1, *Illegitimacy, Patrimonial Rights, and Legal Nationalism in Luso-Brazilian Inheritance (1750–1821)*; vol. 2, *Illegitimacy, Inheritance Rights, and Public Power in the Formation of Imperial Brazil (1822–1889).* Stanford, Calif.: Stanford University Press, 2003.

Lewis, Laura A. *Hall of Mirrors: Power, Witchcraft, and Caste in Colonial Mexico.* Durham: Duke University Press, 2003.

Li, Tania Murray. *The Will to Improve: Governmentality, Development, and the Practice of Politics.* Durham: Duke University Press, 2007.

Lind, Goran. *Common Law Marriage: A Legal Institution for Cohabitation.* New York: Oxford University Press, 2008.

Linebaugh, Peter, and Marcus Rediker. *The Many-Headed Hydra: Sailors, Slaves, Commoners in the Hidden History of the Revolutionary Atlantic.* Boston: Beacon Press, 2000.

Lipsett-Rivera, Sonya, and Lyman L. Johnson, eds. *The Faces of Honor: Sex, Shame, and Violence in Colonial Latin America.* Albuquerque: University of New Mexico Press, 1998.

Littlefield, Daniel C. *Rice and Slaves: Ethnicity and the Slave Trade in Colonial South Carolina.* Urbana: University of Illinois Press, 1991.

Lockhart, James. *Spanish Peru, 1532–1560: A Colonial Society.* Madison: University of Wisconsin Press, 1968.

———. "The Social History of Colonial Spanish America: Evolution and Potential." *Latin American Research Review* 7, no. 1 (1972): 6–45.

———. *The Nahuas after the Conquest: A Social and Cultural History of the Indians of Central Mexico, Sixteenth through Eighteenth Centuries*. Stanford, Calif.: Stanford University Press, 1992.

———. "Trunk Lines and Feeder Lines: The Spanish Reaction to American Resources." In *Transatlantic Encounters: Europeans and Andeans in the Sixteenth Century*, edited by Kenneth J. Andrien and Rolena Adorno, 90–120. Berkeley: University of California Press, 1994.

Lokken, Paul. "Marriage as Slave Emancipation in Seventeenth-Century Rural Guatemala." *The Americas* 58, no. 2 (2001): 175–200.

Lovejoy, Paul E. *Transformations in Slavery: A History of Slavery in Africa*. 2nd ed. Cambridge: Cambridge University Press, 2000.

———. "Identifying Enslaved Africans in the African Diaspora." In *Identity in the Shadow of Slavery*, edited by Paul E. Lovejoy, 1–29. London: Continuum, 2001.

———. "Ethnic Designations of the Slave Trade and the Reconstruction of the History of Trans-Atlantic Slavery." In *Trans-Atlantic Dimensions of Ethnicity in the African Diaspora*, edited by Paul E. Lovejoy and David V. Troutman, 9–42. London: Continuum, 2003.

———, ed. *Identity in the Shadow of Slavery*. New York: Bloomsbury Academic, 2000.

Lovejoy, Paul E., and David Vincent Trotman. "Introduction: Ethnicity and the African Diaspora." In *Trans-Atlantic Dimensions of Ethnicity in the African Diaspora*, edited by Paul E. Lovejoy and David Vincent Trotman, 1–8. London: Continuum, 2003.

Luna, Francisco Vidal, and Herbert S. Klein. *Slavery and the Economy of São Paulo, 1750–1850*. Stanford, Calif.: Stanford University Press, 2003.

Lyons, Clare A. *Sex among the Rabble: An Intimate History of Gender and Power in the Age of Revolution, Philadelphia, 1730–1830*. Chapel Hill: Published for the Omohundro Institute of Early American History and Culture, Williamsburg, Virginia, by the University of North Carolina Press, 2006.

MacGaffey, Wyatt. "Dialogues of the Deaf: Europeans on the Atlantic Coast of Africa." In *Implicit Understandings: Observing, Reporting, and Reflecting on the Encounters between Europeans and Other Peoples in the Early Modern Era*, edited by Stuart B. Schwartz, 249–67. Cambridge: Cambridge University Press, 1994.

MacKay, Ruth. *The Limits of Royal Authority: Resistance and Obedience in Seventeenth-Century Castile*. Cambridge: Cambridge University Press, 1995.

MacLachlan, Colin. *Spain's Empire in the New World: The Role of Ideas in Institutional and Social Change*. Berkeley: University of California Press, 1988.

Magdalena, Léon, and Carmen Diana Deere. "La brecha de género en la propiedad de la tierra en América Latina." *Estudios Sociológicos* 23, no. 68 (2005): 397–439.

Mamigonian, Beatriz G., and Karen Racine, eds. *The Human Tradition in the Black Atlantic, 1500–2000*. Lanham: Rowman & Littlefield Publishers, 2010.

Mangan, Jane E. *Trading Roles: Gender, Ethnicity, and the Urban Economy in Colonial Potosí*. Durham: Duke University Press, 2005.

Mann, Kristin. "Shifting Paradigms in the Study of the African Diaspora and of Atlantic History and Culture." *Slavery and Abolition* 22, no. 1 (2001): 1–2.

Marshall, Ana Maria, and Scott Barclay. "In Their Own Words: How Ordinary People Construct the Legal World." *Law and Social Inquiry* 28, no. 3 (2003): 617–28.

Martin, Cheryl English. *Governance and Society in Colonial Mexico: Chihuahua in the Eighteenth Century*. Stanford, Calif.: Stanford University Press, 1996.

Martínez, María Elena. "The Black Blood of New Spain: *Limpieza de Sangre*, Racial Violence, and Gendered Power in Early Colonial Mexico." *William and Mary Quarterly* 61, no. 3 (2004): 479–520.

———. *Genealogical Fictions: Limpieza de Sangre, Religion, and Gender in Colonial Mexico*. Stanford, Calif.: Stanford University Press, 2008.

———. "The Language, Genealogy, and Classification of 'Race' in Colonial Mexico." In *Race and Classification: The Case of Mexican America*, edited by Ilona Katzew and Susan Deans-Smith, 25–42. Stanford, Calif.: Stanford University Press, 2009.

Marzahl, Peter. *Town in the Empire: Government, Politics, and Society in Seventeenth-Century Popayán*. Austin: University of Texas Press, 1978.

Matory, J. Lorand. "The English Professors of Brazil: On the Diasporic Roots of the Yorùbá Nation." *Comparative Studies in Society and History* 41, no. 1 (January 1999): 72–103.

———. *Black Atlantic Religion: Tradition, Transnationalism, and Matriarchy in the Afro-Brazilian Candomblé*. Princeton: Princeton University Press, 2005.

Matthew, Laura E. *Memories of Conquest: Becoming Mexicano in Colonial Guatemala*. Chapel Hill: University of North Carolina Press, 2012.

Maturana, Humberto R., and Francisco J. Varela. *El árbol del conocimiento: Las bases biológicas del entendimiento humano*. Santiago de Chile: Lumen, 2004.

Mbembe, Achille. *On the Postcolony*. Berkeley: University of California Press, 2001.

McFarlane, Anthony. "Riot and Rebellion in Colonial Spanish America." *Latin American Research Review* 17, no. 2 (1982): 212–21.

———. "Civil Disorders and Popular Protests in Late Colonial New Granada." *Hispanic American Historical Review* 64, no. 1 (1984): 17–54.

———. "*Cimarrones* and *Palenques*: Runaways and Resistance in Colonial Colombia." In *Out of the House of Bondage: Runaways, Resistance, and Maroonage in Africa and the New World*, edited by Gad Heuman, 131–51. London: Frank Cass, 1986.

———. "The Rebellion of the Barrios: Urban Insurrection in Bourbon Quito." In *Reform and Insurrection in Bourbon New Grenada and Peru*, edited by John R. Fisher, Allan J. Keuthe, and Anthony McFarlane, 197–254. Baton Rouge: Louisiana State University Press, 1990.

———. *Colombia before Independence: Economy, Society, and Politics under Bourbon Rule*. Cambridge: Cambridge University Press, 1993.

McKinley, Michelle A. "Fractional Freedoms: Slavery, Legal Activism, and Ecclesiastical Courts in Colonial Lima, 1593–1689." *Law and History Review* 28, no. 3 (2010): 749–90.

———. "'Such Unsightly Unions Could Never Result in Holy Matrimony': Mixed Status Marriages in Seventeenth-Century Colonial Lima." *Yale Journal of Law and the Humanities* 22, no. 2 (2010): 217–55.

———. "Till Death Do Us Part: Testamentary Manumission in Seventeenth-Century Lima, Peru." *Slavery and Abolition* 33, no. 3 (September 2012): 381–401.

McKnight, Kathryn Joy. "'En su Tierra lo Aprendió': An African *Curandero*'s Defense before the Cartagena Inquisition." *Colonial Latin American Review* 12, no. 1 (2003): 63–84.

McKnight, Kathryn Joy, and Leo J. Garofalo, eds. *Afro-Latino Voices: Narratives from the Early Modern Ibero-Atlantic World, 1550–1812*. Indianapolis: Hackett Publishing Company, 2009.

Meiklejohn, Norman A. "The Implementation of Slave Legislation in Eighteenth-Century New Granada." In *Slavery and Race Relations in Latin America*, ed. Robert Brent Toplin, 176–203. Westport, Conn.: Greenwood Press, 1974.

Meillassoux, Claude. *The Anthropology of Slavery: The Womb of Iron and Gold*. Chicago: University of Chicago Press, 1991.

Mercado, Pedro de. *Historia de la Provincia del Nuevo Reino y Quito de la Campañía de Jesús*. Vol. 35. Bogotá: Empresa Nacional de Publicaciones, 1957.

Metcalf, Alida C. *Go-betweens and the Colonization of Brazil, 1500–1600*. Austin: University of Texas Press, 2005.

Meyer, Melissa L. *Thicker Than Water: Origins of Blood as Symbol and Ritual*. New York: Taylor and Francis Group, 2005.

Miers, Suzanne, and Igor Kopytoff, eds. *Slavery in Africa: Historical and Anthropological Perspectives*. Madison: University of Wisconsin Press, 1977.

Mignolo, Walter. *The Darker Side of the Renaissance: Literacy, Territoriality, and Colonization*. Ann Arbor: University of Michigan Press, 2003.

———. *The Idea of Latin America*. Malden, Mass.: Blackwell Publishing, 2005.

———. *Local Histories/Global Designs: Coloniality, Subaltern Knowledges, and Border Thinking*. Princeton: Princeton University Press, 2011.

Miller, Joseph C. *Way of Death: Merchant Capitalism and the Angolan Slave Trade, 1730–1830*. Madison: University of Wisconsin Press, 1988.

———. *The Problem of Slavery as History: A Global Approach*. New Haven: Yale University Press, 2012.

Miller, Peter, and Nikolas Rose. *Governing the Present: Administering Economic, Social and Personal Life*. 2008. Reprint, Cambridge: Polity Press, 2012.

Mills, Kenneth. *Idolatry and Its Enemies: Colonial Andean Religion and Extirpation, 1640–1750*. Princeton: Princeton University Press, 1997.

Milton, Cynthia E. *The Many Meanings of Poverty: Colonialism, Social Compacts and Assistance in Eighteenth-Century Ecuador*. Stanford, Calif.: Stanford University Press, 2007.

Minchom, Martín. *The People of Quito, 1690–1810: Change and Unrest in the Underclass*. Boulder, Colo.: Westview Press, 1994.

Mintz, Sidney, and Richard Price. *The Birth of African-American Culture: An Anthropological Perspective*. Boston: Beacon Press, 1976.

Molineux, Catherine. "Hogarth's Fashionable Slaves: Moral Corruption in Eighteenth-Century London." *English Literary History* 72, no. 2 (2005): 495–520.

———. "Pleasures of the Smoke: 'Black Virginians' in Georgian London's Tobacco Shops." *William and Mary Quarterly* (2007): 327–76.

———. *Faces of Perfect Ebony: Encountering Atlantic Slavery in Imperial Britain*. Cambridge, Mass.: Harvard University Press, 2012.

Morales, Edgardo Pérez. "Naturaleza, paisaje y memoria: Alturas y ciudades del Reino de Quito en la experiencia viajera del siglo XVIII." *Procesos*, no. 28 (2008): 5–28.

Moraña, Mabel, Enrique Dussel, and Carlos A. Jáuregui, eds. *Coloniality at Large: Latin America and the Postcolonial Debate*. Durham: Duke University Press, 2008.

Moreno, Christina Borchert de. "Capital comercial y producción agrícola: Nueva España y Quito en el siglo XVIII." *Anuario de Estudios Americanos* 46 (1989): 131–72.

Morgan, Jennifer L. "'Some Could Suckle Over Their Shoulder': Male Travelers, Female Bodies, and the Gendering of Racial Ideology, 1500–1770." *William and Mary Quarterly* 54, no. 1 (January 1997): 167–92.

———. *Laboring Women: Reproduction and Gender in New World Slavery*. Philadelphia: University of Pennsylvania Press, 2004.

Morgan, Philip D. "The Cultural Implications of the Atlantic Slave Trade: African Regional Origins, American Destination and New World Developments." *Slavery and Abolition* 18, no. 1 (1997): 122–45.

———. *Slave Counterpoint: Black Culture in the Eighteenth-Century Chesapeake and Lowcountry*. Chapel Hill: University of North Carolina Press, 1998.

Mörner, Magnus. *Race Mixture in the History of Latin America*. Boston: Little, Brown, 1967.

Morrison, Karen Y. "Whitening Revisited: Nineteenth-Century Cuban Counterpoints." In *Africans to Spanish America: Expanding the Diaspora*, edited by Sherwin K. Bryant, Rachel Sarah O'Toole, and Ben Vinson III, 163–85. Urbana: University of Illinois Press, 2012.

Mosquera, Claudia, Mauricio Pardo, and Odile Hoffmann, eds. *Afrodescendientes en las Américas: Trayectorias sociales e identitatarias*. Bogotá: Universidad Nacional de Colombia, 2002.

Moten, Fred. *In the Break: The Aesthetics of the Black Radical Tradition*. Minneapolis: University of Minnesota Press, 2003.

Mullin, Gerald. *Flight and Rebellion: Slave Resistance in Eighteenth-Century Virginia*. New York: Oxford University Press, 1972.

Mumford, Jeremy Ravi. "Litigation as Ethnography in Sixteenth-Century Peru: Polo de Ondegardo and the Mitimaes." *Hispanic American Historical Review* 88, no. 1 (2008): 5–40.

———. *Vertical Empire: The General Resettlement of Indians in the Colonial Andes*. Durham: Duke University Press, 2012.

Murphy, Robert Cushman. "The Earliest Spanish Advances Southward from Panama along the West Coast of South America." *Hispanic American Historical Review* 21 (1941): 16–18.

Murra, John V. *Formaciones económicas y políticas del mundo andino*. Lima: Instituto de Estudios Peruanos, 1975.

Nader, Helen. *Liberty in Absolutist Spain: The Habsburg Sale of Towns, 1516–1700*. The Johns Hopkins University Studies in Historical and Political Science, no. 108. Baltimore: Johns Hopkins University Press, 1990.

Navarrete, María Cristina. *Prácticas religiosas de los negros en la colonia: Cartagena, siglo XVII*. Cali: Universidad del Valle, 1995.

———. "Palenques y cimarrones al norte del Nuevo Reino de Granada en el siglo XVII." *Fronteras de la Historia* 6 (2001): 87–107.

———. *Génesis y desarollo de la esclavitud en Colombia, siglos XVI y XVII*. Cali: Universidad del Valle, 2005.

Newson, Linda A. *The Cost of Conquest: Indian Decline in Honduras under Spanish Rule*. Boulder, Colo.: Westview Press, 1986.

———. *Indian Survival in Colonial Nicaragua*. Norman: University of Oklahoma Press, 1987.

———. *Life and Death in Early Colonial Ecuador*. Norman: University of Oklahoma Press, 1995.

Newson, Linda A., and Susie Minchin. "Slave Mortality and African Origins: A View from Cartagena, Colombia, in the Early Seventeenth Century." *Slavery and Abolition* 25, no. 3 (December 2004): 18–43.

———. "Diets, Food Supplies, and the African Slave Trade in Early Seventeenth Century Spanish America." *The Americas* 63, no. 4 (2007): 517–50.

———. *From Capture to Sale: The Portuguese Slave Trade to Spanish South America in the Early Seventeenth Century*. Leiden: Brill, 2007.

Nimako, Kwame, and Glenn Willemsen. *The Dutch Atlantic: Slavery, Abolition and Emancipation*. London: Pluto Press, 2011.

Nishida, Mieko. "From Ethnicity to Race and Gender: Transformations of Black Lay Sodalities in Salvador, Brazil." *Journal of Social History* 32, no. 2 (1998): 329–48.

Northrup, David. "Igbo and Myth Igbo: Culture and Ethnicity in the Atlantic World, 1600–1850." *Slavery and Abolition* 21, no. 3 (2000): 1–20.

———. "The Gulf of Guinea and the Atlantic World." In *The Atlantic World and Virginia, 1550–1624*, edited by Peter Mancall, 170–93. Chapel Hill: University of North Carolina Press, 2007.

Nowara-Schmidt, Christopher. *Slavery, Freedom, and Abolition in Latin America and the Atlantic World*. Albuquerque: University of New Mexico Press, 2011.

O'Hara, Matthew D. *A Flock Divided: Race, Religion, and Politics in Mexico, 1749–1857*. Durham: Duke University Press, 2010.

Olsen, Margaret M. *Slavery and Salvation in Colonial Cartagena de Indias*. Gainesville: University Press of Florida, 2004.

O'Malley, John W. *The First Jesuits*. Cambridge, Mass.: Harvard University Press, 1993.

Ortíz de la Tabla Ducasse, Javier. "El Obispado de Quito en el siglo XVI." *Museo Histórico* (Quito) 18 (1961): 161–209.

———. *Los encomenderos de Quito, 1534–1660: Origen y evolución de una élite colonial*. Seville: CSIC, 1993.

Osorio, Alejandra. "The King in Lima: Simulacra, Ritual, and Rule in Seventeenth-Century Peru." *Hispanic American Historical Review* 84, no. 3 (2004): 447–74.

O'Toole, Rachel Sarah. "'In a War against the Spanish': Andean Protection and African Resistance on the Northern Peruvian Coast." *The Americas* 63, no. 1 (2006): 19–52.

———. "From the Rivers of Guinea to the Valleys of Peru: Becoming a Bran Diaspora within Spanish Slavery." *Social Text* 25, no. 3 (2007): 19–36.

———. *Bound Lives: Africans, Indians, and the Making of Race in Colonial Peru*. Pittsburgh: University of Pittsburgh Press, 2012.

———. "To Be Free and *Lucumí*: Ana de la Calle and Making African Diaspora Identities in Colonial Peru." In *Africans to Spanish America: Expanding the Diaspora*, edited by Sherwin K. Bryant, Rachel Sarah O'Toole, and Ben Vinson III, 73–92. Urbana: University of Illinois Press, 2012.

Owens, J. B. *"By My Absolute Royal Authority": Justice and the Castilian Commonwealth at the Beginning of the First Global Age*. Rochester, N.Y.: University of Rochester Press, 2005.

Owensby, Brian P. "How Juan and Leonor Won Their Freedom: Litigation and Liberty in Seventeenth-Century Mexico." *Hispanic American Historical Review* 85, no. 1 (2005): 39–79.

———. *Empire of Law and Indian Justice in Colonial Mexico*. Stanford, Calif.: Stanford University Press, 2008.

Pacheco, Juan Manuel. *Los Jesuitas en Colombia*. 3 vols. Bogotá: Editorial San Juan Eudes, 1959.

Pagden, Anthony. *The Fall of Natural Man: The American Indian and the Origins of Comparative Ethnology*. 2nd ed. Cambridge: Cambridge University Press, 1986.

———. "Dispossessing the Barbarian: The Language of Spanish Thomism and the Debate over the Property Rights of the American Indians." In *The Languages of Political Theory in Early-Modern Europe*, edited by Anthony Pagden, 79–98. Cambridge: Cambridge University Press, 1987.

———. *Spanish Imperialism and the Political Imagination, 1513–1830*. New Haven: Yale University Press, 1990.

———. *European Encounters with the New World: From Renaissance to Romanticism*. New Haven: Yale University Press, 1993.

———. *Lords of All the World: Ideologies of Empire in Spain, Britain and France, c. 1500–c. 1800*. New Haven: Yale University Press, 1995.

Painter, Nell Irvin. "Representing Truth: Sojourner Truth's Knowledge and Becoming Known." *Journal of American History* 81 (September 1994): 461–92.

———. *Soul Murder and Slavery*. Waco, Tex.: Markham Press Fund, Baylor University Press, 1995.

Palacios Preciado, Jorge. *La trata de negros por Cartagena de Indias, 1650–1750*. Tunja: Universidad Pedagógica y Tecnológica de Colombia, 1973.

Palmer, Colin A. *Slaves of the White God: Blacks in Mexico, 1570–1650*. Cambridge, Mass.: Harvard University Press, 1976.

———. *Human Cargoes: The British Slave Trade to Spanish America, 1700–1739*. Urbana: University of Illinois Press, 1981.

———. "From Africa to the Americas: Ethnicity in the Early Black Communities of the Americas." *Journal of World History* 6, no. 2 (1995): 223–36.

———. "Defining and Studying the Modern African Diaspora." *Perspectives* 36, no. 6 (1998): 22–25.

———. *Eric Williams and the Making of the Modern Caribbean*. Durham: University of North Carolina Press, 2006.

Palmié, Stephan. "Against Syncretism: 'Africanizing' and 'Cubanizing' Discourses in North American Òrìsà Worship." In *Counterworks: Managing the Diversity of Knowledge*, edited by Richard Fardon, 69–100. New York: Routledge, 1995.

——. "A Taste for Human Commodities: Experiencing the Atlantic System." In *Slave Cultures and the Cultures of Slavery*, edited by Stephan Palmié, 40–54. Knoxville: University of Tennessee Press, 1995.

——. *Wizards and Scientists: Explorations in Afro-Cuban Modernity and Tradition*. Durham: Duke University Press, 2002.

——. "Creolization and Its Discontents." *Annual Review of Anthropology* 35 (2006): 433–56.

——. "Ecué's Atlantic: An Essay in Methodology." *Journal of Religion in Africa* 37, no. 2 (2007): 275–315.

——. "Introduction: Out of Africa?" *Journal of Religion in Africa* 37, no. 2 (2007): 159–73.

——, ed. *Slave Cultures and the Cultures of Slavery*. Knoxville: University of Tennessee Press, 1995.

Palomeque, Silvia. *Cuenca en el siglo XIX: La articulación de una región*. Quito: Facultad Latinoamericana de Ciencias Sociales, 1990.

Parker, Freddie. *Running for Freedom: Slave Runaways in North Carolina, 1775–1840*. New York: Routledge, 1993.

Paton, Diana. "Punishment, Crime, and the Bodies of Slaves in Eighteenth-Century Jamaica." *Journal of Social History* 34, no. 4 (2001): 923–54.

——. "Witchcraft, Poison, Law, and Atlantic Slavery." *William and Mary Quarterly* 69, no. 2 (April 2012): 235–64.

Patterson, Orlando. *Slavery and Social Death: A Comparative Study*. Cambridge, Mass.: Harvard University Press, 1982.

——. *Freedom*. Vol. 1, *Freedom in the Making of Western Culture*. New York: Basic Books, 1991.

Patterson, Tiffany, and Robin D. G. Kelley. "Unfinished Migrations: Reflections on the African Diaspora and the Making of the Modern World." In *Africa's Diaspora*, edited by Ralph Faulkingam and Mitzi Goheen, special issue of *African Studies Review* 43, no. 1 (April 2000): 11–45.

Pearce, Adrian J. *British Trade with Spanish America, 1763–1808*. Liverpool: Liverpool University Press, 2007.

Penningroth, Dylan C. *The Claims of Kinfolk: African American Property and Community in the Nineteenth-Century South*. Chapel Hill: University of North Carolina Press, 2003.

Phelan, John Leddy. "Authority and Flexibility in the Spanish Imperial Bureaucracy." *Administrative Science Quarterly* 5 (1960): 47–65.

——. *The Kingdom of Quito in the Seventeenth Century: Bureaucratic Politics in the Spanish Empire*. Madison: University of Wisconsin Press, 1967.

——. *The People and the King: The Comunero Revolution in Colombia, 1781*. Madison: University of Wisconsin Press, 1978.

Philips, Carla Rhan. *Six Galleons for the King of Spain: Imperial Defense in the Early Seventeenth Century*. 1986. Reprint, Baltimore: Johns Hopkins University Press, 1992.

Pike, Ruth. "Sevillian Society in the Sixteenth Century: Slaves and Freedmen." *Hispanic American Historical Review* 47, no. 3 (1967): 344–59.

——. *Aristocrats and Traders: Sevillian Society in the Sixteenth Century*. Ithaca, N.Y.: Cornell University Press, 1972.

Ponce Leiva, Pilar. "El poder informal: Mujeres de Quito en el siglo XVII." *Revista Complutense de Historia de América*, no. 23 (1997): 97–111.

Powers, Karen Vieira. *Andean Journeys: Migration, Ethnogenesis, and the State in Colonial Quito*. Albuquerque: University of New Mexico Press, 1995.

———. "A Battle of Wills: Inventing Chiefly Legitimacy in the Colonial North Andes." In *Dead Giveaways: Indigenous Testaments of Colonial Mesoamerica and the Andes*, edited by Susan Kellogg and Mathew Restall, 183–213. Salt Lake City: University of Utah Press, 1998.

———. "Land Concentration and Environmental Degradation: Town Council Records on Deforestation in Uyumbicho (Quito, 1553–96)." In *Colonial Lives: Documents on Latin American History, 1550–1850*, edited by Richard Boyer and Geoffrey Spurling, 11–17. Oxford: Oxford University Press, 2000.

Pratt, Mary Louise. *Imperial Eyes: Travel Writing and Transculturation*. New York: Routledge, 1992.

Premo, Bianca. *Children of the Father King: Youth, Authority, and Legal Minority in Colonial Lima*. Chapel Hill: University of North Carolina Press, 2005.

———. "An Equity against the Law: Slave Rights and Creole Jurisprudence in Spanish America." *Slavery and Abolition* 32, no. 4 (2011): 495–517.

Price, Richard. *Maroon Societies: Rebel Slave Communities in the Americas*. 2nd ed. Baltimore: Johns Hopkins University Press, 1979.

———. *First-Time.* Baltimore: Johns Hopkins University Press, 1983.

———. "The Miracle of Creolization: A Retrospective." *New West Indian Guide/Nieuwe West-Indische Gids* 75, nos. 1&2 (2001): 35–64.

Proctor, Frank "Trey," III. "Gender and the Manumission of Slaves in New Spain." *Hispanic American Historical Review* 86, no. 2 (2006): 309–36.

———. *Damned Notions of Liberty: Slavery, Culture, and Power in Colonial Mexico, 1640–1769*. Albuquerque: University of New Mexico Press, 2010.

———. "African Diasporic Ethnicity in Mexico City to 1650." In *Africans to Spanish America: New Directions*, edited by Sherwin K. Bryant, Rachel O'Toole, and Ben Vinson III, 50–72. Urbana: University of Illinois Press, 2012.

Puar, Jasbir K. "'I Would Rather Be a Cyborg Than a Goddess': Becoming-Intersectional in Assemblage Theory." *philoSOPHIA* 2, no. 1 (2012): 49–66.

Quijano, AnQuijano, Aníbal. "Coloniality of Power, Eurocentrism, and Latin America." In *Coloniality at Large: Latin America and the Postcolonial Debate,* edited by Mabel Moraña, Enrique Dussel, and Carlos A. Jáuregui, 181–224. Durham: Duke University Press, 2008.

Rabasa, José. *Writing Violence on the Northern Frontier: The Historiography of Sixteenth-Century New Mexico and Florida and the Legacy of Conquest*. Durham: Duke University Press, 2000.

Rama, Angel. *The Lettered City*. Translated by John C. Chasteen. Durham: Duke University Press, 1996.

Ramírez, Susan Elizabeth. *The World Upside Down: Cross-Cultural Contact and Conflict in Colonial Peru*. Stanford, Calif.: Stanford University Press, 1998.

———. *To Feed and Be Fed: The Cosmological Bases of Authority and Identity in the Andes*. Stanford, Calif.: Stanford University Press, 2005.

Ranciére, Jacques. *Dis-agreement: Politics and Philosophy*. Translated by Julie Rose. Minneapolis: University of Minnesota Press, 1999.

Rappaport, Joanne. *The Politics of Memory: Native Historical Interpretation in the Colombian Andes*. Cambridge: Cambridge University Press, 1990.

———. "'Asi lo Paresçe por su Aspeto': Physiognomy and the Construction of Difference in Colonial Bogotá." *Hispanic American Historical Review* 91, no. 4 (November 2011): 601–31.

Rappaport, Joanne, and Tom Cummins. *Beyond the Lettered City: Indigenous Literacies in the Andes*. Durham: Duke University Press, 2012.

Rathbone, Richard. "The Gold Coast, the Closing of the Atlantic Slave Trade, and Africans of the Diaspora." In *Slave Cultures and the Cultures of Slavery*, edited by Stephan Palmié, 55–66. Knoxville: University of Tennessee Press, 1995.

Rediker, Marcus. *The Slave Ship: A Human History*. New York: Penguin Group, 2007.

Reff, Daniel T. *Plagues, Priests, and Demons: Sacred Narratives and the Rise of Christianity in the Old World and the New*. Cambridge: Cambridge University Press, 2005.

Reid-Vazquez, Michele. *The Year of the Lash: Free People of Color in Cuba and the Nineteenth-Century Atlantic World*. Athens: University of Georgia Press, 2011.

———. "Tensions of Race, Gender, and Midwifery in Colonial Cuba." In *Africans to Spanish America: New Directions*, edited by Sherwin K. Bryant, Rachel O'Toole, and Ben Vinson III, 186–205. Urbana: University of Illinois Press, 2012.

Reis, João José. *Slave Rebellion in Brazil: The Muslim Uprising of 1835 in Bahia*. Translated by Arthur Brakel. Baltimore: Johns Hopkins University Press, 1993.

———. *Death Is a Festival: Funeral Rites and Rebellion in Nineteenth-Century Brazil*. Chapel Hill: University of North Carolina Press, 2003.

Restall, Matthew. "Black Conquistadors: Armed Africans in Early Spanish America." *The Americas* 57, no. 2 (2000): 174–96.

———. *Seven Myths of the Spanish Conquest*. New York: Oxford University Press, 2004.

———. *Beyond Black and Red: African-Native Relations in Colonial Latin America*. Albuquerque: University of New Mexico Press, 2005.

———. *The Black Middle: Africans, Mayas, and Spaniards in Colonial Yucatán*. Stanford, Calif.: Stanford University Press, 2009.

Restall, Matthew, and Kris Lane. *Latin America in Colonial Times*. Vol. 1. Cambridge: Cambridge University Press, 2011.

Restrepo, Luz Adriana Maya. *Brujería y reconstrucción de identitidades entre los africanos y sus descendientes en la Nueva Granda, siglo XVII*. Santafé de Bogotá: Imprenta Nacional de Colombia, 2005.

———, ed. *Geografía humana de Colombia: Los Afrocolombianos*. Vol. 6. Santafé de Bogotá: Instituto Colombiano de Cultura Hispánica, 1998.

Robinson, Cedric. *Black Marxism: The Making of the Black Radical Tradition*. Chapel Hill: University of North Carolina Press, 2000.

Rodríguez Jiménez, Pablo Emilio. "Aspectos del comércio y la vida de los esclavos, Popayán, 1780–1850." *Boletín de Antropología* 7, no. 23 (1990): 11–26.

Romero Vergara, Mario Diego. *Poblamiento y sociedad en el Pacífico colombiano, siglos XVI al XVIII*. Cali: Universidad del Valle, 1995.

———. "Familia afrocolombiana y construcción territorial en el Pacífico sur, siglo XVIII." In *Geografía Humana de Colombia: Los Afrocolombianos*, vol. 6, edited by Luz Adriana Maya Restrepo, 103–40. Santafé de Bogotá: Instituto de Cultura Hispánica, 1998.

Rostworowski de Diez, Canseco. *Pachacámac y el Señor de los Milagros: Una trayectoria milenaria*. Lima: Instituto de Estudios Peruanos, 1992.

Rout, Leslie B. *The African Experience in Spanish America, 1502 to the Present Day*. Cambridge: Cambridge University Press, 1976.

Rucker, Walter C. *The River Flows On: Black Resistance, Culture, and Identity Formation in Early America*. Baton Rouge: Louisiana State University Press, 2006.

Sáez, José L. *La iglesia y el negro esclavo en Santo Domingo: Una historia de tres siglos*. Vol. 3. Santo Domingo: El Patronato de la Ciudad Colonial de Santo Domingo, 1994.

Safford, Frank, and Marco Palacios. *Colombia: Fragmented Land, Divided Society*. New York: Oxford University Press, 2002.

Safier, Neil. *Measuring the New World: Enlightenment Science and South America*. Chicago: University of Chicago Press, 2008.

Salas, Mariano. *Pedro Claver, el santo de los esclavos*. Madrid: Ediciones de la Revista de Occidente, 1969.

Salmoral, Manuel Lucena. *Sangre sobre piel negra: La esclavitud quiteña en el contexto del reformismo Borbónico*. Quito: Abya-Yala, 1991.

———. *Los códigos negros de la América Española*. Alcalá de Henares: Universidad de Alcalá, UNESCO, 1996.

Salomon, Frank. *Native Lords of Quito in the Age of the Incas: The Political Economy of North-Andean Chiefdoms*. Cambridge: Cambridge University Press, 1986.

———. *The Cord Keepers: Khipus and Cultural Life in a Peruvian Village*. Durham: Duke University Press, 2004.

Salomon, Frank, and Stuart B. Schwartz, eds. *The Cambridge History of the Native Peoples of the Americas*. Vol. 3, pt. 1, *South America*. Cambridge: Cambridge University Press, 1999.

Sartorius, David. "My Vassals: Free-Colored Militias in Cuba and the Ends of Spanish Empire." *Journal of Colonialism and Colonial History* 5, no. 2 (2004): n.p.

———. "Race in Retrospect: Thinking with History in Nineteenth-Century Cuba." In *Race and Blood in the Iberian World*, edited by Max S. Hering Torres, María Elena Martínez, and David Nirenberg, 169–90. Vol. 3. Münster: LIT Verlag, 2012.

Saunders, A. C. de C. M. *A Social History of Black Slaves and Freedmen in Portugal, 1441–1555*. Cambridge: Cambridge University Press, 1982.

Savoia, P. Rafael. "El negro Alonso de Illescas y sus descendientes (entre 1553–1867)." In *Actas del primer congreso de historia del negro en el Ecuador y sur de Colombia*, edited by P. Rafael Savoia, 29–61. Quito: Centro Cultural Afro-Ecuatoriano, 1988.

———. *El negro en la historia: Aportes para el conocimiento de las raíces en América Latina*. Quito: Centro Cultural Afro-Ecuatoriano, Departamento de Pastoral Afroecuatoriano, 1990.

———. *El negro en la historia: Raíces africanas en la nacionalidad ecuatoriana conferencias del tercer congreso [y] XVI Jornadas de Historia Social y Genealogía.* Quito: Centro Cultural Afroecuatoriano, 1992.

Schechner, Richard. *Between Theater and Anthropology.* Philadelphia: University of Pennsylvania Press, 1985.

Schoenbrun, David L. "Conjuring the Modern in Africa: Durability and Rupture in Histories of Public Healing between the Great Lakes of East Africa." *American Historical Review* 111 (2006): 1403–39.

Schwartz, Stuart B. *Sovereignty and Society in Colonial Brazil: The High Court of Babia and Its Judges.* Berkeley: University of California Press, 1973.

———. *Sugar Plantations in the Formation of Brazilian Society: Bahia, 1550–1835.* Cambridge: Cambridge University Press, 1985.

———. *Slaves, Peasants, and Rebels: Reconsidering Brazilian Slavery.* 1992. Reprint, Urbana: University of Illinois Press, 1996.

———. *Victors and Vanquished: Spanish and Nahua Views of the Conquest of Mexico.* Bedford Series in History & Culture, no. 38. Boston: Bedford/St. Martin's, 2000.

Scott, David. "That Event, This Memory: Notes on the Anthropology of African Diasporas in the New World." *Diaspora: A Journal of Transnational Studies* 1, no. 3 (1991): 261–84.

———. *Refashioning Futures: Criticism after Postcoloniality.* Princeton: Princeton University Press, 1999.

Scott, James C. *Weapons of the Weak: Everyday Forms of Resistance.* New Haven: Yale University Press, 1985.

———. *Domination and the Arts of Resistance: Hidden Transcripts.* New Haven: Yale University Press, 1990.

———. *Seeing Like a State: How Certain Schemes to Improve the Human Condition Have Failed.* New Haven: Yale University Press, 1998.

Scott, Joan W. *Gender and the Politics of History.* New York: Columbia University Press, 1988.

Scott, Rebecca J. *Slave Emancipation in Cuba: The Transition to Free Labor, 1860–1899.* Princeton: Princeton University Press, 1985.

———. *Degrees of Freedom: Louisiana and Cuba after Slavery.* Cambridge, Mass.: Belknap Press of Harvard University Press, 2005.

———. "'She . . . Refuses to Deliver Up Herself as the Slave of Your Petitioner': Émigrés, Enslavement, and the 1808 Louisiana Digest of the Civil Laws." *Tulane European and Civil Law Forum* 24 (2009): 115–36.

———. "Paper Thin: Freedom and Re-enslavement in the Diaspora of the Haitian Revolution." *Law and History Review* 29, no. 4 (2011): 1061–87.

———. "Slavery and Law in Atlantic Perspective: Jurisdiction, Jurisprudence, and Justice." *Law and History Review* 29, no. 4 (2011): 915–24.

———. "Under Color of Law: *Siliadin v. France* and the Dynamics of Enslavement in Historical Perspective." In *The Legal Understanding of Slavery: From the Historical to the Contemporary*, edited by J. Allain, 152–64. Oxford: Oxford University Press, 2012.

Scott, Rebecca J., and Jean M. Hébrard. *Freedom Papers: An Atlantic Odyssey in the Age of Emancipation*. Cambridge, Mass.: Harvard University Press, 2012.

Seed, Patricia. "The Social Dimensions of Race: Mexico City, 1753." *Hispanic American Historical Review* 62, no. 4 (1982): 596–606.

———. *To Love, Honor, and Obey in Colonial Mexico: Conflicts over Marriage Choice, 1574–1821*. Stanford, Calif.: Stanford University Press, 1988.

———. *Ceremonies of Possession in Europe's Conquest of the New World, 1492–1640*. Cambridge: Cambridge University Press, 1995.

Sharpe, William Frederick. *Slavery on the Spanish Frontier: The Colombian Chocó, 1680–1810*. Norman: University of Oklahoma Press, 1976.

Shaw, Stephanie J. "Mothering under Slavery in the Antebellum South." In *Mothering: Ideology, Experience, and Agency*, edited by Evelyn Nakano Glenn, Grace Chang, and Linda Rennie Forcey, 237–58. New York: Routledge, 1994.

———. "Using the WPA Ex-Slave Narratives to Study the Impact of the Great Depression." *Journal of Southern History* 69, no. 3 (2003): 623–58.

———. "Creolization, Decreolization, and Being." *Historically Speaking* 11, no. 3 (2010): 27–28.

Shepherd, Verene, Bridget Brereton, and Barbara Bailey, eds. *Engendering History: Caribbean Women in Historical Perspective*. London: James Currey, 1995.

Silverblatt, Irene. *Moon, Sun, and Witches: Gender Ideologies and Class in Inca and Colonial Peru*. Princeton: Princeton University Press, 1987.

———. *Modern Inquisitions: Peru and the Colonial Origins of the Civilized World*. Durham: Duke University Press, 2004.

Smallwood, Stephanie E. *Saltwater Slavery: A Middle Passage from Africa to American Diaspora*. Cambridge, Mass.: Harvard University Press, 2007.

Smith, Micaela A. "Conditions of Belonging: Life, Historical Preservation, and Tourism Development in the Making of Pelourinho-Maciel, Salvador da Bahia, Brazil, 1965–1985." Ph.D. diss., University of Southern California, 2012.

Smolenski, John. "Hearing Voices: Microhistory, Dialogicality and the Recovery of Popular Culture on an Eighteenth-Century Virginia Plantation." *Slavery and Abolition* 24, no. 1 (2003): 1–23.

Soares, Mariza de Carvalho. *Devotos da cor: Identidade étnica, religiosidade e escravidão no Rio de Janeiro, século XVIII*. Rio de Janeiro: Civilização Brasileira, 2000.

———. "African Barbeiros in Brazilian Slave Ports." In *The Black Urban Atlantic in the Age of the Slave Trade*, edited by Matt Childs, Jorge Cañizares Esguerra, and James Sidbury, 207–32. Philadelphia: University of Pennsylvania Press, 2013.

Soares, Mariza, Jane Landers, Paul E. Lovejoy, and Andrew McMichael. "Slavery in Ecclesiastical Archives: Preserving the Records." *Hispanic American Historical Review* 86, no. 2 (2006): 337–46.

Socolow, Susan Migden. *The Bureaucrats of Buenos Aires, 1769–1810: El Amor al Real Servicio*. Durham: Duke University Press, 1987.

———. *The Women of Colonial Latin America*. Cambridge: Cambridge University Press, 2000.

Solow, Barbara L., ed. *Slavery and the Rise of the Atlantic System*. Cambridge: Cambridge University Press, 2002.

Soulodre–La France, Renée. "Socially Not So Dead! Slave Identities in Bourbon Nueva Granada." *Colonial Latin American Review* 10, no. 1 (2001): 87–103.

Spalding, Karen. "Exploitation as an Economic System: The State and the Extraction of Surplus in Colonial Peru." In *The Inca and Aztec States, 1400–1800*, edited by George Collier, Renato Rosaldo, and John Wirth, 321–42. New York: Academic Press, 1982.

———. *Huarochirí: An Andean Society under Inca and Spanish Rule.* Stanford, Calif.: Stanford University Press, 1988.

Spicker, Jessica. "El cuerpo femenino en cautiverio: Aborto e infanticídio entre las esclavas de la Nueva Granada, 1750–1810." In *Geografía humana de Colombia: Los Afrocolombianos*, vol. 6, edited by Luz Adriana Maya Restrepo, 141–66. Santafé de Bogotá: Instituto de Cultura Hispánica, 1998.

Stavig, Ward. *The World of Túpac Amaru: Conflict, Community, and Identity in Colonial Peru.* Lincoln: University of Nebraska Press, 1999.

Stern, Steve J. *Peru's Indian Peoples and the Challenge of Spanish Conquest: Huamanga to 1640.* Madison: University of Wisconsin Press, 1982.

———. *The Secret History of Gender: Women, Men, and Power in Late Colonial Mexico.* Chapel Hill: University of North Carolina Press, 1995.

Stoler, Ann Laura. *Race and the Education of Desire: Foucault's History of Sexuality and the Colonial Order of Things.* Durham: Duke University Press, 1995.

———. *Along the Archival Grain: Epistemic Anxieties and Colonial Common Sense.* Princeton: Princeton University Press, 2010.

Sweet, James H. "The Iberian Roots of American Racist Thought." *William and Mary Quarterly* 54, no. 1 (1997): 143–66.

———. *Recreating Africa: Culture, Kinship, and Religion in the African-Portuguese World, 1441–1770.* Chapel Hill: University of North Carolina Press, 2003.

———. "Mistaken Identities? Olaudah Equiano, Domingos Álvares, and the Methodological Challenges of Studying the African Diaspora." *American Historical Review* 114, no. 2 (2009): 279–306.

———. *Domingos Álvares, African Healing, and the Intellectual History of the Atlantic World.* Chapel Hill: University of North Carolina Press, 2011.

Tanenhaus, David S., ed. *Law, Slavery, and Justice.* Special issue of *Law and History Review* 29, no. 4 (2011).

Tannenbaum, Frank. *Slave and Citizen: The Classic Comparative Story of Race Relations in the Americas.* New York: A. A. Knopf, 1947.

Tardieu, Jean-Pierre. *Los negros y la iglesia en el Perú, siglos XVI–XVII.* 2 vols. Quito: Centro Cultural Afroecuatoriano, 1997.

———. "Un proyecto utópico de manumisión de los cimarrones del 'palenque de los montes de Cartagena' en 1682." In *Afrodescendientes en las américas: Trayectorias sociales e identitarias*, edited by Claudia Mosquera, Mauricio Pardo, and Odile Hoffmann, 169–80. Bogotá: Universidad Nacional de Colombia, 2002.

———. *El negro en la real audiencia de Quito, siglos XVI–XVIII.* Lima: Instituto Francés de Estudios Andinos, 2006.

———. *Cimarrones de Panamá: La forja de una identidad afroamericana en el siglo XVI.* Madrid: Iberoamericana, 2009.

———. "Negros e indios en el obraje de San Ildefonso: Real audiencia de Quito, 1665–1666." *Revista de Indias* 72, no. 255 (2012): 527–49.

Taussig, Michael T. *The Devil and Commodity Fetishism in South America*. Chapel Hill: University of North Carolina Press, 1980.

Taylor, William B. *Drinking, Homicide, and Rebellion in Colonial Mexican Villages*. Stanford, Calif.: Stanford University Press, 1979.

———. "Between Global Process and Local Knowledge: An Inquiry into Early Latin American Social History, 1500–1900." In *Reliving the Past: The Worlds of Social History*, edited by Olivier Zunz, 115–90. Chapel Hill: University of North Carolina Press, 1985.

———. *Magistrates of the Sacred: Parish Priests and Indian Parishioners in Eighteenth-Century Mexico*. Stanford, Calif.: Stanford University Press, 1999.

Thomas, Hugh. *The Slave Trade: The Story of the Atlantic Slave Trade, 1440–1870*. New York: Simon & Schuster, 1999.

———. *Rivers of Gold: The Rise of the Spanish Empire, from Columbus to Magellan*. New York: Random House, 2005.

Thornton, John. "African Dimensions of the Stono Rebellion." *American Historical Review* (1991): 1101–13.

———. "'I Am the Subject of the King of Congo': African Political Ideology and the Haitian Revolution." *Journal of World History* (1993): 181–214.

———. *Africa and Africans in the Making of the Atlantic World, 1400–1800*. 2nd ed. Cambridge: Cambridge University Press, 1998.

———. *Kongolese Saint Anthony: Dona Beatriz Kimpa Vita and the Antonian Movement, 1684–1706*. Cambridge: Cambridge University Press, 1998.

Tomlich, Dale W. *Slavery and the Circuit of Sugar: Martinique in the World Economy, 1830–1848*. Baltimore: Johns Hopkins University Press, 1990.

———. *Through the Prism of Slavery: Labor, Capital, and World Economy*. Lanham: Rowman & Littlefield, 2003.

Torres, Arlene, and Norman E. Whitten Jr., eds. *Blackness in Latin America and the Caribbean: Social Dynamics and Cultural Transformations*. Blacks in the Diaspora, vol. 2. Bloomington: Indiana University Press, 1998.

Torres, Max S. Hering, María Elena Martínez, and David Nirenberg, eds. *Race and Blood in the Iberian World*. Münster: LIT Verlag, 2012.

Townsend, Camilla. "En busca de la libertad: Los esfuerzos de los esclavos Guayaquileños por garantizar su independencia después de la Independencia." *Procesos: Revista Ecuatoriana de Historia* 4 (1993): 73–86.

———. "'Half My Body Free, the Other Half Enslaved': The Politics of the Slaves of Guayaquil at the End of the Colonial Era." *Colonial Latin American Review* 7, no. 1 (1998): 105–28.

———. *Tales of Two Cities: Race and Economic Culture in Early Republican North and South America: Guayaquil, Ecuador, and Baltimore, Maryland*. Austin: University of Texas Press, 2000.

Trouillot, Michel-Rolph. *Silencing the Past: Power and the Production of History*. Boston: Beacon Press, 2012.

Truhan, Deborah L. *Apuntes para la historia de Cuenca, 1557–1730*. Quito: Fundo Documental Museo Pumapungo del Ministerio de Cultura, 2011.

Tsing, Anna. *Friction: An Ethnography of Global Connection*. Princeton: Princeton University Press, 2005.

Twinam, Ann. *Public Lives, Private Secrets: Gender, Honor, Sexuality, and Illegitimacy in Colonial Spanish America*. Stanford, Calif.: Stanford University Press, 1999.

Tyrer, Robson Brines. *Historia demográfica y económica de la audiencia de Quito: Población indígena e industria textíl, 1600–1800*. Quito: Banco Central del Ecuador, 1988.

Uribe-Uran, Victor M. *Honorable Lives: Lawyers, Family, and Politics in Colombia, 1780–1850*. Pittsburgh: University of Pittsburgh Press, 2000.

Usner, Daniel H., Jr. *Indians, Settlers, and Slaves in a Frontier Exchange Economy: The Lower Mississippi Valley before 1783*. Chapel Hill: University of North Carolina Press, 1992.

Valencia Villa, Carlos Eduardo. *Alma en boca y huesos en costal: Una aproximación a los contrastes socio-económicos de la esclavitud: Santafeó, Mariquita y Mompox, 1610–1660*. Bogotaó: Instituto Colombiano de Antropología y Historia, 2003.

Valtierra, Angel. *San Pedro Claver: El santo que libertó una raza*. New ed. Cartagena: Departamento de Publicaciones, Santuario de San Pedro Claver, 1964.

van Deusen, Nancy E. "Determining the Boundaries of Virtue: The Discourse of *Recogimiento* among Women in Seventeenth-Century Lima." *Journal of Family History* 22, no. 4 (1997): 373–89.

———. "The 'Alienated' Body: Slaves and Free *Castas* in the Hospital de San Bartolomé of Lima, 1680–1700." *The Americas* 56, no. 1 (1999): 1–30.

———. *Between the Sacred and the Worldly: The Institutional and Cultural Practice of Recogimiento in Colonial Lima*. Stanford, Calif.: Stanford University Press, 2001.

———. "Recent Approaches to the Study of Gender Relations among Native Andeans under Colonial Rule." In *New World, First Nations: Native Peoples of Mesoamerica and the Andes under Colonial Rule*, edited by David Cahill and Blanca Tovias de Plaisted, 144–66. Eastbourne: Sussex Academic Press, 2006.

———. "Circuits of Knowledge among Lay and Religious Women in Early Seventeenth-Century Peru." In *Gender, Race, and Religion in the Colonization of the Americas*, edited by Nora E. Jaffary, 137–51. Burlington: Ashgate Press, 2007.

———. "Reading the Body: Mystical Theology and Spiritual Appropriation in Early Seventeenth-Century Lima." *Journal of Religious History* 33, no. 1 (Spring 2009): 1–27.

———. "Diasporas, Bondage, and Intimacy in Lima, 1535 to 1555." *Colonial Latin American Review* 19, no. 2 (August 2010): 247–77.

———. "God Lives among the Pots and Pans: Religious Servants in Seventeenth-Century Lima." In *Africans to Spanish America: New Directions*, edited by Sherwin K. Bryant, Rachel O'Toole, and Ben Vinson III, 136–60. Urbana: University of Illinois Press, 2012.

———. "The Intimacies of Bondage: Female Indigenous Servants and Their Spanish Masters, 1492–1555." *Journal of Women's History* 24, no. 1 (Spring 2012): 13–43.

———. "Seeing *Indios* in Sixteenth-Century Castile." *William and Mary Quarterly* 69, no. 2 (April 2012): 205–34.

Vansina, Jan M. *Paths in the Rainforests: Toward a History of Political Tradition in Equatorial Africa*. Madison: University of Wisconsin Press, 1990.

Varón, Rafael. "Cofradías de indios y poder local en el Perú colonial: Huaraz, siglo XVII." *Allpanchis* 17, no. 20 (1982): 127–46.

Vaughan, Alden T., and Virginia Mason Vaughan. "Before Othello: Elizabethan Representations of Sub-Saharan Africans." *William and Mary Quarterly* 54, no. 1 (January 1997): 19–44.

Vaughan, Megan. *Curing Their Ills: Colonial Power and African Illness*. Cambridge: Polity Press, 1991.

Vega Franco, Marisa. *El tráfico de esclavos con América: Asientos de Grillo y Lomelín, 1663–1674*. Seville: Escuela de Estudios Hispanoamericanos de Sevilla, 1984.

Vila Vilar, Enriqueta. *Hispanoamérica y el comercio de esclavos*. Seville: Escuela de Estudios HispanoAmericanos, 1977.

———. "Cimarronaje en Panamá y Cartagena: El costo de una guerrilla en el siglo XVII." *C.M.H.I.B. Caravelle*, no. 49 (1987): 77–92.

Villa-Flores, Javier. "'To Lose One's Soul': Blasphemy and Slavery in New Spain, 1596–1669." *Hispanic American Historical Review* 82, no. 3 (2002): 435–68.

———. *Dangerous Speech: A Social History of Blasphemy in Colonial Mexico*. Tucson: University of Arizona Press, 2006.

Villegas, Juan. *Negros y mulatos esclavos: Audiencia de Quito*. Montevideo: Centro de Estudios de Historia Americana, 1992.

Vinson, Ben, III. *Bearing Arms for His Majesty: The Free-Colored Militia in Colonial Mexico*. Stanford, Calif.: Stanford University Press, 2001.

———. "African (Black) Diaspora History, Latin American History—A Comment." *The Americas* 63, no. 1 (July 2006): 1–18.

Voekel, Pamela. *Alone before God: The Religious Origins of Modernity in Mexico*. Durham: Duke University Press, 2002.

Von Germeten, Nicole. *Black Blood Brothers: Confraternities and Social Mobility for Afro-Mexicans*. Gainesville: University Press of Florida, 2006.

Wade, Peter. *Blackness and Race Mixture: The Dynamics of Racial Identity in Colombia*. Baltimore: Johns Hopkins University Press, 1993.

———. "Construcciones de lo negro y del África en Colombia: Política y cultura en la música costeña y el rap." In *Afrodescendientes en las américas: Trayectorias sociales e identitarias*, edited by Claudia Mosquera, Mauricio Pardo, and Odile Hoffmann, 245–78. Bogotá: Universidad Nacional de Colombia, 2002.

Walker, Charles F. *Shaky Colonialism: The 1746 Earthquake-Tsunami in Lima, Peru, and Its Long Aftermath*. Durham: Duke University Press, 2008.

Walker, Daniel E. *No More, No More: Slavery and Cultural Resistance in Havana and New Orleans.* Minneapolis: University of Minnesota Press, 2004.

Walker, Geoffrey J. *Spanish Politics and Imperial Trade, 1700–1789*. Bloomington: Indiana University Press, 1979.

Walker, Tamara J. "'He Outfitted His Family in Notable Decency': Slavery, Honor and Dress in Eighteenth-Century Lima, Peru." *Slavery and Abolition* 30, no. 3 (2009): 383–402.

Ware, Rudolph T., III. "Slavery in Islamic Africa, 1400–1800." In *The Cambridge World History of Slavery*, vol. 3, *AD 1420–AD 1804*, edited by David Eltis and Stanley L. Engerman, 47–80. Cambridge: Cambridge University Press, 2011.

———. *The Walking Qur'an: Islamic Education, Embodied Knowledge, and History in West Africa*. Chapel Hill: University of North Carolina Press, 2014.

Watson, Alan. *Roman Slave Law*. Baltimore: Johns Hopkins University Press, 1987.

———. *Slave Law in the Americas*. Athens: University of Georgia Press, 1989.

Weinstein, Barbara. *The Amazon Rubber Boom, 1850–1920*. Stanford, Calif.: Stanford University Press, 1983.

———. "Erecting and Erasing Boundaries: Can We Combine the 'Indo' and the 'Afro' in Latin American Studies?" *Estudios Interdisciplinarios de America Latina y el Caribe* 19, no. 1 (2008): 129–44.

Weismantel, Mary. *Cholas and Pishtacos: Stories of Race and Sex in the Andes.* Chicago: University of Chicago Press, 2001.

West, Robert C. *Colonial Placer Mining in Colombia*. Baton Rouge: Louisiana State University Press, 1952.

Wey-Gómez, Nicolás. *The Tropics of Empire: Why Columbus Sailed South to the Indies.* Cambridge: MIT Press, 2008.

Whitten, Norman E., Jr. *Black Frontiersmen: A South American Case*. Hoboken, N.J.: John Wiley and Sons, 1974.

———. *Sacha Runa: Ethnicity and Adaptation of Ecuadorian Jungle Quichua*. Urbana: University of Illinois Press, 1976.

———. *Black Frontiersmen: Afro-Hispanic Culture of Ecuador and Colombia*. Long Grove, Ill.: Waveland Press, 1986.

Whitten, Norman E., Jr., and Arlene Torres, eds. *Blackness in Latin America and the Caribbean: Social Dynamics and Cultural Transformations.* Blackness in the Diaspora, vol. 1. Bloomington: Indiana University Press, 1998.

Wightman, Ann M. *Indigenous Migration and Social Change: The Forasteros of Cuzco, 1570–1720*. Durham: Duke University Press, 1990.

Williams, Eric Eustace. *Capitalism and Slavery*. Chapel Hill: University of North Carolina Press, 1941.

———. *From Columbus to Castro: The History of the Caribbean, 1492–1969*. New York: Harper and Row, 1970.

Wolf, Eric R. *Europe and the People without History*. Berkeley: University of California Press, 1997.

Wood, Peter H. *Black Majority: Negroes in Colonial South Carolina from 1670 through the Stono Rebellion*. New York: W. W. Norton, 1996.

Wynter, Sylvia. "1492: A New World View." In *Race, Discourse, and the Origin of the Americas: A New World View*, edited by Vera Lawrence Hyatt and Rex Nettleford, 5–57. Washington, D.C.: Smithsonian Institution Press, 1995.

———. "Unsettling the Coloniality of Being/Truth/Freedom: Towards the Human, after Man, Its Overrepresentation—An Argument." *CR: The New Centennial Review* 3, no. 3 (2003): 257–337.

Yáñez, Segundo Moreno. *Sublevaciones indígenas en la audiencia de Quito: Desde comienzos del siglo XVIII hasta finales de la colonia*. Quito: Ediciones de la Universidad Católica, 1985.

Yáñez, Segundo Moreno, and Frank Solomon, eds. *Reproducción y transformación de las sociedades Andinas, siglos XVI–XX*. Quito: Abya-Yala, 1991.

Yannakakis, Yanna. *The Art of Being In-Between: Native Intermediaries, Indian Identity, and Local Rule in Colonial Oaxaca*. Durham: Duke University Press, 2008.

Yarak, Larry. "West African Coastal Slavery in the Nineteenth Century: The Case of the Afro-European Slave Owners of Elmina." *Ethnohistory* 36, no. 1 (1989): 44–60.

Young, Jason R. *Rituals of Resistance: African Atlantic Religion in Kongo and the Low-country South in the Era of Slavery*. Baton Rouge: Louisiana State University Press, 2007.

Zarama Rincón, Rosa Isabel. "Barbacoas: Piña de oro de la gobernación de Popayán, 1750–1810." *Revista de Historia* 10, no. 70 (2004): 173–201.

Zeleza, Paul Tiyambe. "Rewriting the African Diaspora: Beyond the Black Atlantic." *African Affairs* 104, no. 414 (2005): 35–68.

Zeuski, Michael, and Orlando García Martínez. "*La Amistad* de Cuba: Ramón Ferrer, contrabando de esclavos, captividad y modernidad Atlántica." *Caribbean Studies* 37 (January–June 2009): 97–170.

Zulawski, Ann. *"They Eat from Their Labor": Work and Social Change in Colonial Bolivia*. Pittsburgh: University of Pittsburgh Press, 1994.

Zuluaga R., Francisco U. "Clientelismo y guerrillas en el Valle del Patia, 1536–1811." In *La Independencia: Ensayos de historia social*, edited by Germán Colmenares, 111–36. Bogotá: Instituto Colombiano de Cultura, 1986.

———. *Guerrilla y sociedad en el Patía*. Cali: Universidad del Valle, 1994.

———. *La protesta social en el sur-occidente Colombiano, siglo XVIII*. Cali: Universidad del Valle, 1997.

INDEX

Page numbers in italics refer to illustrations.

slaves in, 86; percentage of slaves sold in Popayán, 57, 58; regulation of slaves in, 34; in slave trade routes, 54–59, 55, 62, 167 (n. 76)

Carzedo, Joseph Veltran de, 56

Castas: in ethnic monikers, 64; and *nación,* interchangeable use of terms, 49–50

Castigo, El (*palenque*), 45, 122–23

Castile, crown of. *See* Crown

Castillo, Phelipa del, 127–28

Castro y Guzman, Antonio de, 36

Catholicism: litigation by slaves and, 177 (n. 14); in mining communities, limited presence of, 104–6; in runaway settlements, 122–23; symbolic impact of slaves in, 88, 90–91; whitening of blacks through, 87, 88, 91. *See also* Jesuits; Priests; Religious life of slaves

Central Africa, slaves originating in, 66, 74, 75

Cepeda, Catalina de, 96

Chambers, Douglas, 64–65, 165 (n. 54)

Chamorro, Bernarda Muños, 135

Chandler, David L., 177 (n. 11)

Chaves, Diego Revelo de, 115

Chaves, María Eugenía, 118, 137–38

Children, baptism of: indigenous, 97–100; slave, 92–96, 100

Chiriboga, Martín de, 124

Chocó, church's presence in, 105

Christians in origins of slavery, 11–12, 155 (n. 43)

Christian vassals: New Laws limiting power of, 31; slavery in status and authority of, 7, 12, 31–32, 38, 39, 160 (n. 46); slaves as, 115, 122

Cimaroons. *See* Maroons

Claver, Pedro, 86

Clergy. *See* Priests

Clothing of slaves, 20

Coartados, 82

Cofradía de Morenos, 89

Cofradías de color, 85, 88–89

Colmenares, Germán, 160 (n. 64), 167 (n. 77)

Colonial archive, slaves in, 18–20

Colonial development, 24–45; colonist uprisings and, 25–28; *encomienda* as method of, 24–25; fundamental role of slavery in, 1–2, 3, 6, 24–25, 45; labor as, 25; mining in, 38–39; in Pacific lowlands, 41–45; priests in, 28–29; race governance in, 11, 24, 25, 146; regulation of slavery in, 29–41; slaves as threat to, 26

Colonialism: problems with conceiving slavery as distinct from, 15–16; slavery as basic to, 45

Colonial sovereignty, development of. *See* Colonial development

Colonist uprisings, 25–28

Columbus, Christopher, 13–14

Comte de Lamoignon (ship), 62

Congo, slaves originating in, 75

Coronel, Ildefonso, 138–39

Coronel Feijóo, Rosario, 110, 175 (n. 69), 179 (n. 34)

Corral, Joan de, 164 (n. 37)

Correa, Gerónima, 131

Correa, Gertrudis, 131

Correa, Prudencio, 130–32

Cortés, Miguel, 168 (n. 81)

Country marks (scarification), 67–68, 73–75

Courts, ecclesiastical: slave litigation in, 177 (n. 14). See also *Audiencia;* Litigation by slaves

Creolization. *See* Afro-Creoles

Crown: on baptism of slaves, 53; branding of bodies with insignia of, 67, 68, 79–81, 148; colonial governance of (*see* Colonial development); Columbus's claims on behalf of, 13–14; divine right of kings and, 125; *encomienda* grants from, 24–25, 158 (n. 6); on free blacks' treatment, 33, 34, 159 (n. 34), 178 (n. 27); petitions to, on importation of slaves, 1–3, 151 (n. 2), 153 (n. 18); on punishment for crimes, 30, 159 (n. 29); regulation of slavery by, 30–35; royal slaves owned by, 153 (n. 18); sanction of slave shipments by, 16, 18; slaves as subjects of, 6, 161 (n. 6); subsidies for slave importation from, 1, 21, 153 (n. 18); taxation by (*see* Taxes)

Cruz, Gertrudis de la, 134

Cruz, Maria de la, 60–61, 163 (n. 32)

Cuba, runaway slaves in, 34, 178 (n. 27)

Cuenca, population of slaves in, 157 (n. 80)

Cuesta, Estevan de, 103

Customs inspections and reports on bodies of slaves, 68–73, 80

Davidson, David M., 177 (n. 11)

Davila, Pedrarías, 42

Day laborers, free blacks as, 3

Death penalty, crown endorsement of, 159 (n. 29)

Death rates among slaves, 95, 172 (n. 23)

De Granda, Germán, 76–77, 168 (nn. 83, 89)

De instauranda Aethiopum salute (Sandoval), 170 (n. 2)

Delgado, Claudio, 139–42

Delinquent slaves, 31, 159 (n. 32)

Deracination, 1, 14, 47–48

DeSoto Mayor, Juachin, 132–33, 138

Díaz, María Chiquinquirá, 137–38

Distinguished Woman with Her Negro Slave (Albán), *19*

Divine right of kings, 125

Documentation: of baptism of slaves, 53, 92, 93, 169 (n. 99); of fugitive slaves, 123, 179 (n. 30); of litigation by slaves, 118; of marks on bodies of slaves, 52, 68–73, 80; of marriage among slaves, 91–93; of *nación* in slave trade, 60–61, 164 (n. 44); of religious life of slaves, 91–93; of slaves in colonial archive, 18–20

Dominicans, slaves owned by, 163 (n. 35)

Dutch visual culture, black slavery in, 16, *17*

Ecclesiastical courts, slave litigation in, 177 (n. 14)

Economic value of slaves, 7, 147

Ecuador, contemporary: blackness in, 143

Elites: in contraband slave trade, 76; dependence on slaves, 21; as godparents, 95–96, 100; hierarchy of slaves and indigenous servants in households of, 98; slaves in displays of wealth of, 20

Elizondo, Afonso Cepedas de Arizcum, 137

El Sagrario Parish Church (Quito), 93–96, 97, 100, 172 (n. 21)

Encomienda: colonist uprisings over, 25; definition of, 24–25, 158 (n. 6); as method of colonial expansion, 24–25; New Laws on, 25, 32; in Quito city, 25; reversion back to crown, 25

Endogamy, 101–4

England, black slavery in, 16–18

Erazo, Manuel de, 79

Esclavo and *negro*, interchangeable use of terms, 170 (n. 7)

Esmeraldas, 123, 143–45

Espinosa, Magdalena de, 129

Espinosa de las Monteros, Antonio, 129

Espinosa Montero, Juliana, 129–30

Espinzo, María del Carmen, 137

Estacio, Gaspar de, 77

Estopiñan, Onorio, 140

Ethnicity: country marks (scarification) indicating, 67–68, 73–75; definitions of, 64–65; diversity of slave, 64–75, *74*, 108; European recognition of, 75; in identity formation, 67–68; monikers of, 11, 64, 102, 107

Ethnies, 64–65

Ethnogenesis, 86, 106

Europe, black slavery in visual culture of, 16–18, *17*

Europe and the People without History (Wolf), 46

Exogamy, 106–7

Falabarria, Antonio de, 163 (n. 35)

Fathers at baptisms, 94, 95, 100

Ferdinand (king of Aragon), 1, 14

Fortune (ship), 62

Free blacks: arming of, ban on, 31; Auncibay on role of, 2–3, 130; baptism of
children of, 96, 100; crown on treatment of, 33, 34, 159 (n. 34), 178 (n. 27);
as godparents, 96, 100; litigation by,
127–30; marriage of, 101, 102–3, 104;
population of, in Quito city, 96, 173
(n. 32); religious evangelism among,
88; threats to freedom of, 82

Freedom: litigation by slaves for, 116,
127–39, 176 (n. 8); through manumission, 2–3

French Royal Guinea Company, 79–80

Fuentes, Francisco de, 105

Fugitive (runaway) slaves, 122–24;
documentation of, 123, 179 (n. 30); and
effectiveness of litigation by slaves,
120; in eighteenth century, 122–24;
in Esmeraldas, 123, 143–45; freedom
lawsuits by, 176 (n. 8); as outsiders,
120, 122; vs. petite marronage, 31, 159
(n. 32); punishments for, 29, 30; regulation by crown, 31, 33–34, 178 (n. 27);
regulation by town councils, 29, 36;
settlements of, 45, 120, 122–23, 143–45

Galant (ship), 62

García Salgado, Roque, 53, 60, 169 (n. 99)

Gasca, Pedro de la, 27

Gaudeman, Stephen, 96

Gauisandes, Jasinto, 135–36

Geller, Ernest, 165 (n. 54)

Germendi, Agustín de, 79

Glymph, Thyvolia, 99

Godparents, 92–100; elites as, 95–96, 100;
free blacks as, 96, 100; of indigenous
children, 97–100; in marriage of god-
children, 93, 104; selection of, 92, 93,
94, 96; of slave children, 92–96

Gold Coast, slaves originating in, 66, 74,
75

Gold mining: Auncibay on importation
of slaves for, 1–3, 30, 151–52 (nn. 2–3),

153 (n. 18); decline of, 141; expansion
into new territories, 42–45; illegal
slave trade and, 77–79; by indigenous peoples, 20–21, 151 (n. 2), 157
(n. 74); locations of, 20–21, 157 (n. 73);
religious practice and, 84; by slaves,
20–21, 43–45; along slave trade routes,
54, 56; taxes on, 78. *See also specific
locations*

González, Duarte, 116

Gonzalez, Juan, 161 (n. 2)

Gonzalez, Manuel, 168 (n. 81)

Gonzalez Gordillo, Juan, 100

Governance/Governing/Government:
definition and use of terms, 152 (n. 4);
race (*see* Race governance); slavery as
practice of, 2, 3, 16

Grace, 90, 91

Guaman Poma de Ayala, Felipe, 153 (n. 19)

Guayaquil: arming of slaves in, ban on,
158 (n. 20); baptism of slaves in, 169
(n. 99); industries using slave labor
in, 21, 35; marriage among slaves in,
104; population of slaves in, 18, 21, 157
(n. 80); regulation of slavery by town
council of, 35–37; in slave trade routes,
54, 60–63

Guerra, Joseph de la, 77–79

Guerrero, Antonio, 79

Guerrero de Jelazar, Mariana, 164 (n. 44)

Guerro De Salar, Mariana, 61

Guevara y Cantos, Juan María de, 35

Guinea, slaves originating in, 11, 51

Guinea, Upper: slaves originating in, 66,
74

Habitats. See *Naturaleza*

Hack, William: *An Accurate Description of
the South Sea*, 43

Hapsburg monarchy, 164 (n. 48)

Health inspections of slave ships, 68

Hernández Girón, Francisco, 27, 28

Herzog, Tamar, 29

Hesse, Barnor, 10, 46

Heywood, Linda, 164 (n. 44)

Popayán: arrival and dispersal of *bozales* in, 46, 161 (nn. 2–3); Auncibay on importation of slaves to, 1–2, 30, 152 (n. 3); ethnic diversity of slaves in, 65–66; gold produced in, 20, 157 (n. 73); origins of slaves in, 160 (n. 64); percentage of Cartagena slaves sold in, 57, 58; population of slaves in, 18, 157 (n. 80); as slave trade center, 57; slave trade route to, 54–59

Popayán-Ibarra-Quito passage, 59–60

Popos, 167 (n. 74)

Population of Quito: free blacks, 96, 173 (n. 32); indigenous peoples, 18, 20–21, 157 (n. 74)

—slaves, 5, 18, 20–21, 157 (n. 80); Afro-Creole, 65–66, 98; women, 95; total, 116

Portero, Juan, 93

Porteros, Mariana de, 126

Porto Bello in slave trade routes, 167 (n. 76)

Portrait de Jeanne d'Austriche (Morais), 17

Portuguese crown on baptism of slaves, 53, 162 (n. 15), 169 (n. 99)

Potosí: silver mining at, 38–39; silver strike of 1545 at, 38

Pradeo, Alberto Mathías del, 102

Prado y Zúñiga, Francisco, 42

Premo, Bianca, 118, 180 (n. 43)

Priests: categorization of slaves, 85; in colonial development, 28–29; doubts about morality of slavery, 85, 170 (n. 3); in religious governance of slaves, 84–85

Property ownership by slaves, 33

Puerto Viejo: population of slaves in, 21; in slave trade routes, 61

Purcará, battle of (1554), 28

Pusír, 109

Quajara plantation, 124

Quintamayó, 106

Quito (city): baptism of infants in, 93–100; Chapel of Santo Domingo in, 89;

colonist uprising in, 25–28; Convent of Our Lady of the Rosary in, 89, 171 (n. 12); marriage in, 101–3; population of free blacks in, 96, 173 (n. 32); population of slaves in, 18, 21, 95, 116, 157 (n. 80); regulation of slavery in, 29–30; Spanish conquest of, 24–25; town council of, 24, 29–30

Quito, Kingdom of: map of, 4; population of (*see* Population of Quito); as slave society vs. society with slaves, 5, 40, 45. *See also specific regions and towns*

Race, construction of, 47–48, 162 (n. 9)

Race governance, 9–13; aim of, 10–11; in colonial development, 11, 24, 25, 146; definition of, 7; development of, 11–13; of indigenous peoples, 9–10; nomenclature of, 9–10, 154 (n. 35)

Racial slavery. *See* Slavery

Raíz, Cristoval de, 129

Ramírez Dávalos, Gil, 28

Razón, Juan, 45

Real audiencia. See Audiencia

Reál Cedúla: of 1540, 30, 33, 159 (n. 34); of 1789, 119

Rebels: colonist, 25–28; indigenous, regulation by town councils, 36

—black, 122–24; ban on arming of slaves and, 27–28, 31, 158 (n. 20); in colonist uprisings, 25–27; in effectiveness of litigation by slaves, 120; in eighteenth century, 122–24; as outsiders, 120, 122; regulation by crown, 30–31, 33; and threats of slave resistance, 123–24, 141, 179 (nn. 32, 34)

Records. *See* Documentation

Reducción General de Indios, 32

Religious life of slaves, 84–114; *cofradías* (brotherhoods) in, 85, 88–89; expressions of piety in, 87–88, 90; Jesuits in, 84, 86–88; racialization through, 86; sacramental records of, 91–93; slaveholders' role in, 84, 92–93, 105, 172

(n. 20); symbolic impact of, 88, 90–91. *See also* Baptism of slaves; Marriage of slaves

Restall, Matthew, 152 (n. 14)

Reyes, Miguel de los, 77–79, 168 (n. 83), 169 (n. 93)

Reymundo, Geronima, 127–28

Reymundo, Thomás, 127–28

Rica, Ana, 128–30

Rica, Juana, 128–30

Rica, Magdalena, 128–30

Rights. *See* Legal rights of slaves

Riobamba in slave trade routes, 61

Rios, Juan Philupo de los, 45, 160 (n. 64)

Rivera, Juan de, 105

Robinson, Cedric, 155 (n. 45)

Roman law, slavery in, 6

Romero, Juan, 133

Royal African Company, 74–75

Royal audience, legal right of slaves to, 8, 115–16. See also *Audiencia*

Royal Guinea Company, 167 (n. 77)

Royal insignia, branding of bodies with, 67, 68, 79–81, 148

Royal mercy in litigation by slaves, 125, 132

Royal slaves, 153 (n. 18)

Ruíz Bazán, José, 79

Ruíz Bonifacio, Juan, 60–61

Ruíz de Roxas, Diego, 129

Rumiñahui (Inka general), 24

Runaway slaves. *See* Fugitive slaves

Rural areas, litigation by slaves in, 149–50

Sacramental records, 91–93

Sacred communities. *See* Religious life of slaves

Salazar, Diego de, 126

Saltwater slavery, 46, 52, 146, 161 (n. 1)

Salvatierra, Conde de, 37

Sambrano, Margarita de, 130–31

Sánchez, José, 76

Sánchez, Xavier, 123

Sánchez Gallque, Andrés: *Los mulatos de Esmeraldas*, 143, *144*

Sandoval, Alonso de, 53, 86, 166 (n. 71), 169 (n. 99), 170 (n. 3), 171 (n. 14); *De instauranda Aethiopum salute*, 170 (n. 2)

Santa Fé, Lucía, 45

Santa Fé, Manuel, 45

Santa María del Puerto, 42

São Tomé, slaves originating from, 65

Scarification, 67–68, 73–75

Schwartz, Stuart, 96

"Seasoning" of slaves, 56, 166 (n. 59), 169 (n. 98)

Sevicia in litigation by slaves, 115, 119, 137, 138

Sexual relationships and freedom lawsuits by women, 132–37. *See also* Marriage of slaves

Sezego, 107

Ships, slave: examples of, 62; inspections of, 68; shipwrecks, 143

Siete Partidas. *See* Law

Silva, Pedro de, 127–28

Silver mining: after silver strike of 1545, 38–39; Toledo Reforms on, 32

Sindicats, 8

Slaveholders and slave masters: Auncibay on role of, 2; colonial status and authority of, 160 (n. 46); dispossessed of slaves, 34, 161 (n. 6); as godparents, 95–96, 100; of illegal slaves, 76–79, 167 (nn. 79–80), 168 (nn. 81–83); litigation by slaves against (*see* Litigation by slaves); regulation by crown, 34, 161 (n. 6); regulation by town councils, 29–30, 37; in religious life of slaves, 84, 92–93, 105, 172 (n. 20); slaves in production and performance of wealth by, 19–20; slave threats of violence against, 123–24, 141, 179 (nn. 32, 34)

Slave resistance, threats of, 123–24, 141, 179 (nn. 32, 34)

Slavery: blackness associated with, 13, 16, 47–48, 146, 155 (n. 43), 156 (n. 55); in contemporary social imaginary of Ecuador, 143; in development of colonial sovereignty (*see* Colonial

CPSIA information can be obtained
at www.ICGtesting.com
Printed in the USA
LVHW090741071221
705491LV00005B/814